Professional
Search Engine
Optimization with PHP

Professional
Search Engine
Optimization with PHP

A Developer's Guide to SEO

Jaimie Sirovich

Cristian Darie

Wiley Publishing, Inc.

Professional Search Engine Optimization with PHP: A Developer's Guide to SEO

Published by
Wiley Publishing, Inc.
10475 Crosspoint Boulevard
Indianapolis, IN 46256
www.wiley.com

Copyright © 2007 by Wiley Publishing, Inc., Indianapolis, Indiana
Published simultaneously in Canada
ISBN: 978-0-470-10092-9
Manufactured in the United States of America
10 9 8 7 6 5 4 3 2 1

Library of Congress Cataloging-in-Publication Data:

Sirovich, Jaimie, 1981-
  Professional search engine optimization with PHP : a developer's guide to SEO / Jaimie Sirovich, Cristian Darie.
    p. cm.
  Includes index.
  ISBN 978-0-470-10092-9 (pbk.)
  1. PHP (Computer program language) 2. Web sites--Design. 3. Search engines. I. Darie, Cristian. II. Title.
  QA76.73.P224S525 2007
  005.13'3--dc22

                    2007003317

For general information on our other products and services please contact our Customer Care Department within the United States at (800) 762-2974, outside the United States at (317) 572-3993 or fax (317) 572-4002.

Trademarks: Wiley, the Wiley logo, Wrox, the Wrox logo, Programmer to Programmer, and related trade dress are trademarks or registered trademarks of John Wiley & Sons, Inc. and/or its affiliates, in the United States and other countries, and may not be used without written permission. Microsoft and Excel are registered trademarks of Microsoft Corporation in the United States and/or other countries. All other trademarks are the property of their respective owners. Wiley Publishing, Inc., is not associated with any product or vendor mentioned in this book.

Wiley also publishes its books in a variety of electronic formats. Some content that appears in print may not be available in electronic books.

About the Authors

Jaimie Sirovich is a search engine marketing consultant. He works with his clients to build them powerful online presences. Officially Jaimie is a computer programmer, but he claims to enjoy marketing much more. He graduated from Stevens Institute of Technology with a BS in Computer Science. He worked under Barry Schwartz at RustyBrick, Inc., as lead programmer on e-commerce projects until 2005. At present, Jaimie consults for several organizations and administrates the popular search engine marketing blog, SEOEgghead.com.

Cristian Darie is a software engineer with experience in a wide range of modern technologies, and the author of numerous books and tutorials on AJAX, ASP.NET, PHP, SQL, and related areas. Cristian currently lives in Bucharest, Romania, studying distributed application architectures for his PhD. He's getting involved with various commercial and research projects, and when not planning to buy Google, he enjoys his bit of social life. If you want to say "Hi," you can reach Cristian through his personal web site at http://www.cristiandarie.ro.

Credits

Acquisitions Editor
Kit Kemper

Developmental Editor
Kenyon Brown

Technical Editor
Bogdan Brinzarea

Production Editor
Angela Smith

Copy Editor
Kim Cofer

Editorial Manager
Mary Beth Wakefield

Production Manager
Tim Tate

Vice President and Executive Group Publisher
Richard Swadley

Vice President and Executive Publisher
Joseph B. Wikert

Compositor
Laurie Stewart, Happenstance Type-O-Rama

Proofreader
Ian Golder

Indexer
Melanie Belkin

Anniversary Logo Design
Richard Pacifico

Acknowledgments

The authors would like to thank the following people and companies, listed alphabetically, for their invaluable assistance with the production of this book. Without their help, this book would not have been possible in its current form.

Dan Kramer of Volatile Graphix for generously providing his cloaking database to the public — and even adding some data to make our cloaking code examples work better.

Kim Krause Berg of The Usability Effect for providing assistance and insight where this book references usability and accessibility topics.

MaxMind, Inc., for providing their free GeoLite geo-targeting data — making our geo-targeting code examples possible.

Several authors of WordPress plugins including Arne Brachhold, Lester Chan, Peter Harkins, Matt Lloyd, and Thomas McMahon.

Family and friends of both Jaimie and Cristian — for tolerating the endless trail of empty cans of (caffeinated) soda left on the table while writing this book.

Contents

Contents

Contents

Contents

Introduction

Welcome to *Professional Search Engine Optimization with PHP: A Developer's Guide to SEO!*

Search engine optimization has traditionally been the job of a marketing staff. With this book, we examine search engine optimization in a brand new light, evangelizing that SEO should be done by the programmer as well.

To maximize success in search engine optimization efforts, developers and marketers should work together, starting from a web site's inception and technical and visual design as well as throughout its lifetime. We provide developers and IT professionals with the information they need to create and maintain a search engine–friendly web site and avoid common pitfalls that confuse search engine spiders. This book discusses in depth how to facilitate site spidering and discusses the various technologies and services that can be leveraged for site promotion.

Who Should Read This Book

Professional Search Engine Optimization with PHP: A Developer's Guide to SEO is mainly geared toward web developers, because it discusses search engine optimization in the context of web site programming. You do not need to be a programmer by trade to benefit from this book, but some programming background is important for *fully* understanding and following the technical exercises.

We also tried to make this book friendly for the search engine marketer with some IT background who wants to learn about a different, more technical angle of search engine optimization. Usually, each chapter starts with a less-technical discussion on the topic at hand and then develops into the more advanced technical details. Many books cover search engine optimization, but few delve at all into the meaty technical details of *how* to design a web site with the goal of search engine optimization in mind. Ultimately, this book does just that.

Where programming *is* discussed, we show code with explanations. We don't hide behind concepts and buzzwords; we include hands-on practical exercises instead. Contained within this reference are fully functional examples of using XML-based sitemaps, social-bookmarking functionality, and even working implementations of cloaking and geo-targeting.

What Will You Learn from this Book?

In this book, we have assembled the most important topics that programmers and search engine marketers should know about when designing web sites.

> ## Getting the Most Out of this Book
>
> You may choose to read this book cover-to-cover, but that is strictly not required. We recommend that you read Chapters 1–6 first, but the remaining chapters can be perused in any order. In case you run into technical problems, a page with chapter-by-chapter book updates and errata is maintained by Jaimie Sirovich at `http://www.seoegghead.com/seo-with-php-updates.html`. You can also search for errata for the book at `www.wrox.com`, as is discussed later in this introduction.
>
> If you have any feedback related to this book, don't hesitate to contact either Jaimie or Cristian! This will help to make everyone's experience with this book more pleasant and fulfilling.

At the end of **Chapter 1, You: Programmer and Search Engine Marketer,** you create the environment where you'll be coding away throughout the rest of the book. Programming with PHP can be tricky at times; in order to avoid most configuration and coding errors you may encounter, we will instruct you how to prepare the working folder and your MySQL database.

If you aren't ready for these tasks yet, don't worry! You can come back at any time, later. All programming-related tasks in this book are explained step by step to minimize the chances that anyone gets lost on the way.

Chapter 2, A Primer in Basic SEO, is a primer in search engine optimization tailored for the IT professional. It stresses the points that are particularly relevant to the programmer from the perspective of the programmer. You'll also learn about a few tools and resources that all search engine marketers and web developers should know about.

Chapter 3, Provocative SE-Friendly URLs, details how to create (or enhance) your web site with improved URLs that are easier for search engines to understand and more persuasive for their human readers. You'll even create a URL factory, which you will be able to reuse in your own projects.

Chapter 4, Content Relocation and HTTP Status Codes, presents all of the nuances involved in using HTTP status codes correctly to relocate and indicate other statuses for content. The proper use of these status codes is essential when restructuring information on a web site.

Chapter 5, Duplicate Content, discusses duplicate content in great detail. It then proposes strategies for avoiding problems related to duplicate content.

Chapter 6, SE-Friendly HTML and JavaScript, discusses search engine optimization issues that present themselves in the context of rendering content using HTML, JavaScript and AJAX, and Flash.

Chapter 7, Web Feeds and Social Bookmarking, discusses web syndication and social bookmarking. Tools to create and syndicate feeds and ways to leverage social bookmarking are presented.

Chapter 8, Black Hat SEO, presents black hat SEO from the perspective of preventing black hat victimization and attacks. You may want to skip ahead to this chapter to see what this is all about!

Chapter 9, Sitemaps, discusses the use of sitemaps — traditional and XML-based — for the purpose of improving and speeding indexing.

Chapter 10, Link Bait, discusses the concept of link bait and provides an example of a site tool that could bait links.

Chapter 11, Cloaking, Geo-Targeting, and IP Delivery, discusses cloaking, geo-targeting, and IP Delivery. It includes fully working examples of all three.

Chapter 12, Foreign Language SEO, discusses search engine optimization for foreign languages and the concerns therein.

Chapter 13, Coping with Technical Issues, discusses the various issues that an IT professional must understand when maintaining a site, such as how to change web hosts without potentially hurting search rankings.

Chapter 14, Case Study: Building an E-Commerce Store, rounds it off with a fully functional search engine–optimized e-commerce catalog incorporating much of the material in the previous chapters.

Chapter 15, Site Clinic: So You Have a Web Site?, presents concerns that may face a preexisting web site and suggests enhancements that can be implemented in the context of their difficulty.

Lastly, **Chapter 16, WordPress: Creating an SE-Friendly Blog,** documents how to set up a search engine–optimized blog using WordPress 2.0 and quite a few custom plugins.

We hope that you will enjoy reading this book and that it will prove useful for your real-world search engine optimization endeavors!

Contacting the Authors

Jaimie Sirovich can be contacted through his blog at http://www.seoegghead.com. Cristian Darie can be contacted from his web site at http://www.cristiandarie.ro.

Conventions

To help you get the most from the text and keep track of what's happening, we've used a number of conventions throughout the book.

> **Boxes like this one hold important, not-to-be forgotten information that is directly relevant to the surrounding text.**

Tips, hints, tricks, and asides to the current discussion are offset and placed in italics like this.

As for styles in the text:

- ❑   We *highlight* new terms and important words when we introduce them.
- ❑   We show keyboard strokes like this: Ctrl+A.
- ❑   We show file names, URLs, and code within the text like so: `persistence.properties`.
- ❑   We present code in two different ways:

```
In code examples we highlight new and important code with a gray background.
The gray highlighting is not used for code that's less important in the present
context, or has been shown before.
```

Source Code

As you work through the examples in this book, you may choose either to type in all the code manually or to use the source code files that accompany the book. All of the source code used in this book is available for download at `http://www.wrox.com`. Once at the site, simply locate the book's title (either by using the Search box or by using one of the title lists) and click the Download Code link on the book's detail page to obtain all the source code for the book.

> *Because many books have similar titles, you may find it easiest to search by ISBN; this book's ISBN is 978-0-470-10092-9.*

Once you download the code, just decompress it with your favorite compression tool. Alternatively, you can go to the main Wrox code download page at `http://www.wrox.com/dynamic/books/download.aspx` to see the code available for this book and all other Wrox books.

Errata

We make every effort to ensure that there are no errors in the text or in the code. However, no one is perfect, and mistakes do occur. If you find an error in one of our books, like a spelling mistake or faulty piece of code, we would be very grateful for your feedback. By sending in errata you may save another reader hours of frustration and at the same time you will be helping us provide even higher quality information.

To find the errata page for this book, go to `http://www.wrox.com` and locate the title using the Search box or one of the title lists. Then, on the book details page, click the Book Errata link. On this page you can view all errata that has been submitted for this book and posted by Wrox editors. A complete book list including links to each book's errata is also available at `www.wrox.com/misc-pages/booklist.shtml`.

If you don't spot "your" error on the Book Errata page, go to `www.wrox.com/contact/techsupport.shtml` and complete the form there to send us the error you have found. We'll check the information and, if appropriate, post a message to the book's errata page and fix the problem in subsequent editions of the book.

p2p.wrox.com

For author and peer discussion, join the P2P forums at p2p.wrox.com. The forums are a web-based system for you to post messages relating to Wrox books and related technologies and interact with other readers and technology users. The forums offer a subscription feature to email you topics of interest of your choosing when new posts are made to the forums. Wrox authors, editors, other industry experts, and your fellow readers are present on these forums.

At http://p2p.wrox.com you will find a number of different forums that will help you not only as you read this book, but also as you develop your own applications. To join the forums, just follow these steps:

1. Go to p2p.wrox.com and click the Register link.

2. Read the terms of use and click Agree.

3. Complete the required information to join as well as any optional information you wish to provide and click Submit.

4. You will receive an email with information describing how to verify your account and complete the joining process.

   You can read messages in the forums without joining P2P but in order to post your own messages, you must join.

Once you join, you can post new messages and respond to messages other users post. You can read messages at any time on the web. If you would like to have new messages from a particular forum emailed to you, click the Subscribe To This Forum icon by the forum name in the forum listing.

For more information about how to use the Wrox P2P, be sure to read the P2P FAQs for answers to questions about how the forum software works as well as many common questions specific to P2P and Wrox books. To read the FAQs, click the FAQ link on any P2P page.

You: Programmer and Search Engine Marketer

Googling for information on the World Wide Web is such a common activity these days that it is hard to imagine that just a few years ago this verb did not even exist. Search engines are now an integral part of our lifestyle, but this was not always the case. Historically, systems for finding information were driven by data organization and classification performed by humans. Such systems are not entirely obsolete — libraries still keep their books ordered by categories, author names, and so forth. Yahoo! itself started as a manually maintained directory of web sites, organized into categories. Those were the good old days.

Today, the data of the World Wide Web is enormous and rapidly changing; it cannot be confined in the rigid structure of the library. The format of the information is extremely varied, and the individual bits of data — coming from blogs, articles, web services of all kinds, picture galleries, and so on — form an almost infinitely complex virtual organism. In this environment, making information *findable* necessitates something more than the traditional structures of data organization or classification.

Introducing the ad-hoc query and the modern search engine. This functionality reduces the aforementioned need for organization and classification; and since its inception, it has been become quite pervasive. Google's popular email service, GMail, features its searching capability that permits a user to find emails that contain a particular set of keywords. Microsoft Windows Vista now integrates an instant search feature as part of the operating system, helping you quickly find information within any email, Word document, or database on your hard drive from the Start menu regardless of the underlying file format. But, by far, the most popular use of this functionality is in the World Wide Web search engine.

These search engines are the exponents of the explosive growth of the Internet, and an entire industry has grown around their huge popularity. Each visit to a search engine potentially generates business for a particular vendor. Looking at Figure 1-1 it is easy to figure out where people in Manhattan are likely to order pizza online. Furthermore, the traffic resulting from non-sponsored, or organic, search results costs nothing to the vendor. These are highlighted in Figure 1-1.

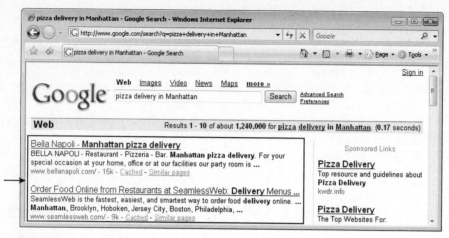

Figure 1-1

The less obvious effect of the search engine explosion phenomenon is that web developers are now directly involved in the search engine marketing process. To rank well in these organic results, it may not be enough to "write relevant content," as your typical search engine marketing tutorial drones. Rather, the web application developer must work together with the marketing team, and he or she must build a web site fully aware that certain features or technologies may interfere with a search engine marketing campaign. An improperly designed web site can interfere with a search engine's need to periodically navigate and index the information contained therein. In the worst case, the search engine may not be able to index the content at all.

So, ironically, while users are becoming less interested in understanding the structure of data on the Internet, the structure of a web site is becoming an increasingly important facet in search engine marketing! This structure — the architecture of a web site — is the primary focus of this book.

We hope that this brief introduction whets your appetite! The remainder of this chapter tells you what to expect from this book. You will also configure your development machine to ensure you won't have any problems following the technical exercises in the later chapters.

Who Are You?

Maybe you're a great programmer or IT professional, but marketing isn't your thing. Or perhaps you're a tech-savvy search engine marketer who wants a peek under the hood of a search engine optimized web site. Search engine marketing is a field where technology and marketing are both critical and interdependent, because small changes in the implementation of a web site can make you or break you in search engine rankings. Furthermore, the fusion of technology and marketing know-how can create web site features that attract more visitors.

The *raison d'être* of this book is to help web developers create web sites that rank well with the major search engines, and to teach search engine marketers how to use technology to their advantage. We assert that neither marketing nor IT can exist in a vacuum, and it is essential that they not see themselves as opposing forces in an organization. They *must* work together. This book aims to educate both sides in that regard.

> ### The Story
>
> So how do a search engine marketer from the USA (Jaimie) and a programmer from Romania (Cristian) meet? To answer, we need to tell you a funny little story. A while ago, Jaimie happened to purchase a book (that shall remain nameless) written by Cristian, and was not pleased with one particular aspect of its contents. Jaimie proceeded to grill him with some critical comments on a public web site. Ouch!
>
> Cristian contacted Jaimie courteously, and explained most of it away. No, we're not going to tell you the name of the book, what the contents were, or whether it is still in print. But things did eventually get more amicable, and we started to correspond about what we do for a living. Jaimie is a web site developer and search engine marketer, and Cristian is a software engineer who has published quite a few books in the technology sector. As a result of those discussions, the idea of a technology-focused search engine optimization book came about. The rest is more or less history.

What Do You Need to Learn?

As with anything in the technology-related industry, one must constantly learn and research to keep apprised of the latest news and trends. *How exhausting!* Fortunately, there are fundamental truths with regard to search engine optimization that are both easy to understand and probably won't change in time significantly — so a solid foundation that you build now will likely stand the test of time.

We remember the days when search engine optimization was a black art of analyzing and improving on-page factors. Search engine marketers were obsessed over keyword density and which HTML tags to use. Many went so far as to recommend optimizing content for different search engines individually, thusly creating different pages with similar content optimized with different densities and tags. Today, that would create a problem called *duplicate content*.

The current struggle is creating a site with interactive content and navigation with a minimal amount of duplicate content, with URLs that do not confuse web spiders, and a tidy internal linking structure. There is a thread on SearchEngineWatch (http://www.searchenginewatch.com) where someone asked which skill everyone reading would like to hone. Almost all of them enumerated programming as one of the skills (http://forums.searchenginewatch.com/showthread.php?t=11945). This does not surprise us. Having an understanding of both programming and search engine marketing will serve one well in the pursuit of success on the Internet.

When people ask us where we'd suggest spending money in an SEO plan, we always recommend making sure that one is starting with a sound basis. If your web site has architectural problems, it's tantamount to trumpeting your marketing message atop a house of cards. *Professional Search Engine Optimization with PHP: A Developer's Guide to SEO* aims to illustrate how to build a solid foundation.

To get the most out of this journey, you should be familiar with a bit of programming (PHP, preferably). You can also get quite a bit out this book by only reading the explanations. And another strategy to reading this book is to do just that — then hand this book to the web developer with a list of concerns and directives in order to ensure the resulting product is search engine optimized. In that case, don't get bogged down in the exercises — just skim them.

We cover a quick introduction to SEO in Chapter 2, which should nail down the foundations of that subject. However, PHP and MySQL are vast subjects; and this book cannot afford to also be a PHP and MySQL tutorial. The code samples are explained step by step, but if you have never written a line of PHP or SQL before, and want to follow the examples in depth, you should also consider reading a PHP and MySQL tutorial book, such as the following:

❑ *PHP and MySQL for Dynamic Web Sites: Visual QuickPro Guide, 2nd edition* (Larry Ulman, Peachpit Press, 2005)

❑ *Build Your Own Database Driven Website Using PHP & MySQL, 3rd Edition* (Kevin Yank, Sitepoint, 2005)

❑ *Teach Yourself PHP in 10 Minutes* (Chris Newman, Sams, 2005)

SEO and the Site Architecture

A web site's architecture is what grounds all future search engine marketing efforts. The content rests on top of it, as shown in Figure 1-2. An optimal web site architecture facilitates a search engine in traversing and understanding the site. Therefore, creating a web site with a search engine optimized architecture is a major contributing factor in achieving and maintaining high search engine rankings.

Architecture should also be considered throughout a web site's lifetime by the web site developer, alongside other factors such as aesthetics and usability. If a feature does not permit a search engine to access the content, hinders it, or confuses it, the effects of good content may be reduced substantially. For example, a web site that uses Flash or AJAX technologies inappropriately may obscure the majority of its content from a search engine.

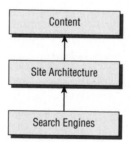

Figure 1-2

We do not cover copywriting concepts in detail, or provide much coaching as to how to create persuasive page titles. These are also very important topics, which are masterfully covered by Bryan and Jeffrey Eisenberg in *Persuasive Online Copywriting: How to Take Your Words to the Bank* (Wizard Academy Press, 2002), and by John Caples and Fred E. Hahn in *Tested Advertising Methods, 5th edition* (Prentice Hall, 1998). Shari Thurow also has an excellent section on creating effective titles in her book, *Search Engine Visibility* (New Riders Press, 2002). Writing copy and titles that rank well is obviously not successful if it does not convert or result in click-throughs, respectively. We do give some pointers, though, to get you started.

We also do not discuss concepts related to search engine optimization such as usability and user psychology in depth, though they are strong themes throughout the book.

Optimizing a site's architecture frequently involves tinkering with variables that also affect usability and the overall user perception of your site. When we encounter such situations, we alert you to why these certain choices were made. Chapter 5, "Duplicate Content," highlights a typical problem with breadcrumbs and presents some potential solutions. Sometimes we find that SEO enhancements run counter to usability. Likewise, not all designs that are user friendly are search engine friendly. Either way, a compromise must be struck to satisfy both kinds of visitors — users and search engines.

SEO Cannot Be an Afterthought

One common misconception is that search engine optimization efforts can be made after a web site is launched. This is frequently incorrect. Whenever possible, a web site can and should be designed to be search engine friendly as a fundamental concern.

Unfortunately, when a preexisting web site is designed in a way that poses problems for search engines, search engine optimization can become a much larger task. If a web site has to be redesigned, or partially redesigned, the migration process frequently necessitates special technical considerations. For example, old URLs must be *properly* redirected to new ones with similar relevant content.

The majority of this book documents best practices for design from scratch as well as how to mitigate redesign problems and concerns. The rest is dedicated to discretionary enhancements.

Communicating Architectural Decisions

The aforementioned scenario regarding URL migration is a perfect example of how the technical team and marketing team must communicate. The programmer must be instructed to add the proper redirects to the web application. Otherwise existing search rankings may be hopelessly lost forever. Marketers must know that such measures must be taken in the first place.

In a world where organic rankings contribute to the bottom line, a one-line redirect command in a web server configuration file may be much more important than one may think. This particular topic, URL migration, is discussed in Chapter 4.

Architectural Minutiae Can Make or Break You

So you now understand that small mistakes in implementation can be quite insidious. Another common example would be the use of JavaScript-based navigation, and failing to provide an HTML-based alternative. Spiders would be lost, because they, for the most part, do not interpret JavaScript.

The search engine spider is "the third browser." Many organizations will painstakingly test the efficacy and usability of a design in Internet Explorer and Firefox with dedicated QA teams. *Unfortunately, many fall short by neglecting to design and test for the spider.* Perhaps this is because you have to design in the abstract for the spider; we don't have a Google spider at our disposal after all; and we can't interview it afterward with regard to what it thought of our "usability." However, that does not make its assessment any less important.

The Spider Simulator tool located at `http://www.seochat.com/seo-tools/spider-simulator/` shows you the contents of a web page from the perspective of a hypothetical search engine. The tool is very simplistic, but if you're new to SEO, using it can be an enlightening experience.

Preparing Your Playground

This book contains many exercises, and all of them assume that you've prepared your environment as explained in the next few pages. If you're a PHP and MySQL veteran, here's the quick list of software requirements. If you have these, you can skip to the end of the chapter, where you're instructed to create a MySQL database for the few exercises in this book that use it.

- ❑ Apache 2 or newer, with the mod_rewrite module
- ❑ PHP 4.1 or newer
- ❑ MySQL

Your PHP installation should have these modules:

- ❑ php_mysql (necessary for the chapters that work with MySQL)
- ❑ php_gd2 (necessary for exercises in Chapter 5 and Chapter 10)
- ❑ php_curl (necessary for exercises in Chapter 11)

> The programming exercises in this book assume prior experience with PHP and MySQL. However, if you follow the exercises with discipline, exactly as described, everything should work as planned.

If you already have PHP but you aren't sure which modules you have installed, view your `php.ini` configuration file. On a default Windows installation, this file is located in the `Windows` folder; if you install PHP through XAMPP as shown in the exercise that follows, the path is `\Program Files\xampp\apache\bin`. To enable a module, remove the leading "`;`" from the `extension=module_name.dll` line, and restart Apache.

After installing the necessary software, you'll create a virtual host named `seophp.example.com`, which will point to a folder on your machine, which will be your working folder for this book. We will add a line to your computer's host file to configure this domain. All exercises you build in this book will be accessible on your machine through `http://seophp.example.com`.

Lastly, you'll prepare a MySQL database named `seophp`, which will be required for a few of the exercises in this book. Creating the database isn't a priority for now, so you can leave this task for when you'll actually need it for an exercise.

> The next few pages cover the exact installation procedure assuming that you're running Microsoft Windows. If you're running Linux or using a web hosting account, we assume you already have Apache, PHP, and MySQL installed with necessary modules.

Installing XAMPP

XAMPP is a package created by Apache Friends (http://www.apachefriends.org), which includes Apache, PHP, MySQL, and many other goodies. If you don't have these already installed on your machine, the easiest way to have them running is to install XAMPP.

Here are the steps you should follow:

1. Visit http://www.apachefriends.org/en/xampp.html, and go to the XAMPP page specific for your operating system.

2. Download the XAMPP installer package, which should be an executable file named like xampp-win32-version-installer.exe.

3. Execute the installer executable. When asked, choose to install Apache and MySQL as services, as shown in Figure 1-3. Then click Install.

4. You'll be asked to confirm the installation of each of these as services. Don't install the FileZilla FTP Server service unless you need it for particular purposes (you don't need it for this book), but do install Apache and MySQL as services.

> Note that you can't have more than 1 web server on port 80 (the default port used for HTTP communication). If you already have a web server on your machine, such as IIS, you should either make it use another port, uninstall it, or deactivate it. Otherwise, Apache won't work. The exercises in this book assume that your Apache server works on port 80; they may not work otherwise.

5. In the end, confirm the execution of the XAMPP Control Panel, which can be used for administering the installed services. Figure 1-4 shows the XAMPP Control Panel.

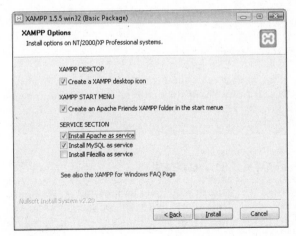

Figure 1-3

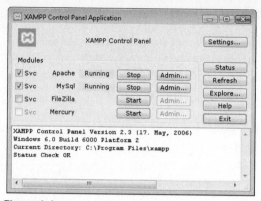

Figure 1-4

> The XAMPP Control Panel is particularly useful when you need to stop or start the
> Apache server. Every time you make a change to the Apache configuration files,
> you'll need to restart Apache.

6. To test that Apache installed correctly, load `http://localhost/` using your web browser. An
XAMPP welcome screen like the one in Figure 1-5 should load.

7. Finally, after you've tested that both Apache and PHP work, it's recommended to turn on PHP
error reporting. Apache logs errors in a file named `error.log`, located in the `xampp\apache\`
`logs` folder; looking at the latest entries of this file when something goes wrong with your application can be very helpful at times. To enable PHP error reporting, open for editing the `php.ini`
configuration file, located by default in the `xampp\apache\bin\` folder. There, locate this entry:

```
display_errors = Off
```

and change it to:

```
display_errors = On
```

8. To configure what kind of errors you want reported, you can alter the value of the PHP
`error_reporting` value. We recommend the following setting to report all errors, except
for PHP notices:

```
error_reporting = E_ALL & ~E_NOTICE
```

Preparing the Working Folder

Now you'll create a virtual host named `seophp.example.com` on your local machine, which will point
to a local folder named `seophp`. The `seophp` folder will be your working folder for all the exercises in
this book, and you'll load the sample pages through `http://seophp.example.com`.

The `seophp.example.com` *as virtual host won't interfere with any existing online applications,
because* `example.com` *is a special domain name reserved by IANA to be used for documentation and
demonstration purposes. See* `http://example.com` *for the official information.*

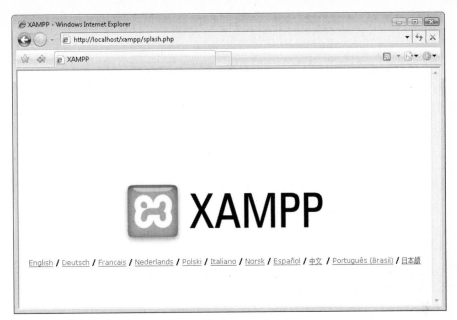

Figure 1-5

Follow these steps to create and test the virtual host on your machine:

1. First, you need to add `seophp.example.com` to the Windows `hosts` file. The following line will tell Windows that all domain name resolution requests for `seophp.example.com` should be handled by the local machine instead of your configured DNS. Open the `hosts` file, which is located by default in `C:\Windows\System32\drivers\etc\hosts`, and add this line to it:

```
127.0.0.1       localhost
127.0.0.1       seophp.example.com
```

2. Now create a new folder named `seophp`, which will be used for all the work you do in this book. You might find it easiest to create it in the root folder (`C:\`), but you can create it anywhere else if you like. If you do so, the `DocumentRoot` directive in your `http-vhosts.conf` file must be changed accordingly.

3. Finally, you need to configure a virtual host for `seophp.example.com` in Apache. Right now, all requests to `http://localhost/` and `http://seophp.example.com/` are handled by Apache's default directory, and both yield the same result. You want requests to `http://seophp.example.com/` to be served from your newly created folder, `seophp`. This way, you can work with this book without interfering with the existing applications on your web server.

   To create the virtual host, you need to edit the Apache configuration file. In typical Apache installations there is a single configuration file named `httpd.conf`. XAMPP ships with more configuration files, which handle different configuration areas. To add a virtual host, add the following lines to `xampp\apache\conf\extra\httpd-vhosts.conf`. (If you installed XAMPP with the default options, the `xampp` folder should be under `\Program Files`.)

```
NameVirtualHost 127.0.0.1:80

<VirtualHost 127.0.0.1:80>
  DocumentRoot "C:/Program Files/xampp/htdocs"
  ServerName localhost
</VirtualHost>

<VirtualHost 127.0.0.1:80>
  DocumentRoot C:/seophp/
  ServerName seophp.example.com
  <Directory C:/seophp/>
    Options Indexes FollowSymLinks
    AllowOverride All
    Order allow,deny
    Allow from all
  </Directory>
</VirtualHost>
```

In order for `http://localhost/` **to continue working after you create a virtual host, you need to define and configure it as a virtual host as well — this explains why we've included it in the vhosts file. If you have any important applications working under** `http://localhost/`**, make sure they continue to work after you restart Apache at the end of this exercise.**

4. To make sure `httpd-vhosts.conf` gets processed when Apache starts, open `xampp\apache\conf\httpd.conf` and make sure this line, located somewhere near the end of the file, isn't commented:

```
# Virtual hosts
include conf/extra/httpd-vhosts.conf
```

5. Restart Apache for the new configuration to take effect. The easiest way to restart Apache is to open the XAMPP Control Panel, and use it to stop and then start the Apache service.

   In case you run into trouble, the first place to check is the Apache error log file. In the default XAMPP installation, this is xampp\apache\logs\error.log.

6. To test your new virtual host, create a new file named `test.php` in your `seophp` folder, and type this code in it:

```
<?php
phpinfo();
?>
```

7. Then load `http://seophp.example.com/test.php` and expect to see a page like the one in Figure 1-6.

   This way you've also tested that your PHP installation is working correctly.

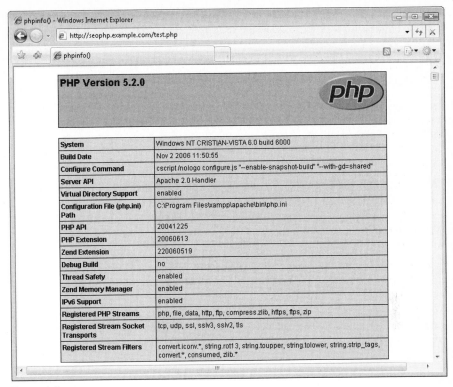

Figure 1-6

Preparing the Database

The final step is to create a new MySQL database. You're creating a database named seophp that you will use for the exercises contained in this book. You'll also create a user named seouser, with the password seomaster, which will have full privileges to the seophp database.

You will be using this database only for the exercises in Chapter 11 and Chapter 14, so you can skip this database installation for now if desired.

To prepare your database environment, follow these steps. Note that this exercise uses the MySQL console application to send commands to the database server.

Follow these steps:

1. Load a Windows Command Prompt window by going to Start ➪ Run and executing cmd.exe. In Windows Vista, you can type cmd or Command Prompt in the search box of the Start menu.

2. Change your current directory to the bin folder of your MySQL installation. With the default XAMPP installation, that folder is \Program Files\xampp\mysql\bin. Change the directory using the following command:

```
cd \Program Files\xampp\mysql\bin
```

3. Start the MySQL console application using the following command (this loads an executable file named `mysql.exe` located in the directory you have just browsed to):

```
mysql -u root
```

If you have a password set for the root account, you should also add the -p option, which will have the tool ask you for the password. By default, after installing XAMPP, the `root` *user doesn't have a password. Needless to say, you may want to change this for security reasons.*

4. Create the `seophp` database by typing this at the MySQL console:

```
CREATE DATABASE seophp;
```

MySQL commands, such as CREATE DATABASE, *are not case sensitive. If you like, you can type* create database *instead of* CREATE DATABASE. *However, database objects, such as the* seophp *database, may or may not be case sensitive, depending on the server settings and operating system. For this reason, it's important to always use consistent casing. (This book uses uppercase for MySQL commands, and lowercase for object names.)*

5. Switch context to the `seophp` database.

```
USE seophp;
```

6. Create a database user with full access to the new `seophp` database:

```
GRANT ALL PRIVILEGES ON seophp.*
TO seouser@localhost IDENTIFIED BY "seomaster";
```

7. Make sure all commands executed successfully, as shown in Figure 1-7.

8. Exit the console by typing:

```
exit;
```

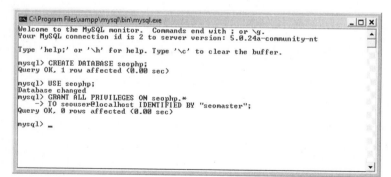

Figure 1-7

Summary

Congratulations! You will soon be ready to write some code and delve into more advanced SEO concepts! The next chapter takes you through a quick SEO tutorial, and builds the foundation for the chapters to come.

2

A Primer in Basic SEO

Although this book addresses search engine optimization primarily from the perspective of a web site's architecture, you, the web site developer, may also appreciate this handy reference of basic factors that contribute to site ranking. This chapter discusses some of the fundamentals of search engine optimization.

If you are a search engine marketing veteran, feel free to skip to Chapter 3. However, because this chapter is relatively short, it may still be worth a skim. It can also be useful to refer back to it, because our intent is to provide a brief guide about what does matter and what probably does not. This will serve to illuminate some of the recommendations we make later with regard to web site architecture.

This chapter contains, in a nutshell:

- ❑ A short introduction to the fundamentals of SEO.
- ❑ A list of the most important search engine ranking factors.
- ❑ Discussion of search engine penalties, and how you can avoid them.
- ❑ Using web analytics to assist in measuring the performance of your web site.
- ❑ Using research tools to gather market data.
- ❑ Resources and tools for the search engine marketer and web developer.

Introduction to SEO

Today, the most popular tool that the users employ to find products and information on the web is the search engine. Consequentially, ranking well in a search engine can be very profitable. In a search landscape where users rarely peruse past the first or second page of search results, poor rankings are simply not an option.

> **Search engine optimization aims to increase the number of visitors to a web site from unpaid, "organic" search engine listings by improving rankings.**

Knowing and understanding the exact algorithms employed by a search engine would offer an unassailable advantage for the search engine marketer. However, search engines will never disclose their proprietary inner workings — in part for that very reason. Furthermore, a search engine is actually the synthesis of thousands of complex interconnected algorithms. Arguably, even an individual computer scientist at Google could not know and understand everything that contributes to a search results page. And certainly, deducing the exact algorithms is impossible. There are simply too many variables involved.

Nevertheless, search engine marketers are aware of several ranking factors — some with affirmation by representatives of search engine companies themselves. There are positive factors that are generally known to improve a web site's rankings. Likewise, there are negative factors that may hurt a web site's rankings. Discussing these factors is the primary focus of the material that follows in this chapter.

You should be especially wary of your sources in the realm of search engine optimization. There are many snake oil salesmen publishing completely misleading information. Some of them are even trying to be helpful — they are just wrong. One place to turn to when looking for answers is reputable contributors on SEO forums. A number of these forums are provided at the end of this chapter.

Many factors affect search engine rankings. But before discussing them, the next section covers the concept of "link equity," which is a fundamental concept in search engine marketing.

Link Equity

Without links, the World Wide Web would just be a collection of unrelated documents. Links provide structure and provide both implicit and explicit information in the aggregate. For example, if a web page is linked from many web sites, it usually implies that it is a more important page than one that has fewer incoming links. Moreover, if the anchor text of those links contains the word "cookie," this indicates to search engines that the cited page is about cookies.

Links assign value to web pages, and as a result they have a fundamental role in search engine optimization. This book frequently references a concept called *URL equity* or *link equity*. Link equity is defined as the equity, or value, transferred to another URL by a particular link. For clarity, we will use the term *link equity* when we refer to the assigning or *transferring* of equity, and *URL equity* when we refer to the actual equity contained by a given URL.

Among all the factors that search engines take into consideration when ranking web sites, link equity has become paramount. It is also important for other reasons, as we will make clear. Link equity comes in the following forms:

1. **Search engine ranking equity.** Modern search engines use the quantity and quality of links to a particular URL as a metric for its quality, relevance, and usefulness. A web site that scores well in this regard will rank better. Thus, the URL contains an *economic* value in tandem with the content that it contains. That, in turn, comprises its URL equity. If the content is moved to a new URL, the old URL will eventually be removed from a search engine index. However,

doing so alone will not result in transference of the said equity, unless all the incoming links are changed to target the new location on the web sites that contain the links (needless to say, this is not likely to be a successful endeavor). The solution is to inform the search engines about the change using redirects, which would also result in equity transference. Without a proper redirect, there is no way for a search engine to know that the links are associated with the new URL, and the URL equity is thusly entirely lost.

2. **Bookmark equity.** Users will often bookmark useful URLs in their browsers, and more recently in social bookmarking web sites. Moving content to a new URL will forgo the traffic resulting from these bookmarks unless a redirect is used to inform the browser that the content has moved. Without a redirect, a user will likely receive an error message stating that the content is not available.

3. **Direct citation equity.** Last but not least, other sites may cite and link to URLs on your web site. That may drive a significant amount of traffic to your web site in itself. Moving content to a new URL will forgo the traffic resulting from these links unless a redirect is used to inform the browser that the content has moved.

Therefore, before changing any URLs, log files or web analytics should be consulted. One must be aware of the value in a URL. Web analytics are particularly useful in this case because the information is provided in an easy, understandable, summarized format. If a URL must be changed, one may want to employ a 301-redirect. This will transfer the equity in all three cases. Redirects are discussed at length in Chapter 4, "Content Relocation and HTTP Status Codes."

Google PageRank

PageRank is an algorithm patented by Google that measures a particular page's importance relative to other pages included in the search engine's index. It was invented in the late 1990s by Larry Page and Sergey Brin. PageRank implements the concept of link equity as a ranking factor.

> **PageRank considers a link to a page as a vote, indicating importance.**

PageRank approximates the likelihood that a user, randomly clicking links throughout the Internet, will arrive at that particular page. A page that is arrived at more often is likely more important — and has a higher PageRank. Each page linking to another page increases the PageRank of that other page. Pages with higher PageRank typically increase the PageRank of the other page more on that basis. You can read a few details about the PageRank algorithm at http://en.wikipedia.org/wiki/PageRank.

To view a site's PageRank, install the Google toolbar (http://toolbar.google.com/) and enable the PageRank feature, or install the SearchStatus plugin for Firefox (http://www.quirk.biz/searchstatus/). One thing to note, however, is that the PageRank indicated by Google is a cached value, and is usually out of date.

> **PageRank values are published only a few times per year, and sometimes using outdated information. Therefore, PageRank is not a terribly accurate metric. Google itself is likely using a more current value for rankings.**

PageRank is just one factor in the collective algorithm Google uses when building search results pages (SERPs). It is still possible that a page with a lower PageRank ranks above one with a higher PageRank for a particular query. PageRank is also relevance agnostic, in that it measures overall popularity using links, and not the subject shrouding them. Google currently also investigates the relevance of links when calculating search rankings, therefore PageRank should not be the sole focus of a search engine marketer. Building relevant links will naturally contribute to a higher PageRank. Furthermore, building too many irrelevant links solely for the purpose of increasing PageRank may actually hurt the ranking of a site, because Google attempts to detect and devalue irrelevant links that are presumably used to manipulate it.

PageRank is also widely regarded by users as a trust-building factor, because users will tend to perceive sites with a high value as more reputable or authoritative. Indeed, this is what PageRank is designed to indicate. This perception is affirmed by the fact that Google penalizes spam or irrelevant sites (or individual pages) by reducing or zeroing their PageRank.

Google PageRank isn't the only link-related ranking algorithm, but it is one of the most popular. Other algorithms include:

- ❑ The Hilltop algorithm (`http://www.cs.toronto.edu/~georgem/hilltop/`)
- ❑ ExpertRank of Ask.com (`http://about.ask.com/en/docs/about/ask_technology.shtml`)
- ❑ HITS (`http://en.wikipedia.org/wiki/HITS_algorithm`)
- ❑ TrustRank (`http://en.wikipedia.org/wiki/TrustRank`)

A Word on Usability and Accessibility

Web site usability is defined as the ease of use exhibited by a web site. Web site accessibility addresses the same concerns, but focuses on those users who have impairments such as limited vision or hearing. The search engine marketer can analogize usability and accessibility as "user optimization."

Having a web site that ranks well is paramount. But the search engine is only one of the consumers of a web site's contents, and your users must also appreciate your web site once they arrive. Developers especially tend to ignore this factor, and they often cower in fear when they hear words like "usability" and "accessibility." Kim Krause Berg of *The Usability Effect* (`http://www.usabilityeffect.com`) suggests an explanation:

"This is because, and they [developers] are not alone in this belief, they fear someone is about to put some serious limitations on their work. Graphic artists often react the same way."

As a hybrid developer and search engine marketer, you must have a wiser reaction. The implementation of a web site must incorporate search engine optimization concerns, as well as usability and accessibility concerns. Where interests conflict, a careful compromise must be struck. "User optimization" must not be forgotten.

Sometimes search engine optimization and usability concerns coincide; other times they hopelessly clash. Ultimately, your users will appreciate attention to usability and accessibility in the form of more conversions. If you want more information on this subject, Steve Krug's *Don't Make Me Think, 2nd* edition (New Riders Press, 2005) is a classic that covers these concepts in detail. *Prioritizing Web Usability* (New Riders Press, 2006) by Jakob Nielsen and Hoa Loranger is also a great book, addressing the areas where usability problems typically present themselves.

Search Engine Ranking Factors

The algorithms used by Google, Yahoo!, or MSN Live Search to calculate search results can change at any time, therefore we generally avoid citing specific details regarding particular search engines and their algorithms. Search engines have been known to periodically modify their algorithms and, as a result, turn the SERPs upside down. Examples of this include Google's Florida and BigDaddy updates. A great place to peruse to see the latest trends are the forums mentioned at the end of this chapter.

Historically, search engine marketers created optimized pages for each particular search engine. This is no longer viable, as mentioned in Chapter 1, because it yields duplicate content. Rankings must be achieved in all search engines using the same web pages. Furthermore, calculations such as "optimal keyword density" and "optimal page content length" for the various search engines are almost entirely obsolete. Calculations like these demonstrate a gross oversimplification of modern search engine information retrieval algorithms.

With these disclaimers out of the way, it is time to briefly discuss the most important factors as a quick primer for the web site developer. We group the factors that affect search engine rankings into the following general categories:

- ❑ Visible on-page factors
- ❑ Invisible on-page factors
- ❑ Time-based factors
- ❑ External factors

> **You can find a great synopsis of the relevance of the various factors, in the opinion of a number of various experts, at** `http://www.seomoz.org/articles/search-ranking-factors.php`.

On-Page Factors

On-page factors are those criteria of a web page that are dictated by the contents of a web page itself. They are critical to a search engine marketing campaign, but less so than they were historically, because they are very easy to manipulate. Because there are obvious incentives for spammers to do so, search engines have begun to place importance on other factors as well. That is *not* to say that on-page factors are not important, however.

It is useful to further divide on-page factors into two categories — those that are visible and those that are invisible. The former are much more important than the latter. Many search engine marketers believe that the latter are now devalued to the extent that they are mostly not worth bothering with. This is because they can be so easily manipulated without influencing page presentation at all. Spam can be carefully hidden in a web page in this way. A search engine's confidence in such factors being honest or accurate, therefore, is low. In short, the search engine's algorithms regard visible content with more confidence, because the user will actually see this content.

Any content that is hidden using CSS or other forms of subterfuge, regardless of intent, may be regarded as an invisible factor and devalued. At worst, if employed excessively, the page or site may be penalized as a whole.

Visible On-Page Factors

The visible on-page factors covered here are the following:

❑ Page title

❑ Page headings

❑ Page copy

❑ Outbound links

❑ Keywords in URLs and domain name

❑ Internal link structure and anchors

❑ Overall site topicality

Page Title

The page title is a string of text, defined by contents of the `<title>` element in the `<head>` section of the HTML document. The title is visible both in the title bar of a browser window, as well as the headline of a search engine result. It is arguably one of the most important factors in search engine optimization because it is both an important factor in search engine rankings, as well as a critical call to action that can enhance the click-through rate (CTR). Certainly, it is one of the most important on-page factors. Vanessa Fox of Google states, "Make sure each page has a descriptive `<title>` tag and headings. The title of a page isn't all that useful if every page has the same one."

> One of the biggest mistakes web developers make is to set the title for all pages on a web site to the same default text. Frequently, this text is the company name and/or a slogan. In this case, at best your pages will be indexed poorly. At worst, the site could receive a penalty if the search engines see the pages as duplicate content. Be sure all pages on a dynamic site have unique and relevant titles.

When writing titles, it is also wise to insert some targeted keywords. You should not lose sight, however, that a title is also a call to action. Even if a title successfully influences a search engine to rank a page highly, that ranking effectiveness is then multiplied by your CTR. Keyword stuffed titles are not always effective for CTR, though they may rank well. As a reminder, these keywords should also appear in the document's copy.

People will also frequently use a page title for the anchor text of an inbound link. Anchor text is an important external factor, and its beneficial effect is discussed later in this chapter.

Page Headings

Page headings are sections of text set off from web page copy to indicate overall context and meaning. They are usually larger in size than the other copy within the document. They are typically created using `<Hx>` tags in HTML, where x is a number between 1 and 6. They have been abused in the past to manipulate search rankings, but they are still an important on-page factor, and they also serve to help the user navigate a page.

Page Copy

It is intuitively clear that a page that contains the keywords that a user is looking for should be relevant to his or her search query. Search engine algorithms take this into account as well. Keyword insertion, however, should not be done in the excess. Mentioning the keywords in various inflections (plural, singular, past, present, and so on) is likely beneficial, as well as varying word order ("chocolate chip cookies" versus "cookies with chocolate chips"). Excessive and contrived keyword repetition — "keyword stuffing" — however, could actually be perceived as spam.

Because the search engine algorithms are unknown, "excessive" is an unfortunately vague qualifier. This is one of the times we will reference something requisitely in an imprecise manner.

SEO copywriting aims to produce content on a web site in such a way that it reads well for the surfer, but also targets specific search terms in search engines. It is a process that legitimately, without the use of spamming techniques, seeks to achieve high rankings in the search engines. SEO copywriting is an art, and it takes time to master. There is no magic solution that will make it easy to create copy that is persuasive, contains relevant keywords a few times, and sounds like it is not contrived specifically to do so. There are a few tricks, and a few useful hints, however.

*One of our favorite tricks is to use the end and beginning of a sentence to repeat a keyword subtly. Example: "Miami Hotels: You may want to try one our fine hotels in **Miami. Hotel** accommodations at the Makebelieve Hotel will exceed your wildest expectations."*

The copy should also contain words that are related, but not necessarily inflections of your targeted key phrase. For example, a search engine algorithm would likely see a page on cookies that also contains the words "chocolate chip" or "cakes" as relevant. This tends to happen naturally with well-written prose, but it is worth mentioning.

Outbound Links

Search engines will evaluate the links that a document contains. A related link on a web page is valuable content in and of itself, and is treated as such by search engines. However, links to totally irrelevant or spam content can potentially hurt the rankings of a page. Linking to a "bad neighborhood" of spam sites or even lots of irrelevant sites can hurt a site's rankings.

Keywords in Page URL and Domain Name

It is likely that keywords contained by a URL, both in the domain name or in the file name, do have a minor but apparently positive effect on ranking. It also likely has an effect on CTR because keywords in the URL may make a user more likely to click a link due to an increase in perceived relevance. The URL, like the page title, is also often selected as the anchor text for a link. This may have the same previously mentioned beneficial effect.

Internal Link Structure and Anchors

Search engines may make the assumption that pages not linked to, or buried within a web site's internal link structure, are less important, just as they assume that pages that are not linked well from external sources are less important than those that are. Linking from the home page to content that you would like to rank can improve that page's rankings, as well as linking to it from a sitemap and from various related content within the site. This models real-world human behavior as well. Popular products are often prominently featured in the front of a store.

One horrible way to push pages down the link hierarchy is to implement pagination using "< prev" and "next >" links, without linking directly to the individual pages. Consider the example of the fourth page of an article that is split into four parts. It is reached like this:

Home Page ⇨ Article Part 1 ⇨ Article Part 2 ⇨ Article Part 3 ⇨ Article Part 4

This fourth page is harder to reach not only by humans (who need to click at least four times), but also by search engines, which would probably consider the content in that page as less important. We call the effect of this link structure "death by pagination," and we suggest two possible approaches for mitigating the problem:

1. Don't use simple pagination. Page with "< prev" and "next >" links, but also add links to the individual pages, that is, "< prev 1 2 3 4 next >." This creates a better navigation scheme to all pages.

2. Add a sitemap with links to all the pages.

Because this problem is pretty common with blogs, in Chapter 16 you create a WordPress plugin that implements pagination with links to the individual pages. This technique is also demonstrated in the e-commerce case study in Chapter 14. You learn more about sitemaps in Chapter 9.

Overall Site Topicality

The fact that a web page is semantically related to other pages within a web site may boost the rankings of that particular page. This means other related pages linked within a site may be used to boost the rankings of the web site as a whole. This tends to happen naturally when writing quality content for a web site regardless.

Invisible On-Page Factors

Invisible on-page factors are, as you correctly guessed, parts of a web page that are not visible to the human readers. They can be read, however, by a search engine parsing a web site. Invisible page factors include:

❑ Meta description

❑ Meta keywords

❑ Alt and title attributes

❑ Page structure considerations

Meta Description

For the most part, the importance of a meta description lies in the fact that search engines may choose to use it in the SERPs, instead of displaying relevant bits from the page (this is not guaranteed, however). Speaking from a marketing point of view, this may improve CTR. A meta description may also have a minor effect on search engine rankings, but it is definitely not a critical factor in that regard. Here is an example:

```
<head>
  <meta name="description" value="The secrets to baking fresh, chewy chocolate chip
  cookies that make you wish thousands of calories were actually good for you!" />
  ...
</head>
```

Meta Keywords

This criterion is widely regarded as totally unimportant because it is completely invisible and subject to manipulation. It is wise to place a few major keywords as well as their misspellings in the meta keywords tag, but the effectiveness of targeting misspellings this way has been disputed:

```
<head>
  <meta name="keywords" value="chocolate chip cookies, baking chocolate chip
cookies, choclate, cokies" />
  ...
</head>
```

Alt and Title Attributes

Because these attributes are mostly invisible, they are likely not an important ranking factor. Many assert that their value is higher on hyperlinked images. They are important, however, for screen readers and text-based browsers — that is, for accessibility and usability in general, so they should not be ignored for that reason alone. Neither of these attributes will make or break you, but blind visitors using screen readers will thank you in any case. This is a case where accessibility, usability, and search engine optimization coincide. The descriptions should be short. Keyword stuffing in an `alt` attribute will irk blind users using screen readers, and possibly "irk" the search engines as well. Alt attributes can only be used in image tags, whereas title attributes can be used in most tags. Here is an example of the `alt` attribute in an image:

```
<img src="/images/chocolate_chip_cookie.jpg" alt="a picture of a really big
chocolate chip cookie">
```

And the `title` attribute on a link:

```
<a href="/chocolate_chip_cookie.html" title="a really big chocolate chip cookie">
```

Page Structure Considerations

Search engines use block-level elements, for example `<div>`, `<p>`, or `<table>` elements to group related text. Using block-level elements indiscriminately for layout, as illustrated in the following example, may be harmful:

```
<div>Dog</div>
<div>food</div> is likely to be less relevant than:
<div>dog food</div>.
```

Time-Based Factors

Try as you might, but the only criterion that cannot be manipulated in any way is time. Old men and women are often sought for their knowledge and experience. And the price of wine is directly proportional to its age for a reason.

This is a useful analogy. Because time cannot be cheated, an old site that slowly accumulates links over time and regularly adds new knowledge is what we term "fine wine." Search engines tend to agree, and give the deserved credit to such fine wines.

Many marketers previously purchased expired domain names that used to house an older popular web site in the interest of tricking search engines into thinking a site is not new. Search engines are now aware of this practice and reset the "aging-value" of any site that is housed by an expired domain name, as well as devalue its preexisting links. In fact, there may also be a penalty applied to such expired domain names, as discussed later in this chapter in the section "The Expired Domain Penalty." There are still opportunities, however, in buying domains directly from users with old existing web sites.

The time-based factors that are used as ranking factors are the site and page age, and the age of the links referring to it. The registration length of a domain name may also influence rankings.

Site and Page Age

A web site that has existed for many years is likely to rank better than a new site, all other variables held constant. Over time, a web site acquires trust. This models human behavior as well — a shopper is more likely to shop at a store that has existed for many years and provided good service than a new store with no reputation at all.

Likewise, a page that has existed for a long time may rank better, both because it probably acquired links over the years, and because search engines may consider age a factor on the page level as well. There are some conflicting views on this, however, and many also suggest changing and updating content on a page over time as well, because it indicates that the site is active and includes fresh content.

Link Age

Links that are present on other sites pointing to a web site acquire more value over time. This is another instance of the "fine wine" analogy. Over time, a link may appreciate in value.

Domain Registration Length

Search engines may view a long domain name registration as an indication that a web site is not engaging in spam. Domain names are relatively inexpensive on a yearly basis, and spammers frequently use them in a disposable fashion. The domains eventually get permanently banned and must be abandoned. A search engine spammer would typically not register a domain name for more than one year, because registering for more than that disrupts the economics of spamming. Search engines are aware of this. Therefore, if possible, it may be wise to register your domain name for more than one year. It certainly cannot hurt.

External Factors

Many external factors can influence the search engine rankings of a web site. The following pages discuss these:

- ❑ Quantity, quality, and relevance of inbound links
- ❑ Link churn
- ❑ Link acquisition rate
- ❑ Link anchor text and surrounding copy
- ❑ Reciprocal links
- ❑ Number of links on a page

- ❑ Semantic relationships among links on a page
- ❑ IP addresses of cross-linked sites
- ❑ TLD of domain name for a link
- ❑ Link location
- ❑ Web standards compliance
- ❑ Detrimental "red-flag" factors

Quantity of Inbound Links

A site with many inbound links is likely to be relevant because many people voted for it by placing the link on their sites. There are some caveats here with regard to whether the links are detected to be part of an artificial link scheme, and quality is also a concern as explained in the next section. However, more is generally better.

Quality of Inbound Links

A popular web site that links to you prominently that itself has many inbound links and a good reputation is likely to mean more than a link from a random page from an unimportant web site with few links. There is no absolute definition that describes "quality." Search engines themselves struggle with this definition and use very complicated algorithms that implement an approximation of the human definition. Use your judgment and intuition.

There are certain exceptions to this rule, as MySpace.com (or other similar social web sites with user-generated content) may have many links pointing to it as a whole, but a link, even from a popular MySpace profile sub page, may not yield the results that would seem reasonable from a direct interpretation of link popularity. The same may also be true for Blogger.com blogs and other subdomain-based sites. This may be because search engines treat such sites as exceptions to stem artificial manipulation.

Relevance of Inbound Links

A search engine is likely to view a link from a semantically related web page or site as more valuable than a link from a random unrelated one. Usually, a series of links with very similar anchor text from unrelated sources is an indicator of an artificial link scheme, and they may be devalued. Too many links from irrelevant sources may result in a penalty. This has led to speculation that competitors can hurt your web site by pointing many such links to your web site. Google states in its Webmaster Help Center, however, that there is "almost nothing a competitor can do to harm your ranking or have your site removed from our index" (`http://www.google.com/support/webmasters/bin/answer.py?answer=34449`). The verdict is out on MSN Live Search, as documented at `http://www.seroundtable.com/archives/006666.html`.

Link Churn

Links that appear and disappear on pages are likely to be part of a linking scheme. The rate at which these links appear and disappear is termed "link churn." If this happens frequently, it may be regarded as spam. Those links will either be devalued, or at worst your web site will be regarded as spam and penalized. Unless you are participating in such a scheme, this should probably not be a concern.

Link Acquisition Rate

An algorithm may view the acquisition of many thousands of links by a new site as suspicious, if not also accompanied by relevant highly ranked authority sites. Usually this is an indicator of an artificial linking scheme. This consideration was affirmed by Google engineer Matt Cutts in one of his videos at http://www.mattcutts.com/blog/more-seo-answers-on-video/.

Link Anchor Text and Surrounding Copy

Inbound links that contain semantically related anchor text to the content they point to have a positive effect on rankings. The copy surrounding the link, if present, may also do the same. Some even posit that this copy is as important as the link anchor text itself. Links with such surrounding copy are widely believed to be valued more by search engines, because links without copy surrounding it are frequently purchased and/or less indicative of a vote.

Manipulating link anchor text and the surrounding copy, if done en masse, can be used to manipulate search results by creating a phenomenon called "Google bombing" (http://en.wikipedia.org/wiki/Google_bomb). *One popular example of this is illustrated, at the time of writing, with a query to Yahoo!, Google, or MSN, with the keyword "miserable failure." The top result is the White House's official biographical page for President George W. Bush, which doesn't contain either of the words "miserable" or "failure" in the copy, but is linked from many sites that contain the words "miserable failure." This particular Google bomb, and a few related ones, are described at* http://en.wikipedia.org/wiki/Miserable_failure.

Reciprocal Links

A long time ago, webmasters used to trade links strategically to achieve radical improvements in rankings. This created an artificial number of self-serving votes. Over time, search engines became wiser and they devalued such reciprocal links. In response, search engine marketers created link-exchanging schemes with multiple parties to avoid detection. Modern search engines can detect such simple subterfuge as well. That is not to say that reciprocal linking is bad, but it should be balanced by several one-way links as well. The combination of the two models something more natural-looking and will result in higher ranking.

Number of Links on a Page

A link on a page with few outbound links is generally worth more than a link on a page with many outbound links. This concept is also implied by the formula for Google's PageRank.

Semantic Relationship among Links on a Page

A search engine may assume that a page with many links to pages that are not semantically related is a links page, or some sort of page designed to manipulate rankings or trade links. It is also believed that even naming a page with the word "links" in it, such as links.php, may actually devalue links contained within that particular page.

IP Addresses of Cross-Linked Sites

It is sometimes useful to think of an IP address as you do a phone number. For this example's sake, format a hypothetical phone number, (123) 555-1212, differently — as if it were an IP:

```
123.555.1212
```

The first number, 123, is the area code, the second, 555, is the exchange, and the third, 1212, is the number within that exchange. The numbers go from most significant to least significant. 123 probably indicates "somewhere in this or that state." 555 means "some county in the state," and so on. So we can assert that the person answering the phone at 123.555.1212 is in the same neighborhood as 123.555.1213.

Likewise, IP addresses located in the same C class — that is, addresses that match for the first three octets (xxx.xxx.xxx.*) — are very likely to be nearby, perhaps even on the same server.

When sites are interlinked with many links that come from such similar IP addresses, they will be regarded suspiciously, and those links may be devalued. For example, a link from domainA on 100.100.1.1 to domainB on 100.100.1.2 is a link between two such sites. Done excessively, this can be an indicator for artificial link schemes meant to manipulate the rankings of those web sites. Matt Cutts affirms that Google scrutinizes this sort of interlinking in his video at http://www.mattcutts.com/blog/seo-answers-on-google-video/.

Perhaps you host quite a few sites with similar themed content for whatever reason, and do not wish to worry about this. There are a few vendors that offer hosting in multiple C classes. We don't have experience working with any of these providers, and do not make any recommendations. This is just a list of hosting services that we've found that offer this particular service. Many of them also offer custom nameserver and netblock information.

- ❑ http://www.dataracks.net/
- ❑ http://www.gotwebhost.com/
- ❑ http://www.seowebhosting.net/
- ❑ http://www.webhostforseo.com/

TLD of Domain Name for a Link

It is widely believed that .edu and .gov domain names are less susceptible to manipulation and therefore weighed more heavily. This is disputed by some search engine marketers as the actual factor, and they assert that the same effect may be as a result of the age (most schools and governmental agencies have had sites for a while), and amount of links that they've acquired over time. Matt Cutts coincides with this view (http://www.mattcutts.com/blog/another-two-videos/). It is mostly irrelevant, however, what the underlying reason is. Getting a link from a site that fits this sort of profile is very desirable — and most .edu and .gov domains do.

Link Location

Links prominently presented in content near the center of the page may be regarded by the search engines as more important. Links embedded in content presented near the bottom of a page are usually less important; and external links at the bottom of a page to semantically unrelated sites may, at worst, be a criterion for spam-detection. Presentation location is different than *physical* location. The physical location within the document was historically important, but is less of a factor more recently. Ideally, the primary content of a page should be early in the HTML source of a web page, as well as prominently displayed in the center region of a web page. More on this topic is discussed in Chapter 6, "SE-Friendly HTML and JavaScript."

Web Standards Compliance

Standards compliance and cleanliness of code is historically unimportant, but the recent accessibility work may eventually make it become a small ranking factor. That said, Matt Cutts downplays it because 40% of the web doesn't validate (http://www.mattcutts.com/blog/more-seo-answers-on-video/). Content on google.com itself does not validate, at the moment of writing this text. You can use the W3C Markup Validation Service at http://validator.w3.org/ to test your web pages for compliance.

Detrimental "Red-Flag" Factors

Obviously writing spammy content, launching thousands of spammy doorway pages simultaneously, or soliciting spammy links that actually get detected as such are detrimental in nature, but we will not continue in that vein. Some of these factors are discussed in more detail in Chapter 8, "Black Hat SEO."

Potential Search Engine Penalties

A penalized web site is much less likely to show up in a SERP, and in some cases it may not appear at all. This section discusses the following:

- ❑ The Google "sandbox effect"
- ❑ The expired domain penalty
- ❑ Duplicate content penalty
- ❑ The Google supplemental index

The Google "Sandbox Effect"

Many search engine optimization experts hypothesize that there is a virtual "purgatory" that all newly launched sites must pass through in order to rank well in Google. In fact, many new sites seem to pass through this stage, and many find that the period is remarkably close to six months. Matt Cutts states in an interview with Barry Schwartz that there may be "things in the algorithm that may be perceived as a sandbox that doesn't apply to all industries" (http://www.seroundtable.com/archives/002822.html).

We believe that while Google may not explicitly have a "sandbox," the effect itself is real. For this reason it is termed an "effect," and not a "penalty." It may be the collective side effect of several algorithms — not an explicit "sandbox algorithm." Some sites seem to be exceptions to the rule, especially those that acquire links from several authority sites early on. A few links from CNN.com and other prominent web sites, for example, may exempt a web site from the sandbox effect.

Some hypothesize that Yahoo! has a similar algorithmic factor, but that it is less severe and pronounced. MSN Search does not appear to have anything similar implemented.

The Expired Domain Penalty

Using a previously expired domain to launch a new web site used to evade this dreaded "sandbox effect." This was likely because Google was unaware that the site was new. Google put a stop to this loophole a while ago, and now it seems to be quite the opposite situation at times.

An expired domain name may now be subject to a temporary penalty. This is important, because it implies an additional delay before a site begins to rank well. In some cases Google will even refuse to index the pages at all during that period, leaving a web site vulnerable to content theft. Content theft is discussed at length in Chapter 5, "Duplicate Content."

It is also likely that Google devalues any links that are acquired before the re-registration of the domain. At the time of writing, other search engines do not appear to penalize previously expired domains.

Duplicate Content Penalty

Search engines attempt to avoid indexing multiple copies of the same content — duplicate content. Many search engine optimization experts hypothesize that not only does a search engine not index such pages, but it also penalizes a site for having the duplicated content.

This is a subject of much debate, but in any case, having duplicate content will not improve the rankings of a site in any of the major search engines. Therefore, duplicate content should be avoided, and this book devotes an entire chapter to the subject.

The Google Supplemental Index

This is not strictly a penalty in and of itself, but it may be the result of one. Google stores its crawled search data in two indexes: the primary index and the *supplemental index*. The supplemental index stores pages that are less important to Google for whatever reason. Results from the supplemental index typically appear at the end of the results for a Google query (unless the query is very specific), and the results are marked as supplemental results.

Figure 2-1 shows how a supplemental result is denoted in a Google search results page. Factors that lead to inclusion of that link in the supplemental index rather than the primary index are the lack of significant unique content or a lack of inbound links to the said content. It may also be as a result of explicit penalization.

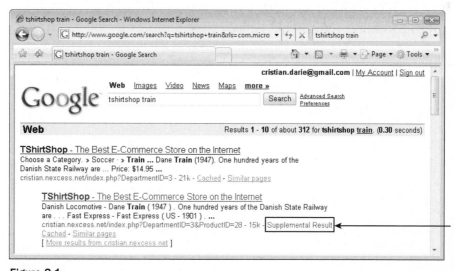

Figure 2-1

Resources and Tools

There are many tools, web sites, and practices that serious search engine marketers must be aware of. As a web developer concerned with SEO, you should also be knowledgeable of at least the most important of them. The rest of this chapter highlights a few such resources that can be helpful in your search engine marketing quest.

Web Analytics

Web analytics measure traffic and track user behavior on a particular web site. Typically web analytics are also used for the purpose of optimizing business performance based on various metrics such as conversion rate and return on investment. They are particularly relevant for tracking return on investment for PPC advertising, where there is a particular cost for each click. However, they are also used to track which keywords from organic traffic are leading to conversions. This informs the search engine marketer which key phrases he or she should target when performing search engine optimization — both to improve and to maintain current positioning.

Google Analytics

Google Analytics is a free and robust web service that performs web analytics. It is located at `http://www.google.com/analytics/`. The service is complex enough to merit its own book; feel free to check out *Google Analytics* (Mary E. Tyler and Jerri L. Ledford, Wiley, 2006). Figure 2-2 shows one of the many reports Google Analytics can deliver.

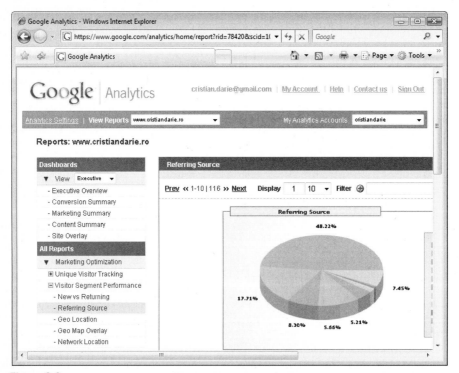

Figure 2-2

Other Web Analytics Tools

Google Analytics is just one of the many analytics tools available today. Here are a few others:

❑ ClickTracks (http://www.clicktracks.com/)

❑ CoreMetrics (http://www.coremetrics.com/)

❑ HitTail (http://www.hittail.com/)

A detailed list of web analytics tools has been aggregated by Carsten Cumbrowski at http://www.cumbrowski.com/webanalytics.html.

Market Research

Just as it is important to know data about your web site, it's equally important to know the market and your competitors. The first skill to learn is how to use the built-in features of the search engines. For example, to find all the pages from http://www.seoegghead.com indexed by Google, Yahoo!, or MSN, you'd need to submit a query for site:www.seoegghead.com. Figure 2-3 shows the results of this query in Google.

Figure 2-3

Yahoo! Site Explorer

Yahoo! Site Explorer shows what pages of a web site were indexed by Yahoo!, and what other pages link to it. A query of linkdomain:www.cristiandarie.ro brings you to the Yahoo! Site Explorer page shown in Figure 2-4.

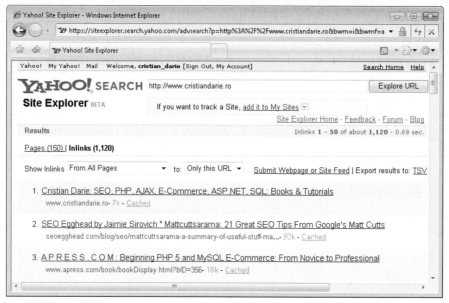

Figure 2-4

Google and MSN Live Search also contain this functionality. It can be accessed in both using the same `linkdomain:` syntax, but at the time of writing they don't provide very accurate information.

Google Trends

Google Trends is a tool from Google that provides the statistics regarding the volume of keyword searches over various time periods. Data are available going back to 2004.

The Google Trends service lets you partition data by language and region and plot multiple key phrases on one graph. This can be used to track and anticipate traffic for a particular period (see Figure 2-5). The service is available at `http://www.google.com/trends`.

Figure 2-5 shows the Google Trends report for "SEO" as of 8/30/2006.

Alexa Rankings

Alexa Rankings attempt to rank all web sites globally by quantity of traffic. The traffic rankings use statistics based on data gathered from the Alexa Toolbar and other tools connected to the service. The service is provided by Alexa Internet, a subsidiary of Amazon Incorporated. Yahoo! is ranked number one at the time of this book's writing.

The statistics aren't generally accepted as accurate, and many speculate that the rankings are subject to manipulation and skewing as a result of a limited dataset. In general, the statistics are more accurate with higher ranking sites (those with *lower* numerical rankings). Despite these caveats, Alexa Rankings can be used to get a handle on increasing traffic trends, and they are generally fun to watch.

Figure 2-6 shows the Alexa Rankings page for `http://www.seoegghead.com`, at the date of November 21, 2006.

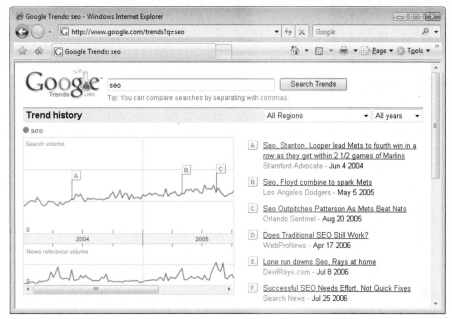

Figure 2-5

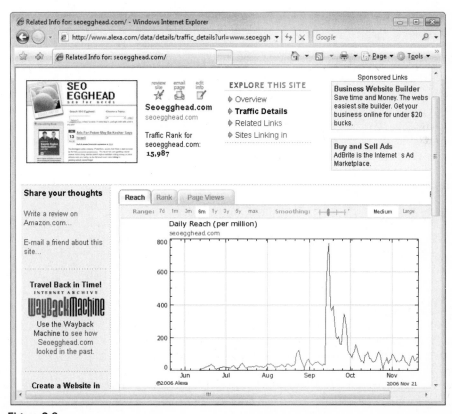

Figure 2-6

Researching Keywords

Brainstorming keywords that seem relevant to your web site may help to identify keywords to target in a search engine marketing campaign. However, the actual keywords used by web searchers may be surprising more often than not. Fortunately, tools are available that mine available search data and conveniently allow one to peruse both related keywords as well as their respective query volumes. Such services include:

- ❏ Wordtracker (`http://www.wordtracker.com`)
- ❏ Keyword Discovery (`http://www.keyworddiscovery.com`)
- ❏ The Yahoo! Search Marketing Keyword Tool (`http://inventory.overture.com/`)

Both Wordtracker and Keyword Discovery are fee-based tools that tap into various smaller search engines to assemble their data. The latter is a free tool that uses the data from Yahoo! Search Marketing's pay-per-click network; Figure 2-7 shows this tool in action for the keyword "seo."

Because none of these tools are immune to data anomalies — and even deliberate manipulation — it may be wise to use two tools and some intuition to assess whether the data is real. For more information on using keyword research tools effectively, we recommend reading *Search Engine Optimization An Hour a Day* (Wiley Publishing, Inc., 2006) by Jennifer Grappone and Gradiva Couzin.

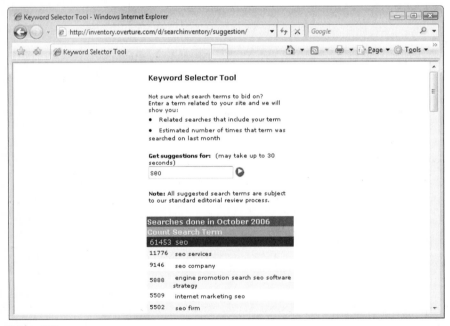

Figure 2-7

Browser Plugins

The Search Engine Marketer may be aided by some Search Engine Optimization tools. Table 2-1 reveals the ones that we've found particularly useful.

Table 2-1

Tool Name	Browser	Web Site	Description
SearchStatus	Firefox	`http://www.quirk.biz/searchstatus/`	This plugin shows both PageRank and Alexa Ranking in the Firefox status bar.
SEO for Firefox	Firefox	`http://www.seobook.com/archives/001741.shtml`	This plugin modifies Google and Yahoo! SERPs to display various metrics regarding a site, such as PageRank, Alexa Ranking, and number of links broken down by several criteria.
Web Developer Extension	Firefox	`http://chrispederick.com/work/webdeveloper/`	A must-have tool for all web developers; the list of features is too long to mention here.
RefControl	Firefox	`http://www.stardrifter.org/refcontrol/`	The plugin lets you control what gets sent as the HTTP Referer on a per-site basis.
View HTTP Headers	Firefox	`http://livehttpheaders.mozdev.org/`	Displays HTTP headers.
View HTTP Headers	Internet Explorer	`http://www.blunck.info/iehttpheaders.html` or `http://www.blunck.se/iehttpheaders/iehttpheaders.html`	Displays HTTP headers.

Community Forums

There are a few great places you can ask your SEO-related questions. It is advisable to search and peruse the forum archives before asking questions, because many of them are likely answered already. Table 2-2 shows resources we find consistently helpful.

Table 2-2

Resource	Link
Digital Point Forums	http://forums.digitalpoint.com/
Cre8asiteforums	http://www.cre8asiteforums.com/
WebmasterWorld Forums	http://www.webmasterworld.com/
SearchEngineWatch Forums	http://forums.searchenginewatch.com/
Search Engine Roundtable Forums	http://forums.seroundtable.com/

Search Engine Blogs and Resources

Table 2-3 lists a number of blogs that are good to read to stay current. You'll discover many more, and eventually make your own list of favorites. This is just *our* list:

Table 2-3

Resource	Link
SearchEngineWatch	http://searchenginewatch.com/
SEO Book	http://www.seobook.com/
Matt Cutts' blog	http://www.mattcutts.com/blog/
Search Engine Roundtable	http://www.seroundtable.com/
ThreadWatch	http://www.threadwatch.org/
SEO Black Hat	http://seoblackhat.com/
Google Blog	http://googleblog.blogspot.com/
Google Blogoscoped	http://blog.outer-court.com/
John Battelle	http://battellemedia.com/
Copyblogger	http://www.copyblogger.com/
Yahoo! Search Blog	http://www.ysearchblog.com/
Carsten Cumbrowski	http://www.cumbrowski.com/
… and let's not forget SEO Egghead	http://www.seoegghead.com/

Summary

Although much of what you've read in this chapter is common sense, we are sure you have learned at least a few new things about the factors that influence the rankings of your web site in modern search engines.

Starting with Chapter 3, we're putting on our programmer hats. So put on your hat and grab a can of Red Bull. Lots of technical content is ahead!

3

Provocative
SE-Friendly URLs

"Click me!" If the ideal URL could speak, its speech would resemble the communication of an experienced salesman. It would grab your attention with relevant keywords and a call to action, and it would persuasively argue that you should choose it instead of the other one. Other URLs on the page would pale in comparison.

URLs are more visible than many realize, and are a contributing factor in CTR. They are often cited directly in copy, and they occupy approximately 20% of the real estate in a given search engine result page. Apart from "looking enticing" to humans, URLs must be friendly to search engines. URLs function as the "addresses" of all content in a web site. If confused by them, a search engine spider may not reach some of your content in the first place. This would clearly reduce search engine friendliness.

Creating search engine friendly URLs becomes challenging and requires more forethought when developing a dynamic web site. A dynamic web site with poorly architected URLs presents numerous problems for a search engine. On the other hand, search engine friendly URLs containing relevant keywords may both increase search engine rankings, as well as prompt a user to click them.

This chapter discusses how well-crafted URLs can make the difference between highly ranked web pages and pages at the bottom of the search results. It then illustrates how to generate optimized URLs for dynamic web sites using the Apache mod_rewrite module in coordination with application code written in PHP. Lastly, this chapter considers some common caveats — and addresses how to avoid them.

By the end of this chapter you will acquire the skills that will enable you to employ search engine friendly URLs in a dynamic PHP-based web site. More specifically, in the rest of this chapter you will:

- ❑ Understand the differences between static URLs and dynamic URLs.
- ❑ Understand the benefits of URL rewriting.

❑ Use mod_rewrite and regular expressions to implement URL rewriting.

❑ Follow exercises to practice rewriting numeric and keyword-rich URLs.

❑ Create a PHP "link factory" library to help you keep the URLs in your site consistent.

Why Do URLs Matter?

Many search engine marketers have historically recommended placing relevant keywords in URLs. The original rationale was that a URL's contents are one of the major criteria in search engine ranking.

Over time, this has changed. It is now a less important criterion with regard to search engine ranking. On top of that, dynamic sites make employing such URLs more difficult. That does not mean, however, that creating such URLs with relevant keywords is obsolete and unnecessary!

So let's enumerate all of the benefits of placing keywords in URLs:

1. Doing so still has a small beneficial effect on search engine ranking in and of itself.

2. The URL is roughly 20% of the real estate you get in a SERP result. It functions as a call to action and increases perceived relevance. Keywords in a URL that match a query will also be bolded or otherwise set off by major search engines.

3. The URL appears in the status bar of a browser when the mouse hovers over anchor text that references it. Again — it functions as a call to action and increases perceived relevance.

4. Keyword-based URLs tend to be easier to remember than `?product_id=5&category_id=2`.

5. Often, the URL is cited as the actual anchor text, that is:

```
<a href="http://www.example.com/foo.html">http://www.example.com/foo.html</a>
```

In the case mentioned at point 5:

❑ A user would likely click the anchor text including relevant keywords over a dynamic string. Same story here — you know the effects.

❑ Because keywords in anchor text *are* a decisive ranking factor, having keywords in the URL anchor text *will* help you rank better for "foos."

Static URLs and Dynamic URLs

Initially, the World Wide Web was comprised predominantly of static web sites. Each URL within a web site pointed to an actual physical file located on a web server's file system. Therefore, a search engine spider had very little to worry about. The spider would crawl throughout the web site and index every URL in a relatively straightforward manner. Problems such as duplicate content and spider traps did not typically exist.

Today, dynamic web sites dominate the World Wide Web landscape. Unfortunately, they frequently present problems when one looks at their URLs from a search engine's perspective — especially with regard to spidering.

For example, many dynamic web sites employ query string parameters that generate different URLs that host very similar or identical content. This is interpreted as *duplicate content* by search engines, and this may result in a page penalization. The use of many URL parameters may also result in *spider traps* (http://en.wikipedia.org/wiki/Spider_trap), or in linking structures that are hard to follow by a search engine. Needless to say, both scenarios reduce the web site's ranking performance with the search engines. Duplicate content is discussed in Chapter 5.

Because the web developers reading this book are architecting dynamic sites, these subjects must be examined in depth. And we start by categorizing URLs into two groups based on their anatomy:

- ❑ Static URLs
- ❑ Dynamic URLs

Static URLs

Static URLs do *not* include a query string. By this definition, a URL referencing a PHP script *without* parameters is still static. Two examples of static URLs are as follows:

```
http://www.example.com/about-us.html
http://www.example.com/site-map.php
```

Static URLs — even those generated by a PHP script — typically pose no challenges for a search engine.

Dynamic URLs

Dynamic URLs are those that include a query string, set off by ?, a question mark. This string is used to pass various parameters to a PHP script. Multiple parameters are delimited by & and then appended to the query string. A typical dynamic URL looks like the following:

```
http://www.example.com/product.php?category_id=1&product_id=2
```

In this example, product.php is the name of a physical file containing a PHP script on a web server. The highlighted section is the query string. When a web browser makes a request to the PHP script with a particular query string, the script may then present differing content based on the various parameters.

> **Because the query string values affect the script's output, a search engine typically considers the same file name with differing query strings as completely different web pages, despite the fact that those pages originate from the same physical script file.**

However, the script does not necessarily have to present different content based on different permutations of the query string — which is the basis of the most common cause of duplicate content. The most trivial example of this is when you add a parameter that does not change the presented content at all, such as in these examples:

```
http://www.example.com/product.php?product_id=2&extra_param=123
http://www.example.com/product.php?product_id=2&another_extra_param=456
```

Session IDs and various other tracking IDs are two very common culprits. In the worst case, a search engine may not index such URLs at all. Therefore, the use of such parameters should be avoided as much as possible.

Dynamic URLs — especially those with more than two parameters — may pose problems for search engines, due to the increased difficulty in ascertaining how to spider the site. Matt Cutts of Google affirms all of this on his blog at `http://www.mattcutts.com/blog/seo-answers-on-google-video/`. Lastly, a dynamic URL may look less appealing or relevant than a well-constructed static URL to a human user.

> *In some cases, search engines may attempt to eliminate an extra parameter, such as a session-related parameter, and index site URLs without it. Depending on this functionality is neither realistic nor wise, however.*

Fortunately, there are many ways to improve URLs with regard to indexability as well as aesthetics. This typically involves eliminating any unnecessary parameters, and/or obscuring the dynamic parameters using keyword-rich static URLs.

The solution to the latter is to employ Apache's mod_rewrite module to present URLs that are static — or at least appear to be static — but are, in actuality, mapped to dynamic URLs. This is a process called URL-rewriting, and is detailed later in this chapter.

> *Note that URL rewriting is done differently depending on the server-side technology employed for a web site. This book focuses on mod_rewrite, because this is the de facto standard in the PHP community. You are introduced to working with mod_rewrite later in this chapter. For an ASP.NET implementation, check out the ASP.NET edition of this book,* Professional Search Engine Optimization with ASP.NET: A Developer's Guide to SEO.

Dynamic URLs may also benefit from some of the concepts in this chapter, such as using functions (URL factories) to generate URLs to enhance URL consistency, and strategies to reduce the number of parameters — rewritten or not — required for site navigation.

URLs and CTR

It is clear that users are more likely to click a search result that *looks* more relevant. One way to do this is to include relevant keywords — such as the product name in the URL. Although the effect on rankings due to keywords in URLs may be small in current search engine algorithms, the effect of a better CTR may be noticed.

> **Static-looking keyword-rich URLs are more aesthetically pleasing, and may enhance your CTR. Query keywords are also highlighted in the results pages if their URLs contain those keywords.**

A better CTR means a better ad. The most important factor in a search engine result may be the page title, but if you're shopping for blue widgets, and you see the following two results, which one would you click if you were looking for "blue widgets," all other variables equal?

```
http://www.example.com/Products/Blue-Widget.html
http://www.example.com/product.php?id=1
```

For a real-world example, see Figure 3-1, where I was searching for "Mickey Mouse t-shirt."

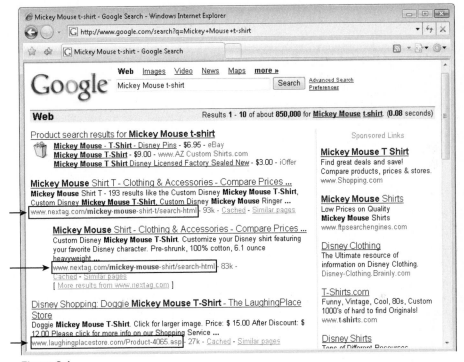

Figure 3-1

URLs and Duplicate Content

As mentioned earlier, if a search engine establishes that many different URLs in a web site contain the same content, it may not index them at all; in the worst case, if it is done excessively, it may designate the site as a spam site and penalize it.

Unfortunately, many web sites have been "forced" to create duplicate content because of technical considerations and business rules. However, sometimes there are better solutions to these considerations and rules. The concepts of the URLs and duplicate content are intimately related. This chapter and the next discuss the technicalities related to URL rewriting and redirection respectively, and Chapter 5 analyzes the concept of duplicate content.

URLs of the Real World

Before proceeding to write code, this section looks at three examples of URLs that you'll see frequently while browsing, and discusses the technical details involved in creating these URLs. This will help you understand where we're heading, and why you'll write the code from the exercises in this chapter. You will see examples with:

❑ Dynamic URLs

❑ Numeric rewritten URLs

❑ Keyword-rich URLs

Example #1: Dynamic URLs

Data displayed by dynamic web sites is usually stored in some sort of backend database. Typically, a numeric ID is associated with each data row of a database table, and all database operations with the table (such as selecting, inserting, deleting, or updating rows) are done by referencing that ID.

More often than not, the same ID used to identify an item in the database is also used in PHP scripts to refer to that particular item — such as a product in an e-commerce web site, an article of a blog, and so on. In a dynamic URL, these IDs are passed via the query string to a script that presents differing content accordingly.

Figure 3-2 shows a page from `http://www.cristiandarie.ro/BalloonShop/`. This is a demo e-commerce site presented in one of Cristian's books, and employs dynamic URLs. As you can see, the page is composed using data from the database, and the ID that identifies the data item is taken from the dynamic URL.

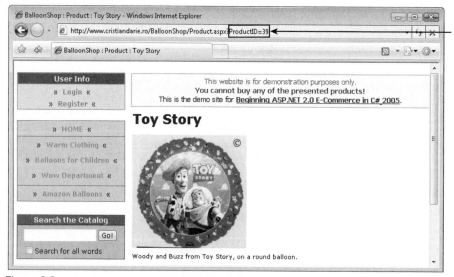

Figure 3-2

This is probably the most common approach employed by dynamic web sites at present, because you frequently meet URLs such as the following:

- ❑   `http://www.example.com/catalog.php?cat_id=1`

- ❑   `http://www.example.com/catalog.php?cat_id=2&prod_id=3&ref_id=4`

This approach is certainly the easiest and most straightforward when developing a dynamic site. However, it is frequently sub-optimal from a search engine spider's point of view. It also doesn't provide relevant keywords or a call to action to a human viewing the URL.

Some programmers also tend to use extra parameters freely — as shown in the second URL example. For example, if the parameter `ref_id` is used for some sort of tracking mechanism, and search engine friendliness is a priority, it should be removed. Lastly, any necessary duplicate content should be excluded from search engines' view using a `robots.txt` file or a `robots` meta tag. This topic is discussed in Chapter 5.

> If URLs on your site are for the most part indexed properly, it may not be wise to restructure URLs. However, if you decide that you must, please also read Chapter 4, which teaches you how to make the transition smoother. Chapter 4 shows how to preserve link equity by properly redirecting old URLs to new URLs. Also, not all solutions to URL-based problems require restructuring URLs; as mentioned earlier, duplicate content can be excluded using the `robots.txt` file or the `robots` meta tag, which are discussed in Chapter 5.

Example #2: Numeric Rewritten URLs

An improved version of the previous example is a modified URL that removes the dynamic parameters and hides them in a static URL. This static URL is then mapped to a dynamic URL using an Apache module called mod_rewrite. The `ref_id` parameter previously alluded to is also not present, because those types of tracking parameters usually can and should be avoided:

- ❑   `http://www.example.com/Products/1/` (1 parameter)

- ❑   `http://www.example.com/Products/2/1/` (2 parameters)

The impact of numeric URL rewriting will likely be negligible on a page with one parameter, but on pages with two parameters or more, URL-rewriting is desirable.

This form of URL is particularly well-suited to the adaptation of existing software. Retrofitting an application for keyword-rich URLs, as discussed in the next section, may present additional difficulty in implementation.

It is important to realize that rewriting a dynamic URL only *obscures* the parameters. It prevents a search engine from perceiving that a URL structure is problematic as a result of having many parameters. If underlying problems still exist on a web site — usually in the form of duplicate content — a search engine still may still have difficulty indexing it effectively.

Lastly, this improvement should not be implemented on a currently indexed site unless the old URLs are redirected to their new counterparts. Other web sites may cite them even if you do not, and this may create a duplicate content issue, as well as squander link equity.

Example #3: Keyword-Rich Rewritten URLs

Finally, here are two examples of ideal keyword-rich URLs:

- ❏ `http://www.example.com/Products/High-Powered-Drill-P1.html`

- ❏ `http://www.example.com/Products/Tools-C2/High-Powered-Drill-P1.html`

This is often the best approach to creating URLs, but also presents an increased level of difficulty in implementation — especially if you are modifying preexisting source code for software. In that case this solution may not have an easy and apparent implementation, and it requires more interaction with the database to extract the copy for the URLs.

> *The decision whether to use the* `.html` *suffix in the URL is mostly a non-issue. You could also use a URL such as* `http://www.example.com/Products/High-Powered-Drill-P1/` *if you prefer the look of directories.*

This "ideal" URL presents a static URL that indicates both to the search engine and to the user that it is topically related to the search query. Usually the keyword-rich URLs are created using keywords from the name or description of the item presented in the page itself. Characters in the keyword string that are not alphanumeric need to be removed, and spaces should be converted to a delimiting character. Dashes are desirable over underscores as the delimiting character because most search engines treat the dash as a space and the underscore as an actual character, though this particular detail is probably not terribly significant. On a new site, dashes should be chosen as a word-delimiter.

> **Don't get URL-obsessive! For example, it would not be recommended to change underscores to dashes in existing URLs in an existing web site, all other things left equal. However, in the initial design phase it would be wise to use the dash rather than the programmer's tendency to prefer the underscore character. The effects of this "optimization" are marginal at best, and changing URLs for marginal gains is not recommended because the side effects may cause more harm than the gains — even if everything is done properly. Use your best judgment when deciding whether to change your current URL structure.**

Maintaining URL Consistency

Regardless of whether your URLs are static or dynamic, it's important to maintain consistency. In the case of dynamic URLs, it's important to maintain consistent parameter order in URLs with more than one parameter.

In PHP, the parameters of a query string are typically accessed by name rather than by ordinal. The order in which the parameters appear does not affect the output of the PHP script, unless your script is specifically written to take parameter order into consideration. Here is an example where a PHP web site would generate the exact same content, but using different URLs:

```
http://www.example.com/catalog.php?product_id=1&category_id=2
http://www.example.com/catalog.php?category_id=2&product_id=1
```

If the catalog.php script accesses the parameters as $_GET['product_id'] and $_GET['category_id'], respectively, these two different URLs would generate the same content. There's no standard specifying that URL parameters are commutative. If both dynamic links are used within the web site, search engines may end up spidering different URLs with identical content, which could get the site penalized.

In conclusion, it's wise to be consistent and follow a standard parameter order to avoid problems and improve your rankings. Consider an example where the parameter order may make a difference:

```
http://www.example.com/compare_products.php?item[]=1&item[]=2
http://www.example.com/compare_products.php?item[]=2&item[]=1
```

Here, the parameter name is item, and it's used to populate a PHP array called $_GET['item']. In the former case the item array contains (1,2), and in the latter it contains (2,1). In this case, a search engine cannot assume these URLs are equivalent — and indeed they may not be.

The programmer should also try to use consistent capitalization on file names and query strings. Search engines resolve such simple differences, especially because file names in Windows are not case sensitive, but the following URLs are technically different in both Windows and Unix operating systems:

```
http://www.example.com/products.php?color=red
```

and

```
http://www.example.com/PRODUCTS.php?color=RED
```

Again, maintaining a consistent style is desirable. The developer should also try to reference directories in a web site with the trailing "/" consistently. For example, if you're using numeric rewritten URLs, it would be best to avoid referencing a particular product using both of the following links, even if your script can successfully parse them:

```
http://www.example.com/Products/1/
```

and

```
http://www.example.com/Products/1
```

In practice, search engines *can* resolve many of these ambiguities. Matt Cutts asserts that Google can "*do things like keeping or removing trailing slashes, [and try] to convert URLs with upper case to lower case*" (http://www.mattcutts.com/blog/seo-advice-url-canonicalization/), but this is only a subset of the aforementioned ambiguities. It is best to remove all of the offending ambiguities regardless.

In order to enforce consistency as a whole, you can create a function for each type of URL required by a site. Through the logic in that function URLs are consistently formatted. As you will see in Chapter 5, consistency also makes it easier to exclude files in `robots.txt`, because the preceding problems having to do with ordering and casing also apply there.

For example, if you're building an e-commerce web site, you could create a function such as the following:

```
function create_link($category_id, $product_id)
{
  return 'product.php?category_id=' . $category_id . '&product_id=' . $product_id;
}
```

Calling this function providing 5 and 6 as parameters, it will return `product.php?category_id=5&product_id=6`. Using this function throughout the web site will ensure all your links follow a consistent format.

This implementation of `create_link()` is overly simplistic and not really useful for real-world scenarios. If you want to improve your URLs more significantly, you need to utilize more advanced functions in coordination with URL rewriting. The benefits of URL consistency will also apply there. So without further ado, the next section discusses this subject.

URL Rewriting

Taking into consideration the guidelines and recommendations mentioned earlier, this section presents solutions you can apply in your web applications to accomplish URL-rewriting using the mod_rewrite Apache module.

> From now on, the chapter tends to be very technical. As a rule of thumb, most exercises you'll find in this book involve writing code, which at times can get quite complex. We've done our best to explain it, but if you don't have the technical background assumed by this book — experience with PHP development — you may need assistance in following the examples.

The hurdle you must overcome when implementing the URLs shown earlier is that they don't actually exist anywhere in your web site. Your site still contains a script — named, say, `product.php` — which expects to receive parameters through the query string and generate content depending on those parameters. This script would be ready to handle a request such as this:

```
http://seophp.example.com/product.php?product_id=123
```

But your web server would normally generate a 404 error if you tried any of the following:

```
http://seophp.example.com/Products/123.html
http://seophp.example.com/my-super-product.html
```

URL rewriting allows you to transform the URL of such an incoming request to a different URL according to a defined set of rules. You could use URL rewriting to transform the previous non-existent URLs to `product.php?product_id=123`, which *does* exist.

The URL rewriting service is provided by the Apache web server through the mod_rewrite module. PHP does not have anything to do with it (beyond generating the links with our URL factory), because the PHP engine takes charge only once the .php file is executed. The mod_rewrite module is the de-facto standard for URL rewriting in the Apache world, and is typically supported by any Apache-based hosting package. It is used in the examples in this chapter and throughout this book.

Figure 3-3 describes how mod_rewrite fits into the picture. Its role is to rewrite the URL of the incoming requests, but doesn't affect the output of the PHP script in any way.

At first sight, the rewriting rules can be added easily to an existing web site, but in practice there are other issues to take into consideration. For example, as shown a bit later, you'd also need to modify the existing links within the web site content. In Chapter 4 you'll continue by learning how to properly redirect old links to the new links in a preexisting web site.

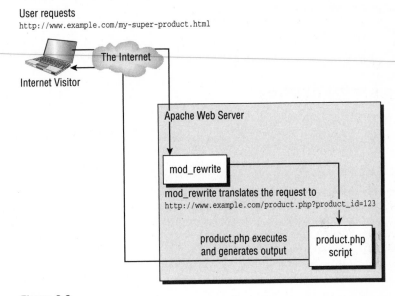

Figure 3-3

The mod_rewrite Apache module is an invaluable tool to web developers tasked with architecting complex dynamic sites that are still search engine friendly. It allows the programmer to declare a set of rules that are applied by Apache on-the-fly to map static URLs requested by the visitor to dynamic query strings sent to various PHP scripts. As far as a search engine spider is concerned, the URLs are static.

> Learning how to properly use mod_rewrite involves a lot of work, but the final result is beautiful and elegant. It allows visitors and search engines to access your site using aesthetically pleasing and search engine friendly static URLs. However, in the background your PHP scripts still work with query string parameters, in the typical parameter-driven fashion. As you can see in Figure 3-3, the PHP script is still driven by a dynamic URL.

You can find the official documentation of mod_rewrite at `http://httpd.apache.org/docs/2.2/rewrite/`. The introduction to mod_rewrite is located at `http://httpd.apache.org/docs/2.2/rewrite/rewrite_intro.html`. There are multiple books dedicated to mod_rewrite. We recommend *The Definitive Guide to Apache mod_rewrite* (Apress, 2006).

The rest of this chapter is dedicated to URL rewriting, using various exercises covering the following:

❑   Installing mod_rewrite

❑   Testing mod_rewrite

❑   Working with regular expressions

❑   Rewriting numeric URLs with two parameters

❑   Rewriting keyword-rich URLs

❑   Building a link factory

❑   Pagination and URL rewriting

❑   Rewriting images and streaming content

Installing mod_rewrite

If you're implementing the exercises in this book using an external hosting provider, it's very likely that mod_rewrite is already installed and enabled. In that case, you can simply skip to the next section, "Testing mod_rewrite." Consult your web host for information regarding whether mod_rewrite is supported and enabled.

If you've installed Apache yourself, read on. Because of its popularity, mod_rewrite is now included with all common Apache distributions. If desired, you can verify if your Apache installation has the mod_rewrite module by looking for a file named `mod_rewrite.so` under the `modules` folder in your Apache installation directory.

However, mod_rewrite may not be enabled by default in your Apache configuration. To make sure, open the Apache configuration file, named `httpd.conf`. If you've installed Apache using the XAMPP package as instructed in Chapter 1, the full path of the file will be `\Program Files\xampp\apache\conf\httpd.conf`.

Open `httpd.conf` and find the following line:

```
#LoadModule rewrite_module modules/mod_rewrite.so
```

The leading # means the line is commented, so remove it in order to have Apache load the mod_rewrite module upon its startup:

```
LoadModule rewrite_module modules/mod_rewrite.so
```

After any change to `httpd.conf`, you need to restart the Apache server in order for the changes to take effect. In case you run into trouble, you can check Apache's error log file (`/logs/error.log`), which should contain the details of the error.

> Older versions of Apache (1.3 and older) may also require you to add the following line to `httpd.conf`:
>
>   AddModule mod_rewrite.c
>
> For this reason, older mod_rewrite tutorials mention this line as obligatory, but it's no longer required by new versions of Apache.

Testing mod_rewrite

Once mod_rewrite is installed and enabled, you add the rewriting rules to the Apache configuration file, `httpd.conf`. Apache also lets you save configuration options (including rewriting rules) on a per-directory basis to a configuration file named `.htaccess`. All you have to do is create a file named `.htaccess` into a directory of your application, and Apache will read it automatically when accessing that directory and directories within.

As with mod_rewrite, `.htaccess` isn't related to PHP in any way. The `.htaccess` file is strictly an Apache configuration file. You'll see how it works in the exercise that follows.

Using `.htaccess` is useful in the following scenarios:

❑ You don't have access to the global configuration file, `httpd.conf` (this tends to be true in a shared hosting account).

❑ You want to have customized configuration options for a particular directory of the application.

❑ You want to be able to change the configuration options without restarting Apache. You *are* required to restart Apache after modifying `httpd.conf`, and this is problematic if you have other applications running on the web server.

All of the exercises in this book are designed to work with the `.htaccess` file. This is the method we generally recommend for defining rewriting rules, especially in the development stage when the rules change frequently. This way you avoid restarting Apache every time you change a rewriting rule. It is also the only solution in a shared hosting environment, where you do not have access to `httpd.conf` and you cannot restart the server, either.

In the upcoming exercise you create a simple rewrite rule that translates `my-super-product.html` to `product.php?product_id=123`. This is the exact scenario that was presented in Figure 3-3.

The `product.php` script is designed to simulate a real product page. The script receives a query string parameter named `product_id`, and generates a very simple output message based on the value of this parameter. Figure 3-4 shows the sample output that you'll get by loading `http://seophp.example.com/product.php?product_id=123`.

To improve search engine friendliness, you want to be able to access the same page through a static URL: `http://seophp.example.com/my-super-product.html`. In order to implement this feature, you'll use — you guessed it! — mod_rewrite.

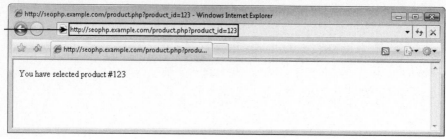

Figure 3-4

As you know, what mod_rewrite basically does is to translate an input string (the URL typed by your visitor) to another string (a URL that can be processed by your PHP scripts). In this exercise you make it rewrite my-super-product.html to product.php?product_id=123.

---

httpd.conf versus .htaccess

There are also some subtle differences in the way Apache handles rules for mod_rewrite in .htaccess vs. httpd.conf. If for any reason you prefer using httpd.conf, you'll need to take this into consideration while going through the exercises:

1. You should place your rewrite rules inside the <VirtualHost> element of the httpd.conf or vhosts.conf file instead of .htaccess.

2. When working with htppd.conf, the slash (/) that follows the domain name in a URL is considered to be part of the URL.

In the next exercise, you are presented this URL rewriting code:

```
RewriteEngine On
RewriteRule ^my-super-product\.html$ /product.php?product_id=123
```

When using httpd.conf, the rule would need to contain a leading slash:

```
RewriteEngine On
RewriteRule ^/my-super-product\.html$ /product.php?product_id=123
```

This exercise, as all the other exercises in this book, assumes that you've installed Apache and PHP as shown in Chapter 1.

Please visit Jaimie Sirovich's web page dedicated to this book — http://www.seoegghead.com/seo-with-php-updates.html — for updates and additional information regarding the following code.

Testing mod_rewrite

1. Create a file named `product.php` in your `seophp` folder, and add this code to it:

```php
<?php

// display product details
echo 'You have selected product #' . $_GET['product_id'];

?>
```

2. Test your simple PHP script by loading `http://seophp.example.com/product.php?product_id=3`. The result should resemble Figure 3-4.

3. Create a file named `.htaccess` in your `seophp` folder, and add the following lines to it. Their functionality is explained in the section that follows.

```
RewriteEngine On

# Translate my-super.product.html to /product.php?product_id=123
RewriteRule ^my-super-product\.html$ /product.php?product_id=123
```

Here's a little detail that's worth a mention. The `.htaccess` *file is technically a file with an empty name, and the* `htaccess` *extension. Depending on the settings of your Windows system, this file may not be easily visible in Windows Explorer.*

4. Switch back to your browser again, and this time load `http://seophp.example.com/my-super-product.html`. If everything works as it should, you should get the output that's shown in Figure 3-5.

If you get a server error at this point, most probably the mod_rewrite module isn't correctly enabled. Make sure you've restarted the Apache server after enabling mod_rewrite in `httpd.conf`*. Open the* `error.log` *file from the Apache logs directory to read details about the error.*

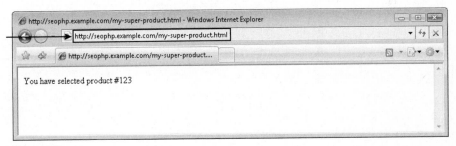

Figure 3-5

Congratulations! You've taken your first step into the world of mod_rewrite! The example is indeed very simplistic and without much practical value — at least compared with what you'll learn next! But you need to fully understand the basics of URL rewriting first.

You started by creating a very simple PHP script that takes a numeric parameter through the query string. You could imagine this is a more involved page that displays lots of details about the product with the ID mentioned by the `product_id` query string parameter, but in your case you're simply displaying a text message that confirms the ID has been correctly read from the query string. The `product.php` script is indeed very simple! Here's its code again:

```php
<?php

// display product details
echo 'You have selected product #' . $_GET['product_id'];

?>
```

This script is easy to understand even if you're relatively new to PHP. The `echo` command is used to output text, and `$_GET['product_id']` tells PHP to access the value of `product_id` contained by the query string.

For a visual example of how the predefined server variables are interpreted, see Figure 3-6.

After testing that `product.php` script works, you moved on to access this same script, but through a URL that doesn't physically exist on your server. This is done through URL rewriting, and you implemented this by adding a rule to be processed by the mod_rewrite module.

The `.htaccess` file you've created in the `phpseo` folder contains two program lines. The first enables the URL rewriting engine:

```
RewriteEngine On
```

URL Rewriting and PHP

As Figure 3-3 describes, the PHP script is executed *after* the original URL has been rewritten. This explains why `$_GET['product_id']` reads the value of `product_id` from the *rewritten* version of the URL. This is helpful, because the script works fine no matter whether you accessed `product.php` directly, or the initial request was for another URL that was rewritten to `product.php`.

The `$_GET` predefined variable, as well as almost all the other predefined PHP variables, work with the rewritten URL. The PHP documentation pages for the predefined variables are `http://www.php.net/reserved.variables` and `http://www.php.net/variables.predefined`.

PHP, however, also allows you retrieve the originally requested URL through `$_SERVER['REQUEST_URI']`, which returns the path (excluding the domain name) of the original request. This is helpful whenever you need to know what was the original URL of the request initiated by the client.

Table 3-1 describes the most commonly used server variables.

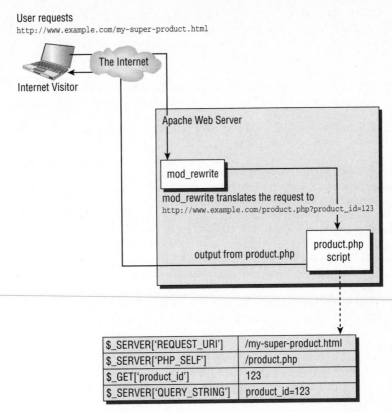

Figure 3-6

Table 3-1

Server Variable	Description
$_SERVER['REQUEST_URI']	Returns the URI (Uniform Resource Identifier) of the original request. In practice, this returns the path of the *original* request excluding the domain name.
$_GET['parameter_name']	Returns the value of the *parameter_name* query string parameter from the rewritten URL.
$_POST['parameter_name']	Returns the value of the *parameter_name* POST parameter of the request.
$_COOKIES['cookie_name']	Returns the value of the *cookie_name* cookie.
$_SESSION['variable_name']	Returns the value of the *variable_name* session variable.
$_SERVER['QUERY_STRING']	Returns the query string from the *rewritten* URL.
$_SERVER['PHP_SELF']	Returns the file name of the running script.

The second line specifies the rewrite rule using the mod_rewrite `RewriteRule` command. You use this to have mod_rewrite translate `my-super-product.html` to `product.php?product_id=123`. The line that precedes the `RewriteRule` line is a comment; comments are marked using the pound (character) at the beginning of the line, and are ignored by the mod_rewrite parser:

```
# Translate my-super.product.html to /product.php?product_id=123
RewriteRule ^my-super-product\.html$ /product.php?product_id=123
```

You can find the official documentation for `RewriteRule` *at* `http://www.apacheref.com/ref/mod_rewrite/RewriteRule.html`.

In its basic form, `RewriteRule` takes two parameters. The first parameter *describes* the original URL that needs to be rewritten, and the second specifies what it should be rewritten to. The pattern that describes the original URL is delimited by ^ and $, which assert that the string has nothing before or after the matching text (explained further in the following sections), and its contents are written using *regular expressions*, which you learn about next.

In case you were wondering why the `.html` *extension has been written as* `\.html` *in the rewrite rule, we will explain it now. In regular expressions — the programming language used to describe the original URL that needs to be rewritten — the dot is a character that has a special significance. If you want that dot to be read as a literal dot, you need to escape it using the backslash character. As you'll learn, this is a general rule with regular expressions: when special characters need to be read literally, they need to be escaped with the backslash character (which is a special character in turn — so if you wanted to use a backslash, it would be denoted as* `\\`*).*

Using RewriteBase

The regular expressions and scripts in this book assume that your application runs in the root folder of their domain. This is the typical scenario. If, however, you host your application in a subfolder of your domain, such as `http://www.example.com/seophp`, you'd need to make a few changes to accommodate the new environment.

The most important change would be to use the `RewriteBase` directive of mod_rewrite to specify the new location to act as a root of your rewriting rules. This directive is explained at `http://www.apacheref.com/ref/mod_rewrite/RewriteBase.html`. Also, the rewritten URL should lose its leading slash, because you're not rewriting to root any more. Basically, if you host your first example in a subfolder named `seophp`, your `.htaccess` file for the previous exercise should look like this:

```
RewriteEngine On
RewriteBase /seophp
RewriteRule ^my-super-product\.html$ product.php?product_id=123
```

Introducing Regular Expressions

Many love regular expressions, while others hate them. Many think they're very hard to work with, while many (or maybe not so many) think they're a piece of cake. Either way, they're one of those topics you can't avoid when URL rewriting is involved. We'll try to serve a gentle introduction to the subject, although entire books have been written on the subject. You may even find entire books on mod_rewrite, including in-depth discussion of regular expressions. The Wikipedia page on regular expressions is great for background information (http://en.wikipedia.org/wiki/Regular_expression).

A regular expression (sometimes referred to as a *regex*) is a special string that describes a text *pattern*. With regular expressions you can define rules that match strings, extract data from strings, and transform strings, which enable very flexible and complex text manipulation using concise rules. Regular expressions aren't specific to mod_rewrite and URL rewriting. On the contrary, they've been around for a while, and they're implemented in many tools and programming languages, including PHP.

To demonstrate their usefulness with a simple example, assume your web site needs to rewrite links as shown in Table 3-2.

Table 3-2

Original URL	Rewritten URL
Products/P1.html	product.php?product_id=1
Products/P2.html	product.php?product_id=2
Products/P3.html	product.php?product_id=3
Products/P4.html	product.php?product_id=4
...	...

If you have 100,000 products, without regular expressions you'd be in a bit of a trouble, because you'd need to write just as many rules — no more, no less. *You don't want to manage an* .htaccess *file with 100,000 rewrite rules!* That would be unwieldy.

However, if you look at the Original URL column of the table, you'll see that all entries follow the same *pattern*. And as suggested earlier, regular expressions can come to rescue! Patterns are useful because with a single pattern you can match a theoretically infinite number of possible input URLs, so you just need to write a rewriting rule for every *type* of URL you have in your web site.

In the exercise that follows, you use a regular expression that matches Products/P*n*.html, and use mod_rewrite to translate URLs that match that pattern to product.php?product_id=*n*. This will implement exactly the rules described in Table 3-1.

Working with Regular Expressions

1. Open the .htaccess file you created earlier in your seophp folder, and add the following high-lighted rewriting rule to it:

```
RewriteEngine On

# Translate my-super.product.html to /product.php?product_id=123
RewriteRule ^my-super-product\.html$ /product.php?product_id=123
```

```
# Rewrite numeric URLs
RewriteRule ^Products/P([0-9]+)\.html$ /product.php?product_id=$1 [L]
```

2. Switch back to your browser again, and this time load http://seophp.example.com/
Products/P1.html. If everything works as it should, you will get the output that's shown
in Figure 3-7.

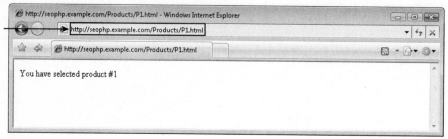

Figure 3-7

3. You can check that the rule really works, even for IDs formed of more digits. Loading
http://seophp.example.com/Products/P123456.html would give you the ou[0-9]+tput
shown in Figure 3-8.

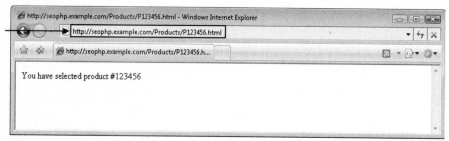

Figure 3-8

Congratulations! The exercise was quite short, but you've written your first regular expression! Take a
closer look at your new rewrite rule:

```
RewriteRule ^Products/P([0-9]+)\.html$ /product.php?product_id=$1 [L]
```

If this is your first exposure to regular expressions, it must look scary! Just take a deep breath and read
on: we promise, it's not as complicated as it looks.

> **Appendix A contains a gentler introduction to regular expressions.**

As you learned in the previous exercise, a basic `RewriteRule` takes two arguments. In this example it also received a special flag — `[L]` — as a third argument. The meaning of these arguments is discussed next.

The first argument of `RewriteRule` is a regular expression that describes the *matching* URLs you want to rewrite. The second argument specifies the destination (*rewritten*) URL. So, in geek-speak, the `RewriteRule` line basically says: rewrite any URL that *matches* the `^Products/P([0-9]+)\.html$` pattern to `/product.php?product_id=$1`. In English, the same line can be roughly read as: "delegate any request to a URL that looks like `Products/P`**n**`.html` to `/product.php?product_id=`**n**".

Let's analyze in detail the regular expression that describes the matching URLs that need to be rewritten. That regular expression is:

```
^Products/P([0-9]+)\.html$
```

Most characters, including alphanumeric characters, are read literally and simply match themselves. Remember the first `RewriteRule` you've written in this chapter to match `my-super-product.html`, which was mostly created of such "normal" characters.

What makes regular expressions so powerful (and sometimes complicated), are the special characters (or *metacharacters*), such as ^, ., or *, which have special meanings. Table 3-3 describes the metacharacters you'll meet.

> *Remember that this theory applies to regular expressions in general. URL rewriting is just one of the many areas where regular expressions are used.*

Table 3-3

Metacharacter	Description
^	Matches the beginning of the line. In our case, it will always match the beginning of the URL. The domain name isn't considered part of the URL, as far as `RewriteRule` is concerned. It is useful to think of ^ as "anchoring" the characters that follow to the beginning of the string, that is, asserting that they be the first part.
.	Matches any single character.
*	Specifies that the preceding character or expression can be repeated zero or more times — not at all to infinite.
+	Specifies that the preceding character or expression can be repeated one or more times. In other words, the preceding character or expression must match at least once.
?	Specifies that the preceding character or expression can be repeated zero or one time. In other words, the preceding character or expression is optional.
{m,n}	Specifies that the preceding character or expression can be repeated between *m* and *n* times; *m* and *n* are integers, and *m* needs to be lower than *n*.

Table continued on following page

Metacharacter	Description
( )	The parentheses are used to define a *captured expression*. The string matching the expression between parentheses can then be read as a variable. The parentheses can also be used to group the contents therein, as in mathematics, and operators such as *, +, or ? can then be applied to the resulting expression.
[ ]	Used to define a character class. For example, [abc] will match any of the characters a, b, c. The - character can be used to define a range of characters. For example, [a-z] matches any lowercase letter. If - is meant to be interpreted literally, it should be the last character before]. Many metacharacters lose their special function when enclosed between [and], and are interpreted literally.
[^]	Similar to [ ], except it matches everything except the mentioned character class. For example, [^a-c] matches all characters except a, b, and c.
$	Matches the end of the line. In our case, it will always match the end of the URL. It is useful to think of it as "anchoring" the previous characters to the end of the string, that is, asserting that they be the last part.
\	The backslash is used to escape the character that follows. It is used to escape metacharacters when you need them to be taken for their literal value, rather than their special meaning. For example, \. will match a dot, rather than "any character" (the typical meaning of the dot in a regular expression). The backslash can also escape itself — so if you want to match C:\Windows, you'll need to refer to it as C:\\Windows.

Using Table 3-2 as reference, analyze the expression ^Products/P([0-9]+)\.html$. The expression starts with the ^ character, matching the beginning of the requested URL (remember, this doesn't include the domain name). The characters Products/P assert that the next characters in the URL string match those characters.

Let's recap: the expression ^Products/P will match any URL that starts with Products/P.

The next characters, ([0-9]+), are the crux of this process. The [0-9] bit matches any character between 0 and 9 (that is, any digit), and the + that follows indicates that the pattern must occur one or more times, so you can have an entire number rather than just a digit. The enclosing parentheses around [0-9]+ indicate that the regular expression engine should store the matching string (which will be a number) inside a variable called $1. (You'll need this variable to compose the rewritten URL.)

Finally, you have \.html$, which means that string should end in .html. The \ is the escaping character, which indicates that the . should be taken as a literal dot, not as "any character" (which is the significance of the . metacharacter). The $ matches the end of the string — the URL in this case.

The second argument of RewriteRule, /product.php?product_id=$1, plugs the variables that you stored into your script URL mapping, and indicates to the web server that requests by a browser for URLs matching that previous pattern should be delegated to that particular script with those numbers substituted for $1.

The second argument of RewriteRule *isn't written using the regular expressions language. Indeed, it doesn't need to, because it's not meant to match anything. Instead, it simply supplies the form of the rewritten URL. The only part with a special significance here is the* $1 *variable, whose value is extracted from the expression between parentheses of the first argument of* RewriteRule.

As you can see, this rule does indeed rewrite any request for a URL that ends with Products/P*n*.html to product.php?product_id=*n*, which can be executed by the product.php script you wrote earlier.

At the end of a rewrite rule you can also add special flags for the new URL by appending one or more flag arguments, delimited by commas. These arguments are specific the RewriteRule command, and not to regular expressions in general. Table 3-4 lists the possible RewriteRule arguments. These rewrite flags must always be placed in square brackets at the end of an individual rule. Multiple flags are delimited by commas, i.e., [NC, L].

Table 3-4

RewriteRule Option	Significance	Description
R	Redirect	Sends an HTTP redirect
F	Forbidden	Forbids access to the URL
G	Gone	Marks the URL as gone
P	Proxy	Passes the URL to mod_proxy
L	Last	Stops processing further rules
N	Next	Starts processing again from the first rule, but using the current rewritten URL
C	Chain	Links the current rule with the following one
T	Type	Forces the mentioned MIME type
NS	Nosubreq	The rule applies only if no internal sub-request is performed
NC	Nocase	URL matching is case-insensitive
QSA	Qsappend	Appends a query string part to the new URL instead of replacing it
PT	Passthrough	Passes the rewritten URL to another Apache module for further processing
S	Skip	Skips the next rule
E	Env	Sets an environment variable

Some of these flags are used in later chapters as well.

RewriteRule commands are processed in sequential order as they are written in the configuration file. If you want to make sure that a rule is the last one processed in case a match is found for it, you need to use the [L] flag as listed in the preceding table:

```
RewriteRule ^Products/P([0-9]+)\.html$ ./product.php?product_id=$1 [L]
```

This is particularly useful if you have a long list of RewriteRule commands, because using [L] improves performance and prevents mod_rewrite from processing all the RewriteRule commands that follow once a match is found. This is usually what you want regardless.

URL Rewriting and PHP

Regular expressions are also supported by PHP. Whenever you need to do string manipulation that is too hard to implement using the typical PHP string functions (http://www.php.net/strings), the regular expression functions can come in handy, as soon as you get accustomed to working with regular expressions.

> One detail worth keeping in mind is that the regular PHP string manipulation functions execute much faster than regular expressions, so you should use them only when necessary. For example, if you simply want to check whether one string literal is included in another, using strpos() or strstr() would be much more efficient than using preg_match(), the regular expression matching function we use.

PHP has many regular expression functions, the most common of which are listed in Table 3-5 for your convenience. The examples in this book use only preg_match and preg_replace, which are the most frequently used, but it's good to know there are others. For more information, visit http://www.php.net/pcre.

Table 3-5

PHP Function	Description
preg_grep	Receives as parameters a regular expression, and an array of input strings. The function returns an array containing the elements of the input that match the pattern. More details at http://www.php.net/preg_grep.
preg_match	Receives as parameters a regular expression and a string. If a match is found, the function returns 1. Otherwise, it returns 0. The function doesn't search for more matches: after one match is found, the execution stops. More details at http://www.php.net/preg_match.

PHP Function	Description
preg_match_all	Similar to preg_match, but all matches are attempted. After one match is found, the subsequent searches are performed on the rest of the string. More details at http://www.php.net/preg_match_all.
preg_quote	Escapes all special regular expression characters of the input string using the backslash character. More details at http://www.php.net/preg_quote.
preg_replace	Replaces matching parts of a string with a replacement expression. It receives three non-optional parameters: the pattern used for matching, the replacement expression, and the input string. More details at http://www.php.net/preg_replace.
preg_replace_callback	Similar to preg_replace, except instead of a replacement expression, you specify a function that returns the replacement expression. More details at http://www.php.net/preg_replace_callback.
preg_split	Splits a string on the boundaries matched by a regular expression. The resulting substrings are returned in the form of an array. More details at http://www.php.net/preg_split.

Unlike with mod_rewrite, when you supply a regular expression to a PHP function you need to enclose the regular expression definition using a delimiter character. The delimiter character can be any character, but if the same character needs to appear in the regular expression itself, it must be escaped using the backslash (\) character. The examples here use # as the delimiter. So if your expression needs to express a literal #, it should be indicated as \#.

Rewriting Numeric URLs with Two Parameters

What you've accomplished in the previous exercise is rewriting numeric URLs with one parameter. You now expand that little example to rewrite URLs with two parameters.

The URLs with one parameter that you supported looked like http://seophp.example.com/Products/Pn.html. Now assume that your links need to support a category ID as well, not only a product ID. The new URLs will look like this:

```
http://seophp.example.com/Products/C2/P1.html
```

The existing product.php script will be modified to handle links such as:

```
http://seophp.example.com/product.php?category_id=2&product_id=1
```

For a quick reminder, here's the rewriting rule you used for numeric URLs with one parameter:

```
RewriteRule ^Products/P([0-9]+)\.html$ /product.php?product_id=$1
```

For rewriting two parameters, the rule would be a bit longer, but not much more complex:

```
RewriteRule ^Products/C([0-9]+)/P([0-9]+)\.html$ ↵
/product.php?category_id=$1&product_id=$2 [L]
```

Go ahead and put this to work in a quick exercise.

Rewriting Numeric URLs

1. In your `seophp` folder, modify the `product.php` script that you created earlier like this:

```php
<?php

// display product details
echo 'You have selected product #' . $_GET['product_id'] .
     ' from category #' . $_GET['category_id'];

?>
```

2. Test your script by loading `http://seophp.example.com/product.php?category_id=5&product_id=99` in your web browser. You should get the expected output as shown in Figure 3-9.

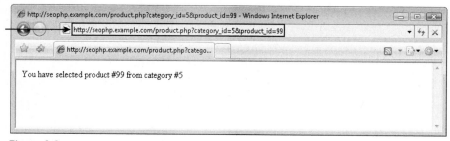

Figure 3-9

3. Change the current rewriting rule in your `.htaccess` file as shown in the following code. Also remove any old rules, because they wouldn't work well with the new `product.php` script, which receives two parameters now.

```
RewriteEngine On

# Rewrite numeric URLs
RewriteRule ^Products/C([0-9]+)/P([0-9]+)\.html$ ↵
/product.php?category_id=$1&product_id=$2 [L]
```

Note that the entire `RewriteRule` *command and its parameters **must be written on a single line** in your* `.htaccess` *file. If you split it in two lines as printed in the book, you'll get a 500 error from the web server when trying to load scripts from that folder.*

4. Load `http://seophp.example.com/Products/C5/P99.html`, and expect to get the same output as with the previous request, as shown in Figure 3-10.

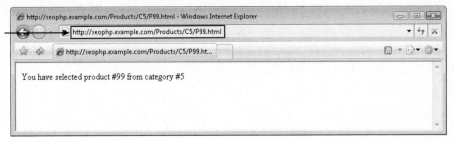

Figure 3-10

In this example you started by modifying `product.php` to accept product URLs that accept a product ID and a category ID. Then you added URL rewriting support for URLs with two numeric parameters. You created a rewriting rule in your `.htaccess` file, which handles URLs with two parameters:

```
RewriteRule ^Products/C([0-9]+)/P([0-9]+)\.html$ ↵
/product.php?category_id=$1&product_id=$2 [L]
```

The rule looks a bit more complicated, but if you look carefully, you'll see that it's not so different from the rule handling URLs with a single parameter. The rewriting rule has now two parameters — $1 is the similarly designed number that comes after `Products/C`, and is defined by (`[0-9]+`), and the second parameter, $2, is the number that comes after `/P`.

Figure 3-11 is a visual representation of how this rewrite rule matches the incoming link.

The result is that you now delegate any URL that looks like `Products/Cm/Pn.html` to `product.php?category_id=m&product_id=n`.

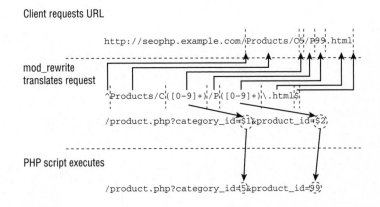

Figure 3-11

Rewriting Keyword-Rich URLs

Here's where the real fun begins! This kind of URL rewriting is a bit more complex, and there are more strategies you could take. When working with rewritten numeric URLs, it was relatively easy to extract the product and category IDs from a URL such as `/Products/C5/P9.html`, and rewrite the URL to `product.php?category_id=5&product_id=9`.

A keyword-rich URL doesn't necessarily have to include any IDs. Take a look at this one:

```
http://www.example.com/Products/Tools/Super-Drill.html
```

(You met a similar example in the first exercise of this chapter, where you handled the rewriting of `http://seophp.example.com/my-super-product.html`.)

This URL refers to a product named "Super Drill" located in a category named "Tools." Obviously, if you want to support this kind of URL, you need some kind of mechanism to find the IDs of the category and product the URL refers to.

One solution that comes to mind is to add a column in the product and category tables that associate such strings with their respective IDs that your application can handle. In such a request you could look up the information in the Category and Product tables, get their IDs, and use them.

However, we propose an easier solution that is more easily implemented and still brings the benefits of a keyword-rich URL. Look at the following URLs:

```
http://www.products.com/Products/Super-Drill-P9.html
http://www.products.com/Products/Tools-C5/Super-Drill-P9.html
```

These URLs include keywords. However, we've sneaked IDs in these URLs, in a way that isn't unpleasant to the human eye, and doesn't distract attention from the keywords that matter, either.

In the case of the first URL, the rewriting rule can simply extract the number that is tied at the end of the product name (`-P9`), and ignore the rest of the URL. For the second URL, the rewriting rule can extract the category ID (`-C5`) and product ID (`-P9`), and then use these numbers to build a URL such as `product.php?category_id=5&product_id=9`.

The rewrite rule for keyword-rich URLs with a single parameter looks like this:

```
RewriteRule ^Products/.*-P([0-9]+)\.html?$ /product.php?product_id=$1 [L]
```

The rewrite rule for keyword-rich URLs with two parameters looks like this:

```
RewriteRule ^Products/.*-C([0-9]+)/.*-P([0-9]+)\.html$ ↵
/product.php?category_id=$1&product_id=$2 [L]
```

Take a look at this latter rule at work in an exercise.

> As you will see in Chapter 14 in the e-commerce demo, you will use one-parameter URLs to implement the category pages (which contain lists of products), and two-parameter URLs to implement

the individual product pages. These URLs are "hackable," in that the products will be placed in an intuitive-looking directory structure. Users can intuitively modify such URLs to navigate the site.

Rewriting Keyword-Rich URLs

1. Modify the .htaccess file in your seophp folder like this:

```
RewriteEngine On

# Rewrite numeric URLs
RewriteRule ^Products/C([0-9]+)/P([0-9]+)\.html$ ↵
/product.php?category_id=$1&product_id=$2 [L]

# Rewrite keyword-rich URLs
RewriteRule ^Products/.*-C([0-9]+)/.*-P([0-9]+)\.html$ ↵
/product.php?category_id=$1&product_id=$2 [L]
```

2. Load http://seophp.example.com/Products/Tools-C5/Super-Drill-P9.html, and voila, you should get the result that's shown in Figure 3-12.

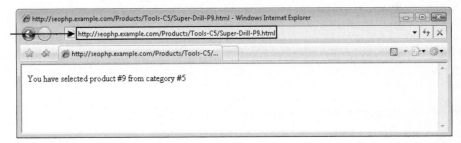

Figure 3-12

You currently have two rules in your .htaccess file, and they are working beautifully!

The new rule matches URLs that start with the string Products/, then contain a number of zero or more characters (.*) followed by -C. This is expressed by ^Products/.*-C. The next characters must be one or more digits, which as a whole are saved to the $1 variable, because the expression is written between parentheses — ([0-9]+). This first variable in the URL, $1, is the category ID.

After the category ID, the URL must contain a slash, then zero or more characters (.*), then -P, as expressed by /.*-P. Afterward, another captured group follows, to extract the ID of the product, ([0-9]+), which becomes the $2 variable. The final bit of the regular expression, \.html$, specifies the URL needs to end in .html.

The two extracted values, $1 and $2, are used to create the new URL, /product.php?category_id=$1&product_id=$2. Figure 3-13 describes the process visually.

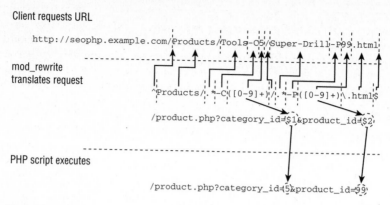

Figure 3-13

Building a Link Factory

Back in the days when you worked only with dynamic URLs, it was easy to build the URLs right in the application code without much planning. You cannot do that here. If you want to use keyword-rich URLs in your web site, just having a RewriteRule in your .htaccess file isn't enough! You also need to ensure that all the links in your web site use these keyword-rich versions consistently throughout the web site. Obviously, including the URLs manually in the web site is not an option — it's a dynamic site after all, and the link management task would quickly become impossible to handle when you have a large number of products in your catalog!

Fortunately, there's a very straightforward solution to this problem, which as soon as it's put in place, removes any additional link management effort. The solution we're proposing is to use a function to generate the new URLs based on data already existing in your database, such as product or category names. As mentioned before, this also enforces consistency.

Say that you have a product called Super Drill, located in the category Tools. You know the product ID is 9, and the category ID is 5. It's quite easy to create a PHP function that uses this data to generate a link such as /Products/Tools-C5/Super-Drill-P9.html.

In the exercise that follows you create and then use two PHP functions:

❑ _prepare_url_text receives as a parameter a string that will be included into the beautified URL, such as a product or category name, and transforms it into a form that can be included in a URL. For example, this function would transform Super Drill to Super-Drill.

❑ make_product_url takes as parameters the names of a product and a category, and their IDs, and uses the _prepare_url_text function to generate a URL such as /Products/Tools-C5/Super-Drill/P9.html.

> If you're a PHP OOP (object-oriented programming) fan, you might like to place these functions into a class. In this case, the `_prepare_url_text()` function should be a private method because it's only intended for internal use, and the `make_product_url()` would be a public method. OOP features are not used in this chapter to keep the examples simple and brief, but the underscore character is used to prefix functions that are meant for internal use only — such as in `_prepare_url_text()` — to make an eventual migration to object-oriented code easier. Later the book uses PHP OOP features when that is recommended by the specifics of the exercises.

You create these functions and put them to work step by step in the following exercise.

Building the Link Factory

1. In your `seophp` folder, create a new folder named `include`.

2. In the `include` folder, create a file named `config.inc.php`, and add this code to it:

```php
<?php

// site domain; no trailing '/' !
define('SITE_DOMAIN', 'http://seophp.example.com');

?>
```

3. Also in the `include` folder, create a file named `url_factory.inc.php`, and add the `_prepare_url_text()` and `make_product_url()` functions to it as shown in the code listing:

```php
<?php

// include config file
require_once 'config.inc.php';

// prepares a string to be included in an URL
function _prepare_url_text($string)
{
  // remove all characters that aren't a-z, 0-9, dash, underscore or space
  $NOT_acceptable_characters_regex = '#[^-a-zA-Z0-9_ ]#';
  $string = preg_replace($NOT_acceptable_characters_regex, '', $string);

  // remove all leading and trailing spaces
  $string = trim($string);

  // change all dashes, underscores and spaces to dashes
  $string = preg_replace('#[-_ ]+#', '-', $string);

  // return the modified string
  return $string;
}
```

```php
// builds a link that contains a category and a product
function make_category_product_url($category_name, $category_id,
                                   $product_name, $product_id)
{
  // prepare the product name and category name for inclusion in URL
  $clean_category_name = _prepare_url_text($category_name);
  $clean_product_name = _prepare_url_text($product_name);

  // build the keyword-rich URL
  $url = SITE_DOMAIN . '/Products/' .
        $clean_category_name . '-C' . $category_id . '/' .
        $clean_product_name . '-P' . $product_id . '.html';

  // return the URL
  return $url;
}

?>
```

4. In your `seophp` folder, create a file named `catalog.php` with these contents:

```php
<?php
// load the URL factory library
require_once 'include/url_factory.inc.php';
?>

<!DOCTYPE html PUBLIC "-//W3C//DTD XHTML 1.1//EN"
 "http://www.w3.org/TR/xhtml11/DTD/xhtml11.dtd">
<html>
  <head>
    <title>The SEO Egghead Shop</title>
  </head>
  <body>
    <h1>Products on Promotion at SEO Egghead Shop</h1>
    <ul>
      <li>
        <a href="<?php echo make_category_product_url("Carpenter's Tools", 12, ↵
"Belt Sander", 45); ?>">
          Carpenter's Tools: Belt Sander
        </a>
      </li>
      <li>
        <a href="<?php echo make_category_product_url("SEO Toolbox", 6, "Link ↵
Juice", 31); ?>">
          SEO Toolbox: Link Juice
        </a>
      </li>
      <li>
        <a href="<?php echo make_category_product_url("Friends' Shed", 2, "AJAX ↵
PHP Book", 42); ?>">
          Friends' Shed: AJAX PHP Book
        </a>
```

```
        </li>
      </ul>
    </body>
  </html>
```

5. You're making use of the `product.php` file you created in the previous exercise. Here's its code again for your reference:

```php
<?php

// display product details
echo 'You have selected product #' . $_GET['product_id'] .
    ' from category #' . $_GET['category_id'];

?>
```

6. Add one last rule to your `.htaccess` file:

```
RewriteEngine On

# Rewrite numeric URLs
RewriteRule ^Products/C([0-9]+)/P([0-9]+)\.html$
/product.php?category_id=$1&product_id=$2 [L]

# Rewrite keyword-rich URLs
RewriteRule ^Products/.*-C([0-9]+)/.*-P([0-9]+)\.html$
/product.php?category_id=$1&product_id=$2 [L]

# Rewrite catalog.html
RewriteRule ^catalog.html$ /catalog.php [L]
```

7. Load `http://seophp.example.com/catalog.html` in your web browser. You should be shown a page like the one shown in Figure 3-14.

8. Click one of the links, and ensure the rewriting correctly loads the `product.php` script as shown in Figure 3-15.

9. Just for the fun of it, or if you want to refresh your memory about how the `product.php` script works, load `http://seophp.example.com/product.php?category_id=6&product_id=31`. You should get the same output that's shown in Figure 3-15, but this time through a dynamic URL.

Figure 3-14

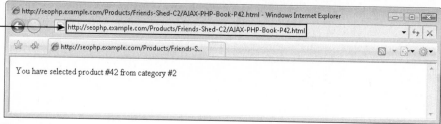

Figure 3-15

Congratulations! You've just implemented a very organized and powerful strategy that you can use to rewrite all the URLs in your catalog, and you've also implemented the URL rewriting scheme that makes them work.

Let's analyze the code you've written piece by piece, starting with the `_prepare_url_text()` function. This function prepares a string such as a product name or a category name to be included into a URL, by either deleting or changing to dashes those characters in a string that are invalid or not aesthetically pleasing in a URL. It retains all alphanumeric characters as-is. For example, if the function receives as a parameter the string "Friends' Shed", it will return "Friends-Shed."

The `_prepare_url_text()` function starts by using `preg_replace()` to delete all characters that aren't alphanumerical, a dash, a space, or an underscore, ensuring there are no characters left that could break your URL:

```
// remove all characters that aren't a-z, 0-9, dash, underscore or space
$NOT_acceptable_characters_regex = '#[^-a-zA-Z0-9_ ]#';
$string = preg_replace($NOT_acceptable_characters_regex, '', $string);
```

The `preg_replace()` PHP function allows for string manipulation using regular expressions. The original string is supplied as the third parameter. The function replaces the string portions matched by the regular expression supplied as the first parameter, with the string supplied as the second parameter.

In this case, the regular expression `[^-a-zA-Z0-9_ ]` matches all characters not (^) in the set of letters, numbers, dashes, underscores, or spaces. You indicate that the matching characters should be replaced with `''`, the empty string, effectively removing them. The pound (#) character used to enclose the regular expression is the delimiter character that you need to use with regular expressions in PHP functions.

Then you continue by removing the leading and trailing spaces from the string it receives as parameter, using the PHP `trim()` function:

```
// remove all leading and trailing spaces
$string = trim($string);
```

Finally, you use `preg_replace()` once again to transform any groups of spaces, dashes, and underscores to dashes. For example, a string such as SEO___Toolbox (note there are three underscores) would be replaced to SEO-Toolbox. Then you return the transformed URL string:

```
// change all dashes, underscores and spaces to dashes
$string = preg_replace('#[-_ ]+#', '-', $string);

// return the modified string
return $string;
```

Here are some examples of this transformation:

```
// displays Carpenters-Tools
echo _prepare_url_text("Carpenter's Tools");

// displays Black-And-White
echo _prepare_url_text("Black and White");
```

`_prepare_url_text()` is used by `make_category_product_url()` to create product URLs. The `make_category_product_url()` function receives as parameters a category name, a product name, a category ID, and a product ID, and it uses this data to create the keyword-rich URL. The code in this function is pretty straightforward. It starts by using `_prepare_url_text()` to prepare the product and category names for inclusion in a URL:

```
// builds a link that contains a category and a product
function make_category_product_url($category_name, $category_id,
                                   $product_name, $product_id)
{
  // prepare the product name and category name for inclusion in URL
  $clean_category_name = _prepare_url_text($category_name);
  $clean_product_name = _prepare_url_text($product_name);
```

Then it simply joins strings to create a string of the form `./Products/Category-Name-Cm/Product-Name-Pn.html`. Finally, it returns this string:

```
  // build the keyword-rich URL
  $url = './Products/' .
         $clean_category_name . '-C' . $category_id . '/' .
         $clean_product_name . '-P' . $product_id . '.html';
  // return the URL
  return $url;
}
```

Here are some examples of this function's use, and the results:

```
// display /Products/Carpenters-Tools-C12/Belt-Sander-P45.html
echo make_product_url("Carpenter's Tools", 12, 'Belt Sander', 45);

// display /Products/Hammers-C3/Big-and-Mighty-Hammer-P4.html
echo make_product_url('Hammers', 3, 'Big and Mighty Hammer', 4);
```

71

The web site application should be retrofitted with `make_product_url()`. All instances of a web site application's code where URLs are displayed should be replaced. For example (assume the following variables refer to product database information):

```
echo "/products.php?category_id=$category_id&product_id=$product_id";
```

These kinds of instances should be changed to:

```
echo make_product_url($category_name, $category_id, $product_name, $product_id);
```

We've demonstrated how you can do this by creating a fictional catalog page of an e-commerce web site, `catalog.php`, and we've even created a rewrite rule for it so you could access it using a static URL.

In a real-world web site the product and category names and IDs would be retrieved from the database, but for the purposes of this exercise we've typed them by hand to simplify the example.

```
<a href="<?php echo make_category_product_url("Carpenter's Tools", 12, 'Belt ↵
Sander', 45); ?>">
  Carpenter's Tools: Belt Sander
</a>
```

Pagination and URL Rewriting

It is often necessary to paginate series of pages on a web site. Ideally, the URLs of those the pages should also be rewritten. This rule is not illustrated in action until the e-commerce store in Chapter 14, but here is the rule to whet your appetite:

```
RewriteRule ^Products/.*-C([0-9]+)/Page-([0-9]+)/?$ ↵
category.php?category_id=$1&page_num=$2 [L]
```

Rewriting Images and Streaming Media

Some recommend using keywords not only in HTML document names, but also embedded in the image and media file names. Especially if you are in the image and streaming media distribution business, this may be more important.

Depending on your particular application, you may find it easier to use proper physical file names. However, if the solution is more complex, rewriting image file URLs may make sense. Rewriting can be accomplished here with little effort. All files should be placed in one directory with only ids as their file names, that is, ("1", "2", "3") — no extensions. You delegate the requests *directly* to physical files on the file system — and not through a PHP application. You do this because streaming media use extensions in a web server that cannot be easily implemented in PHP scripts. The URLs are generated using a PHP function as in previous examples.

Rewriting Image Files

1. Copy the `media` folder from the code download to your `seophp` folder. In your `seophp/media` folder, you should have five files named 1, 2, 3, 4, and 5. These are jpeg image files.

2. Add the following rewrite rule to the `.htaccess` file:

```
RewriteEngine On

# Rewrite numeric URLs
RewriteRule ^Products/C([0-9]+)/P([0-9]+)\.html$ ↵
/product.php?category_id=$1&product_id=$2 [L]

# Rewrite keyword-rich URLs
RewriteRule ^Products/.*-C([0-9]+)/.*-P([0-9]+)\.html$ ↵
/product.php?category_id=$1&product_id=$2 [L]

# Rewrite catalog.html
RewriteRule ^catalog.html$ /catalog.php [L]

# Rewrite cartoons.html
RewriteRule ^cartoons.html$ /cartoons.php [L]

# Rewrite media files
RewriteRule ^.*-M([0-9]+)\..*$ /media/$1 [L]
```

3. Create a new file named `cartoons.php` in your `seophp` folder, and add the following code to it:

```
<!DOCTYPE html PUBLIC "-//W3C//DTD XHTML 1.1//EN"
  "http://www.w3.org/TR/xhtml11/DTD/xhtml11.dtd">
<html>
  <head>
    <title>URL Rewriting Media Files</title>
  </head>
  <body>
    <img src="http://seophp.example.com/Tweety-M1.jpg" alt="Tweety" />
    <img src="http://seophp.example.com/Toy-Story-M2.jpg" alt="Toy Story" />
    <img src="http://seophp.example.com/Tweety-Sylvester-M3.jpg" alt="Tweety & ↵
Sylvester" />
    <img src="http://seophp.example.com/Mickey-M4.jpg" alt="Mickey" />
    <img src="http://seophp.example.com/Minnie-M5.jpg" alt="Minnie" />
  </body>
</html>
```

4. Load `http://seophp.example.com/cartoons.html`, and expect to see five images, as shown in Figure 3-16.

Figure 3-16

5. At this moment the image rewriting works perfectly. However, in order to implement it in a real-world web site you also need to extend the URL factory to build the image file names for you. Open the URL factory file, `url_factory.inc.php`, and add this function to it:

```
// builds a link to a media file
function make_media_url($id, $name, $extension)
{
  // prepare the medium name for inclusion in URL
  $clean_name = _prepare_url_text ($name);

  // build the keyword-rich URL
  $url = SITE_DOMAIN . '/' . $clean_name . '-M' . $id . '.' . $extension;

  // return the URL
  return $url;
}
```

6. Open `cartoons.php`, and change the hard-coded file names to calls to the `make_media_url()` function, like this:

```
<?php
// load the URL factory library
require_once 'include/url_factory.inc.php';
?>

<!DOCTYPE html PUBLIC "-//W3C//DTD XHTML 1.1//EN"
  "http://www.w3.org/TR/xhtml11/DTD/xhtml11.dtd">
<html>
  <head>
    <title>URL Rewriting Media Files</title>
  </head>
  <body>
    <img src="<?php echo make_media_url(1, "Tweety", "jpg"); ?>" alt="Tweety" />
    <img src="<?php echo make_media_url(2, "Toy Story", "jpg"); ?>" alt="Toy Story"↵
/>
    <img src="<?php echo make_media_url(3, "Tweety & Sylvester", "jpg"); ?>" ↵
alt="Tweety & Sylvester" />
    <img src="<?php echo make_media_url(4, "Mickey", "jpg"); ?>" alt="Mickey" />
    <img src="<?php echo make_media_url(5, "Minnie", "jpg"); ?>" alt="Minnie" />
  </body>
</html>
```

7. Load `http://seophp.example.com/cartoons.html` again. Expect to get the same links as before, and the results shown in Figure 3-16.

The exercise was pretty much similar to the previous ones, except Apache rewrites the image URLs to physical files on your disk. The regular expression looks a bit more complicated this time, but it's really not very different from the other ones you've dealt with:

```
RewriteRule ^.*-M([0-9]+)\..*$ /media/$1 [L]
```

The rule matches any random set of characters followed by -M (`^.*-M`), followed by a group of digits that is captured as $1 — (`[0-9]+`). Next you have a literal dot — `\.` (note that it's escaped using the backslash), and followed again by a random set of characters — (`.*`).

In English, the rule matches URLs such as `Some-Media-Name-Mn.some-extension`, and rewrites them directly to a physical file `/media/n`.

The new function you've added to the URL factory generates such beautified URLs. In case you want to use search engine friendly image file names, you should either give them proper names from the start, or use the URL factory together with the rewriting rule to ensure consistency throughout the web site.

Problems Rewriting Doesn't Solve

URL-rewriting is not a panacea for all dynamic site problems. In particular, URL-rewriting in and of itself does not solve any duplicate content problems. If a given site has duplicate content problems with a dynamic approach to its URLs, the problem would likely also be manifest in the resulting rewritten static URLs as well. In essence, URL-rewriting only obscures the parameters — however many there are, from the search engine spider's view. This is useful for URLs that have many parameters as we mentioned. Needless to say, however, if the varying permutations of obscured parameters *do not* dictate significant changes to the content, the same duplicate content problems remain.

A simple example would be the case of rewriting the page of a product that can exist in multiple categories. Obviously, these two pages would probably show duplicate (or very similar content) even if accessed through static-looking links, such as:

```
http://www.example.com/Products/College-Books-C1/Some-Book-Title-P2.html
http://www.example.com/Products/Out-of-Print-Books-C2/Some-Book-Title-P2.html
```

Additionally, in the case that you have duplicate content, using static-looking URLs may actually exacerbate the problem. This is because whereas dynamic URLs make the parameter values and names obvious, rewritten static URLs obscure them. Search engines are known to, for example, attempt to drop a parameter they heuristically guess is a session ID and eliminate duplicate content. If the session parameter were rewritten, a search engine would not be able to do this at all.

There are solutions to this problem. They typically involve removing any parameters that can be avoided, as well as excluding any of the remaining the duplicate content. These solutions are explored in depth in Chapter 5.

A Last Word of Caution

URLs are much more difficult to revise than titles and descriptions once a site is launched and indexed. Thus, when designing a new site, special care should be devoted to them. Changing URLs later requires you to redirect all of the old URLs to the new ones, which can be extremely tedious, and has the potential to influence rankings for the worse if done improperly and link equity is lost. Even the most trivial changes to URL structure should be accompanied by some redirects, and such changes should only be made when it is absolutely necessary.

This is relatively simple process. In short, you use the URL factory that you just created to create the new URLs based on the parameters in the old dynamic URLs. Then you employ what is called a "301-redirect" to the new URLs. The various types of redirects are discussed in the following chapter.

So, if you are retrofitting a web application that is powering a web site that is already indexed by search engines, you must redirect the old dynamic URLs to the new rewritten ones. This is especially important, because without doing this every page would have a duplicate and result in a large quantity of duplicate content. You can safely ignore this discussion, however, if you are designing a new web site.

Summary

This chapter covered a lot of material! It detailed how to employ static-looking URLs in a dynamic web site step-by-step. Such URLs are both search engine friendly and more enticing to the user. This is accomplished by using mod_rewrite in coordination with a "URL factory." This also enforces consistency in URLs. It is important to realize, however, that URL rewriting is not a panacea for all dynamic site problems — in particular, duplicate content problems. That is the focus of Chapter 5, "Duplicate Content."

Content Relocation and HTTP Status Codes

One of the perks of PHP is that it abstracts away many low-level implementation details from the web developer. It does such a great job, in fact, that you can typically build complex web applications without understanding much at all about the protocol web servers used to speak to the world, HTTP (**H**yper**T**ext **T**ransport **P**rotocol).

Though most of the time this ignorance is bliss, it is sometimes not so with regard to search engine optimization. Using the protocol improperly has the potential to wreak havoc for search engine rankings. On the other hand, knowing how to use it effectively can be of great help to the very same end.

HTTP status codes are a small but critical part of this protocol. They provide information regarding the state of an HTTP request. You can use them, for example, to indicate that the requested information should be retrieved from a different location henceforth. In modern search engines, doing so also may also result in a transference of link equity to that new location. This example alone highlights the importance of knowing how to use these codes.

In this chapter you will:

❑   Learn about the HTTP status codes that are pertinent to the search engine marketer.

❑   Understand how to use the redirection status codes properly, how to signal deleted pages, and how to avoid indexing errors.

❑   Learn how to implement redirection using PHP and mod_rewrite.

❑   Follow step-by-step exercises to implement automatic URL correction and canonicalization.

HTTP Status Codes

Each time a user agent requests a URL from a web site, the server replies with a set of HTTP headers; the requested content follows after them. Most users never see this part of the communication, however, because web browsers do not normally display them.

If you've never seen how these headers look, it's time to get your feet wet. The easiest way to get started is to use a web-based tool that does all of the work for you. One such tool is located at http://www .seoegghead.com/tools/view-http-headers.php.

Figure 4-1 shows the results of using this tool for http://www.cristiandarie.ro. The status code is highlighted.

A more convenient way to view these headers is by using a plugin for your browser. One plugin you can use with Firefox is LiveHTTPHeaders (http://livehttpheaders.mozdev.org/). For Internet Explorer you can use ieHTTPHeaders (http://www.blunck.se/iehttpheaders/iehttpheaders.html).

Figure 4-2 shows LiveHTTPHeaders in action.

The part of the HTTP headers you're predominantly interested in for the purpose of this chapter is the line containing the *status code* of the request, as indicated in the figure. The most common status code is 200, which specifies the request was processed by your web server successfully without any surprises, and that the content the user requested follows.

Figure 4-1

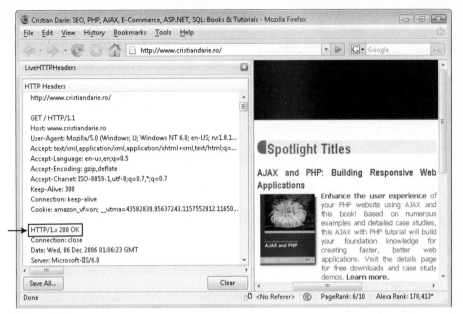

Figure 4-2

However, there are many other status codes you need to know about as a search engine marketer. The status codes considered in this chapter are:

❑   Redirection: 301 and 302

❑   Removal: 404

❑   Server Error: 500

The official descriptions for all HTTP status codes are available at http://www.w3.org/Protocols/rfc2616/rfc2616-sec10.html.

Redirection Using 301 and 302

The 301 and 302 codes are the HTTP status codes used for redirection. These codes indicate that another request must be made in order to fulfill the HTTP request — the content is located elsewhere. When a web page replies with either of these codes, it does not return any HTML content, but includes an additional Location: HTTP header that indicates another URL where the content is found.

Figure 4-3 shows an example of how redirects occur in practice. As you can see, when a redirect occurs, the URL that issues the redirect doesn't return any content, but indicates the new URL that should be referenced instead.

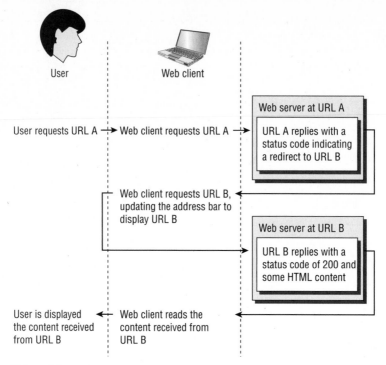

Figure 4-3

Note that in the case the user agent is a search engine spider or a software application, there is not a user involved in the process, as shown in Figure 4-3. Search engines follow the same basic process to update SERPs when they encounter a redirect.

Redirections can be chained, that is, one redirect can point to a page that, in turn, redirects again. However, multiple redirects should be avoided to the extent that it is possible. A maximum of five redirections was stipulated by an older version of RFC 2616, but that limit was later lifted. Regardless, it is wise to avoid chained redirects because they can slow down site spidering — spiders may only *schedule* the result of the redirection for spidering instead of immediately fetching it.

We recommend chaining no more than three redirects.

The HTTP standard actually contains many redirection status codes. They are listed in Table 4-1.

In practice only the 301 and 302 status codes are used for redirection. Furthermore, because browsers are known to struggle with certain of the other status codes, it is probably wise to avoid them, even if they seem more relevant or specific. It can only be assumed that search engines may also struggle with them, or at least that it is not entirely understood how they should be interpreted.

Table 4-1

Status Code	Description
300	Multiple choices
301	Moved permanently
302	Found
303	See other
304	Not modified
305	Use Proxy
307	Temporary Redirect

301

The 301 status code indicates that a resource has been permanently moved to the new location specified by the `Location:` header that follows. It indicates that the old URL is obsolete and should replace any references to the old URL with the indicated URL.

Take as an example a fictional page named `http://www.example.com/old_page.php`, which returns this header:

```
HTTP/1.1 301 Moved Permanently
Date: Wed, 14 Jun 2006 09:50:39 GMT
Server: Apache/2.0.54 (Unix)
X-Powered-By: PHP/5.0.4
Location: http://www.example.com/new_page.php
Content-Length: 0
Connection: close
Content-Type: text/html; charset=ISO-8859-1
```

When loading the page in a web browser, one will be automatically redirected to the new location specified by the `Location` header. After the redirection, the back button in your browser won't reference the initially requested page, as a result of the old page being *permanently* redirected.

The 301 status code also indicates to search engines that link equity from the previous URL should be credited to the new one. In theory, the new page will inherit the rankings of the original page. In practice, however, it may take some time for this to occur. It would be wise not to frivolously change URLs regardless, if this is a concern.

The 301 status code is arguably the most important one when it comes to search engine optimization. The largest part of this chapter is dedicated to this status code, and to exercises demonstrating its use. But before getting to the exercises, the following sections examine the 302, 404, and 500 status codes. These are important to understand as well.

302

The 302 status code is a bit ambiguous in meaning. It indicates that a resource is "temporarily" moved. The old URL is not obsolete at all, and clients will not cache the result unless indicated explicitly by a `Cache-Control` or `Expires` header. To confuse things even further, 302 is also used for some paid advertising links, but that is not the usage discussed here.

The big problem with the 302 status code is that its meaning for search engines depends on its context. In practice, it is worth dividing them into *internal* temporary redirects, that is, from a page on domain A to another page on domain A, and *external* temporary redirects, from a page on domain A to a page on domain B.

Browsers always abide by the definitions for interpreting a 302 redirect — both internal and external. However, today, most search engines (Google and Yahoo! included) only use it for an *internal* 302. For an internal 302 redirect, then, search engines will not cache the result of the redirect, and continue to list domain A in the SERPs. This is consistent with the definition.

External 302 redirects are more of a problem. Matt Cutts of Google states that more than 99% of the time, Google will list the result with the destination result, that is, domain B, instead of domain A. This is against the standard, and Google behaves like this to mitigate a vulnerability called "302 hijacking."

302 hijacking refers to the practice of using a page on domain A to reference a page on domain B, which has fresh quality content. Typically, that page would rank well based on that "stolen" fresh content from domain B, and employ a form of cloaking to redirect users to another page. This practice became prevalent enough to warrant a change in policy from both Google and Yahoo!, and, according to Matt Cutts, *"Google is moving to a set of heuristics that return the destination page more than 99% of the time. Why not 100% of the time? Most search engines reserve the right to make exceptions when we think the source page will be better for users, even though we'll only do that rarely."*

In the article at `http://www.mattcutts.com/blog/seo-advice-discussing-302-redirects/`, Matt Cutts discusses external 302s. In this case, the RFC definition is not the rule — it is the exception! For the most part, external 302s are treated as 301s, except that they do not effect the transference of link equity.

In practice, on a dynamic site, you should evaluate whether 302s are necessary anyway. If you want a URL to host some different content than the usual temporarily, it is better to change the content transparently. Possible implementations include using an `include()`, or fetching and displaying the alternative content remotely, obviating the need for the 302 in the first place. To do this you can use the cURL functions in PHP — Client URL Library.

Supposing the old page was called `old_page.php`, and the page that contains the required content is called `new_page.php`, you could simply include the content from the latter page as follows:

```
include('new_page.php');
```

To include the content from a different server using cURL, you could do something like this:

```
$ch = curl_init();
curl_setopt($ch, CURLOPT_URL,'http://www.example.com/new_page.php');
curl_setopt($ch, CURLOPT_RETURNTRANSFER,1);
echo curl_exec($ch);
```

Removing Deleted Pages Using 404

Everyone with "fat fingers" has seen the 404 status code at some point. It means that the URL you requested does not exist. However, there are a few technical details related to this status code that are less obvious.

First of all, it's less understood that along with a 404 status code, the web server can also deliver any HTML content — just like it does with the 200 status code. Indeed, people usually associate 404 with the generic Apache error page; but this is not necessarily the case. Some web sites customize their 404 pages to enhance the user experience. Advanced web sites may even try to give the visitors suggestions as to what they might have meant based on the keywords in the invalid URL.

Regardless of whether a 404 page is generic or custom, it always tells search engines the page does not exist; and if so, that it should be removed from the index.

> Search engines *never* index a page that arrives with the 404 status code.

For a static site, presenting a 404 error is automatic — simply delete the file. Unfortunately, many dynamic sites abandon the concept of 404s, because it takes some extra effort to implement. Typically when a product is deleted from a database, the product's page is no longer linked from the other pages of the web site. The product's page may, however, be linked from pages of external web sites, have acquired link equity, and remain indexed by search engines.

The worst thing you can do is return a blank page with a 200 status code — as happens often when a product ID no longer exists in a database. This will result in a number of blank pages indexed by a search engine over time, resulting in duplicate content. Instead, you should return a 404 status code, perhaps with a friendly error message as well.

> A common mistake is to deliver a "page not found" message that is meant to handle 404, but with a 200 status code instead. Web hosting services often allow setting a custom 404 page — that is, the page that is to be fed when a non-existent URL is requested. However, they may not set the 404 status code correctly. This can result in a theoretically infinite number of duplicate pages in your web site. You can verify that the correct headers are sent using the tools cited earlier in this chapter.

The moral of the story? Keep a tidy shop. Return 404s for all deleted pages. Some search engine marketers suggest redirecting old products to semantically related products instead of 404ing. This preserves link equity, whereas a 404 does not. This can be done in .htaccess or PHP with a 301 redirect, and is demonstrated later in this chapter.

Avoiding Indexing Error Pages Using 500

Once upon a time, in a place far away, your web server is chugging along; everything is fine and dandy. Then, all of a sudden, something terrible happens, and the database goes down. Because this is an unanticipated error condition (all of us could do better error checking!), many pages return erroneous blank pages or perhaps 404s. Perhaps the web server goes down altogether. Worse still, you don't have a hot standby to replace it. Meanwhile, search engines are trying to index your pages, not finding anything, getting blank pages, and so on. Here are the possibilities:

❑ **Returning 404s or blank pages.** This is a real problem. If a server returns a 404, a search engine will de-list your pages. If a search engine sees blank pages, or pages full of errors, it may do the same. This should be avoided at all costs.

❑ **Not finding anything (no connection).** This is actually more desirable than it sounds in terms of indexing. Although it may look extremely unprofessional, a search engine is likely to assume that there are intermittent connectivity problems and try again later. Your users may, however, be annoyed. At least from a spider's point of view, though, as long as this is resolved in a day or so, there is no major problem.

So what is the proper solution? It's actually fairly simple. A "500" status code can be returned, along with a custom page describing the error. This indicates to search engines that there is a temporary technical problem. Perhaps the site is down for maintenance. Say it politely and provide the time it will be back up. Or perhaps there was a national disaster as in the case of certain web servers in the New Orleans area in 2006. Put up a global error page for every URL with a polite message, and wait for things to clear up. One could do this automatically if, for example, the database cannot be accessed.

To do this in PHP use this line of PHP, and then add whatever content you wish:

```
header('HTTP/1.0 500 Internal Server Error');
echo 'The bank is closed until the scary aliens leave on their space ship; sorry
for the inconvenience, thank you for being a Bank of Mars customer.';
exit();
```

Redirecting with PHP and mod_rewrite

From now on, this chapter primarily discusses uses of the 301 HTTP status code. You can implement it with either mod_rewrite or PHP.

When using mod_rewrite, redirecting is implemented similarly to URL rewriting, except that you specify a redirection status code as a parameter. The following rule does a 301 redirect to bar.php when the initial request is for foo.php:

```
RewriteRule ^foo\.php$ /bar.php [R=301,L]
```

Except for the new R option at the end, there's nothing new for you here — but that option represents an important difference! With or without the R option, the visitor would end up transparently seeing the content provided by bar.php. However, when redirection is used, the user's web client actually makes two calls to the web server. First it asks for foo.php; as a response, it gets a 301 redirect code in the HTTP header, indicating bar.php as the new location. Then the web client requests bar.php, and informs the user that a new URL has been loaded by updating the URL displayed in the address bar.

In PHP, you redirect by adding HTTP headers using the header() function. If you want foo.php to do a 301 redirect to bar.php, your foo.php should look like this:

```php
<?php

header('HTTP/1.1 301 Moved Permanently');
header('Location: http://www.example.com/bar.php');

?>
```

> When just the Location **header is mentioned without explicitly mentioning the status code, a *302* temporary redirect is implied. Keep this in mind.**

In practice, when a site redesign involves changing URLs, the webmaster should at least 301 redirect the most important URLs to their new counterparts. Otherwise link equity will be lost.

Using a series of 301 redirects mitigates this problem. If your site is already indexed by search engines, you need to systematically rewrite old URLs to new URLs.

Using Redirects to Change File Names

In the exercise that follows you update the product pages you created in Chapter 3 to redirect all the dynamic URLs to their keyword-rich versions. Currently, the same content can be retrieved using both dynamic URLs and keyword-rich URLs (see Figure 3-9 and Figure 3-12 from Chapter 3); the following two links would get to the same content:

```
http://seophp.example.com/Products/SEO-Toolbox-C6/Link-Juice-P31.html
```

and

```
http://seophp.example.com/product.php?category_id=6&product_id=31
```

To avoid any problems that can result from two links generating this duplicate content, make sure that the visitor is always redirected to the proper keyword-rich URL, if a different URL was used. This is critical during a migration to such URLs on a preexisting web site, because the old URLs will be definitely indexed.

Alright, we're sure you're eager to write some code!

Redirecting Dynamic URLs to Keyword-Rich URLs

1. Add this code to your `config.inc.php` file. These global associative arrays define a line of products and categories, simulating a real product database. You'll need the data from these arrays to generate the keyword-rich versions of URLs automatically, using PHP code. (Arrays are used instead of a real database to keep the exercise easier for you to follow.)

```php
<?php

// site domain; no trailing '/' !
define('SITE_DOMAIN', 'http://seophp.example.com');

// create a fictional database with products and categories
$GLOBALS['products'] = array
       ("45" => "Belt Sander",
        "31" => "Link Juice",
        "42" => "AJAX PHP Book");
$GLOBALS['categories'] = array
       ("12" => "Carpenter's Tools",
         "6" => "SEO Toolbox",
         "2" => "Friend's Shed");

?>
```

2. Create `include/url_redirect.inc.php` and type this code:

```php
<?php

// load the URL factory library
require_once 'url_factory.inc.php';

// redirects to proper URL if not already there
function fix_category_product_url()
{
  // obtain the proper URL of the current category/product page
  $proper_url = get_proper_category_product_url();

  // 301 redirect to the proper URL if necessary
  if (SITE_DOMAIN . $_SERVER['REQUEST_URI'] != $proper_url)
  {
    header('HTTP/1.1 301 Moved Permanently');
    header('Location: ' . $proper_url);
    exit();
  }
}

// returns the proper keyword-rich URL
function get_proper_category_product_url()
{
```

```
    // retrieve product and category IDs from the query string
    $product_id = $_GET['product_id'];
    $category_id = $_GET['category_id'];

    // retrieve product and category names from fictional database
    $product_name = $GLOBALS['products'][$product_id];
    $category_name = $GLOBALS['categories'][$category_id];

    // create keyword-rich URL
    $proper_url = make_category_product_url($category_name, $category_id,
                                            $product_name, $product_id);

    // redirect to keyword-rich URL if not already there
    return $proper_url;
  }

?>
```

3. Add these lines to `product.php`:

```php
<?php

// load library that handles redirects
require_once 'include/url_redirect.inc.php';

// redirect requests proper keyword-rich URLs when not already there
fix_category_product_url();

// display product details
echo 'You have selected product #' . $_GET['product_id'] .
     ' from category #' . $_GET['category_id'];

?>
```

4. Load `http://seophp.example.com/product.php?category_id=2&product_id=42` in your web browser, and see some magic happen to the URL! Figure 4-4 shows how this request was redirected to its keyword-rich ("proper") version of the URL.

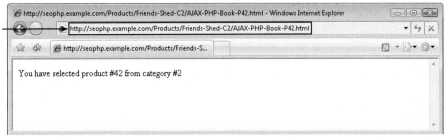

Figure 4-4

You start by modifying product.php to include a reference to url_redirect.inc.php, and then call its fix_category_product_url() function:

```php
<?php

// load library that handles redirects
require_once 'include/url_redirect.inc.php';

// redirect requests proper keyword-rich URLs when not already there
fix_category_product_url();
```

The fix_category_product_url() function is executed every time a product page is loaded, and verifies if the URL used to reach the page is the "proper" one. The "proper" version of the URL is composed using a helper function named get_proper_category_product_url():

```php
// redirects to proper URL if not already there
function fix_category_product_url()
{
  // obtain the proper URL of the current category/product page
  $proper_url = get_proper_category_product_url();
```

How get_proper_category_product_url() works is discussed in a second. For now, just assume the $proper_url variable contains something like http://seophp.example.com/Products/Friends-Shed-C2/AJAX-PHP-Book-P42.html. As soon as you obtain this "proper" URL, you verify that the URL used by the visitor to reach the product page matches:

```php
// 301 redirect to the proper URL if necessary
if (SITE_DOMAIN . $_SERVER['REQUEST_URI'] != $proper_url)
{
```

The $_SERVER['REQUEST_URI'] returns the URL used to reach the page, without the domain name. For example, if you navigate to http://seophp.example.com/product.php?category_id=2&product_id=42, $_SERVER['REQUEST_URI'] will return /product.php?category_id=2&product_id=42. By joining the domain name with this value, you obtain a complete URL.

If there is no match, you do a 301 redirect to the proper URL by setting the necessary header values:

```php
// 301 redirect to the proper URL if necessary
if (SITE_DOMAIN . $_SERVER['REQUEST_URI'] != $proper_url)
{
  header('HTTP/1.1 301 Moved Permanently');
  header('Location: ' . $proper_url);
  exit();
}
```

Now look at get_proper_category_product_url(). This function starts by loading the product and category IDs passed through the URL in the $_GET variable:

```php
// returns the proper keyword-rich URL
function get_proper_category_product_url()
{
  // retrieve product and category IDs from the query string
  $product_id = $_GET['product_id'];
  $category_id = $_GET['category_id'];
```

Then you read the names of the product and the category from your fictional database:

```
// retrieve product and category names from fictional database
$product_name = $GLOBALS['products'][$product_id];
$category_name = $GLOBALS['categories'][$category_id];
```

The fictional database consists of two global associative arrays, associating IDs with names. These are defined in `config.inc.php`, and simulate a real database of products. This example uses associative arrays to keep things simple. You would need a real database in a production scenario, however.

```
// create a fictional database with products and categories
$GLOBALS['products'] = array
        ("45" => "Belt Sander",
         "31" => "Link Juice",
         "42" => "AJAX PHP Book");
$GLOBALS['categories'] = array
        ("12" => "Carpenter's Tools",
         "6" => "SEO Toolbox",
         "2" => "Friend's Shed");
```

With this data at hand, `get_proper_category_product_url()` continues by creating the keyword-rich URL using the `make_category_product_url()` function of the URL factory:

```
// create keyword-rich URL
$proper_url = make_category_product_url($category_name, $category_id,
                                        $product_name, $product_id);
```

Finally, the function returns this value:

```
// redirect to keyword-rich URL if not already there
return $proper_url;
```

URL Correction

The great advantage with your current keyword-rich URLs is that you aren't really relying on the product or category names to find their data, but rather only on their IDs, which are subtly inserted in the URLs. This works great because the text in the URL can change without disabling it.

One potential problem with these links, though, is that when the text for a product or category name changes, its link will automatically be changed as well. As you already know, this has the potential to generate duplicate content problems, and that's certainly not something that you want!

With your current site, there are an infinite number of variations that lead to the same content. Take these two "different" links:

```
http://seophp.example.com/Products/SEO-Toolbox-C6/Link-Juice-P31.html
```

and

```
http://seophp.example.com/Products/SEO-Toolbox-C6/New-Link-Juice-With-Vitamin-L-P31
.html
```

The solution we're proposing is to do 301 redirects to a single "standard" version of the link. Lucky you, the functionality is already there! The `fix_category_product_url()` function from `url_redirect.inc.php` already takes care to redirect any errant or outdated link to its "proper" version, in case the URL isn't already what it should be.

Trying to load any of the two previously mentioned links would simply redirect you to:

```
http://seophp.example.com/Products/SEO-Toolbox-C6/Link-Juice-P31.html
```

Dealing with Multiple Domain Names Properly

Though it's less popular these days, some people desire to have multiple domain names pointing to the same site. For example, say you have three domain names:

```
www.example.com
www.example.org
www.example.net
```

The problem is that, especially if you market all three domains, people are free to link to any of these domains. That's a major duplicate content issue. You must pick a "standard" domain and permanently redirect the other domains to that domain.

Let's pick `www.example.com`. This is how to do it with mod_rewrite:

```
RewriteEngine on
RewriteCond %{HTTP_HOST} !^www\.example\.com
RewriteRule ^(.*)$ http://www.example.com/$1 [R=301,L]
```

Done! Now everything will get redirected to `www.example.com`. Let's analyze the rules in detail.

This is the first time you're using `RewriteCond`. You use `RewriteCond` to place a condition for the rule that follows. In this case, you're interested in verifying that the site has been accessed through `www.example.com`. Take another look at the `RewriteCond` line:

```
RewriteCond %{HTTP_HOST} !^www\.example\.com
```

This line specifies a condition that is true when the host name (`HTTP_HOST`) is not (`!`) `www.example.com`. The rewrite rule captures the entire URL and query string of the original URL, as (`.*`), and passes it to `http://www.example.com`, doing a 301 redirect to the new location. This way, for example, a query to `http://www.example.org/foo?query=string` would be 301 redirected to `http://www.example.com/foo?query=string`.

Using Redirects to Change Domain Names

Sometimes you *have* to change your domain name. Usually this happens in M&A (mergers and acquisitions) cases. Although undesirable, there is a right way to do this, and many wrong ones. Typically both domains need to point to the same web site now that the merger occurred. The *worst* thing you can do is simply point both domains to the same content via DNS. This will result in search engines not knowing which is authoritative. Many links have presumably built up over the years for both domain names, and a search engine will have considerable difficulty ascertaining which version to index. The result is a massive duplicate content problem. You could also take down the old domain, or put a page up on the old domain indicating to users that they should visit the new domain. Both of these methods avert the duplicate content penalty, but do not result in transference of link equity. The proper way to handle such a necessity is to use a 301 redirect to the new domain.

Simply place this in your `.htaccess` file:

```
RewriteEngine on
RewriteCond %{HTTP_HOST} ^old\.example\.com [OR]
RewriteCond %{HTTP_HOST} ^www\.old\.example\.com
RewriteRule ^(.*)$ http://www.new.example.com/$1 [R=301,L]
```

This says that if a request for `old.example.com` or `www.old.example.com` comes in, it should be permanently redirected to `www.new.example.com`, keeping all the query string parameters. Note the way the RewriteRule is only executed if one of the `RewriteCond` rules is satisfied.

Alternatively, you can assert something with another (similar) meaning:

```
RewriteEngine on
RewriteCond %{HTTP_HOST} !^www\.new.example\.com
RewriteRule ^(.*)$ http://www.new.example.com/$1 [R=301,L]
```

This says, similar to the canonicalization situation, anything that's not the right domain should be redirected.

URL Canonicalization: www.example.com versus example.com

This is another topic that comes up again and again. Because every search engine (including Google — even after the BigDaddy update) has issues when a web site is accessible under both `www.example.com` and `example.com` domains, we should be responsible webmasters and remove the ambiguity altogether. Otherwise both versions may be indexed and cause duplicate content problems. This is a fairly simple task.

Simply place this in your `.htaccess` file:

```
RewriteCond %{HTTP_HOST} ^example\.com
RewriteRule ^(.*)$ http://www.example.com/$1 [R=301,L]
```

This says that if a request for `example.com[path]` comes in, it should be permanently redirected to `www.example.com[path]`.

Alternatively, you can assert something with another (similar meaning):

```
RewriteEngine on
RewriteCond %{HTTP_HOST} !^www\.example\.com
RewriteRule ^(.*)$ http://www.example.com/$1 [R=301,L]
```

This says that if any request designated to this site comes in with something other than www.example.com, it should be changed to that. This is a slightly broader definition, and may or may not be desirable. It will also redirect any other domains that resolve to your site to www.example.com.

Please note: It is *not* a good idea to use a site removal tool to remove the example.com pages for a site, even after these changes have been applied! This can result in complete site removal. Matt Cutts of Google says "If you remove one of the www vs. non-www hostnames, it can end up removing your whole domain for six months. Definitely don't do this" (http://www.mattcutts.com/blog/seo-advice-url-anonicalization/). Instead, simply 301 the non-desirable domain to the desirable one, and the problem should slowly be resolved over time.

URL Canonicalization: /index.php versus /

Unfortunately, the concept of index pages (index.php, Default.aspx, and so on) causes yet another duplicate content problem. If no file name in a directory is provided to a web server, the "index" page is typically provided by default, but without redirection to this page. The problem arises when both URLs are linked, either internally or from other sites. This results in the duplicate content because there are two URLs that are used to access the same content. Strictly speaking, neither URL is more correct, though shorter URLs are usually desirable, and hence we favor / over /index.php.

The solution is similar to the one for the www.example.com vs. example.com issue. You must use a 301 redirect to the containing directory whenever you get a request for a file path ending in index.php or index.html. The redirection code can simply be implemented using a mod_rewrite rule or in PHP.

Using mod_rewrite, you'd just need to add these lines to the .htaccess file:

```
RewriteCond %{THE_REQUEST} ^GET\ .*/index\.(php|html)\ HTTP
RewriteRule ^(.*)index\.(php|html)$ /$1 [R=301,L]
```

After making this change, trying to load http://seophp.example.com/index.php should redirect you to http://seophp.example.com/. This rule will also work for subdirectories, i.e. http://www.example.com/Products/index.php gets redirected to http://www.example.com/Products/.

Alternatively, you can take care of the redirection in PHP code. You do that in the next exercise.

Eliminating index.php

1. Add a file named index.php to your seophp folder, with the following code:

```php
<?php
// redirect the current request if necessary
require_once 'include/url_redirect.inc.php';

// redirect requests to index.php and index.html to the root
fix_index_url();
?>

<!DOCTYPE html PUBLIC "-//W3C//DTD XHTML 1.1//EN"
  "http://www.w3.org/TR/xhtml11/DTD/xhtml11.dtd">
<html>
```

```
  <head>
    <title>SEO Egghead: SEO for Nerds</title>
  </head>
  <body>
    <h1>Welcome to SEO Egghead!</h1>
  </body>
</html>
```

2.   Add this code to your `url_redirect.inc.php` file:

```php
<?php

// load the URL factory library
require_once 'url_factory.inc.php';

// redirect requests to index.php and index.html to the root
function fix_index_url()
{
  // if the request is for index.php we redirect to ./
  if (preg_match('#(.*)index\.(html|php)$#', $_SERVER['REQUEST_URI'], $captures))
  {
    // perform a 301 redirect to the new URL
    header('HTTP/1.1 301 Moved Permanently');
    header('Location: ' .SITE_DOMAIN . $captures[1]);
  }
}

...
?>
```

3.   Load `http://seophp.example.com/index.php`, and expect to be redirected to
     `http://seophp.example.com/` (see Figure 4-5).

The code is pretty straightforward. You started by creating a very simple version of `index.php.`, which contains only a title. However, what's special about this `index.php` file is that in the beginning it loads the `url_redirect.inc.php` script. This script checks if the page was accessed through a URL that ends either with `index.php` or `index.html`:

```php
// if the request ends in index.php we redirect to the same path without it.
if (preg_match('#(.*)index\.(html|php)$#', $_SERVER['REQUEST_URI'], $captures))
```

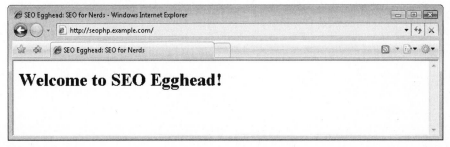

Figure 4-5

Here you use a regular expression to check if the URL ends with the aforementioned file names. You use the `preg_match()` function, and instruct it to store any characters that precede the file name by placing `.*` within parentheses — `(.*)`. These characters, now stored in `$captures[1]`, will be the location you want to redirect to.

If you have a match, you then perform the 301 redirect:

```
{
    // perform a 301 redirect to the new URL
    header('HTTP/1.1 301 Moved Permanently');
    header('Location: ' .SITE_DOMAIN . $captures[1]);
}
```

Other Types of Redirects

Although there are other types of redirects, such as meta refresh and JavaScript redirects, we do not generally recommend their use. Spammers have historically abused them, and for this reason their use is almost *always* suspect. It is recommended that a meta refresh is never used with a delay of less than 10 seconds. A typical meta refresh is illustrated here:

```
<!-- Redirect to SEO Egghead in 10 seconds -->
<meta http-equiv="refresh" content="10;url=http://www.seoegghead.com/">
```

We do not recommend using JavaScript-based redirects at all. If discovered, it will most likely result in some sort of penalty.

Summary

This chapter has illustrated that a fundamental understanding of relevant HTTP status codes is vital to the search engine marketer. Business decisions dictate that pages move, domains change, or that content is removed. Informing the search engine of these decisions using these status codes can avert a very costly "misunderstanding."

5

Duplicate Content

We humans often find it frustrating to listen to people repeat themselves. Likewise, search engines are "frustrated" by web sites that do the same. This problem is called *duplicate content*, which is defined as web content that is either exactly duplicated or substantially similar to content located at different URLs. Duplicate content clearly does not contain anything *original*.

This is important to realize. Originality is an important factor in the human perception of value, and search engines factor such human sentiments into their algorithms. Seeing several pages of duplicated content would not please the user. Accordingly, search engines employ sophisticated algorithms that detect such content and filter it out from search engine results.

Indexing and processing duplicate content also wastes the storage and computation time of a search engine in the first place. Aaron Wall of `http://www.seobook.com/` states that "if pages are too similar, then Google [or other search engines] may assume that they offer little value or are of poor content quality." A web site may not get spidered as often or as comprehensively as a result. And though it is an issue of contention in the search engine marketing community as to whether there is an *explicit* penalty applied by the various search engines, everyone agrees that duplicate content can be harmful.

Knowing this, it would be wise to eliminate as much duplicate content as possible from a web site. This chapter documents the most common causes of duplicate content as a result of web site architecture. It then proposes methods to eliminate or remove it from a search engine's view. You will:

❏   Understand the potential negative effects of duplicate content.

❏   Examine the most common types of duplicate content.

❏   Learn how to exclude duplicate content using `robots.txt` and `meta` tags.

❏   Use PHP code to properly implement an affiliate program.

A common question asked by search engine marketers is "how much duplicate content is too much?" There is no good answer to that question, as you may have predicted. It is best to simply take the conservative approach of eliminating as much of it as possible.

Causes and Effects of Duplicate Content

You know duplicate content can have a negative effect on web site rankings. But how do you examine whether a particular web site exhibits this problem, and how do you mitigate or avoid it?

To begin, you can divide duplicate content into two main categories:

❑   Duplicate content as a result of site architecture

❑   Duplicate content as a result of content theft

These are discussed separately, because they are essentially completely different problems.

Duplicate Content as a Result of Site Architecture

Some examples of site architecture itself leading to duplicate content are as follows:

❑   Print-friendly pages

❑   Pages with substantially similar content that can be accessed via different URLs

❑   Pages with items that are extremely similar, such as a series of differently colored shirts in an e-commerce catalog having similar descriptions

❑   Pages that are part of an improperly configured affiliate program tracking application

❑   Pages with duplicate title or `meta` tag values

❑   Using URL-based session IDs

❑   Canonicalization problems

All of these scenarios are discussed at length in this chapter.

To look for duplicate content as a result of site architecture, you can use a "`site:www.example.com`" query to examine the URLs of a web site that a search engine has indexed. All major search engines (Google, Yahoo!, Microsoft Live Search) support this feature. Usually this will reveal quickly if, for example, "print-friendly" pages are being indexed.

Google frequently places content it perceives as duplicate content in the "supplemental index." This is noted at the bottom of a search engine result with the phrase "supplemental result." If your web site has many pages in the supplemental index, it may mean that those pages are considered duplicate content — at least by Google. Investigate several pages of URLs if possible, and look for the aforementioned cases. Look especially at the later pages of results. It is extremely easy to create duplicate content problems without realizing it, so viewing from the vantage point of a search engine may be useful.

Duplicate Content as a Result of Content Theft

Content theft creates an entirely different problem. Just as thieves can steal tangible goods, they can also steal content. This, unsurprisingly, is the reason why it is called content theft. It creates a similar problem for search engines, because they strive to filter duplicate content from search results — across different web sites as well — and will sometimes make the wrong assumption as to which instance of the content is the original, authoritative one.

This is an insidious problem in some cases, and can have a disastrous effect on rankings. CopyScape (`http://www.copyscape.com`) is a service that helps you find content thieves by scanning for similar content contained by a given page on other pages. Sitemaps can also offer help by getting new content indexed more quickly and therefore removing the ambiguity as to who is the original author. Sitemaps are discussed at length in Chapter 9.

If you are a victim of content theft, and want to take action, first present the individual using the content illicitly with a cease and desist letter. Use the contact information provided on his web site or in the WHOIS record of the domain name. Failing that, the major search engines have procedures to alert them of stolen content. Here are URLs with the directions for the major search engines:

- ❑ Google: `http://www.google.com/dmca.html`
- ❑ Yahoo!: `http://docs.yahoo.com/info/copyright/copyright.html`
- ❑ MSN: `http://search.msn.com/docs/siteowner.aspx?t=SEARCH_WEBMASTER_CONC_AboutDMCA.htm`

Unfortunately, fighting content theft is ridiculously time-consuming and expensive — especially if lawyers get involved. Doing so for all instances is probably unrealistic; and search engines generally *do* accurately assess who is the original author and display that one preferentially. In Google, the illicit duplicates are typically relegated to the supplemental index. However, it may be necessary to take this action in the unlikely case that the URLs with the stolen content actually rank better than yours.

Excluding Duplicate Content

When you have duplicate content on your site, you can remove it entirely by altering the architecture of a web site. But sometimes a web site *has* to contain duplicate content. The most typical scenario of this is when the business rules that drive the web site require the said duplicate content.

To address this, you can simply exclude it from the view of a search engine. Here are the two ways of excluding pages:

- ❑ Using the `robots` meta tag
- ❑ `robots.txt` pattern exclusion

In the following sections, you learn about the `robots` meta tag and about `robots.txt`.

Using the Robots Meta Tag

This is addressed first, not because it's universally the optimal way to exclude content, but rather because it has virtually no limitations as to its application. Using the `robots` meta tag you can exclude any HTML-based content from a web site on a page-by-page basis, and it is frequently an easier method to use when eliminating duplicate content from a preexisting site for which the source code is available, or when a site contains many complex dynamic URLs.

To exclude a page with meta-exclusion, simply place the following code in the `<head>` section of the HTML document you want to exclude:

```
<meta name="robots" content="noindex, nofollow" />
```

This indicates that the page should not be indexed (`noindex`) and none of the links on the page should be followed (`nofollow`). It is relatively easy to apply some simple programming logic to decide whether or not to include such a meta tag on the pages of your site. It will always be applicable, so long as you have access to the source code of the application, whereas `robots.txt` exclusion may be difficult or even impossible to apply in certain cases.

To exclude a specific spider, change "robots" to the name of the spider — for example `googlebot`, `msnbot`, or `slurp`. To exclude multiple spiders, you can use multiple meta tags. For example, to exclude `googlebot` and `msnbot`:

```
<meta name="googlebot" content="noindex, nofollow" />
<meta name="msnbot" content="noindex, nofollow" />
```

Table 5-1 shows the common user agent names used by the various major search engines. The name attribute is note case sensitive; "google" or "Google" will do.

In theory, this method is equivalent to the next method that is discussed, `robots.txt`. The only downside is that the page must be fetched in order to determine that it should not be indexed in the first place. This is likely to slow down indexing. Dan Thies also notes in *The Search Engine Marketing Kit* that "if your site serves 10 duplicate pages for every page of unique content, spiders may still give up indexing ... you can't count on the search engines to fish through your site looking for unique content."

There are two technical limitations are associated with using the meta-exclusion method:

❏ It requires access to the source code of the application. Otherwise, meta tag exclusion becomes impossible because the tag must be placed in the web pages generated by the application.

❏ It only works with HTML files, not with clear text, CSS, or binary/image files.

These limitations can be addressed by using the `robots.txt` file, which is discussed next. However, `robots.txt` also has some limitations as to its application. If you do not have access to the source code of a web application, however, `robots.txt` is your only option.

Table 5-1

Search Engine	User Agent
Google	Googlebot
Yahoo!	Slurp
MSN Search	Msnbot
Ask	Teoma

robots.txt Pattern Exclusion

robots.txt is a text file located in the root directory of a web site that adheres to the robots.txt standard. Taking the risk of repeating ourselves and generating a bit of "duplicate content," here are three basic things to keep in mind regarding robots.txt:

❏ There can be only one robots.txt file.

❏ The proper location of robots.txt is in the root directory of a web site.

❏ robots.txt files located in subdirectories will not be accessed (or honored).

The official resource with the official documentation of robots.txt *is* http://www.robotstxt .org/. *There you can find a Frequently Asked Questions page, the complete reference, and a list with the names of the robots crawling the web.*

If you peruse your logs, you will see that search engine spiders visit this particular file very frequently. This is because they make an effort not to crawl or index any files that are excluded by robots.txt and want to keep a very fresh copy cached. robots.txt excludes URLs from a search engine on a very simple pattern-matching basis, and it is frequently an easier method to use when eliminating entire directories from a site, or, more specifically, when you want to exclude many URLs that start with the same characters.

Sometimes for various internal reasons within a (usually large) company, it is not possible to gain access to modify this file in the root directory. In that case, so long as you have access to the source code of the part the application in question, use the meta robots tag.

> robots.txt is *not* a form of security! It does not prevent access to any files. It *does* stop a search engine from indexing the content, and therefore prevents users from navigating to those particular resources via a search engine results page. However, users could access the pages by navigating directly to them. Also, robots.txt itself is a public resource, and anyone who wants to peruse it can do so by pointing their browser to /robots.txt. If anything, using it for "security" would only make those resources even more obvious to potential hackers if used for that incorrect purpose. To protect content, you should use the traditional ways of authenticating users, and authorizing them to visit resources of your site.

A robots.txt file includes User-agent specifications, which define your exclusion targets, and Disallow entries for one or more URLs you want to exclude therein. Lines in robots.txt that start with # are comments, and are ignored.

The following robots.txt file, placed in the root folder of your site, would not permit any robots (*) to access any files on the site:

```
# Forbid all robots from browsing your site
User-agent: *
Disallow: /
```

The next example disallows any URLs that start with `/directory` from being indexed by Google:

```
# Disallow googlebot from indexing anything that starts with /directory
User-agent: googlebot
Disallow: /directory
```

`googlebot` is Google's user-agent name. It is useful to think of each `Disallow` as matching *prefixes*, not files or URLs. Notably, `/directory.html` (because `/directory` is a prefix of `/directory.html`) would also match that rule, and be excluded. If you want only the contents of the `directory` folder to be excluded, you should specify `/directory/` instead. That last `/` prevents `/directory.html` from matching. Note also that the leading `/` is always necessary on exclusions. The following would be invalid:

```
Disallow: directory
```

> To elaborate, a string specified after `Disallow:` is equivalent to the regular expression `^<your string>.*$` — which means that it matches anything that begins with that string.

The `*` we used for `User-agent` doesn't function as a wildcard "glob" operator. Not that it would be useful for anything, but `goo*bot` would not match `googlebot`, and is invalid.

Wildcard "glob" operators are also not *officially* valid in the `Disallow:` directive either, but Google, MSN, and more recently Yahoo!, support this non-standard form of wildcard matching. We generally do not recommend its use, however, both because it is not part of the standard, and because various other search engines do *not* support it.

> If you must use wildcards in the `Disallow` clause, it is wise to do so only under a specific user-agent clause; for example, `User-agent: googlebot`.

For information regarding the implementations of wildcard matching from search engine vendors, read:

- ❑ Google: `http://www.google.com/support/webmasters/bin/answer.py?answer=35303`

- ❑ MSN: `http://search.msn.com.sg/docs/siteowner.aspx?t=SEARCH_WEBMASTER_REF_RestrictAccessToSite.htm#b`

- ❑ Yahoo!: `http://www.ysearchblog.com/archives/000372.html`

Using wildcards, the following `robots.txt` file would tell Google not to index any URL containing the substring `print=` anywhere within the URL:

```
User-agent: googlebot
Disallow: /*print=
```

It may seem counterintuitive and rather annoying that there is no `Allow` directive to complement `Disallow`. Certain search engines (Google and Yahoo! included) do indeed permit its use, but nuances of their interpretations may vary, and it is not part of the standard. We strongly recommend not using this directive.

More robots.txt Examples

One strange-looking edge case is where you don't place any restrictions on the robot explicitly. In the following snippet, the empty `Disallow` directive means "no exclusion" for any robot. It is equivalent to having no `robots.txt` file at all:

```
User-agent: *
Disallow:
```

To exclude multiple URLs, simply enumerate them under a single `User-agent` directive. For example:

```
User-agent: *
Disallow: /directory
Disallow: /file.html
```

This will exclude any file that begins with `/directory` (including, perhaps, `directory.html`), and any file that begins with `/file.html`.

To use the same rules for multiple search engines, list the `User-agent` directives before the list of `Disallow` entries. For example:

```
User-agent: googlebot
User-agent: msnbot
Disallow: /directory
Disallow: /file.html
```

robots.txt Tips

In theory, according to the `robots.txt` specification, if a `Disallow:` for user agent * exists, as well a `Disallow:` for a specific robot user agent, and that robot accesses a web site, only the more specific rule for that particular robot should apply, and only one `Disallow:` would be excluded. Accordingly, it is necessary to repeat all rules in * under, for example, googlebot's user agent as well to exclude the items listed for `User-agent: *`.

Thus, the following rules would only exclude Z from googlebot, not X, Y, and Z as you may think:

```
User-agent: *
Disallow: X
Disallow: Y

User-agent: googlebot
Disallow: Z
```

If you want X, Y, and Z excluded for googlebot, you should use this:

```
User-agent: *
Disallow: X
Disallow: Y

User-agent: googlebot
Disallow: X
Disallow: Y
Disallow: Z
```

One last example:

```
User-agent: googlebot
Disallow:

User-agent: *
Disallow: /
```

These rules would only allow Google to spider your site. This is because the more specific rule for googlebot overrides the rule for *.

We recommend that webmasters place the exclusions for the default rule, *, last. According to the standard, this should not matter. However, there is some ambiguity as to whether a web spider picks the *first* matching rule, or the *most specific* matching rule. In the former case, if the * rule is placed first, it could conceivably be applied. Listing the * rules last removes that ambiguity.

Generating robots.txt On-the-Fly

Nothing prevents a site developer from programmatically generating the robots.txt file on-the-fly, dynamically. Include the following rule in .htaccess to map robots.php to robots.txt, and use the robots.php script to generate it. In this fashion, you can use program logic similar to that used for meta tag exclusion in order to generate a robots.txt file.

The following rule in .htaccess delegates the requests for robots.txt to robots.php:

```
RewriteEngine On
RewriteRule ^robots.txt$ /robots.php
```

The robots.php file could look like this:

```
<?
header('Content-type: text/plain');
...
...
?>
# static parts of robots.txt can be added here
```

You will see a real-life example of generating robots.txt on the fly in Chapter 14.

Handling robots.txt Limitations

Suppose a site has a number of products at URLs that look like /products.php?product_id=<number>, and a number of print-friendly product pages at the URL /products.php?product_id=<number>&print=1.

A standard robots.txt file cannot conveniently be used to eliminate these print-friendly pages, because the match has to be from the left. There would have to be a robots.txt entry for every page, and at that point it degenerates into a case similar to meta tag exclusion. In that case it is simpler to use meta-exclusion. Furthermore, it is reported that there is a limit of 5000 characters for a robots.txt file in Google (http://www.seroundtable.com/archives/003932.html), so if the list gets too long, it may be problematic.

> *Wildcard matching can be used to accomplish this as mentioned earlier in this chapter, but its use is not standard. The rule would like Disallow:* /products.php*print=*.*

However, in this case there is a standards-based solution. If you reverse the order of the parameters, such that the print-friendly URLs look like /products.php?print=1&product_id=<number>, you can easily exclude /products.php?print=1 in robots.txt.

In general, reordering parameters can make robots.txt more palatable for dynamic sites. However, in the case of preexisting sites, it can involve changing your URLs, may involve redirects, and that may be undesirable for many reasons. This topic was covered in Chapter 4. In this case it is fine, because the pages are to be excluded anyway.

When dealing with an entire directory, on static files, or, in general, cases where many fully qualified file names have the same prefix, it is usually advisable to use robots.txt exclusion. Doing so is simpler and reduces stress on your server as well as the robot. In cases where the "left-pattern-matching" logic of a robots.txt exclusion will not work, a meta-exclusion will usually work. These methods can complement each other, so feel free to mix and match them as you see fit.

Solutions for Commonly Duplicated Pages

So you've got the tools. Now where can you use them, and when are they appropriate? Sometimes the solution is exclusion, other times there are more fundamental solutions addressing web site architecture. And though there are an infinite number of causes for duplicate content, there are a number of common culprits worth mentioning. Some of the most frequently observed are the following:

- ❑ Print-friendly pages
- ❑ Navigation links and breadcrumb navigation
- ❑ Affiliate pages
- ❑ Pages with similar content
- ❑ Pages with duplicate meta tag or title values
- ❑ URL canonicalization problems
- ❑ Pages with URL-based session IDs

Print-Friendly Pages

One of the most common sources of duplicate content is the "print-friendly" page. A throwback from the day where CSS did not provide a means to provide multiple media for formatting (print, screen, and so on), many programmers simply provided two versions for every page — the standard one and the printable one.

In fact, many programmers still do this today. And though it is not wrong to do so — unless you're a CSS zealot, all print-friendly pages should be excluded using either exclusion method, otherwise a search engine will see two versions of those pages on your site.

Navigation Links and Breadcrumb Navigation

Friendly navigation is clearly desirable for any web site. Unfortunately, it sometimes creates duplicate content. Take the example of a web site that inserts category IDs in URLs of products that are in multiple categories in order to provide breadcrumb navigation. In this way the developer creates many different URLs (one per category, actually) of substantially duplicate content. This section examines breadcrumb navigation now in more detail.

Breadcrumbs are navigational aid elements, usually found on the top of a web page that look something like `home > products > fortune cookies`. They especially help users navigate when they are deeply within a web site. In this case, using the back button is typically frustrating. And in the case that a user arrives from a search engine results page, the back button also certainly doesn't do what you wish it would!

> It's worth noting that breadcrumb navigation is not the only problematic site navigation scheme around. Matrix, faceted, and dynamic drill-down navigation systems are gaining rapidly in popularity. A considerable number of large retailers, such as Wal-Mart, eToys, The Home Depot, and the Discovery Channel Store implement these types of site navigation, and show where the industry is heading.

> The duplicate content issues resulting from these complex systems are problematic as well, but this is outside the scope of this book. The same general principles apply.

The SEO consequences of breadcrumb navigation are none when a site product is in only one category. The category can be implied by the database, because there is a 1:1 relationship of product to category. Therefore, there is no need to pass the category ID in the URL — but even if it is present, there will be only one permutation of product and category. Hence there is no duplicated content.

Rewriting the URLs does nothing to resolve this. For example:

```
/Products/Category-A-C1/Product-A-P10.html and

/Products/Category-B-C2/Product-A-P10.html and

/Products/Category-C-C3/Product-A-P10.html
```

These three URLs are just as problematic as

```
/Products.php?category_id=1&product_id=10 and

/Products.php?category_id=2&product_id=10 and

/Products.php?category_id=3&product_id=10
```

It's just obscured in the former version.

The problem arises when a product is in more than one category, and a parameter must be passed in order to build the breadcrumb programmatically. Without breadcrumbs, the parameter would be unnecessary, and presumably the user would navigate back to the category page using his or her back button, but now you have a problem. If every product is in an average of three categories, you have three essentially duplicated pages for every product on the site.

The only difference on your pages is the breadcrumb:

```
Home > products > fortune cookies > frosted fortune cookie
Home > products > novelty cookies > frosted fortune cookie
```

This creates a particularly sticky problem. The benefits of friendly site navigation cannot be denied, but it also causes duplicate content issues. This is a topic that we feel is largely ignored by the SEM community. Breadcrumbs are clearly a help for navigation, but can cause problems with regard to duplicate content. In general, using tracking variables in URLs that do not effect substantial changes in the content creates duplicate content.

There are other ways to cope with this issue. Following is a presentation of the ways that you *can* address the duplicate content issues associated with breadcrumbs if you do want to address it.

Using One Primary Category and robots.txt or Meta-Exclusion

This involves setting one category that a product falls into as "primary." It involves adding a field to a database in the application to indicate as such. This is the idea espoused by Dan Thies in his SEM book *The Search Engine Marketing Kit* as well. The upside is that it's bulletproof, in that you will never be penalized by a search engine for having duplicated pages. But there are two downsides:

1. Very often the keywords from your products placed in multiple categories (in the title, perhaps under the breadcrumb, or in the "suggested" products) may yield unexpected rankings for what we call "permutation" keywords. Obviously, with this solution, you only get one of the permutations — the primary one.

   Example: Assume a cake is in two categories: "birthday" and "celebration." The resulting titles are "Super Cheesecake: Birthdays" and "Super Cheesecake: Celebration." If the webmaster picks "birthday" as the primary category, a search engine will never see the other page that may rank better for the hypothetical less-competitive keywords "celebration cheesecake," because that page is excluded via robots.txt or meta-exclusion.

2. Users may passively "penalize" you by linking the non-primary page. A link to an excluded page has questionable link-equity, arguably none for that page — but perhaps also none to the domain in general.

Changing Up the Content on the Various Permutations

Done right this can also work, but it must be done carefully. If done inadequately, it can, in the worst case, result in a penalty. You could change the description of a hypothetical product on a per-category basis, or add different related products to the page. As you may have guessed, the exact threshold for how much unique content is required is elusive. Use this technique with caution.

Some Thoughts

Which method do we suggest in most cases? The first method — exclusion. If you look closely at the following two links on a web site created by one of the authors of this book:

```
http://www.lawyerseek.com/Practice/In-the-News-C20/Protopic-P38/
http://www.lawyerseek.com/Practice/Pharmaceutical-Injury-C1/Protopic-P38/
```

There are two URLs, but one is excluded in the `robots.txt` file. The former is excluded. The `robots.txt` file at `http://www.lawyerseek.com/` contains the following entry that excludes the following URL:

```
User-agent: *
...
...
Disallow: /Practice/In-The-News-C20/Protopic-P38/
```

Similar Pages

If you have several very similar products that exist on multiple URLs, think about changing your web application to contain the various permutations of the products on one page. Consider the example of a product that comes in several different colors. The resulting product pages would typically contain different pictures but substantially duplicate descriptions. The business logic may dictate that these are different products with different SKUs, but you can still present them on one page with a pull-down menu to select the color/SKU to be added to the shopping cart.

The shopping cart page of an e-commerce site, login pages, and other like pages should also not be indexed, because there is typically no valuable content on such pages. For example, it is easy to see how the following shopping cart URLs could create duplicate content:

```
http://www.example.com/cart.php?product_id=1
...
...
http://www.example.com/cart.php?product_id=99
```

Pages with Duplicate Meta Tag or Title Values

A common mistake is to set the `meta keywords`, `meta description`, or title values on a web site to the same default value programmatically for every page. Aaron Wall of SEOBook states *"If you have complete duplication of any element (page title, meta keywords, meta description) across your site then it is at best a wasted opportunity, but may also hurt your ability to get your site indexed or ranked well in some search engines."* If time and resources cannot be dedicated to creating unique meta tags, they should probably not be created at all, because using the same value for every page is certainly not beneficial. Having identical titles for every page on a web site is also particularly detrimental. Many programmers make this mistake, because it is very easy not to notice it.

URL Canonicalization

Many web sites exhibit subtle but sometimes insidious duplicate problems due to URL canonicalization problems. The two most common of such problems are documented in Chapter 4 in the sections "URL Canonicalization: www.example.com versus example.com," and "URL Canonicalization: /index.php versus /."

URL-Based Session IDs

URL-based session management causes major problems for search engines, because each time a search engine spiders your web site, it will receive a different session ID and hence a new set of URLs with the same content. Needless to say, this creates an enormous amount of duplicate content. The PHP feature that automatically tracks user sessions using a query string parameter is named trans_sid. You can disable this feature, and permit only cookie-based session support.

> **URL-based sessions may be important on large e-commerce sites, or in certain demographics, because a small number of users disable cookies in their browsers.**

To turn off URL-based session IDs, you'd need to add these lines to your .htaccess file:

```
php_value session.use_only_cookies 1
php_value session.use_trans_sid 0
```

The same effect can be achieved using this PHP code:

```php
<?php

// store the session ID using cookies
@ini_set ('session.use_only_cookies', 1);
// disable trans_sid
@ini_set ('session.use_trans_sid', 0);

?>
```

The URL factory you created in Chapter 3, together with the redirect library from Chapter 4, can be used to redirect any URLs that contain the session ID to the "proper" versions of the URLs in case this feature was inadvertently left on and such URLs are indexed by a search engine.

Chapter 11 also discusses a method using cloaking that dynamically turns URL-based session IDs off for search engines, but leaves it on for human users.

Other Navigational Link Parameters

In general, parameters in URLs such as those that indicate that a user came from a particular page can create a large amount of duplicate content. Covering all examples would be impossible, but consider the following imaginary URLs:

```
http://www.example.com/Some-Product.html?from_url=about-us.php
http://www.example.com/Some-Product.html?from_url=contact-us.php
```

The list could get quite long depending on how many pages link to that product. In practice, whenever possible, it may be advisable to use session-based or HTTP_REFERER-based data to track things such as these, even if imperfect solutions.

Affiliate Pages

Imagine that you have a product, The Ultimate Widget. You set up a great web affiliate program that pays 50% of revenue on the product, and everyone wants to join. Soon, you have thousands of affiliates applying. To indicate to your application which affiliate it was, you add a parameter `?aff=<aff_id>`.

In this scenario, your main page for The Ultimate Widget would be located at an URL such as this:

```
http://www.example.com/Products/The-Ultimate-Widget/
```

Your associates would sell the exact same product, which has (naturally) the same product details, through links like these:

```
http://www.example.com/Products/The-Ultimate-Widget/?aff=123
http://www.example.com/Products/The-Ultimate-Widget/?aff=456
```

Unfortunately, assuming all these links were spidered, you now have thousands of pages of duplicate content. This can be a profound problem. As mentioned in the introduction to this chapter, in the worst case, excessive duplicate content can get a site penalized. Special care must be taken to mitigate this problem. Fortunately, there are a few fairly easy solutions.

Using Referrers and Cookies instead of Query String Parameters

Using referrers is effective in that it completely transparently informs your application of where the traffic comes from; simply match the `$_SERVER['HTTP_REFERER']` variable against a domain name (or a complete URL if desired), and if there is a match, set a session variable or a cookie accordingly.

One major caveat of this method is that certain security software deliberately masks the content of `HTTP_REFERER`, and thus a small amount of affiliate traffic will be unaccounted for. Whether this is acceptable is between you and your affiliates. The obvious upside is that all links are entirely without parameters, and to a search engine it looks like a natural link, not an affiliate link. This is potentially great for a link-building campaign.

Such a system also presents more maintenance if a particular affiliate wants to promote your product on more than one site (you would have to set up associations on a per-referring-domain basis), and by the same token such links could not be used effectively on public forums such as bulletin boards and blog comments.

This method is not demonstrated here because it is typically not a viable solution.

Using Excluded Affiliate URLs

You can also use `robots.txt` or meta-exclusion, as previously discussed, to exclude all URLs that are associated with the affiliate program. For example, you could add the following tag to every affiliate page:

```
<meta name="robots" content="noindex, nofollow">
```

Alternatively, you could place the affiliate script in a subdirectory and exclude it in `robots.txt`:

```
User-agent: *
Disallow: /aff/
```

Redirecting Parameterized Affiliate URLs

It is also possible to use parameterized affiliate URLs, so long as the URLs are redirected to the "main" URL after setting a cookie or session variable for your reference. This section presents two examples, implementing them step-by-step in exercises.

One common theme in these presented solutions is that when a URL containing an affiliate ID is requested, you retain the affiliate ID somewhere else, and then do a 301 redirect to the URL without the affiliate parameters. The examples use the visitor's session to store the affiliate ID, but you may choose to use cookies instead.

In Chapter 4 you learned that the 301 status code means "Moved permanently," so the page you redirect to is interpreted as the new permanent location of the requested page. This eliminates any potential duplicate content problems.

Example #1

This example assumes that you have affiliate URLs that look like `http://seophp.example.com/Products/SEO-Toolbox-C6/Link-Juice-P31.html?aff_id=987`. The URL you're finally redirecting to is `http://seophp.example.com/Products/SEO-Toolbox-C6/Link-Juice-P31.html`.

Redirecting Keyword-Rich Affiliate URLs

1. Open `.htaccess` and find the line that rewrites keyword-rich product URLs:

```
# Rewrite keyword-rich URLs
RewriteRule ^Products/.*-C([0-9]+)/.*-P([0-9]+)\.html$ ↵
/product.php?category_id=$1&product_id=$2 [L]
```

Modify this line by adding this bit to its end, like this:

```
# Rewrite keyword-rich URLs
RewriteRule ^Products/.*-C([0-9]+)/.*-P([0-9]+)\.html$ ↵
/product.php?category_id=$1&product_id=$2&%{QUERY_STRING} [L]
```

2. Modify `product.php` like this:

```php
<?php

// load library that handles redirects
require_once 'include/url_redirect.inc.php';

// start PHP session
session_start();

// save affiliate ID
if (isset($_REQUEST['aff_id']))
{
  $_SESSION['aff_id'] = $_REQUEST['aff_id'];
}

// redirect requests proper keyword-rich URLs when not already there
fix_category_product_url();
```

```
// display product details
echo 'You have selected product #' . $_GET['product_id'] .
    ' from category #' . $_GET['category_id'];

// display affiliate details
echo '<br /><br /> You got here through affiliate: ';
if (!isset($_SESSION['aff_id']))
{
  echo '(no affiliate)';
}
else
{
  echo $_SESSION['aff_id'];
}

?>
```

3. Test your new script now. The first test consists of loading a product page without an affiliate ID, such as `http://seophp.example.com/Products/SEO-Toolbox-C6/Link-Juice-P31.html`. Figure 5-1 shows the result.

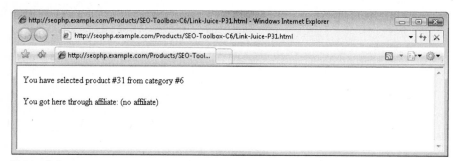

Figure 5-1

4. Now add an affiliate ID. Load `http://seophp.example.com/Products/SEO-Toolbox-C6/Link-Juice-P31.html?aff_id=987`. Expect to be correctly redirected to the main product page, and still get the affiliate ID retained. Figure 5-2 shows the expected output.

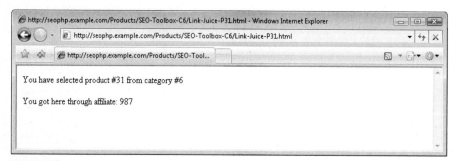

Figure 5-2

As you can see in Figure 5-2, the URL doesn't include any affiliate IDs any more, yet the page retained the affiliate ID. And you achieved this with only a few lines of PHP code! Everything starts, again, with a mod_rewrite rule:

```
RewriteRule ^Products/.*-C([0-9]+)/.*-P([0-9]+)\.html$ ↵
/product.php?category_id=$1&product_id=$2&%{QUERY_STRING} [L]
```

The {QUERY_STRING} bit is a special variable provided by mod_rewrite that stores the query string in the URL. The RewriteRule still matches URLs as it did before (such as http://seophp.example.com/Products/SEO-Toolbox-C6/Link-Juice-P31.html?aff_id=987), but this time you append those parameters to the rewritten URL.

This way, when product.php is executed, it'll have access to the aff_id parameter. The only code you've added to product.php is minimal, and it consists of verifying if the aff_id parameter exists in the query string. In the case that it does, you save the affiliate ID value in the user session:

```php
// start PHP session
session_start();

// save affiliate ID
if (isset($_REQUEST['aff_id']))
{
  $_SESSION['aff_id'] = $_REQUEST['aff_id'];
}
```

The redirection itself is done by our old friend, the fix_category_product_url() function. This function verifies if the URL is identical to our generated product URL, and in case it's not, it does an automatic 301 redirect to the "proper" URL; in this case, that proper URL will be a product URL that doesn't contain the aff_id parameter.

```php
// redirect requests proper keyword-rich URLs when not already there
fix_category_product_url();
```

The first time a product page is loaded with an affiliate ID, it will be redirected to its proper version that doesn't contain any query string parameters. When product.php reloads, it will reach the code that displays the product details, and the affiliate ID. This time, the affiliate ID is read from the session:

```php
// display affiliate details
echo '<br /><br /> You got here through affiliate: ';
if (!isset($_SESSION['aff_id']))
{
  echo '(no affiliate)';
}
else
{
  echo $_SESSION['aff_id'];
}
```

Example #2

The second technique involves dynamic URLs. When working with dynamic URLs, the solution is slightly different. In this case you don't need to deal with mod_rewrite anymore, but you need a way to read and remove the affiliate IDs from a dynamic URL, and then redirect to this version of the URL.

111

In the exercise that follows you create a simple affiliate page named `aff_test.php`. When this script will be loaded with an `aff_id` query string parameter, you'll retain the affiliate ID value, then remove the `aff_id` parameter and do a 301 redirect to the new URL.

When removing query string parameters, special care needs to be taken not to alter the already existing parameters, so you'll create a few specialized functions that perform these tasks.

Redirecting Dynamic Affiliate URLs

1. Create a new file named `url_utils.inc.php` in your `seophp/include` folder, and type this code in:

```php
<?php

// transforms a query string into an associative array
function parse_query_string($query_string)
{
  // split the query string into individual name-value pairs
  $items = explode('&', $query_string);

  // initialize the return array
  $qs_array = array();

  // create the array
  foreach($items as $i)
  {
    // split the name-value pair and save the elements to $qs_array
    $pair = explode('=', $i);
    $qs_array[urldecode($pair[0])] = urldecode($pair[1]);
  }

  // return the array
  return $qs_array;
}

// removes a parameter from the query string
function remove_query_param($url, $param)
{
  // extract the query string from $url
  $tokens = explode('?', $url);
  $url_path = $tokens[0];
  $query_string = $tokens[1];

  // transform the query string into an associative array
  $qs_array = parse_query_string($query_string);

  // remove the $param element from the array
  unset($qs_array[$param]);

  // create the new query string by joining the remaining parameters
  $new_query_string = '';
  if ($qs_array)
  {
    foreach ($qs_array as $name => $value)
```

```
      {
        $new_query_string .= ($new_query_string == '' ? '?' : '&')
                            . urlencode($name) . '=' . urlencode($value);
      }
    }

    // return the URL that doesn't contain $param
    return $url_path . $new_query_string;
  }

?>
```

2.   In your `seophp` folder, create a new script named `aff_test.php` and type the following code:

```
<?php

// include URL utils library
require_once 'include/url_utils.inc.php';

// load configuration script
require_once 'include/config.inc.php';

// start PHP session
session_start();

// redirect affiliate links
if (isset($_REQUEST['aff_id']))
{
  // save the affiliate ID
  $_SESSION['aff_id'] = $_REQUEST['aff_id'];

  // obtain the URL with no affiliate ID
  $clean_url = SITE_DOMAIN . remove_query_param($_SERVER['REQUEST_URI'], 'aff_id');

  // 301 redirect to the new URL
  header('HTTP/1.1 301 Moved Permanently');
  header('Location: ' . $clean_url);
}

// display affiliate details
echo 'You got here through affiliate: ';
if (!isset($_SESSION['aff_id']))
{
  echo '(no affiliate)';
}
else
{
  echo $_SESSION['aff_id'];
}

?>
```

3.   Load `http://seophp.example.com/aff_test.php` and expect to get the results displayed in Figure 5-3.

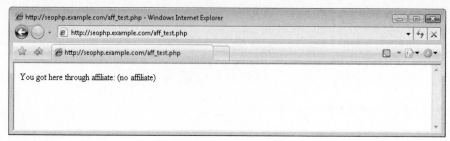

Figure 5-3

4. Load `http://seophp.example.com/aff_test.php?a=1&aff_id=34&b=2`, and expect to be redirected to `http://localhost/seophp/aff_test.php?a=1&b=2`, with the affiliated ID being retained, as shown in Figure 5-4.

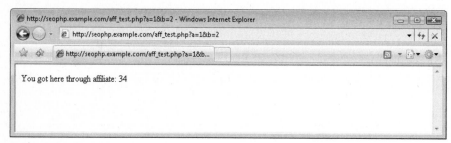

Figure 5-4

Although you've written quite a bit of code, it's pretty straightforward. There's no URL rewriting involved, so you're working with plain-vanilla PHP scripts this time.

Your `aff_test.php` script starts by loading `url_utils.inc.php` and `config.inc.php`, and starting the PHP session:

```php
<?php

// include URL utils library
require_once 'include/url_utils.inc.php';

// load configuration script
require_once 'include/config.inc.php';

// start PHP session
session_start();
```

Then you verify if the `aff_id` query string parameter is present. In case it is, you save its value to the user's session, and redirect to a version of the URL that doesn't contain `aff_id`. The `remove_query_param()` function from the URL utils library is very handy, because it correctly preserves all existing parameters:

```php
// redirect affiliate links
if (isset($_REQUEST['aff_id']))
```

```
{
  // save the affiliate ID
  $_SESSION['aff_id'] = $_REQUEST['aff_id'];

  // obtain the URL with no affiliate ID
  $clean_url = SITE_DOMAIN . remove_query_param($_SERVER['REQUEST_URI'], 'aff_id');

  // 301 redirect to the new URL
  header('HTTP/1.1 301 Moved Permanently');
  header('Location: ' . $clean_url);
}
```

Finally, `aff_test.php` checks whether there's a session parameter named `aff_id` set. In case it is, your user got to the page through an affiliate link, and you'll need to take this into account when dealing with this particular user. For the purposes of this simple exercise, you're simply displaying the affiliate ID, or (`no affiliate`) in case the page was first loaded without an `aff_id` parameter.

```
// display affiliate details
echo 'You got here through affiliate: ';
if (!isset($_SESSION['aff_id']))
{
  echo '(no affiliate)';
}
else
{
  echo $_SESSION['aff_id'];
}

?>
```

It's also worth analyzing what happens inside the `remove_query_param()` function from `url_utils.inc.php`. The strategy you took for removing one query string parameter is to transform the existing query string to an associative array, and then compose the associative array back to a query string, after removing the `aff_id` element.

To keep the code cleaner, you have a separate function that transforms a query string to an associative array. This function is named `parse_query_string()`, and receives as parameter a query string, such as `a=1&aff_id=34&b=2`, and returns an associative array with these elements:

```
'a' => '1'
'aff_id' => '34'
'b' => '2'
```

The function starts by using `explode()` to split the query string on the `&` character:

```
// transforms a query string into an associative array
function parse_query_string($query_string)
{
  // split the query string into individual name-value pairs
  $items = explode('&', $query_string);
```

If `$query string` is a=1&aff_id=34&b=2, then the `items` array will have these three elements:

```
$items[0] => 'a=1'
$items[1] => 'aff_id=34'
$items[2] => 'b=2'
```

You then parse each of these items using the `foreach`, and you split each item on the = character using explode. Using the resulting data you build an associative array named `$qs_array`, which is returned at the end. You use the `urldecode()` function when saving each query string parameter, because special characters may have been encoded:

```
// initialize the return array
$qs_array = array();

// create the array
foreach($items as $i)
{
   // split the name-value pair and save the elements to $qs_array
   $pair = explode('=', $i);
   $qs_array[urldecode($pair[0])] = urldecode($pair[1]);
}

// return the array
return $qs_array;
}
```

We looked at `parse_query_string()` because it's used by `remove_query_param()`, which is the function of interest — as you remember, it's called from `aff_test.php` to remove the `aff_id` parameter from the query string.

The `remove_query_param()` function receives two parameters: the URL and the parameter you want to remove from that URL. The URL will be something like /aff_test.php?a=1&b=2. Because the query string is what you need for further processing, `remove_query_param()` starts by splitting the `$url` parameter into an `$url_path` and a `$query_string`:

```
// removes a parameter from the query string
function remove_query_param($url, $param)
{
   // extract the query string from $url
   $tokens = explode('?', $url);
   $url_path = $tokens[0];
   $query_string = $tokens[1];
```

Next, you use the `parse_query_string()` function to transform the query string into an associative array:

```
// transform the query string into an associative array
$qs_array = parse_query_string($query_string);
```

As mentioned earlier, the associative array will be something like this:

```
'a' => '1'
'aff_id' => '34'
'b' => '2'
```

The good thing with associative arrays, and the reason for which it's sometimes worth using them, is that they're easy to manipulate. Now that you have the query string broken into an associative array, you only need to unset() the parameter you want to remove. In this case, $param will be 'aff_id':

```
// remove the $param element from the array
unset($qs_array[$param]);
```

You now have an associative array that contains the elements you need in the new query string, so you join these elements back in a string formatted like a query string. Note that you only do this if the associative array is not empty, and that you use the ternary operator to compose the query string:

```
// create the new query string by joining the remaining parameters
$new_query_string = '';
if ($qs_array)
{
  foreach ($qs_array as $name => $value)
  {
    $new_query_string .= ($new_query_string == '' ? '?' : '&')
                         . urlencode($name) . '=' . urlencode($value);
  }
}
```

> **What about the ternary operator? If you aren't familiar with it, here's a quick explanation. The ternary operator has the form** (condition ? valueA : valueB). **In case the condition is true, it returns** valueA, **otherwise it returns** valueB.
>
> **In your case, you verify if** $new_query_string **is empty; if this is true, then you first add the** ? **character to it, which is the delimiter for the first query string parameter. For all the subsequent parameters you use the** & **character.**

As soon as the new query string is composed, you join in back with the URL path you initially stripped (which in this case is /aff_test.php), and return it:

```
// return the URL that doesn't contain $param
return $url_path . $new_query_string;
}
```

We hope this has proven to be an interesting string handling exercise. For those of you in love with regular expressions, we're sure you may guess they can be successfully used to strip the aff_id parameter from the query string. Here it is if you're curious:

```
function remove_query_param($url, $param)
{
  // remove $param
  $new_url = preg_replace("#aff_id=?(.*?(&|$))?#", '', $url);

  // remove ending ? or &, in case it exists
  if (substr($new_url, -1) == '?' || substr($new_url, -1) == '&')
  {
    $new_url = substr($new_url, 0, strlen($new_url) - 1);
  }
```

```
    // return the new URL
    return $new_url;
}
```

We'll leave understanding this regular expression for you as homework.

Summary

We would summarize the entire chapter right here in this paragraph, but that would be duplicate content! Because we don't wish to frustrate our readers, we will keep it short.

Ideally, every URL on a web site would lead to a page that is unique. Unfortunately, it is rarely possible to accomplish this in reality. You should simply eliminate as much duplication as possible. Parameters in URLs that do not effect significant changes in presentation should be avoided. Failing that, as in the problems posed by using breadcrumb navigation, URLs that yield duplicate content should be excluded. The two tools in your arsenal you can use to accomplish this are robots.txt exclusion and meta-exclusion.

6

SE-Friendly HTML and JavaScript

In a perfect world, all other ranking factors held constant, a web site's presentation details would not affect its search engine rankings more so than it affects a human visitor's perception of value — his "rankings." *Relevant content* is what users are after, and the goal of a search engine is to provide it. In this perfect world, web pages that contain the same information would rank similarly regardless of the on-page technologies used in their composition.

Unfortunately, in many cases, quite the opposite is true. Using Flash or AJAX to present information, for example, may render much of your web site invisible to search engines. Likewise, using JavaScript-based links for navigation may bring about the same unfortunate result.

The good news, however, is that applying a deep understanding of these presentation concerns will yield an advantage for you over other web sites that exhibit more naiveté. This chapter explores these concerns. It provides solutions and outlines best practices for web site content presentation.

By the end of this chapter you will acquire knowledge that will enable you to use on-page technologies effectively without detriment to search engine rankings. Don't worry. A search engine friendly site does not mean the end of AJAX, Flash, or JavaScript. Don't run back to 1994 . . . yet. This chapter will teach you how to:

❑ Implement SE-friendly JavaScript site functionality.

❑ Generate crawlable images and graphical text using two techniques.

❑ Improve the search engine-friendliness of your HTML.

❑ Analyze when and how to use AJAX and Flash in your web site.

Overall Architecture

Before diving into gory technical details, it is worth mentioning that there are certain architectural decisions that are categorically problematic for any search engine optimization campaign. If upper management, for example, demands a web site be entirely built in Flash, the search engine marketer will not have much leg room to the end of achieving search engine friendliness.

Likewise, if business logic requires that user agents log in before they can see any content, it is easy to anticipate the problems that will cause for search engine optimization. A spider will *not* log in, and therefore see nothing except the login page.

> *Technically, you could employ cloaking to detect the presence of spiders and deliver the content to them without requiring them to log in. However, this is an especially controversial use of an already controversial technique, cloaking. See Chapter 11 for more details on cloaking.*

Unless there are circumstances that impose contradictory restrictions, we would advise that the following general guidelines be followed:

❏ Do *not* require visitors to log in before they can view your content. A search engine spider cannot fill out forms to create an account or log in!

❏ Present copy as clear text, not images (or use one of the techniques presented in this chapter to the same end). Use an HTML/CSS-based design — do not use AJAX or Flash pervasively.

❏ Do *not* require visitors to support JavaScript for navigation to be functional.

The rest of this chapter details how to improve the search engine friendliness of a web site by example, through the appropriate use of HTML, JavaScript, and Flash. It explores specific problems, and proposes their solutions.

Search Engine–Friendly JavaScript

Search engines are designed to index content rather than execute application code. Therefore, JavaScript, when used the wrong way, can degrade a web site's search engine friendliness. On the other hand, JavaScript is not *categorically* problematic, and has its appropriate uses.

This section discusses JavaScript's use in the context of the following:

❏ Links

❏ DHTML menus

❏ Popups

❏ Crawlable images and graphical text

JavaScript Links

The first scenario discussed is the use of JavaScript code for navigation. A JavaScript link is any button or text that, when clicked, navigates to another page. A typical JavaScript link looks like this:

```
<a href="#" onClick="location.href='http://www.example.com'; return false;">Some
Text Here</a>
```

The primary objection to using this sort of link is its use of JavaScript where a regular link would suffice. Doing so will typically prevent a search engine spider from following the links, and also prevent users who disable JavaScript from navigating your site. Using them for *all* navigation may prevent a site from being spidered at all. If you must use such links, provide alternative navigation somewhere else on the site.

The same issues would also be apparent in navigation involving other client-side dynamic technologies such as Java applets, AJAX content, and Flash. In general, any navigation not achieved using a standard anchor (<a>) tag will hinder site spidering.

Some webmasters have reported that spiders, especially Google, seem to be following some obvious-looking JavaScript links in their sites. However, because this is the exception rather than the rule, depending on this is not recommended.

By the same token, using JavaScript as a sort of page exclusion protocol, that is, assuming spiders do not see or crawl links in JavaScript, is also unwise. Even if the JavaScript does achieve the end of obscuring the link from spiders, other sites may link to the URL, which would likely get the page indexed regardless. As discussed in Chapter 5, if you don't want a link to be indexed, you should exclude it using robots.txt or using the meta exclusion tag.

DHTML Menus

Because they're based on JavaScript, DHTML drop-down menus usually present problems for search engines as well. It is wise to provide alternative navigation to all elements listed in the menus. You can do this using a set of links at the bottom of the page, a sitemap, or a combination thereof. This way not only search engines, but visitors with JavaScript support disabled, will be able to navigate the site with ease.

Many drop-down menus are somewhat spider-friendly, whereas others are not at all. The ones that are *not* tend to generate and display HTML on-the-fly using JavaScript. The ones that *are* typically hide and unhide an HTML div element dynamically. The key here is that the HTML and links are actually present, though hidden, in the document. Search engine algorithms may not, however, appreciate the hidden aspect — rendering it an *invisible* on-page factor. It is wise to list the links *visibly* elsewhere in either case.

Popup Windows

The typical method of displaying popups employs JavaScript. And, as you learned, a search engine will likely not spider a page only referred to by JavaScript. So what if you *do* want a popup to be indexed?

The solution is pretty simple. A typical popup link looks like this:

```
<a href="#" onClick="window.open('page.html', 'mywindow', 'width=800,height=600');↵
return false;">Click here.</a>
```

You could make the popup spiderable by changing the link to this:

```
<a href="page.html" onclick="window.open(this.href, 'mywindow', 'width=800,height↵
=600'); return false;" target="_blank">Click here.</a>
```

This still presents a popup in a JavaScript-enabled browser. The `onclick` event uses the `window.open` method to open `this.href` — the `href` attribute of that link. Then it returns `false` to prevent the link itself from being honored. On the other hand, the link is still present, so a search engine is able to navigate to it without executing the JavaScript code.

Alternatively, you could simulate a popup by using a regular link that opens a new window via the `target="_blank"` attribute, and have the page itself automatically resize after it displays. Technically, it's not *really* a popup. It's a new window that automatically resizes — but the effect is similar. The link for such a "popup" would look like this:

```
<a href="page.html" target="_blank">Click here</a>
```

You must include JavaScript on the linked page to resize the window. To do so, place the following code in the `onload` attribute of the document's body tag with the appropriate parameters:

```
<body onload="window.resizeTo(800, 600);">
```

Additionally, you can handle the window's `resize` event to keep the window's size constant:

```
<body onresize='setTimeout("window.resizeTo(800, 600);", 100);'>
```

Using `setTimeout` (which in this example causes the window to be resized after 100 milliseconds) ensures the code will work with all browsers.

In addition to improving search engine visibility for your popups, you have also accomplished a usability enhancement, because both of these popup varieties will degrade to opening content in a new browser window via the `target="_blank"` attribute if a user's JavaScript functionality is disabled.

These techniques are demonstrated in the upcoming exercise. You'll also explore a usability concern with spiderable popups.

Implementing Popup Navigation

Some sort of navigation should be present to allow the user to get back to the parent page if he or she arrives at the popup through a search engine, or from an external web site. Because popups are not usually created to contain contextual and navigational elements, this presents a problem.

You should at least provide a link back to the home page, and ideally to some more relevant parent page. Otherwise, the user may be completely lost and will proceed to the nearest back button.

It is not always desirable to have a popup spidered by a search engine. Between the navigational concerns, and the fact that popups very often do not contain substantial information, it may be wiser not to. Unless the popup has substantial information, we advise excluding the popups from the spiders' view entirely.

You can obtain the page from which the user navigated to the popup by reading the $_SERVER['HTTP_REFERER'] header value. This information allows you to show navigational elements only if the user has arrived from an external web site, such as a SERP.

This method is not 100% reliable, because some firewall applications block the REFERER information. Also, if the referring page is secured via HTTPS, the REFERER information won't be available. In this exercise, when there is no REFERER data, we err on the safe side and display the navigational elements.

You can try out this technique by going through a short exercise.

Implementing Spiderable Popups

1. Add a link to your popup file in your catalog.php script, as highlighted in the following code snippet. Note that this assumes you're working on the code that you built in the previous chapters. If you don't have it ready, feel free to use the code download of this chapter.

```php
<?php
// load the URL factory library
require_once 'include/url_factory.inc.php';
?>
...
...
...
    <li>
      <a href="<?php echo make_category_product_url("Friends' Shed", 2, "PHP
E-Commerce Book", 42); ?>">
        Friends' Shed: PHP E-Commerce Book
      </a>
    </li>
  </ul>
  <center>
    <a href="popup.php" target="_blank">Find more about Professional Search
Engine Optimization with PHP!</a>
  </center>
 </body>
</html>
```

2. Load http://seophp.example.com/catalog.html to ensure your script loads correctly and displays the new link, as shown in Figure 6-1. Note that this exercise assumes you have built your simple catalog as shown in Chapter 3.

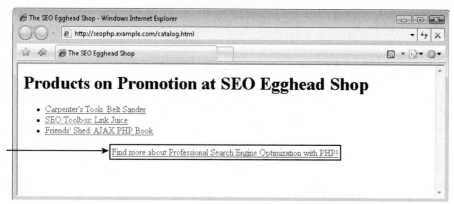

Figure 6-1

3. Create a new file named `popup.php` in your `seophp` folder, and type this code in:

```php
<?php
// load the popup utils library
require_once 'include/popup_utils.inc.php';
?>

<!DOCTYPE html PUBLIC "-//W3C//DTD XHTML 1.1//EN"
 "http://www.w3.org/TR/xhtml11/DTD/xhtml11.dtd">
<html>
  <head>
    <title>Professional Search Engine Optimization with PHP: Table of
Contents</title>
  </head>
  <body onload="window.resizeTo(800, 600);"
        onresize='setTimeout("window.resizeTo(800, 600);", 100);'>
    <h1>Professional Search Engine Optimization with PHP: Table of Contents</h1>

<?php
// display popup navigation only when visitor comes from a SERP
display_navigation();
?>

    <ol>
      <li>You: Programmer and Search Engine Marketer</li>
      <li>A Primer in Basic SEO</li>
      <li>Provocative SE-Friendly URLs</li>
      <li>Content Relocation and HTTP Status Codes</li>
      <li>Duplicate Content</li>
      <li>SE-Friendly HTML and JavaScript</li>
      <li>Web Syndication and Social Bookmarking</li>
      <li>Black Hat SEO</li>
```

```
      <li>Sitemaps</li>
      <li>Link Bait</li>
      <li>IP Cloaking, Geo-Targeting, and IP Delivery</li>
      <li>Foreign Language SEO</li>
      <li>Coping with Technical Issues</li>
      <li>Case Study: Building an E-Commerce Catalog</li>
      <li>Site Clinic: So You Have a Web Site?</li>
      <li>WordPress: Creating a SE-Friendly Weblog?</li>
      <li>Introduction to Regular Expressions</li>
    </ol>
  </body>
</html>
```

4. Create a new file named `popup_utils.inc.php` in your `seophp/include` folder, and write this code:

```php
<?php

// include config file
require_once 'config.inc.php';

// display popup navigation only when visitor comes from a SERP
function display_popup_navigation()
{
  // display navigation?
  $disp_nav = false;

  // if there is no REFERER (visitor loaded popup directly), display navigation
  if (!isset($_SERVER['HTTP_REFERER']))
  {
    $disp_nav = true;
  }
  // if the REFERER not from our domain, display navigation
  else
  {
    // parse the REFERER and the local site using parse_url()
    $parsed_referer = parse_url($_SERVER['HTTP_REFERER']);
    $parsed_local = parse_url(SITE_DOMAIN);

    // extract the domain of the referer, and that of the local site
    $referer_host = $parsed_referer['host'];
    $local_host = $parsed_local['host'];

    // display navigation if the REFERER URL is not from the local domain
    if ($referer_host != $local_host)
    {
      $disp_nav = true;
    }
  }
```

```
  // display navigation if necessary
  if ($disp_nav == true)
  {
    echo '<a href="catalog.html">Visit our catalog page!</a>';
  }
}

?>
```

5. Load `http://seophp.example.com/catalog.html`, and click the popup link. No navigation should show up. If you get to the popup page through Google, Yahoo!, or MSN, or if you load `http://seophp.example.com/popup.php` directly from the address bar of your browser, the navigation link should appear (see Figure 6-2).

6. Now is a great time to test the RefControl Firefox plugin mentioned in Chapter 2. This plugin allows you to display and modify REFERER information. Install the plugin and navigate to `http://seophp.example.com/catalog.html`. In the page, click the link that opens the popup window, and note the HTTP REFERER displayed in the status bar (see Figure 6-3). You can see that the catalog link doesn't show up when the popup is opened as a result of navigation from within your site.

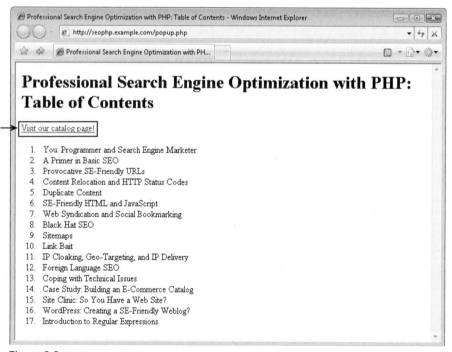

Figure 6-2

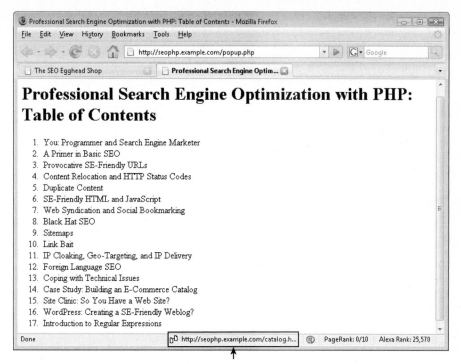

Figure 6-3

That was quite a bit of code, but this is a useful technique! Once your popup library is in place, it becomes really easy to make the navigation link show up whenever it is needed. Here you use the simulated popup window method, but you could have also used a regular JavaScript popup with the same results.

In order to add the navigational link to any popup, there are only two steps you need to take. First, you need to include the `popup_utils.inc.php` script in your popup script. This is what you did in `popup.php`:

```php
<?php
// load the popup utils library
require_once 'include/popup utils.inc.php';
?>
```

Then, you need to call the `display_popup_navigation()` function that's defined in `popup_-utils.inc.php`, in the place where you want the navigational link included:

```php
<?php
// display popup navigation only when visitor comes from a SERP
display_popup_navigation();
?>
```

This function verifies if the REFERER is from the local domain, and if it is, it doesn't display the navigation link. If the REFERER is from any other domain, or if it is empty, the navigation link *is* displayed.

The function starts by telling if a REFERER does exist. If it doesn't, you set a temporary variable, named $display_nav, to true. The default value of this variable is false. At the end of the function you verify its value and decide whether or not to display the navigation links:

```
// display popup navigation only when visitor comes from a SERP
function display_popup_navigation()
{
  // display navigation?
  $disp_nav = false;

  // if there is no REFERER (visitor loaded popup directly), display navigation
  if (!isset($_SERVER['HTTP_REFERER']))
  {
    $disp_nav = true;
  }
```

If there is a REFERER, you verify if the host name of the REFERER is the same one as the host of the SITE_DOMAIN constant, which you've defined in config.inc.php. If the host names are different, the visitor arrived at the popup from an external web site, and you must display the navigation link:

```
  // if the REFERER not from our domain, display navigation
  else
  {
    // parse the REFERER and the local site using parse_url()
    $parsed_referer = parse_url($_SERVER['HTTP_REFERER']);
    $parsed_local = parse_url(SITE_DOMAIN);

    // extract the domain of the referer, and that of the local site
    $referer_host = $parsed_referer['host'];
    $local_host = $parsed_local['host'];

    // display navigation if the REFERER URL is not from the local domain
    if ($referer_host != $local_host)
    {
      $disp_nav = true;
    }
  }
```

In the end, if $disp_nav is true, you display the navigation link:

```
  // display navigation if necessary
  if ($disp_nav == true)
  {
    echo '<a href="catalog.html">Visit our catalog page!</a>';
  }
```

DHTML Popup Windows

As a last alternative, popups can be simulated using DHTML. To accomplish this you can place an invisible `<div>` element at a particular location, then use JavaScript events to hide and unhide it. A robust example is beyond the scope of this book, but the following code is a proof of concept:

```
<span onmouseover="document.getElementById('dhtml_popup_test').style.visibility=
'visible';" onmouseout="document.getElementById('dhtml_popup_test').style.
visibility='hidden';">put your mouse here</span>

<div style="position:absolute; visibility:hidden; border:1px solid black"
id="dhtml_popup_test">This is only visible if your mouse is over the above
text</div>
```

One caveat with this method is that although the text is spiderable, it will likely be regarded as an invisible on-page factor because it is not visible by default.

Crawlable Images and Graphical Text

This is a topic that frequently puts designers and search engine marketers at war! Designers tend to balk at the thought of not having graphical text at their disposal. But spiders cannot read any text that is embedded in an image, regardless of how clear and obvious it may be to a human reader. Therefore regular text styled by CSS should be employed whenever possible.

Unfortunately, CSS does not always provide all the flexibility that a designer needs for typesetting. Furthermore, users do not have a uniform set of fonts installed on all computers. This restricts the fonts that can be used reliably in CSS typesetting substantially. Table 6-1 lists the common fonts that are available on typical Windows and Mac installations.

Table 6-1

Font Type	Font Name
Cursive	Comic Sans MS
Monospace	Courier New
Serif	Times New Roman
	Georgia
Sans-serif	Andale Mono
	Arial
	Arial Black
	Impact

Table continued on following page

Font Type	Font Name
Sans-serif	Trebuchet MS
	Verdana

For further reference, you can check out a more detailed list you can find at http://www.kdweb-pagedesign.com/tut_4.asp.

So in lieu of depending completely on CSS typesetting, a number of techniques can be used to implement "crawlable images." Using client-side JavaScript, you can walk the document tree of an HTML file and selectively replace text portions with graphical elements after it loads. This is called "text replacement."

The following few pages introduce you to two of the most common implementations of text replacement:

❑ *The "sIFR" replacement method* works by replacing specified text with Flash files. This method is documented at length at http://www.mikeindustries.com/sifr/.

❑ *Stewart Rosenberger's text replacement implementation* does the same thing, but replaces the text with images instead. The images are generated at the server-side by a PHP script. The method is described at http://www.alistapart.com/articles/dynatext.

Using these techniques, spiders will be able to read the text present in the document (because spiders do not execute the JavaScript code), and human visitors will see either a Flash file or an image containing the text. This keeps *both* humans and robots happy. This method is not considered black hat, so long as the replacement is faithful to what it replaces.

The "sIFR" Replacement Method

We must admit, we love sIFR! sIFR is an acronym for "Scalable Inman Flash Replacement." It functions by replacing specified portions of plain text from a web page with a parameterized Flash file on the client side.

sIFR brings these benefits:

❑ sIFR doesn't require users to have the necessary fonts installed, because the fonts are included in the Flash file.

❑ If a font is used in multiple pages or headings, it's downloaded by the user's browser only once.

❑ sIFR doesn't hurt search engine rankings, because the plain text is still right there in your web page.

❑ If the user doesn't have Flash or JavaScript installed, the text is simply rendered as normal text.

Before attempting to use sIFR, here's what you need to keep in mind:

❑ For testing purposes, you can use the two Flash files that ship with sIFR — tradegothic.swf and vandenkeere.swf. However, if you want to embed your own fonts into .swf files, you'll need Macromedia Flash. At the time of writing, Macromedia Flash 8 Basic costs $349 and Macromedia Flash 8 Professional costs $699. You can download a trial version from http://www.adobe.com/downloads/ after you register with Adobe; the download size is about 100MB.

❑ You need to have a license to distribute the fonts you're using for the replacement.

You put sIFR to work in the next exercise, where you modify your product catalog to use a font that isn't supported by default by many web browsers. Look ahead at Figures 6-8 and 6-9 to see the difference between the "before" and "after" versions of the catalog's title.

Using sIFR Properly

If you decide to use sIFR for your projects, we recommend that you also check its documentation at http://wiki.novemberborn.net/sifr/, and its description at http://www.mikeindustries.com/sifr/, because they contain more tips and hints that we could not include in the book. You can find a very useful walkthrough at http://wiki.novemberborn.net/sifr/How+to+use. This quote is particularly pertinent: *"sIFR is for headlines, pull quotes, and other small swaths of text. In other words, it is for display type — type which accents the rest of the page. Body copy should remain browser text. Additionally, we recommend not replacing over about 10 blocks of text per page. A few more is fine, but once you get into the 50s or so, you'll notice a processor and speed hit."*

In this exercise you learn how to embed a font into an .swf **file. If you don't have Macromedia Flash, or you don't want to install a trial version, you can use one of the two Flash files that ship with sIFR. To do that, instead of following steps 4 through 9 of the exercise, simply rename** tradegothic.swf **or** vandenkeere.swf **from the** sirf **folder to** super_font.swf.

Using sIFR

1. Start by creating a subfolder in your site where you store the sIFR code. Create a folder named sifr under your seophp folder, so the complete path to it will be /seophp/sifr/.

2. Download sIFR. Navigate to http://www.mikeindustries.com/sifr/ and find the Download link at the bottom of the page. At the time of writing, the direct link to the latest zip package is http://www.mikeindustries.com/blog/files/sifr/2.0/sIFR2.0.2.zip.

3. Unzip the package into your /seophp/sifr folder. The contents of the folder should look the same as Figure 6-4.

4. You need to open the sifr.fla file located in your sifr folder with Macromedia Flash (not the Flash Player!). If you don't have it, you can find the trial download at http://www.adobe.com/downloads/, or at a software catalog web site such as http://www.softpedia.com.

5. If you installed Macromedia Flash correctly, it should open up sifr.fla (see Figure 6-5).

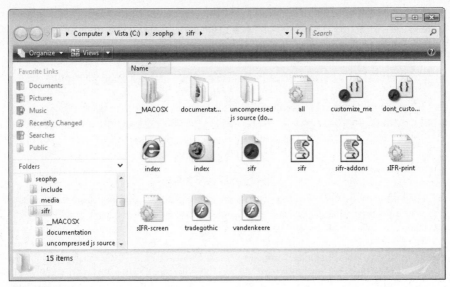

Figure 6-4

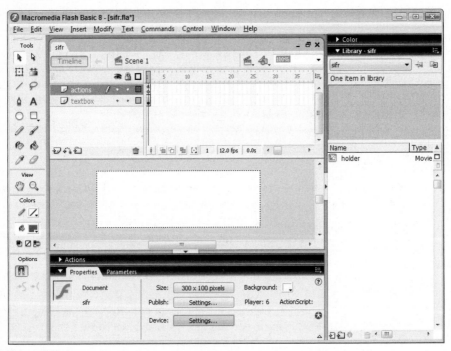

Figure 6-5

6. The `sifr.fla` script that you've just loaded allows you to embed fonts into the `.swf` files that render your graphical text. You'll need to follow the same procedure for each font you want to use. For the purpose of this example choose the Trebuchet MS font (but you can use the font of your choice if you prefer). Double-click the white box in the center of the stage. The "Do not remove this text." text should appear, and the Properties window should be highlighted. Click the font combo box from the Properties window, and choose the font you want to use. This process is shown in Figure 6-6.

7. Export the new file to an `.swf` file by going to File ⇨ Export ⇨ Export Movie. When asked for the name, you should name the file depending on the font you've chosen, because that's what the exported file is used for — to store the font. For the purpose of this exercise, choose `super_font.swf` and click Save (see Figure 6-7).

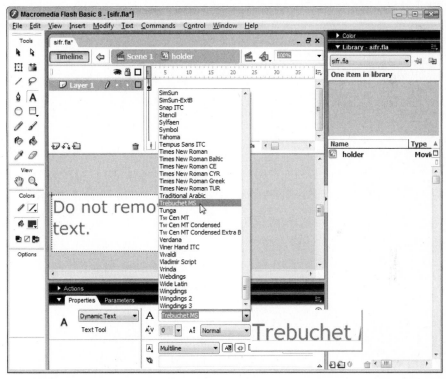

Figure 6-6

Figure 6-7

8. In the options form that shows up after clicking Save, leave the default options, making sure you're exporting to Flash Player 6 format, and click OK.

9. After exporting your file, it's OK to close Macromedia Flash. You don't need to save any changes to `sifr.fla`.

10. Open `catalog.php` and add a reference to the `sifr.js` file. Note that you're working on the `catalog.php` file you created in the previous chapters. Use the code provided by the book's code download if you didn't follow the first six chapters in sequence.

```
<?php
// load the URL factory library
require_once 'include/url_factory.inc.php';
?>

<!DOCTYPE html PUBLIC "-//W3C//DTD XHTML 1.1//EN"
 "http://www.w3.org/TR/xhtml11/DTD/xhtml11.dtd">
<html>
  <head>
    <title>The SEO Egghead Shop</title>
    <script src="sifr/sifr.js" type="text/javascript"></script>
    <link rel="stylesheet" href="sifr/sIFR-screen.css" type="text/css" ↵
media="screen" />
    <link rel="stylesheet" href="sifr/sIFR-print.css" type="text/css" ↵
media="print" />
  </head>
```

11. The final step required to see sIFR in action is to select the strings you want replaced. You do this by including JavaScript code that makes the changes when the page loads. Add this code before the closing `</body>` tag in `catalog.php`, as shown in the following code snippet. (Note there are additional ways to do this, as explained in sIFR's documentation.)

```
<!-- sIFR replacement code -->
<script type="text/javascript">

// continue only if the sIRF code has been loaded
if(typeof sIFR == "function")
{
  // replace the <h1> text
  sIFR.replaceElement(named({sSelector:"body h1", sFlashSrc:"./sifr/super_font.↵
swf"}));
};

</script>

  </body>
</html>
```

12. You're done! If you disable JavaScript and load `http://seophp.example.com/catalog.html`, you get to your catalog page that uses the default heading font, which you can see in Figure 6-8. You may use CSS to style the text for non-JavaScript enabled users if desired.

13. Loading the very same page with JavaScript and Flash enabled, you get your title drawn with the new font! (See Figure 6-9.)

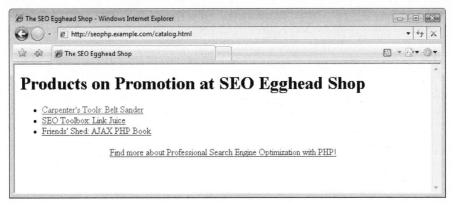

Figure 6-8

Figure 6-9

After all the configuration work is done, sIFR is really easy to use! For starters, you needed to create a Flash application that contains the font you want to distribute to your users. You could use different fonts for various elements, but for the purposes of this exercise just one font was enough.

In order to be able to effectively use sIFR, you needed to reference the sIFR JavaScript library and its two CSS files in your catalog.php script:

```
<script src="sifr/sifr.js" type="text/javascript"></script>
<link rel="stylesheet" href="sifr/sIFR-screen.css" type="text/css"↵
media="screen" />
<link rel="stylesheet" href="sifr/sIFR-print.css" type="text/css"↵
media="print" />
```

After referencing the JavaScript library, you need, of course, to use it. Just referencing sifr.js doesn't have any effect by itself — and here the fun part comes. The following code, which you added at the end of `catalog.php`, uses the `sIFR.replaceElement()` function to replace all `<h1>` tags with Flash files that render text:

```
<!-- sIFR replacement code -->
<script type="text/javascript">

// continue only if the sIRF code has been loaded
if(typeof sIFR == "function")
{
  // replace the <h1> text
  sIFR.replaceElement(named({sSelector:"body h1", sFlashSrc:"./sifr/super_font.↵
swf"}));
};

</script>
```

The `(typeof sIFR == "function")` condition verifies that the sIFR library has been loaded success-fully, so the script won't attempt to call `sIFR.replaceElement()` in case you forgot to reference the sIFR JavaScript library.

The `replaceElement()` function supports more parameters, but the necessary ones are `sSelector` (which defines which HTML elements should be replaced), and `sFlashSrc` (which references the Flash movie containing the font to be used). However, many more parameters are supported, and can be used when you need to fine-tune the replacement options. Table 6-2 contains the list of parameters that you can use with `replaceElement()`.

Table 6-2

replaceElement() Parameter	Description
sSelector	The CSS element you want to replace. Include whitespace in the string *only* when selecting descendants, such as in `body h1`. You can separate multiple CSS elements using commas.
sFlashSrc	The Flash file that contains the font.
sColor	The text color using hex notation.
sLinkColor	The link color using hex notation.
sHoverColor	The hover link color using hex notation.
sBgColor	The background color using hex notation.
nPaddingTop	Top padding in pixels.
nPaddingRight	Right padding in pixels.
nPaddingBottom	Bottom padding in pixels.

replaceElement() Parameter	Description
nPaddingLeft	Left padding in pixels.
sFlashVars	Parameters to send to the Flash movie. When multiple parameters are used, separate them by &. Supported parameters are `textalign`, `offsetLeft`, `offsetTop`, and `underline`.
sCase	Set this to `upper` to transform the text to uppercase, and `lower` to transform the text to lowercase.
sWmode	Supported values are `opaque` (the default) and `transparent` (to enable transparent background).

See the "How to use" documentation at `http://wiki.novemberborn.net/sifr/How+to+use` for more details about using sIFR.

After adding this last bit of code, you're done! Your page will now work by default with replaced text. If Flash or JavaScript aren't supported by the user agent, it falls back gracefully to the default page font.

Stewart Rosenberger's Text Replacement Method

This method uses JavaScript to replace page headings with images. The images are created by a PHP script on-the-fly, so you don't have to build the images yourself. It is otherwise very similar to sIFR.

For this technique to work, there are two prerequisites:

❑ The PHP server must have the GD2 library installed. This is PHP's image manipulation library, and you can learn more about it at `http://www.php.net/image/`.

❑ You need to have access to the font file of the font you want to use, because you'll need to copy it in your web site folder.

Assuming these two conditions are met, you can go on and modify the `popup.php` script that you created earlier in this chapter, and have its header replaced by graphically rendered text when the page loads. Figure 6-10 shows how the page will look after the exercise is completed, and Figure 6-2 shows how the page looks right now.

Replacing Text with Images

1. Start by enabling the GD2 PHP library, which you need for generating images on-the-fly with PHP. If you set up your machine as described in Chapter 1, you have GD2 already installed, but it may not be enabled by default. Open for editing the `php.ini` configuration file. In the typical XAMPP configuration, this file is located in the `\xampp\apache\bin` folder. In other scenarios, you'll find it in your Windows folder.

2. In `php.ini`, remove the leading semicolon in the front of the following line. The semicolon comments the line; if there is no semicolon, then GD2 is already enabled on your system.

```
extension=php_gd2.dll
```

3. Restart the Apache web server for the new configuration to take effect.

4. Create a folder named `dynatext` in your `seophp` folder.

5. Copy the font files you want to use for headers to your `dynatext` folder. On a Windows machine, you can find the font files in the hidden `\Windows\Fonts` folder, or via the Fonts applet that you can find in Control Panel. For the purposes of this exercise, copy `trebuc.ttf` to the `dynatext` folder.

For legal reasons, we're not including any font files in the code download of this book. If you use the code download, you'll still need to copy a font file to your `dynatext` *folder before this exercise will work properly.*

6. Download `http://www.alistapart.com/d/dynatext/heading.php.txt` and save it as `heading.php` in your `dynatext` folder.

7. Modify `heading.php` by setting `$font_file` to the font file name that you copied earlier to the `dynatext` folder, and change `$font_size` to 23:

```php
<?php
/*
    Dynamic Heading Generator
    By Stewart Rosenberger
    http://www.stewartspeak.com/headings/

    This script generates PNG images of text, written in
    the font/size that you specify. These PNG images are passed
    back to the browser. Optionally, they can be cached for later use.
    If a cached image is found, a new image will not be generated,
    and the existing copy will be sent to the browser.

    Additional documentation on PHP's image handling capabilities can
    be found at http://www.php.net/image/
*/

$font_file = 'trebuc.ttf' ;
$font_size = 23 ;
$font_color = '#000000' ;
$background_color = '#ffffff' ;
$transparent_background  = true ;
$cache_images = true ;
$cache_folder = 'cache' ;
```

8. Download `http://www.alistapart.com/d/dynatext/replacement.js` and save the file to your `dynatext` folder.

9. Modify the `replaceSelector` function call at the beginning of `replacement.js` by changing h2 to h1, and changing the value of `hideFlickerTimeout` to a small value, such as 100. Also, alter the references to `heading.php` and `test.png` to reflect their location under the `dynatext` folder, as shown here:

```
function com_stewartspeak_replacement() {
/*
    Dynamic Heading Generator
    By Stewart Rosenberger
    http://www.stewartspeak.com/headings/

    This script searches through a web page for specific or general elements
    and replaces them with dynamically generated images, in conjunction with
    a server-side script.
*/


    replaceSelector("h1","dynatext/heading.php",true);
    var testURL = "dynatext/test.png" ;

    var doNotPrintImages = false;
    var printerCSS = "replacement-print.css";

    var hideFlicker = false;
    var hideFlickerCSS = "replacement-screen.css";
    var hideFlickerTimeout = 100;
```

10. You now need to create a PNG image file named `test.png` in your `seophp` folder. This file can contain anything, but it's best if it's as small as possible — such as a 1x1 pixel image. This is a probe file used by the scripts for testing browser features. **If `test.png` is not present, your text won't be replaced.** You can copy this file from the code download of this chapter.

11. Modify `popup.php` by adding a reference to the `replacement.js` script:

```
<?php
// load the popup utils library
require_once 'include/popup_utils.inc.php';
?>

<!DOCTYPE html PUBLIC "-//W3C//DTD XHTML 1.1//EN"
 "http://www.w3.org/TR/xhtml11/DTD/xhtml11.dtd">
<html>
  <head>
    <title>Professional Search Engine Optimization with PHP: Table of
Contents</title>
    <script src="dynatext/replacement.js" type="text/javascript"></script>
  </head>
  <body onload="window.resizeTo(800, 600);"
        onresize='setTimeout("window.resizeTo(800, 600);", 100);'>
    <h1>Professional Search Engine Optimization with PHP: Table of Contents</h1>
```

12. Load `http://seophp.example.com/popup.php`. If you followed the steps correctly and your machine is configured with GD2 support, you should get your title replaced with an image as shown in Figure 6-10. Compare Figure 6-10 with Figure 6-2 in order to see the difference!

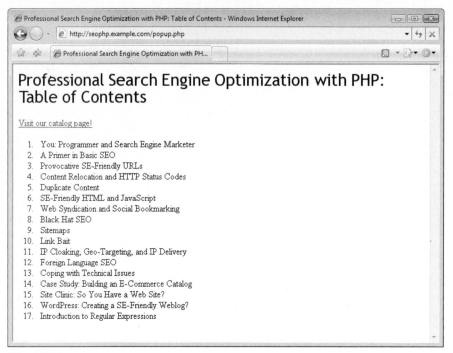

Figure 6-10

Both the PHP script that generates (and eventually caches) the images for text elements on the server, and the JavaScript script that handles the client-side replacing, can be configured to fine-tune the image replacement to your tastes.

We're leaving the subtle configuration options to you as an exercise in case you intend to use Stewart's library in your projects. The next section moves on to discuss improving HTML itself.

Search Engine–Friendly HTML

With some JavaScript-related issues out of the way, there are a number of HTML issues to explore:

❑ HTML structural elements

❑ Copy prominence and tables

❑ Frames

❑ Forms

HTML Structural Elements

In general, HTML provides structural elements that may help a search engine understand the overall topicality of documents, as well as where logical divisions and important parts are located, such as <h1> and <h2> tags, <b> tags, and so on. If you don't include these elements in your HTML code, the search engine must make such decisions entirely itself.

Although most hand-coded sites do well in this regard, especially when a search engine marketer is involved, many content management systems are abysmally bad at it. Also, WYSIWYG (What You See Is What You Get) editors typically do not use these tags, and tend to generate HTML with CSS embedded pervasively in style attributes. This is not ideal with regard to search engine optimization. For example, this structure:

```
<ol>
  <li>Item 1</li>
  <li>Item 2</li>
  <li>Item 3</li>
</ol>
```

provides more semantic information than this:

```
<img src='bullet.gif'>Item 1<br>
<img src='bullet.gif'>Item 2<br>
<img src='bullet.gif'>Item 3<br>
```

even if they look entirely identical onscreen with the currently applied style sheets.

If you've developed web content using a WYSIWYG editor, it may be wise to hand-edit the generated HTML to optimize the content after the fact. You may also choose to create your HTML directly instead of using such an editor. An additional solution of using a custom markup language is explored later in this chapter.

Copy Prominence and Tables

Copy prominence is the physical depth — that is, the actual position (counted in bytes) in the HTML document where the copy starts within your document. Because search engines may consider the content closest to the top of the HTML document more important, it is wise to avoid placing repetitive or irrelevant content before the primary content on a page.

A common form of content that doesn't need to be at the top of an HTML file is JavaScript code. It is wise to move any JavaScript code located at the top of an HTML document either to the bottom, or to a separate file, because JavaScript has a large footprint and is mostly uninteresting to a spider. You can reference external JavaScript files as follows:

```
<script language="JavaScript" src="my_script.js"></script>
```

When referencing external JavaScript files, don't omit the </script> *tag. If you do that, Internet Explorer won't execute your script.*

The other common manifestation of this problem is that many tables-based sites place their site navigation element on the left. This use of tables tends to push the primary content further down physically, and because of this, may contribute to poorer rankings. If there are many navigational elements above the primary content, it may confuse the search engine as to what is actually the primary content on the page, because the navigational elements are higher physically in the document.

> *Search engines do try to detect repetitive elements, such as a navigation elements placed physically before the primary content on a page, and at least partially ignore them. Modern search engines also examine the actual displayed location of content rather than just their physical location in a source document. However, avoiding the situation entirely may improve the odds of proper indexing regardless.*

There are three solutions for this:

❑ Instead of using a tables-based layout, use a pure CSS-type layout where presentation order is arbitrary. An in-depth discussion of CSS is beyond the scope of this book. For more information, you can consult one of the many books on CSS, such as *Beginning CSS: Cascading Style Sheets for Web Design* (Wiley Publishing, Inc., 2004).

❑ Place the navigation to the right side of the page in a tables-based layout. Figure 6-11 shows an example from `http://www.lawyerseek.com`.

❑ Apply a technique that designers typically call *the table trick*, which uses an HTML sleight-of-hand to reverse the order of table cells physically in the document without reversing their presentation.

Even if your site uses tables, typically, parts of a document can be rendered using CSS layout on a selective basis. Doing so does not force you to abandon a tables-based layout completely. A good place to look is in repetitive elements (that is, those generated within loops), such as navigational elements and repeated blocks to shrink HTML size, because tables tend to have a large footprint.

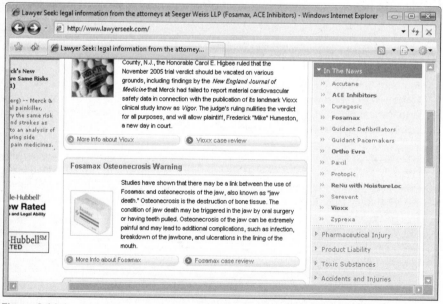

Figure 6-11

The Table Trick Explained

The table trick basically boils down to employing a two-by-two table with an empty first cell, using a second cell with a rowspan set to two, and then putting the navigation in the second row "under" the empty first cell.

Take this simple HTML example:

```
<table>
  <tr>
    <td valign="top">Navigation</td>
    <td valign="top">Content</td>
  </tr>
</table>
```

The rendered content would look like Figure 6-12.

| Navigation | Content |

Figure 6-12

Now, you could rewrite the HTML code to place the relevant content closer to the beginning in the document, while keeping the visual appearance equivalent, this way:

```
<table>
  <tr>
    <td><!-- empty table cell --></td>
    <td rowspan="2" valign="top">Content</td>
  </tr>
  <tr>
    <td valign="top">Navigation</td>
  </tr>
</table>
```

Figure 6-13 shows the result.

This way, the navigation code appears below the content in the physical file, yet it displays on the left when loaded in a browser.

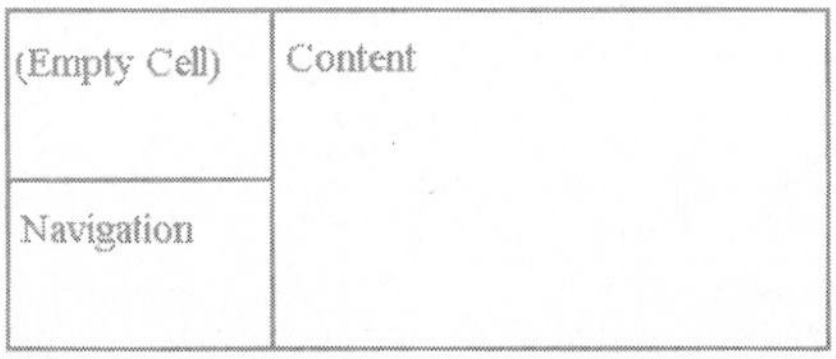

| (Empty Cell) | Content |
| Navigation | |

Figure 6-13

Frames

There have been so many problems with frames since their inception that it bewilders us as to why anyone would use them at all. Search engines have *a lot* of trouble spidering frames-based sites. A search engine cannot index a frames page within the context of its other associated frames. Only individual pages can be indexed. Even when individual pages are successfully indexed, because another frame is often used in tandem for navigation, a user may be sent to a bewildering page that contains no navigation. There is a workaround for that issue (similar to the popup navigation solution), but it creates still other problems. The `noframes` tag also attempts to address the problem, but it is an invisible on-page factor and mercilessly abused by spammers. Any site that uses frames is at such a disadvantage that we must simply recommend not using them at all.

Jacob Nielsen predicted these problems in 1996, and recommended not to use them at the same date. Now, more than ten years later, there is still no reason to use them, and, unlike the also relatively benign problems associated with tables, there is no easy fix. See `http://www.useit.com/alertbox/9612.html`.

Using Forms

A search engine spider will never submit a form. This means that any content that is behind form navigation will not be visible to a spider. There is simply no way to make a spider fill out a form; unless the form were to consist of only pull-downs, radios, and checkboxes — where the domain is defined by permutations of preset values, it could not know what combinations it submits regardless. This is not done in practice, however.

> *There are some reports that Google, in particular, does index content behind very simple forms. Forms that consist of one pull-down that directs the user to a particular web page are in this category. However, as with the example of JavaScript links being spidered, we do not recommend depending on this behavior. As a corollary, if such a form points to content that should be excluded, it may be wise to exclude the content with an explicit exclusion mechanism, such as* `robots.txt` *or the robots* `meta` *tag!*

There is no magic solution for this problem. However, there is a workaround. As long as your script is configured to accept the parameters from a GET request, you can place the URLs of certain form requests in a sitemap or elsewhere in a site.

So if a form submits its values and creates a dynamic URL like the following:

```
/search.php?category_id=1&color=red
```

that same link could be placed on a sitemap and a spider could follow it.

Using a Custom Markup Language to Generate SE-Friendly HTML

As mentioned earlier, using a WYSIWYG editor frequently presents a problem with regard to on-page optimization. Frequently, these editors do not generate HTML that uses tags that adequately delineate the structural meaning of elements on a page.

If you are developing a large web site where non-technical personnel contribute content frequently, you could add support for a simple custom markup language. The markup language can ease the management of content for copywriters who are not familiar with HTML. Additionally, it gives the site developer total control over what the HTML looks like after you transform the custom markup language into HTML.

To implement this you use a simple parser. As a bonus, this parser can implement programmatic features and make global changes that are well beyond the scope and possibilities of the CSS realm.

Here is an example snippet of copy using a custom markup language:

```
{HEADING}Using a Custom Markup Language to Generate Optimized HTML{/HEADING}
As we mentioned earlier, using a WYSIWYG editor frequently presents a problem with
regard to on-page optimization.  Frequently, the editors do not generate HTML that
uses tags that adequately delineate the structural meaning of elements on a page.
Since heading tags, such as h1, ul, and strong are indicators of the structure
within a document, not using them will probably {BOLD}{ITALIC}decrease{/ITALIC}
{/BOLD} the rankings of a page, especially when a search engine is relying on
on-page factors.
```

Which can be automatically translated to this:

```
<h1 class="custom_markup">Using a Custom Markup Language to Generate Optimized
HTML</h1>
As we mentioned earlier, using a WYSIWYG editor frequently presents a problem with
regard to on-page optimization. Frequently, the editors do not generate HTML that
uses tags that adequately delineate the structural meaning of elements on a page.
Since heading tags, such as h1, ul, and strong are indicators of the structure
within a document, not using them will probably <strong><em>decrease</em></strong>
the rankings of a page, especially when a search engine is relying on on-page
factors.
```

In this way, you accomplish two goals. You create very clean and optimized HTML. And you do it without making a copywriter run for the hills. In fact, using a markup language like this, which only presents a copywriter with the necessary elements and styles them according to a set of translation rules, may be even easier than using a WYSIWYG tool in our opinion. Whenever needed, the markup language allows the copywriter to break into HTML for particularly complex cases by using an "{HTML}" tag.

This solution is employed later in the example e-commerce site, but try a quick example of its use now.

Implementing a Custom Markup Translator

1. Create a new file named custom_markup.inc.php in your seophp/include folder, and type this code in:

```php
<?php
function custom_markup_translate($str)
{
  // array with regular expressions that match custom tags
  $search = array(
    '#\{bold}(.*?)\{/bold}#is',
    '#\{italic}(.*?)\{/italic}#is',
    '#\{underline}(.*?)\{/underline}#is',
    '#\{heading}(.*?)\{/heading}#is',
    '#\{subheading}(.*?)\{/subheading}#is',
    '#\{link:(.*?)}(.*?)\{/link}#is',
    '#\{elink:(.*?)}(.*?)\{/elink}#is',
    '#\{unordered-list}(.*?)\{/unordered-list}\s*#is',
    '#\{ordered-list}(.*?)\{/ordered-list}\s*#is',
    '#\s*{list-element}(.*?)\{/list-element}\s*#is',
    '#\{picture:(.*?)}#is',
    '#\t#',
    '#\{comment}(.*?)\{/comment}#is'
    );

  // array with HTML replacements
  $replace = array(
    '<b>\\1</b>',
    '<i>\\1</i>',
    '<u>\\1</u>',
    '<h1 class=some_class>\\1</h1>',
    '<h2 class=some_other_class>\\1</h2>',
    '<a href=\'\\1\'>\\2</a>',
    '<a href=\'\\1\' target="_blank">\\2</a>',
    '<ul>\\1</ul>',
    '<ol>\\1</ol>',
    '<li>\\1</li>',
    '<img src="\\1" border="0">',
    '',
    ''
    );

  // perform the replacement
  $step_1 = preg_replace($search, $replace, $str);
  $step_2 = preg_split('#(\{HTML\}.*?\{/HTML\})#is', $step_1, -1,
PREG_SPLIT_DELIM_CAPTURE);

  $return = '';
```

```php
  foreach ($step_2 as $s2)
  {
    if (preg_match('#\{HTML\}#', $s2))
    {
      $return .= preg_replace('#\{/?HTML\}#is', '', $s2);
    }
    else
    {
      $return .= nl2br($s2);
    }
  }


  // return HTML markup
  return $return;
}
?>
```

2.   Create a file named `markup.txt` in your `seophp` folder, and type this code in:

```
{HEADING}Using a Custom Markup Language to Generate Optimized HTML{/HEADING}As we
mentioned earlier, using a WYSIWYG editor frequently presents a problem with regard
to on-page optimization.  Frequently, the editors do not generate HTML that uses
tags that adequately delineate the structural meaning of elements on a page.  Since
heading tags, such as h1, ul, and strong are indicators of the structure within a
document, not using them will probably {BOLD}{ITALIC}decrease{/ITALIC}{/BOLD} the
rankings of a page, especially when a search engine is relying on on-page factors.
```

3.   Create a file named `test_markup.php` in your `seophp` folder, and write this code:

```php
<!DOCTYPE html PUBLIC "-//W3C//DTD XHTML 1.1//EN"
  "http://www.w3.org/TR/xhtml11/DTD/xhtml11.dtd">
<html>
  <head>
    <title>Testing HTML Markup Translator</title>
  </head>
  <body>

<?php

// include custom markup library
require_once 'include/custom_markup.inc.php';

// set input file name
$file_name = 'markup.txt';

// open markup file from disk
$handle = fopen($file_name, 'r');

// check if the files was opened successfully
if ($handle)
{
  // read file contents
  $markup = fread($handle, filesize("markup.txt"));

  // translate and display custom markup
```

```
    $translated = custom_markup_translate($markup);
    echo $translated;
}
else
{
    // display error message
    echo "Couldn't open $file_name!";
}

?>

    </body>
</html>
```

4. Load `http://seophp.example.com/test_markup.php`, and expect to get the results shown in Figure 6-14.

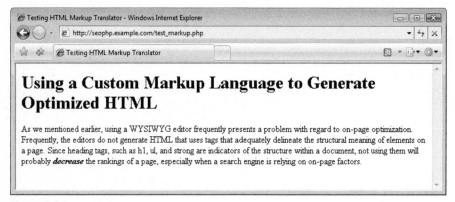

Figure 6-14

This was a simple example, but we're sure you can intuit how useful this system can be when building a more complex content management system. This little script currently knows how to handle these custom markup tags, whose significance is obvious: {bold}, {italic}, {underline}, {heading}, {subheading}, {link}, {elink} (this is a link that opens a new window), {unordered-list}, {ordered-list}, {list-element}, {picture}, and {comment}.

The markup file, `markup.txt`, doesn't contain any HTML elements, but custom markup elements. However, with the help of a simple (but quite long) custom markup library, you're replacing on-the-fly all the custom markup elements with standard HTML tags.

The `custom_markup_translate()` function consists mainly of a number of regular expression replacements, which transform the custom markup code to HTML. We're leaving understanding this function for you as an exercise.

Flash and AJAX

Unfortunately, both Flash and AJAX technologies can pose major problems for search engines when used pervasively. Sites that are entirely Flash or AJAX based will not be indexed very well, if it all. The rationale is fairly simple. Search engines are designed to index pages, not applications.

> Sites built entirely with Flash or entirely with AJAX involve a huge paradigm shift. They do not employ pages for the various elements of a site; rather, they are, more or less, an application embedded on a single page.

Furthermore, even if a search engine could figure out how to interpret a Flash file or AJAX application adequately, parsing and indexing its pertinent content, there would be no way to navigate to that particular part of the application using a URL. Therefore, because the primary goal of a search engine is to provide relevant results to a user, a search engine will be hesitant to rank content in those media well. Lastly, both Flash and AJAX would invite several more innovative and harder-to-detect forms of spam.

The Blended Approach

But before you assume that we vilify Flash and AJAX completely, there is somewhat of a solution. A site designer should only use Flash and AJAX for the areas of the site that require it. This is called *the blended approach*. He or she should design an HTML-based site, and employ Flash and AJAX technologies where they will provide a tangible benefit to the user. He or she should attempt to keep as much of the textual content HTML-based as possible.

Frequently, a mix of HTML and JavaScript (DHTML) can also approximate most of the interactivity of these technologies. For example, clicking a button could hide or unhide an HTML `div` element. This will involve employing the use of smaller Flash or AJAX elements placed inside a traditional HTML layout. In other words, you should use Flash and AJAX as elements on a page, not as the page itself.

Some SEM authorities also recommend providing a non-Flash or AJAX version of content using `<noembed>` *or* `<noscript>`, *respectively. Unfortunately, because those tags are invisible (and have been used so pervasively for spam), their efficacy is questionable. Search engines may choose to ignore the content therein completely. They may, however, enhance usability for users with disabilities, so it is not unwise to employ them for that purpose.*

This solution also misses the mark for another reason — a typical Flash or AJAX site exists on a single "page," therefore further limiting the utility of the tag, because all content would presumably have to exist on that one page!

Figure 6-15 shows an image of a site that looks like a full Flash application, but was changed to HTML with DHTML and hidden layers. The presented link is `http://www.xactcommunication.com/WristLinx-9/X33XIF-WristLinx-TwoWay-Wristwatch-Radio-35.html`.

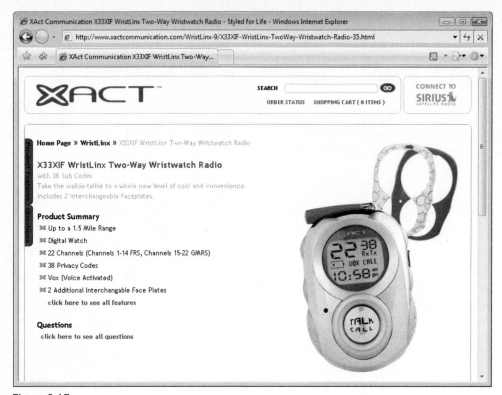

Figure 6-15

Summary

On-page technologies are a double-edged sword. New technologies — such as Flash and AJAX — may be boons for usability and have a certain "cool factor," but may make a site entirely invisible to a search engine spider if not used properly. Even seemingly superficial things like the structure of a link may severely impact web site spiderability, and hence search engine friendliness. Lastly, as stated in Chapter 2, invisible on-page factors are not regarded with any confidence by search engines. So despite the fact that tags such as <noembed> and <noscript> were created to address these issues, your success with them will likely be limited.

7

Web Feeds and Social Bookmarking

You've just added some great new content to your web site. *Now what?* Of course, your current visitors will appreciate the content. They may even tell a few friends about it. But there are technologies that you can leverage to facilitate and encourage them to do some free marketing for you.

This chapter explores web feeds and social bookmarking, two technologies that web site visitors can use to access and promote content that they enjoy. Encouraging visitors to do so is a vital part of viral marketing. This chapter discusses various ways to accomplish this, and walks you through three exercises where you:

❑   Create your own RSS feeds.

❑   Syndicate RSS and Atom feeds.

❑   Add social bookmarking icons to your pages and feeds.

Web Feeds

The *web feed* is a mechanism used to distribute content over the web, in XML-based formats, without attaching any visual presentation to it. The typical way for a person to read your content is to visit your web pages, retrieving their content laid out in HTML format. This doesn't work with web feeds, because they contain no presentation. Instead, people use specialized programs that retrieve and display the data.

Web feeds are used to disseminate information automatically — to humans as well as other web sites. They are a very effective vehicle for information distribution, and they've become very popular because they make it easy for somebody to read news, or recent blog posts, from his or her favorite sources. Web feeds are also nicely described at `http://en.wikipedia.org/wiki/Web_feed`.

Feeds encouraged the development of several applications for their consumption. Modern web browsers (including Internet Explorer 7 and Firefox 2.0), desktop applications such as Microsoft Office 2007, and web applications such as Google Reader (http://www.google.com/reader/) allow users to access the feeds they subscribe to from one convenient location. These applications are called aggregators, or feed readers.

Your web site can provide access to some or all of its content through web feeds. They may include links to the actual content as well as other links to elsewhere within your site. Over time, this will garner traffic and links from users who subscribe to your feeds, as well as the various sites that *syndicate* the information.

Web syndication permits other web sites to promote your content. Other webmasters have an incentive to syndicate feeds on their sites as fresh content, because including relevant syndicated content in *moderation* can be a useful resource. It may, however, be wise to abbreviate the amount of information you provide in a feed, because the *full* content appearing on various sites may present duplicate content problems. You may also choose to syndicate others web sites' content.

> *Moderation means that the web site could stand on its own without the syndicated content as well. If it cannot, it is probably a spam site.*

Today, all major blogging platforms provide feeds of some sort. Most other types of content management systems provide them as well. The custom applications that you develop may also benefit from their addition. This chapter demonstrates how to do so.

In order to be usable by everyone, feeds must be provided in a standardized format. RSS and Atom are the most popular choices.

RSS and Atom

Unfortunately, as usual, there are the requisite format wars. There are many competing formats for web syndication. Two of them are discussed here — RSS and Atom.

Both RSS and Atom are XML-based standards. The virtue of XML is that it provides a common framework that applications can use to communicate among multiple architectures and operating system platforms. RSS and Atom feeds can be viewed as plain text files, but it doesn't make much sense to use them like that, because they are meant to be read by a feed reader or specialized software that uses it in the scheme of a larger application. Figure 7-1 shows Jamie Sirovich's SEO Egghead feed in Cristian's Google Reader list.

RSS has a long and complicated history, with many versions and substantial modifications to the standard. There are two fundamental branches of RSS with two different names. RDF Site Summary (RSS 0.9) was created by Netscape in the late nineties. In response to criticism that it was too complex, a simplified and substantially different version, RSS 0.91, was released. To make things even more interesting, RSS 1.0 is largely a descendant of RSS 0.9, whereas RSS 2.0 is closer to RSS 0.91. RSS 2.0 now stands for *Really Simple Syndication*, and RSS 1.0 still stands for RDF Site Summary. Because this is not a history book on RSS, we will stop here and state that RSS 2.0 is by far the most popular and most adopted at this point. The standard is also now frozen, and no new changes are underway. The standard for RSS 2.0 is located at http://blogs.law.harvard.edu/tech/rss.

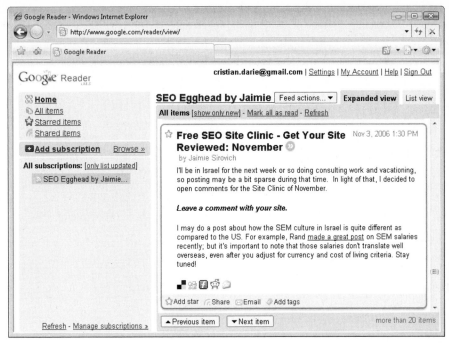

Figure 7-1

Atom was created because of the standards issues that have plagued RSS over time. It was born in 2003. There are two versions, Atom 0.3 and Atom 1.0. It is far more standardized but also more complicated and less commonly used. It has recently been gaining ground, however. For a more detailed comparison of RSS and Atom, consult `http://www.intertwingly.net/wiki/pie/Rss20AndAtom10Compared`.

We are ambivalent about which standard is employed. RSS 2.0 does have a higher adoption rate, it is simpler by most metrics, and that is the format demonstrated here when you create a web feed. To syndicate feeds, however, you will employ the use of a PHP library called SimplePie, which reads *all* versions of RSS and Atom feeds transparently.

A typical RSS 2.0 feed might look like this:

```
<rss version="2.0">
  <channel>
    <title>example.com breaking news</title>
    <link>http://www.example.org</link>
    <description>A short description of this feed</description>
    <language>en</language>
    <pubDate>Tue, 12 Sep 2006 07:56:23 EDT</pubDate>
    <item>
      <title>Catchy Title</title>
      <link>http://www.example.org/catchy-title.html</link>
      <description>
```

```
         The description can hold any content you wish, including XHTML.
      </description>
      <pubDate>Tue, 12 Sep 2006 07:56:23 EDT</pubDate>
    </item>
    <item>
      <title>Another Catchy Title</title>
      <link>http://www.example.org/another-catchy-title.html</link>
      <description>
        The description can hold any content you wish, including XHTML.
      </description>
      <pubDate>Tue, 12 Sep 2006 07:56:23 EDT</pubDate>
    </item>
  </channel>
</rss>
```

The feed may contain any number of <item> elements, each item holding different news or blog entries — or whatever content you want to store.

You can either create feeds for others to access, or you can syndicate feeds that others create. The following section discusses how to create feeds, and the next demonstrates the use of a third-party library called SimplePie to syndicate feeds.

Creating RSS Feeds

To make generating feeds for your content easier, create a class called the "**RSS Factory**." For the first time, you'll use object-oriented programming (OOP).

Previous exercises avoided using PHP's object-oriented programming support. It's used for this one because it actually makes things easier. Some explanations on its usage follow the exercise.

The class is aptly named RSSFactory, and it will provide all necessary functionality for generating RSS feeds. You'll implement this class and then use it to create a feed for "new SEO Egghead products" in the exercise that follows.

Creating the RSS Factory

1. Create a new file named rss_factory.inc.php in your seophp/include folder. You'll keep your RSS Factory class in this file. Type this code in rss_factory.inc.php:

```php
<?php

class RSSFactory
{
  var $_title;
  var $_link;
  var $_description;
  var $_language;
  var $_items;

  // escape string characters for inclusion in XML structure
```

```php
function _escapeXML($str)
{
  $translation = get_html_translation_table(HTML_ENTITIES, ENT_QUOTES);
  foreach ($translation as $key => $value)
  {
    $translation[$key] = '&#' . ord($key) . ';';
  }
  $translation[chr(38)] = '&';
  return preg_replace("/&(?![A-Za-z]{0,4}\w{2,3};|#[0-9]{2,3};)/","&#38;",
                      strtr($str, $translation));
}

// the class constructor is executed when creating an instance of the class
function RSSFactory($title, $link, $description,
                    $language = 'en-us', $items = array())
{
  // save feed data to local class members
  $this->_title = $title;
  $this->_link = $link;
  $this->_description = $description;
  $this->_language = $language;
  $this->_items = $items;
}

// adds a new feed item
function addItem($title, $link, $description, $additional_fields = array())
{
  // add feed item
  $this->_items[] =
    array_merge(array('title' => $title,
                      'link' => $link,
                      'description' => $description),
                $additional_fields);
}

// generates feed
function get()
{
  // initial preparations
  ob_start();
  header('Content-type: text/xml');

  // generate feed header
  echo '<rss version="2.0">' .
      '<channel>' .
        '<title>' . RSSFactory::_escapeXML($this->_title) . '</title>' .
        '<link>' . RSSFactory::_escapeXML($this->_link) . '</link>' .
        '<description>' .
          RSSFactory::_escapeXML($this->_description) .
        '</description>';

  // add feed items
  foreach ($this->_items as $feed_item)
  {
```

```
        // add a feed item and its contents
        echo '<item>';
        foreach ($feed_item as $item_name => $item_value)
        {
          echo "<$item_name>" .
                 RSSFactory::_escapeXML($item_value) .
               "</$item_name>";
        }
        echo '</item>';
      }

      // close channel and rss elements
      echo '</channel></rss>';

      // return feed data
      return ob_get_clean();
    }
  }

?>
```

2. Create a new file in your `seophp` folder named `feed.php`, and type this code in it:

```php
<?php

// load the URL factory library
require_once 'include/rss_factory.inc.php';

// create feed
$rss_feed = new RSSFactory('SEOEgghead.com New Products Feed',
                           'http://www.seoegghead.com/seo-with-php-updates.html',
                           'Exciting new products, updated daily');

// add feed item
$rss_feed->addItem('New Link Juice with Orange Flavor!',
  'http://seophp.example.com/Products/SEO-Toolbox-C6/Link-Juice-P31.html',
  'The new Link Juice product of SEOEgghead.com can do wonders for your website!');

// add feed item
$rss_feed->addItem('Enhance Your PHP Applications with AJAX!',
  'http://seophp.example.com/Products/Friends-Shed-C2/AJAX-PHP-Book-P42.html',
  'Check out this AJAX tutorial for PHP developers!');

// display feed
echo $rss_feed->get();

?>
```

3. Load `http://seophp.example.com/feed.php`. A modern web browser will ask if you want to subscribe to this feed, as shown in Figure 7-2.

4. Clicking the "Subscribe to this feed" link displays a dialog where you can choose subscription options. In Internet Explorer 7 that dialog looks like Figure 7-3, but it will vary depending on the application used.

5. After subscribing to the feed, you will have quick access to the latest entries through your particular feed reader application.

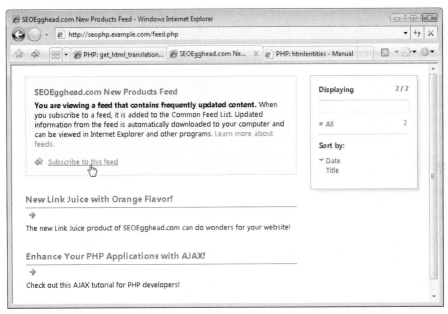

Figure 7-2

Figure 7-3

You have just created the RSSFactory *class*, and then did a quick test by having an RSSFactory *object* ($rss_feed) generate a simple feed in RSS format.

Class? Object? An OOP Primer

The term *class* comes from the lexicon of object-oriented programming (OOP). If you do not know much about OOP, here is a very quick primer that will help you understand the RSSFactory, as well as other examples in this book that use this language feature.

As the name implies, OOP puts objects at the center of the programming model. The *object* is the most important concept in the world of OOP — a self-contained entity that has state and behavior, just like a real-world object.

A class acts as a blueprint for the object, and an object represents an instance of the class defined by its state. You may have objects of class Car, for example, and create as many Car objects as desired — named $myCar, $johnsCar, $davesCar, and so on. But $davesCar may be stopped while John is busy outrunning a police officer on the freeway at 100MPH.

So you get the idea; the class defines the *functionality* provided by the objects. All objects of type Car will have the same basic capabilities — for example, the ability to accelerate to a new speed. However, each individual Car object may register a different speed on its speedometer at any particular time.

The object's state is described by its variable fields, also called "properties." Its functionality is defined by its "methods." These methods are functions inside a class, except that they are called through (->) an object and reference the functions in the context of the state provided by its properties.

In the particular example of the RSS Factory exercise, the class is named RSSFactory, and the object you create is named $rss_feed. When you needed to call the addItem method of the $rss_feed object, you typed $rss_feed->addItem to add an item to the object. You did this twice to add two feed items. Finally, to output the feed you called echo $rss_feed->get(), which displays the feed in accordance with the items that you added to it.

Using this class is simple — you start by referencing the rss_factory.inc.php file (which contains the class), and creating your $rss_feed object:

```php
<?php

// load the URL factory library
require_once 'include/rss_factory.inc.php';

// create feed
$rss_feed = new RSSFactory('SEOEgghead.com New Products Feed',
                        'http://www.seoegghead.com/seo-with-php-updates.html',
                        'Exciting new products, updated daily');
```

Your class is named RSSFactory, and the object you create is named $rss_feed. You create the object using the new operator, and, as you can see, you provide parameters in parentheses after the class name.

These parameters you provide when creating an object are passed to the class *constructor* upon object creation. The constructor is a special method inside the class that gets called automatically when the object is created. You use it to set up some things based on the parameters. In this case, when creating an RSSFactory object, you pass the feed title, link, and description. These are the attributes that are associated with the overall feed itself, not its individual elements. The constructor definition looks like this, in the RSSFactory class:

```
// the class constructor is executed when creating an instance of the class
function RSSFactory($title, $link, $description,
                    $language = 'en-us', $items = array())
{
  // save feed data to local class members
  $this->_title = $title;
  $this->_link = $link;
  $this->_description = $description;
  $this->_language = $language;
  $this->_items = $items;
}
```

So the constructor saves the parameter values to its properties, setting the object's state. Note the usage of $this, which means "the current class instance" when used inside a class. (If you create more objects of type RSSFactory, the $this reference in each of those objects will be different.)

Back in feed.php, after the $rss_feed object is created, its addItem method is called twice to add two feed items:

```
// create feed
$rss_feed = new RSSFactory('SEOEgghead.com New Products Feed',
                           'http://www.seoegghead.com/seo-with-php-updates.html',
                           'Exciting new products, updated daily');

// add feed item
$rss_feed->addItem('New Link Juice with Orange Flavor!',
   'http://localhost/seophp/Products/SEO-Toolbox-C6/Link-Juice-P31.html',
   'The new Link Juice product of SEOEgghead.com can do wonders for your website!');

// add feed item
$rss_feed->addItem('Enhance Your PHP Applications with AJAX!',
   'http://seophp.example.com/Products/Friends-Shed-C2/AJAX-PHP-Book-P42.html',
   'Check out this AJAX tutorial for PHP developers!');
```

Finally, the get() method is called to echo the RSS feed structure. The output of this particular exercise will be as follows:

```
<rss version="2.0">
  <channel>
    <title>SEOEgghead.com New Products Feed</title>
    <link>http://www.seoegghead.com/new-products.html</link>
    <description>Exciting new products, updated daily</description>
    <item>
      <title>New Exciting Product</title>
```

```
            <link>
               http://localhost/seophp/Products/SEO-Toolbox-C6/Link-Juice-P31.html
            </link>
            <description>
               The new Link Juice product of SEOEgghead.com can do wonders for your
website!
            </description>
         </item>
         <item>
            <title>Learn PHP E-Commerce Programming with PostgreSQL</title>
            <link>

http://localhost/seophp/Products/Friends-Shed-C2/PHP-E-Commerce-Book-P42.html
            </link>
            <description>
               This book will teach you PHP E-Commerce programming step by step!
            </description>
         </item>
      </channel>
</rss>
```

To promote your web feed, you should prominently feature it on your web site. In Chapter 16 you will also see how to place "chicklets" on a WordPress blog to facilitate the addition of your web site to specific web application–based feed readers.

Syndicating RSS and Atom Feeds

As explained earlier, many differing format standards are used for web feeds. Luckily, as you saw, there are many tools that help you keep track of your favorite feeds. These tools let you forget about the format wars entirely. However, when you need to programmatically read and parse external feeds for syndication, things get complicated.

Thankfully, Skyzyx Technologies (http://www.skyzyx.com/) has developed a PHP library called SimplePie (http://simplepie.org/) that abstracts the details from the programmer's view and provides a common API used for all feed types and versions. They say:

> "SimplePie is a very fast and easy-to-use class, written in PHP, for reading RSS and Atom syndication feeds. By keeping it simple, and focusing on what's important, we've built a pretty sweet little API. SimplePie's focus has been two-fold: speed and ease of use, and has been very successful on both fronts."

You can find installation instructions at http://simplepie.org/docs/installation/getting-started/ and you can find a guide at http://simplepie.org/docs/installation/from-scratch/.

Here you use SimplePie in a quick exercise. You'll build a page that uses SimplePie to read the feed you've just created, and display it for your visitors.

Reading Feeds using SimplePie

1. To function properly, SimplePie needs a few libraries, as shown in Figure 7-4. If you've prepared Apache and PHP as instructed in Chapter 1, you should have all the necessary libraries installed and enabled, except cURL. To enable cURL, open the `php.ini` configuration file (located by default in `\xampp\apache\bin`), uncomment the following line by removing the leading semicolon, and then restart Apache:

```
extension=php_curl.dll
```

2. Download the SimplePie package from `http://simplepie.org/downloads/`.

3. Unzip the downloaded file, which should be called something like `simplepie_ver.zip`, somewhere on your disk. Then copy `simplepie.inc`, which is the PHP file you're interested in, to your `seophp/include` folder.

4. SimplePie is very developer friendly. Apart from the excellent documentation, SimplePie also ships with a script that tests if your PHP installation supports SimplePie. If you are not sure if your machine supports SimplePie, copy `sp_compatiliby_test.php` from the downloaded package to your `seophp` folder. Then, loading `sp_compatibility_test.php` in your web browser would provide a useful assessment — see Figure 7-4.

5. Create a folder named `cache` under your `seophp` folder. The `seophp/cache` folder will be used by SimplePie for caching purposes.

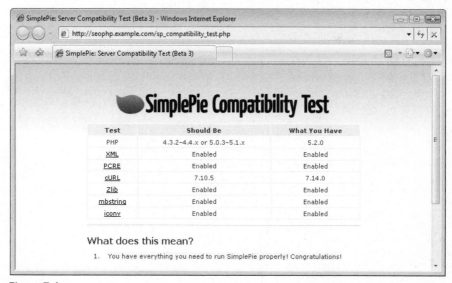

Figure 7-4

6. Create a new file in your `seophp` folder, named `read_feed.php`, and type the following code:

```php
<?php
// load the SimplePie library
require_once 'include/simplepie.inc';

// create and configure SimplePie object
$feed = new SimplePie();
$feed->feed_url('http://seophp.example.com/feed.php');
$feed->cache_location('cache');
$feed->init();
$feed->handle_content_type();
?>

<!DOCTYPE html PUBLIC "-//W3C//DTD XHTML 1.1//EN"
 "http://www.w3.org/TR/xhtml11/DTD/xhtml11.dtd">
<html>
<head>
  <title>Feed Reading Test</title>
</head>
<body>

<?php
if ($feed->data)
{
  // display the title
  echo '<h1>' .
          '<a href="' . $feed->get_feed_link() . '">' .
            $feed->get_feed_title() .
          '</a>' .
        '</h1>';

  // display a maximum of 5 feed items
  $max = $feed->get_item_quantity(5);
  for ($x=0; $x<$max; $x++)
  {
    $item = $feed->get_item($x);

    // display feed link and title
    echo '<h2>' .
            '<a href="' . $item->get_permalink() . '">' .
              $item->get_title() .
            '</a>' .
          '</h2>';

    // display feed description
    echo '<p>' . $item->get_description() . '</p>';
  }
}
?>

</body>
</html>
```

7. Load `http://seophp.example.com/read_feed.php`, and you should get the results shown in Figure 7-5.

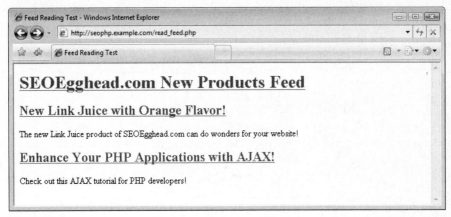

Figure 7-5

So far, so good! Using `SimplePie`, it was almost too easy to read data from an external feed.

Again, you meet the advantages that OOP brings. The whole SimplePie library is based on a class named SimplePie: all you have to do is to create an object of this class, and then start using the appropriate methods:

```php
<?php
// load the SimplePie library
require_once 'include/simplepie.inc';

// create and configure SimplePie object
$feed = new SimplePie();
$feed->feed_url('http://seophp.example.com/feed.php');
$feed->cache_location('cache');
$feed->init();
$feed->handle_content_type();
?>
```

For a detailed reference, please consult the SimplePie documentation at `http://simplepie.org/docs/installation/getting-started/`.

Other Sources of Syndicated Content

Various other sources of syndicated content are available, usually in the form of *web services*. These are outside the scope of this book; they are just mentioned for completeness.

Somewhat similar to RSS or Atom feeds in that they deliver data to external sources upon request, web services provide more complex communication mechanisms. Communication between clients and web services also occurs in XML-based formats; the most common protocols for web services communication are SOAP and REST.

Many major web-based companies, such as Amazon, eBay, Yahoo!, Google, MSN, and Alexa offer access to their vast amount of content through their web services. You can also provide your own web services to the same end. Numerous books have been written to cover some of these services. For more information on web services, consider *Professional Web APIs with PHP: eBay, Google, Paypal, Amazon, FedEx plus Web Feeds* (Wiley Publishing, Inc., 2006).

Social Bookmarking

Social bookmarking web sites offer users convenient storage of their bookmarks remotely for access from any location. Examples of these sites include del.icio.us, digg, Reddit, and so on. These sites usually allow these bookmarks to be private, but many choose to leave them public. And when a particular web page is publicly bookmarked by many users, that is a major positive contributing factor in the ranking algorithm of the search function on a social bookmarking site. Ranking well in these searches presents another *great* source of organic traffic. Furthermore, if a web page is bookmarked by a large number of people, it may result in a front page placement on such a site. This usually results in a landslide of traffic.

Many blogs present links to streamline the process of bookmarking a page. As is typical with facilitating any action desired from a web site user, this may increase the number of bookmarks achieved by a page on your web site. Figure 7-6 shows an example of SEO Egghead with icons for bookmarking a page; highlighted (from left to right) are del.icio.us, digg, Furl, and Reddit.

These little icons make it easy for people browsing a web site to do some free marketing for you — in case they like the content at that particular URL and want to bookmark it. To make adding these icons easy, you create a class that will work for any web application. We referenced the icons and list of social bookmarking sites from Sociable, a plugin for WordPress (it's the same plugin used for that purpose on the SEO Egghead blog) and it's explored in Chapter 16; kudos to Peter Harkins for putting all those icons together.

You create the social bookmarking library in the following exercise, where you'll add those icons to your catalog page, `catalog.php`. You created this script back in Chapter 3, but if you skipped that chapter, feel free to use the code download for Chapter 7. The catalog page is accessible through `http://seophp.example.com/catalog.html`.

> *Note that you wouldn't normally add social bookmarking items on e-commerce catalog pages — except perhaps if it's a very new and exciting product. We've chosen this example to keep the implementation simple for the purposes of the demonstration.*

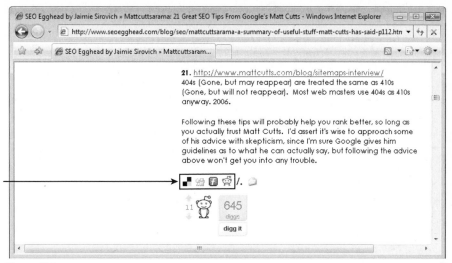

Figure 7-6

Adding Social Bookmarking Support

1. Create a folder named `social_icons` in your `seophp` folder.

2. Download the code archive of this book, and copy the social bookmarking images from the archive to your `social_icons` folder. (The `welcome.html` document from the code download contains details about the exact locations of the necessary files.)

3. Create a new file named `social_bookmarking.inc.php` in your `seophp/include` folder, and type this code in:

```php
<?php
// +------------------------------------------------------------+
// | SocialBookmarking                                          |
// | Displays links for various social bookmarking services     |
// +------------------------------------------------------------+
// | Copyright (c) 2005 Jaimie Sirovich                         |
// +------------------------------------------------------------+
// | Author: Jaimie Sirovich <jsirovic@gmail.com>               |
// | Icons taken from WordPress Plugin Sociable by Peter Harkins |
// | (http://push.cx)                                           |
// +------------------------------------------------------------+

class SocialBookmarking
{
  var $_link;
  var $_title;
  var $_site_name;

  var $_templates = array(
    'blinkbits' => array(
      'icon' => 'blinkbits.tif',
```

```
        'url' => 'http://www.blinkbits.com/bookmarklets/save.php?v=1&source_url=↵
{LINK}&title={TITLE}&body={TITLE}'),

    'BlinkList' => array(
        'icon' => 'blinklist.tif',
        'url' => 'http://www.blinklist.com/index.php?Action=Blink/addblink.php&↵
Description=&Url={LINK}&Title={TITLE}'),

    'blogmarks' => array(
        'icon' => 'blogmarks.tif',
        'url' => 'http://blogmarks.net/my/new.php?mini=1&simple=1&url={LINK}&↵
title={TITLE}'),

    'co.mments' => array(
        'icon' => 'co.mments.gif',
        'url' => 'http://co.mments.com/track?url={LINK}&title={TITLE}'),

    'connotea' => array(
        'icon' => 'connotea.tif',
        'url' => 'http://www.connotea.org/addpopup?continue=confirm&uri={LINK}&↵
title={TITLE}'),

    'del.icio.us' => array(
        'icon' => 'delicious.tif',
        'url' => 'http://del.icio.us/post?url={LINK}&title={TITLE}'),

    'De.lirio.us' => array(
        'icon' => 'delirious.tif',
        'url' => 'http://de.lirio.us/rubric/post?uri={LINK}&title={TITLE};↵
when_done=go_back'),

    'digg' => array(
        'icon' => 'digg.tif',
        'url' => 'http://digg.com/submit?phase=2&url={LINK}&title={TITLE}'),

    'Fark' => array(
        'icon' => 'fark.tif',
        'url' =>
'http://cgi.fark.com/cgi/fark/edit.pl?new_url={LINK}&new_comment={TITLE}&new_comment
={SITENAME}&linktype=Misc'),

    'feedmelinks' => array(
        'icon' => 'feedmelinks.tif',
        'url' => 'http://feedmelinks.com/categorize?from=toolbar&op=submit&↵
url={LINK}&name={TITLE}'),

    'Furl' => array(
        'icon' => 'furl.tif',
        'url' => 'http://www.furl.net/storeIt.jsp?u={LINK}&t={TITLE}'),

    'LinkaGoGo' => array(
```

```
        'icon' => 'linkagogo.tif',
        'url' => 'http://www.linkagogo.com/go/AddNoPopup?url={LINK}&title={TITLE}'),

    'Ma.gnolia' => array(
        'icon' => 'magnolia.tif',
        'url' => 'http://ma.gnolia.com/beta/bookmarklet/add?url={LINK}&↵
title={TITLE}&description={TITLE}'),

    'NewsVine' => array(
        'icon' => 'newsvine.tif',
        'url' => 'http://www.newsvine.com/_tools/seed&save?u={LINK}&h={TITLE}'),

    'Netvouz' => array(
        'icon' => 'netvouz.tif',
        'url' => 'http://www.netvouz.com/action/submitBookmark?url={LINK}&↵
title={TITLE}&description={TITLE}'),

    'Reddit' => array(
        'icon' => 'reddit.tif',
        'url' => 'http://reddit.com/submit?url={LINK}&title={TITLE}'),

    'scuttle' => array(
        'icon' => 'scuttle.tif',
        'url' => 'http://www.scuttle.org/bookmarks.php/maxpower?action=add&↵
address={LINK}&title={TITLE}&description={TITLE}'),

    'Shadows' => array(
        'icon' => 'shadows.tif',
        'url' => 'http://www.shadows.com/features/tcr.htm?url={LINK}&title={TITLE}'),

    'Simpy' => array(
        'icon' => 'simpy.tif',
        'url' => 'http://www.simpy.com/simpy/LinkAdd.do?href={LINK}&title={TITLE}'),

    'Smarking' => array(
        'icon' => 'smarking.tif',
        'url' => 'http://smarking.com/editbookmark/?url={LINK}&description={TITLE}'),

    'Spurl' => array(
        'icon' => 'spurl.tif',
        'url' => 'http://www.spurl.net/spurl.php?url={LINK}&title={TITLE}'),

    'TailRank' => array(
        'icon' => 'tailrank.tif',
        'url' => 'http://tailrank.com/share/?text=&link_href={LINK}&title={TITLE}'),

    'Wists' => array(
        'icon' => 'wists.tif',
        'url' => 'http://wists.com/r.php?c=&r={LINK}&title={TITLE}'),

    'YahooMyWeb' => array(
```

```php
        'icon' => 'yahoomyweb.tif',
        'url' => 'http://myweb2.search.yahoo.com/myresults/bookmarklet?u={LINK}↵
&t={TITLE}')
  );

  // the constructor
  function SocialBookmarking($link, $title, $site_name)
  {
    $this->_link = $link;
    $this->_title = $title;
    $this->_site_name = $site_name;
  }

  // returns the HTML with social bookmarking symbols
  function getHTML($sites =
                  array('del.icio.us', 'digg', 'Furl', 'Reddit', 'YahooMyWeb'))
  {
    // build the output
    $html_feed = '<ul class="social_bookmarking">';
    // create HTML for each of the sites received as parameter
    foreach($sites as $s)
    {
      if ($_site_info = $this->_templates[$s])
      {
        $html_feed .= '<li class="social_bookmarking">';
        $url = str_replace(array('{LINK}', '{TITLE}', '{SITENAME}'),
                           array(urlencode($this->_link),
                           urlencode($this->_title),
                           urlencode($this->_site_name)),
                           $_site_info['url']);
        $html_feed .= '<a rel="nofollow" href="' . $url . '" title="' . $s . '">';
        $html_feed .= '<img src="' . SITE_DOMAIN .
                '/social_icons/' . $_site_info['icon'] . '" alt="' . $s .
                '" class="social_bookmarking" />';
        $html_feed .= '</a></li>';
      }
    }
    $html_feed .= '</ul>';
    return $html_feed;
  }

  // returns HTML with social bookmarking links for inclusion in feeds
  function getFeedHTML($sites =
                  array('del.icio.us', 'digg', 'Furl', 'Reddit', 'YahooMyWeb'))
  {
    // initialize $html_feed
    $html_feed = '';

    // build the HTML feed
    foreach($sites as $s)
    {
      if ($_site_info = $this->_templates[$s])
      {
        $url = str_replace(array('{LINK}', '{TITLE}', '{SITENAME}'),
                           array(urlencode($this->_link),
```

```
                                  urlencode($this->_title),
                                  urlencode($this->_site_name)),
                           $_site_info['url']);
        $html_feed .= '<a rel="nofollow" href="' . $url .
                      '" title="' . $s . '">';
        $html_feed .= '<img src="/social_icons/' . $_site_info['icon'] .
                      '" alt="' . $s . '" class="social_bookmarking" />';
        $html_feed .= '</a> ';
      }
    }

    // return the HTML feed
    return '<p>' . $html_feed . '</p>';
  }
}
?>
```

4. Modify `seophp/catalog.php` like this:

```php
<?php
// load the URL factory library
require_once 'include/url_factory.inc.php';
// load social bookmarking helper class
require_once 'include/social_bookmarking.inc.php';
?>

<!DOCTYPE html PUBLIC "-//W3C//DTD XHTML 1.1//EN"
 "http://www.w3.org/TR/xhtml11/DTD/xhtml11.dtd">
<html>
...
...
...

    <center>
      <?php
        // instantiate class by providing link, title, and site name
        $social = new SocialBookmarking('http://seophp.example.com/catalog.html',
                                        'Exciting SEOEgghead Products!',
                                        'SEOEgghead');
        // display social bookmarking links
        echo $social->getHTML();
      ?>
    </center>
    <center>
      <a href="popup.php" target="_blank">Find more about Professional Search
Engine Optimization with PHP!</a>
    </center>
...
...
...
</html>
```

5. Load `http://seophp.example.com/catalog.html`, and you should get the result you see in Figure 7-7.

6. Now take a look at how to add the same functionality to feeds. The `SocialBookmarking` class has a method named `getFeedHTML()`, which can be used for that purpose. Essentially, `getHTML` and `getFeedHTML` are very similar, but your output will be a bit different for feeds. In this case, `getHTML()` uses an unordered list to display the links, whereas `getFeedHTML()` simply separates the links using spaces. Modify the code in `rss_factory.inc.php` to add social bookmarking links at the end of each feed, like this:

```php
<?php

// load social bookmarking helper class
require_once 'social_bookmarking.inc.php';

class RSSFactory
{
...
...
...
  // generates feed
  function get()
  {
...
...
...
    // add feed items
    foreach ($this->_items as $feed_item)
    {
      // add a feed item and its contents
      echo '<item>';
      foreach ($feed_item as $item_name => $item_value)
      {
        // add social bookmarking icons to feed description
        if ($item_name == 'description')
        {
          // instantiate class by providing link, title, and site name
          $social = new SocialBookmarking($feed_item['link'],
                                          $feed_item['title'],
                                          $this->_title);

          // add social bookmarking icons to the feed
          $item_value = $item_value . $social->getFeedHTML();
        }

        // output feed item
        echo "<$item_name>" .
             RSSFactory::_escapeXML($item_value) .
           "</$item_name>";
      }
...
...
...
  }
}

?>
```

7. Load the feed at `http://seophp.example.com/feed.php` again in your browser, and notice the new social bookmarking links, as shown in Figure 7-8.

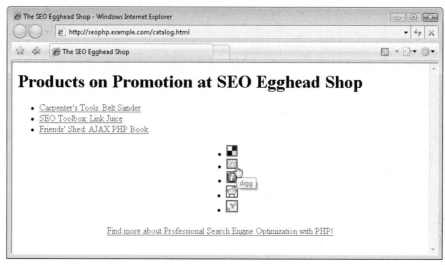

Figure 7-7

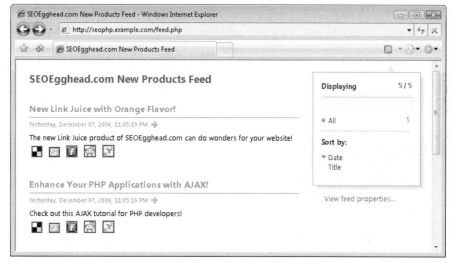

Figure 7-8

The newly created library knows how to generate links for many social networking web sites: blinkbits, blinklist, blogmarks, co.mments, connotea, del.icio.us, de.lirio.us, digg, Fark, feedmelinks, Furl, LinkaGoGo, Ma.gnolia, NewsVine, NetVouz, Reddit, scuttle, Shadows, Simply, Smarking, Spurl, TailRank, Wists, and YahooMyWeb. Wow, this is quite an impressive list, isn't it?

Whenever you add something interesting that other people may want to talk about, you want to facilitate them in doing so. After creating the `SocialBookmarking` class and referencing it from the page where your content is located, you simply need to use it like you did in `catalog.php`:

```
<center>
  <?php
    // instantiate class by providing link, title, and site name
    $social = new SocialBookmarking('http://seophp.example.com/catalog.html',
                                    'Exciting SEOEgghead Products!',
                                    'SEOEgghead');
    // display social bookmarking links
    echo $social->getHTML();
  ?>
</center>
```

The HTML output, of course, can be customized. We won't insist on such customization here though.

Also, note the `getHTML()` method has an optional array parameter that contains the services for which to create links. The default value is `array('del.icio.us', 'digg', 'Furl', 'Reddit', 'YahooMyWeb')`, but you can specify any of the known services if you don't like the default list.

Summary

Feeds provide a streamlined method for users to access content, as well as allow other sites to syndicate content. Links that are embedded in the feeds will both provide traffic directly as well as indirectly over time. Users will click the embedded links in the syndicated content. And search engines will see a gradually increasing number of links. This chapter demonstrated a class to easily create an RSS 2.0 feed, as well as a third-party class to read all of the various formats employed today.

Social bookmarking services offer another sort of organic traffic that should also not be ignored. Streamlining the process of bookmarking on your web site will likely increase the number of bookmarks your site receives, and hence its ranking in the social bookmarking site search function — and perhaps even earn a place on its home page.

8

Black Hat SEO

It may sound quite obvious, but system administrators — those who manage the computers that host your web site, for example, must be acutely aware of computer security concerns. When a particular piece of software is indicated to be vulnerable to hackers, they should find out quickly because it is their priority to do so. Then they should patch or mitigate the security risk on the servers for which they are responsible as soon as possible. Consequently, it may also not surprise you that some of the best system administrators used to be hackers, or are at least very aware of what hacking entails.

Why is this relevant? Although it is *totally unfair* to compare "black hat" search engine marketers to hackers on an ethical plane, the analogy is useful. The "white hat" search engine marketer — that is, a search engine marketer who follows all the rules, must be aware of how a "black hat" operates.

Understanding black hat techniques can help a webmaster protect his or her web sites. Nobody, after all, wants to be caught with his pants down advertising "cheap Viagra." In this chapter you learn how to avoid such problems. In this chapter you will:

- ❑ Learn about black hat SEO.
- ❑ Learn about the importance of properly escaping input data.
- ❑ Learn how to automatically add the nofollow attribute to links.
- ❑ Sanitize input data by removing unwanted tags and attributes.
- ❑ Request human input to protect against scripts adding comments automatically.
- ❑ Protect against redirect attacks.

There is quite a bit to go through, so we'd better get started!

What's with All the Hats?

The "hat" terminology, as just alluded to, has been borrowed from the lexicon of hackers. "White hat" search engine marketers play by the rules, following every rule in a search engine's terms of service to the letter. They will never exploit the work of others. "Black hats," on the other hand, to varying degrees, do not follow the rules of a search engine, and may also exploit the work or property of others. In practice, few search engine marketers fit exactly in either "hat" classification. Rather, it is a spectrum, giving rise to a further confusing "gray hat" classification for people on neither side of the fence exclusively.

> *The black hat versus white hat hacker terminology derives, in turn, from the practice in early Western movies of dressing the bad cowboys in black hats, and the good cowboys in white hats. Hollywood has since matured and no longer uses such simplistic symbolism, but its embarrassing memory lives on in the search engine marketing community.*

Dan Thies sums it up well in *The Search Engine Marketing Kit*. He states that it *"... boils down to whether you, as an SEO consultant, see yourself as a lawyer or an accountant."*

A lawyer, according to Mr. Thies, must put a client's interests first. Lawyers do the best they can for a client, and view the search engine as an adversary. A "black hat" search engine marketer is a lawyer. He or she will do anything within reason to conquer the adversary — the search engines. The definition of "within reason" varies by the individual's ethical compass. Some of the various methods employed by the "black hat" are discussed in this chapter.

An accountant, on the other hand, has a strict set of rules that are followed by rote. His rules are somewhat arbitrarily defined by a governmental agency. A search engine typically also publishes such rules. And a "white hat" search engine marketer follows them just as an accountant does. He or she is dogmatic about it. A site that does not rank well is assumed to be inadequate. And to fix it, only solutions recommended by a search engine's terms of service are employed.

The distinctions aren't as black and white as the terminology seems to indicate. However, at least being aware of "black hat" agenda and techniques is helpful to any search engine marketer, regardless of "hat color" for many reasons. Despite the fact that this book primarily addresses the "accountants," there may be times when bending the rules is necessary due to technical or time constraints (though it usually entails risk). At the same time, it is wise to know and understand your opponents' search marketing strategies so they can be analyzed.

> *Please be aware that this chapter is by no means a comprehensive manual on "black hat" techniques. We have taken the approach of highlighting those areas that contain pertinent information for a web developer. A printed reference on the topic would become stale rather quickly anyway because the methods change rapidly as the search engines and the cowboys in black hats duke it out on a perpetual basis. And though it is possible to read this chapter cynically, it aims mostly to educate the web developer with what he needs to do to beat the black hat cowboy in a duel. Some resources on "black hat" SEO are SEO Black Hat (*`http://www.seoblackhat.com`*), and David Naylor's blog (*`http://www.davidnaylor.co.uk/`*).*

Lastly, because many black hat practices exploit other sites' security vulnerabilities, it is useful to know some common vectors, because they typically improve the rankings of another (spam) web site at the potential expense of *your* web site's rankings. For that reason alone, a basic understanding of black hat techniques is important to any search engine marketer.

Bending the Rules

A typical situation when "bending the rules" may be useful is when a site already exists and presents a flaw that cannot be overcome without a complete redesign. Usually a complete redesign, in the context of a functioning web site, is a complex and arduous undertaking. At best, it cannot be done within the time limits prescribed. At worst, it is completely impossible either due to budget or internal politics.

Perhaps the site is designed entirely in Flash (see Chapter 6), or it employs a URL-based session-handler that could throw a spider into a spider-trap of circular, or infinite references. If a total application rewrite is not an option — as is usually the case — *cloaking* may be employed. Cloaking implies delivering different content depending on whether the user agent is a human or a search engine spider. In the former case, an HTML-based version of the site could be presented to the search engine spiders instead of the Flash version. In the latter case, when the user agent is a spider, the site could use cloaking to remove the session ID and other potentially confusing parameters from the URL, hence removing the spider-trap.

A well-known example of cloaking is that employed by the *New York Times*. Essentially, the *New York Times* web site requests users to create (and pay for) an account with them for certain premium content — as shown in Figure 8-1.

However, this restriction isn't imposed on search engines. Indeed, the *New York Times* allows search engines to browse and index its content without an account, which most probably gets `http://www.nytimes.com/` a lot of incoming traffic from search engines. A full write-up is available at `http://searchenginewatch.com/showPage.html?page=3613561`.

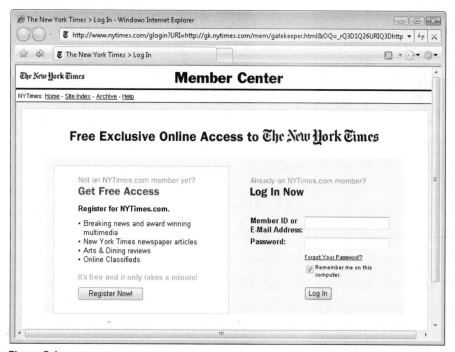

Figure 8-1

A simple Google `site:` query shows that Google has indexed five million pages from `nytimes.com` — see Figure 8-2. In this SERP, it's interesting to note that the results don't have the "view cache" link. This is because `nytimes.com` is using a meta `noarchive` tag that prevents search engines from caching the content (and clever users from circumventing the need for subscriptions). Upon close inspection, one discovers that the search engines are indexing the content of many pages from `nytimes.com` to present relevant results in the SERPs, but the content is not actually available to *you*.

This example does highlight quite well the concept that employing techniques that a search engine considers "black hat" can be used for normatively acceptable purposes. It also highlights that Google is willing to bend its rules for certain high-profile web sites.

Google's stated policies are *not* ambiguous on the cloaking front — cloaking is considered "black hat" and subject to site penalization. Examples like this one cloud the issue, however. Yahoo! and MSN are less strict and allow cloaking so long as it is not misleading for the user. Cloaking, and the technical and ethical issues it entails, is further explained in Chapter 11.

Figure 8-2

Technical Analysis of Black-Hat Techniques

When you view the SERPs for keywords that you would like to acquire, it is often useful to compare your site to the competitions'. If one of your competitors employs a black hat technique, the technique is worthwhile to understand just for that reason alone. Perhaps your competitor has several thousand spam sites pointing at his site, or perhaps his web site is sending optimized content to the search engines via cloaking methods. Some search engine marketers believe in reporting such sites to search engines, whereas some would just like to be aware. That decision is yours.

This chapter details several black hat techniques that are pertinent to every site developer.

Attack Avoidance

Search engine marketers must be aware of several things in black hat SEO from a security perspective. Some black hat search engine marketers exploit faulty or lax software to place links from your site to theirs in order to increase their rankings. This can be either through a bulletin board post, a blog comment, or a generally faulty script. Frequently, black hat techniques employ automated software to seek and exploit such weaknesses.

A black hat marketer may also use some sort of signature in a web application to find many sites using a search engine, such as a version number or tagline. Therefore, it is imperative that any web developer understands this, because being exploited may be to your detriment in rankings, not to mention corporate image. It's clear that nobody wants hundreds of links to spam sites on his forums or comments.

Security notwithstanding, the first step to protect your web site is to keep software that is not under your auspices, that is, third-party software, up-to-date. For example, not too long ago, many blogging applications did not apply the `rel="nofollow"` attribute to links in comments — because it had not been adopted yet! This weakness had been exploited extensively in the past by black hat SEOs.

One more recent exploit was the HTML insertion flaw in Movable Type, a very popular blogging application, and the problem has been documented at `http://seoblackhat.com/2006/06/10/moveable-type-backlink-exploit/`.

Such problems can be avoided by manually patching the software for vulnerabilities, but updating your software frequently would certainly help, because they are usually corrected on your behalf eventually anyway.

HTML Insertion Attacks

A programmer must escape *all* data processed by your web application's code. Escaping means altering the text and other data received from a non-trusted source, such as a comment added by a visitor on your web site, so that it doesn't cause any unwanted side effects when that data is further processed or displayed by your application.

Input data validation and escaping is a common security issue, but most web developers are only accustomed to it, these days, in the context of SQL. Most experienced web developers know that they must escape or sanitize data sent to a SQL database. Otherwise, carefully constructed input can form a malicious query that exposes and/or vandalizes data. Despite this, many programmers forget to escape SQL input; and even more of them forget to do the same for HTML input.

Even the terminology reflects the apathy. You "escape" SQL with the `mysql_real_escape_string()` PHP function, but you "convert special characters" using the `htmlspecialchars()` or `htmlentities()` PHP functions. In addition, there are huge glaring comments about why you should escape SQL.

The `mysql_real_escape_string()` documentation says that *"This function must always (with few exceptions) be used to make data safe before sending a query to MySQL."*

But none of the documentation pages for the HTML escaping functions say anything along the lines of "You must escape your user-generated HTML, otherwise people can use carefully crafted parameters to tell the world you advocate and link to something terribly unethical." Obviously, your site could also show support for other sites engaging questionable but otherwise mundane destinations; but either way, you probably want to make sure you don't advocate any of the above without actually knowing it.

> **We cannot stress enough that this is a major problem that is largely ignored. You must fix your vulnerable sites, or someone else will eventually *make* you fix it.**

Here is an example of code before and after the proper escaping practice. First, here's the version that doesn't use a proper escaping technique:

```php
<?php
// don't try this at home
echo 'Your query for ' .
    $_GET['parameter'] .
    ' has no results.';
?>
```

And here's the version that correctly escapes the input data:

```php
<?php
// proper escaping technique
echo 'Your query for ' .
    htmlspecialchars($_GET['parameter']) .
    ' has no results.";
?>
```

The following short exercise illustrates the difference.

> **All the exercises assume that you have configured your machine as described in Chapter 1. Visit** http://www.seoegghead.com/seo-with-php-updates.html **for updates related to this code.**

Escaping Input Data

1. In your seophp folder, create a script named param_no_escape.php and type this code:

```php
<?php
// don't try this at home
echo 'Your query for ' .
    $_GET['parameter'] .
    ' has no results.';
?>
```

2. Create a new script named param_escape.php with this code:

```php
<?php
// proper escaping technique
echo 'Your query for ' .
```

```
        htmlspecialchars($_GET['parameter']) .
        ' has no results.';
?>
```

3. Load `http://seophp.example.com/param_no_escape.php?parameter=<a href=http://too.much.spam>spam spam spam</a>`. Your innocent, but vulnerable script, nicely takes the parameter and transforms it into an HTML link. You end up linking to `http://too.much.spam`, as shown in Figure 8-3.

4. Now provide the same parameter to your other script, `param_escape.php`. The link would be `http://seophp.example.com/param_escape.php?parameter=<a href= http://too.much.spam>spam spam spam</a>`, and the result is shown in Figure 8-4.

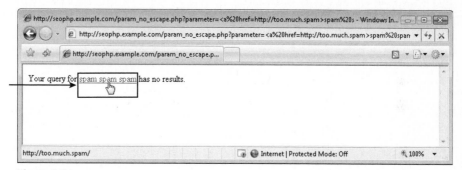

Figure 8-3

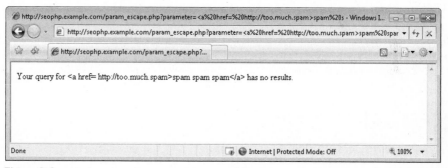

Figure 8-4

The escaping makes a difference, doesn't it! Of course, you don't want anyone to post anything like that on your web site regardless of whether you escape your input data. However, you're much better off when escaping your data for three main reasons:

❑ Carefully escaped data is much less likely to cause damage when further processed by your scripts in general. Doing so has security implications as well — preventing cross-site scripting attacks.

- ❑ You aren't providing free links to spammers.
- ❑ Spammers are less motivated to spend time on your site.

Avoiding Comment Attacks Using Nofollow

Many black hat spammers will use the comment section of a blog or guestbook, or forums, to post spam messages and links that promote their web sites.

Adding the `rel="nofollow"` attribute to a link will inform the search engine that that particular link is not audited by your site, and should therefore not count as a trusted vote for the popularity of the linked site. And though this strictly doesn't prevent spam, it does remove a lot of the motivation that results in a spammer targeting your site. The link will still work, but it will no longer be as desirable to a spammer because it offers a diminished link equity value.

> *In reality,* nofollow *has far from eliminated comment and guestbook spamming. Unfortunately, it does not eliminate the need for manual auditing and spam filtering. It is just a deterrent.*

You can use the same technique when including links to sites that you don't want to "vote." Here's an example:

```
<a rel="nofollow" href="http://too.much.spam">Bad site!</a>
```

It is also important to realize that too many links without `rel="nofollow"` may hurt your rankings if they are linking to "bad neighborhoods" as well as damage your reputation and credibility. All major search engines currently support this the `nofollow` feature.

> *Automated scripts may still target your site, only because, frequently, the spamming is done in bulk, and the spammer has not investigated your site specifically. In practice, however, using* nofollow *is likely to cut down on spam. Either way, if* nofollow *is employed, the damage is mitigated as it can only damage visitor perception, not search engine rankings, because the links will not be seen as votes to a bad neighborhood by a search engine. Collectively, because most web sites will begin using this feature, it will yield inferior results, and spammers will use such techniques less frequently.*

In the exercise that follows you create a little PHP "nofollow library," which employs a regular expression that alters all links in a text buffer by adding the `rel="nofollow"` attribute, but only to links that are not in a predefined "white list."

Creating and Using a Nofollow Library

1. If you haven't already done so by following the previous chapters, create a folder named `include` in your `seophp` folder. Then create a file named `nofollow.inc.php` in your `seophp/include` folder, and add this code to it:

```php
<?php

// include config file
require_once 'config.inc.php';

// finds all the links in $str and processes them using fixLink()
function noFollowLinks($str)
```

```
{
  // replaces every link with the version provided by fixLink()
  return preg_replace_callback(
    "#(<a.*?>)#i",
    create_function('$matches', 'return fixLink($matches[1]);'),
    $str);
}

// receives a string that contains a link such as <a href="http://too.much.spam/">
// and adds the ref="nofollow" attribute if the domain isn't in the white list
function fixLink($input)
{
  // retrieve the whitelist from the config file
  $whitelist = $GLOBALS['whitelist'];

  // if the link in $input already contains ref="nofollow", return it as it is
  if (preg_match('#rel\s*?=\s*?[\'"]?.*?nofollow.*?[\'"]?#i', $input))
  {
    return $input;
  }

  // extract the URL from $input
  preg_match('#href\s*?=\s*?[\'"]?([^\'"]*)[\'"]?#i', $input, $captures);

  // $href will contain the extracted URL, such as http://seophp.example.com
  $href = $captures[1];

  // if URL doesn't contain http://, assume it's a local link
  if (!preg_match('#^\s*http://#', $href))
  {
    return $input;
  }

  // extract the host name of the URL, such as seophp.example.com
  $parsed = parse_url($href);
  $host = $parsed['host'];

  // if the URL is in the whitelist, send $input back as it is
  if (in_array($host, $whitelist))
  {
    return $input;
  }

  // assuming the URL already has a rel attribute, change its value to nofollow
  $x = preg_replace('#(rel\s*=\s*([\'"]?))((?(3)[^\'"]*|[^\'" ]*))([\'"]?)#i',
                    '\\1\\3,nofollow\\4', $input);

  // if the string has been modified, it means it already had a rel attribute,
  // whose value has been changed to nofollow, so we return the new version
  if ($x != $input)
  {
    return $x;
  }
  // if the link in the input string doesn't have ref attribute, we add it
```

```
    else
    {
      return preg_replace('#<a#i', '<a rel="nofollow"', $input);
    }
}

?>
```

2. Edit your existing `include/config.inc.php` file by adding the whitelist definition, as high-lighted in the following code snippet. If you don't have this file from previous exercises, create it and write the necessary code. (Only the definition for `$GLOBALS['whitelist']` is required for this exercise.)

```
<?php

// site domain; no trailing '/' !
define('SITE_DOMAIN', 'http://seophp.example.com');

// create a fictional database with products and categories
$GLOBALS['products'] = array
        ("45" => "Belt Sander",
         "31" => "Link Juice",
         "42" => "AJAX PHP Book");
$GLOBALS['categories'] = array
        ("12" => "Carpenter's Tools",
         "6" => "SEO Toolbox",
         "2" => "Friend's Shed");

// define array of accepted links
$GLOBALS['whitelist'] = array('seophp.example.com', 'www.seoegghead.com');

?>
```

3. Create a file named `comments.php` in the `seophp` folder, with this code:

```
<?php
// load the nofollow library
require_once 'include/nofollow.inc.php';
?>

<!DOCTYPE html PUBLIC "-//W3C//DTD XHTML 1.1//EN"
 "http://www.w3.org/TR/xhtml11/DTD/xhtml11.dtd">
<html>
  <head>
    <title>Professional Search Engine Optimization with PHP: Comments</title>
  </head>
  <body>
    <h1>Old comments:</h1>

<?php

// display first comment
echo noFollowLinks('<p>Hello! Take a look at <a
href="http://too.much.spam">cool@@ta
```

```
link</a>!</p>');

// display second comment
echo noFollowLinks('<p>We\'ve just released our new product, <a href="http://@@ta
seophp.example.com/Products/SEO-Toolbox-C6/Link-Juice-P31.html">Link Juice</a>@@ta
.</p>');

?>

    </body>
</html>
```

4. Load `http://seophp.example.com/comments.php`, and expect to get the result shown in Figure 8-5.

5. Excellent, the links show up correctly on the web page. To verify this worked as expected, view the HTML source. If you're using Internet Explorer, right-click the page and choose View Source. The HTML source should reveal you have generated `nofollow` just for the first link — see Figure 8-6.

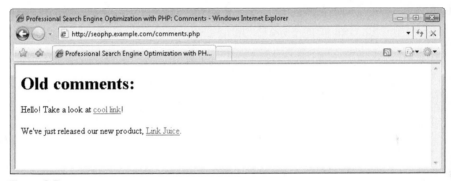

Figure 8-5

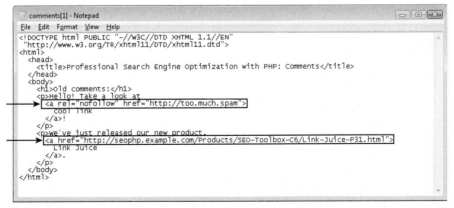

Figure 8-6

Note that we've formatted the HTML code in Figure 8-6 manually in the file for better clarity. Web browsers read the HTML code in the same way regardless of how it's formatted.

The script gracefully handles modifying the `rel` attribute if it already exists. Your `$whitelist` should include the host of the current site, or other sites that you you're happy to link to. This allows fully qualified internal links to work as they should. It also does not touch any link that does not start with `http://` because those links, by definition, are from the current site.

Using the "nofollow library" is very simple. Instead of displaying content that may contain a link as-is, you should filter it through the `noFollowLinks` function, as you did in `comments.php`:

```php
<?php

// display first comment
echo noFollowLinks('<p>Hello! Take a look at <a
href="http://too.much.spam">cool@@ta
link</a>!</p>');

// display second comment
echo noFollowLinks('<p>We\'ve just released our new product, <a href="http://@@ta
seophp.example.com/Products/SEO-Toolbox-C6/Link-Juice-P31.html">Link Juice</a>@@ta
.</p>');

?>
```

For this to work properly, you need to define the "white list," which is the list of allowed hosts, in `config.inc.php`. The exercise only defined `seophp.example.com` and `www.seoegghead.com`:

```php
// define array of accepted links
$GLOBALS['whitelist'] = array('seophp.example.com', 'www.seoegghead.com');
```

The logic of the code in the function is pretty clear, until you get into the details of the regular expressions involved, which are more complex than those from the previous chapters. We leave understanding the code to you as an exercise. If you haven't already, you should read Chapter 3 for a practical introduction to regular expressions. Appendix A is an even more friendly and thorough introduction to regular expressions.

Sanitizing User Input

A similar problem exists with regard to any user-provided content, such as blog comments, guest books, and forum posts. In that case as well, you must take care to remove any potentially malicious content. There are two approaches to achieving this.

You can entirely disable HTML by escaping it as you did in the exercise with `htmlspecialchars()`. Here's an example:

```php
echo htmlspecialchars($guest_book_post_content)
```

instead of

```php
echo($guest_book_post_content);
```

Sometimes, however, it is desirable to permit a limited dialect of HTML tags. To that end it is necessary to sanitize the input by removing only potentially malicious tags and attributes (or, because achieving security is easier as such — allow only tags and attributes that *cannot* be used maliciously).

Some applications take the approach of using a proprietary markup language instead of HTML. A similar topic was discussed in Chapter 6 in the section "Using a Custom Markup Language to Generate SE-Friendly HTML," but to a different end — enhancing on-page HTML optimization. It can also be used to ensure that content is sanitized. In this case, you would execute htmlspecialchars() *over or strip the HTML, then also use a translation function and a limited set of proprietary tags such as* {link} *and* {/link}, {image} *and* {/image}, *to permit only certain functionality. This is the approach of many forum web applications such as vBulletin and phpBB. And indeed for specific applications where users are constantly engaged in dialog and willing to learn the proprietary markup language, this makes sense. However, for such things as a comment or guest book, HTML provides a common denominator that most users know, and allowing a restrictive dialect is probably more prudent with regard to usability. That is the solution discussed here.*

As usual, in order to keep your code tidy, group the HTML sanitizing functionality into a separate file. Go through the following quick exercise, where you create and use this new little library. The code is discussed afterwards.

Sanitizing User Input

1. Create a new file named `sanitize.inc.php` in your `seophp/include` folder, and write this code:

```php
<?php

// sanitizes the HTML code in $inputHTML
function sanitizeHTML(
    $inputHTML,
    $allowed_tags = array('<h1>', '<b>', '<i>', '<a>',
                          '<ul>', '<li>', '<pre>', '<hr>',
                          '<blockquote>', '<img>'))
{
  $_allowed_tags = implode('', $allowed_tags);
  $inputHTML = strip_tags($inputHTML, $_allowed_tags);
  return preg_replace('#<(.*?)>#ise', "'<' . removeBadAttributes('\\1') . '>'" ,
$inputHTML);
}

// removes the unallowed attributes from $inputHTML
function removeBadAttributes($inputHTML)
{
  // define the list of unallowed attributes
  $bad_attributes = 'onerror|onmousemove|onmouseout|onmouseover|' .
                    'onkeypress|onkeydown|onkeyup|javascript:';

  // remove the bad attributes and return the result
  return stripslashes(preg_replace("#($bad_attributes)(\s*)(?==)#is" ,
                    'SANITIZED', $inputHTML));
}

?>
```

2. Modify `comments.php` by adding a third comment that contains an unaccepted `onerror` attribute. You're also including a reference to `sanitize.inc.php`:

```php
<?php
// load the nofollow library
require_once 'include/nofollow.inc.php';
// load the sanitize library
require_once 'include/sanitize.inc.php';
?>

<!DOCTYPE html PUBLIC "-//W3C//DTD XHTML 1.1//EN"
 "http://www.w3.org/TR/xhtml11/DTD/xhtml11.dtd">
<html>
  <head>
    <title>Professional Search Engine Optimization with PHP: Comments</title>
  </head>
  <body>
    <h1>Old comments:</h1>

<?php
// display first comment
echo noFollowLinks('<p>Hello! Take a look at <a href="http://too.much.spam">cool
link</a>!</p>');

// display second comment
echo noFollowLinks('<p>We\'ve just released our new product, <a
href="http://seophp.example.com/Products/SEO-Toolbox-C6/Link-Juice-P31.html">Link
Juice</a>.</p>');

// display third comment
$inHTML = '<p>Sanitizing <img src="INVALID-IMAGE"' .
          'onerror="location.href=\'http://too.much.spam/\'">!</p>';
echo $inHTML;

?>

  </body>
</html>
```

3. Note you haven't sanitized the input `$inHTML` yet. Take a look at what happens without the sanitizing function applied. Loading `http://seophp.example.com/comments.php` should redirect you automatically to `http://too.much.spam/`, as shown in Figure 8-7. This address doesn't exist, obviously, but the exercise proved how easy is to implement such redirects if the data isn't escaped.

4. Now, try to take out the sanitizing function by updating `comments.php`. Find this line:

```php
echo $inHTML;
```

    and replace it with this line:

```php
echo sanitizeHTML($inHTML);
```

5. Now load `http://seophp.example.com/comments.php` once again. Fortunately, this time you will not be redirected to the spam site, as it happened earlier. You should get the output shown in Figure 8-8.

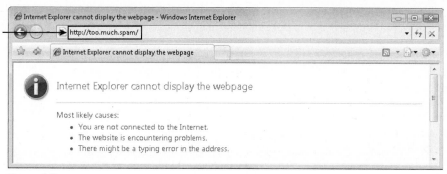

Figure 8-7

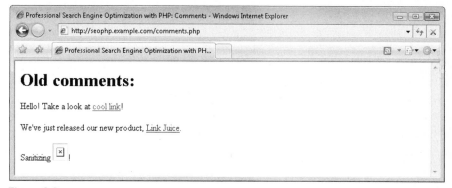

Figure 8-8

6. It's also worth looking at the source code of the page. In Figure 8-9 you can see that your script changed the `onerror` attribute to `SANITIZED`. (Once again, we've reformatted the HTML source manually a little bit to make it more readable.)

```
comments[1] - Notepad
File  Edit  Format  View  Help
<!DOCTYPE html PUBLIC "-//W3C//DTD XHTML 1.1//EN"
 "http://www.w3.org/TR/xhtml11/DTD/xhtml11.dtd">
<html>
  <head>
    <title>Professional Search Engine Optimization with PHP: Comments</title>
  </head>
  <body>
    <h1>old comments:</h1>
      <p>
        Hello! Take a look at <a rel="nofollow" href="http://too.much.spam">cool link</a>!
      </p>
      <p>
        we've just released our new product,
        <a href="http://seophp.example.com/Products/SEO-Toolbox-C6/Link-Juice-P31.html">
        Link Juice</a>.
      </p>
      Sanitizing <img src="INVALID-IMAGE" SANITIZED="location.href='http://too.much.spam/'">
  </body>
</html>
```

Figure 8-9

To sanitize user input, you simply call the `sanitizeHTML()` function on the user-provided input. It will strip any tags that are not in the variable `$allowed_tags`, as well as common attributes that can be cleverly used to execute JavaScript.

Without executing `sanitizeHTML()` over the input HTML, the cleverly constructed HTML would redirect to `http://too.much.spam`. The event `onerror` is executed upon an error. Because the image `INVALID-IMAGE` does not exist (which causes an error), it executes the `onerror` event, `location.href='http://www.spamsite.com'`, causing the redirection.

After executing `sanitizeHTML()`, `onerror` is replaced with `SANITIZED`, and nothing occurs.

> The `sanitizeHTML` function does not typically return valid HTML. In practice, this does not matter, because this function is really designed as a stopgap method to prevent spam. The modified HTML code will not likely cause any problems in browsers or search engines, either. Eventually, the content would be deleted or edited by the site owner anyway.

Having such "black hat" content within a web site can damage both the human as well as a search engine perception of reputation. Embedding JavaScript-based redirects can raise red flags in search engine algorithms and may result in penalties and web site bans. It is therefore of the utmost importance to address and mitigate these concerns.

Note that the nofollow library was not used in this latest example, but you could combine nofollow with sanitize to obtain a better result, like this:

```
// display third comment
$inHTML = '<p>Sanitizing <img src="INVALID-IMAGE"' .
          'onerror="location.href=\'http://too.much.spam/\'">!</p>';
$sanitized = noFollowLinks(sanitizeHTML($inHTML));
echo $sanitized;
```

Lastly, your implementations — both `noFollowLinks()` and `sanitizeHTML()` — will not exhaustively block *every* attack, or allow the flexibility some programmers require. They do, however, make a spammer's life much more difficult, and he or she will likely proceed to an easier target. A project called safe-html by Pixel-Apes is a more robust solution. It is open-source and written in PHP. You can find it at `http://pixel-apes.com/safehtml/`.

Requesting Human Input

One common problem webmasters and developers need to consider are the automatic spam robots, which submit comments on unprotected blogs or other web sites that support comments.

The typical solution to this problem is to use what is called a "CAPTCHA" image that requires the visitor to read a graphical version of text with some sort of obfuscation. A typical human can read the image, but an automated script cannot. This approach, however, unfortunately presents usability problems, because blind users can no longer access the functionality therein. For more information on this type of CAPTCHA, visit `http://freshmeat.net/projects/kcaptcha/`. An improvement on this scheme is an alternative recording of the same information. This is used to overcome the usability issues presented by CAPTCHA.

As a more simple but effective example, in the following exercise you create a small library that asks simple math questions with random operands. Call it SimpleCAPTCHA.

Using SimpleCAPTCHA

1. Start off by installing a required external library. Numbers_Words is a PEAR library that transforms numbers to words, and you're using it to make it harder for an automated script to parse your forms and calculate the results. The official page of the package is http://pear.php.net/package/Numbers_Words.

   PEAR offers a simple installation script. Open a command-line editor in the folder that contains pear.php. If you're using XAMPP as instructed in Chapter 1, the folder will be \Program Files\xampp\php. To browse to that folder using a command-line console, type this command:

   ```
   cd \Program Files\xampp\php
   ```

   At this moment your command-line console will look as shown in Figure 8-10.

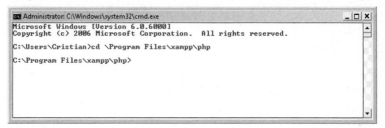

   Figure 8-10

2. To install the Numbers_Words package, you need to execute this command:

   ```
   pear install Numbers_Words
   ```

   If the Numbers_Words package hasn't reached a stable version (as is the case at the moment of writing this chapter), you need to explicitly mention the beta version that you want to install, like this:

   ```
   pear install channel://pear.php.net/Numbers_Words-0.15.0
   ```

   You should get a package confirmation message such as the following:

   ```
   >pear install channel://pear.php.net/Numbers_Words-0.15.0
   downloading Numbers_Words-0.15.0.tgz ...
   Starting to download Numbers_Words-0.15.0.tgz (44,854 bytes)
   ...........done: 44,854 bytes
   install ok: channel://pear.php.net/Numbers_Words-0.15.0
   ```

   At this point you can close the command-line console.

3. In your `seophp/include` library, create a file named `simple_captcha.inc.php`, and then type this code in:

```php
<?php
// load Words library
require_once('Numbers/Words.php');

// SimpleCAPTCHA library
class SimpleCAPTCHA
{
  // verify answer
  function check_answer($answer, $hash)
  {
    return (md5(trim($answer) . $_SERVER['SERVER_ADDR']) == $hash);
  }

  // generate question
  function get_question($max_1, $max_2)
  {
    // define standard question formats
    $question_formats = array(
    'What is %s plus %s?',
    'What is the sum of %s and %s?',
    'What is %s added to %s?',
    'What is %s + %s?'
    );

    // generate random numbers
    $number_1 = rand(0, $max_1);
    $number_2 = rand(0, $max_2);

    // transforms the numbers to words
    $number_1_words = Numbers_Words::toWords($number_1);
    $number_2_words = Numbers_Words::toWords($number_2);

    // generate a random question
    $question = sprintf($question_formats[rand(0,
                          sizeof($question_formats) - 1)],
                    $number_1_words,
                    $number_2_words);

    // returns the question and the hash of the result
    return array('question' => $question,
      'hash' => md5(($number_1 + $number_2) . $_SERVER['SERVER_ADDR']));
  }

  // generates demo form
  function display_demo_form()
  {
  $gq = SimpleCAPTCHA::get_question(1000, 10);
  echo '<form>';
  echo $gq['question'];
```

```php
echo '<input type="text" name="response">';
echo '<input type="hidden" name="hash" value="' . $gq['hash'] . '">';
echo '</form>';
}
}

?>
```

4. Modify `comments.php` as highlighted:

```php
<?php
// load the nofollow library
require_once 'include/nofollow.inc.php';
// load the sanitize library
require_once 'include/sanitize.inc.php';
// load simple CAPTCHA library
require_once 'include/simple_captcha.inc.php';
?>


...
...


// display third comment
$inHTML = '<p>Sanitizing <img src="INVALID-IMAGE"' .
          'onerror="location.href=\'http://too.much.spam/\'">!</p>';
echo sanitizeHTML($inHTML);

// display CAPTCHA question
SimpleCAPTCHA::display_demo_form();
// display answer
if (isset($_GET['response']) && isset($_GET['hash']))
{
  if(SimpleCAPTCHA::check_answer($_GET['response'], $_GET['hash']))
  {
    echo 'Correct!';
  }
  else
  {
    echo 'Wrong answer!';
  }
}

?>

  </body>
</html>
```

5. Load `http://seophp.example.com/comments.php` and type an answer in the text box, as shown in Figure 8-11.

6. After hitting Enter, you should be told if the answer was correct or not, as shown in Figure 8-12.

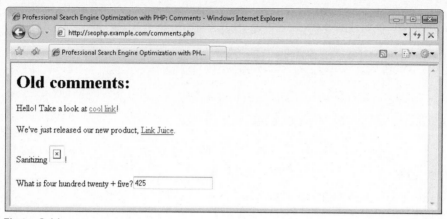

Figure 8-11

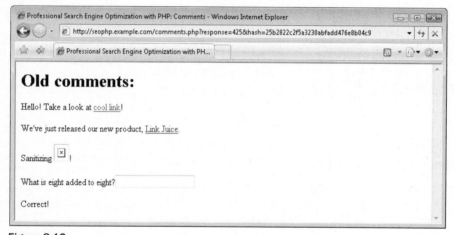

Figure 8-12

Using the simple CAPTCHA library, it's quite easy to implement a simple "human" check before you accept a comment submission.

This little script is still not bulletproof. It can be improved by implementing a more complex mechanism such as the use of obfuscated images. However, the script does its job nicely and it's appropriate to be used on small web sites.

To include the CAPTCHA question in a page, you simply need to include the simple CAPTCHA library, and then call the `display_demo_form()` method somewhere on the page:

```
// display CAPTCHA question
SimpleCAPTCHA::display_demo_form();
```

This call will generate a form like this:

```
<form>What is six hundred fifty-seven + five?
  <input type="text" name="response">
  <input type="hidden" name="hash" value="be3159ad04564bfb90db9e32851ebf9c">
</form>
```

The hidden hash field contains the *hashed* version of the correct answer.

What Is Hashing?

Hashing is a means by which you obtain a unique calculated value that represents another object. Different objects should always have different hash values. The two most popular hashing algorithms are MD5 (Message Digest 5 — http://en.wikipedia.org/wiki/MD5) and SHA (Secure Hash Algorithm — http://en.wikipedia.org/wiki/SHA-1).

The hash value of a piece of data is calculated by applying a mathematical function (the hash algorithm) to that data. The property of these hashing algorithms that makes it very useful when security is involved is that you can't easily obtain the original data from its hashed version (the algorithm is effectively one-way).

Take the example at hand: the hashed value of "662" is "be3159ad04564bfb90db-9e32851ebf9c," but you couldn't obtain the original "662" value if someone told you the hash value. This property makes hashing particularly useful when storing user passwords into a database. When the user tries to authenticate, the typed password is hashed, and the resulting hash value is compared to the hash value of the original (correct) password, which was stored when the user initially created his or her password. If the two values are identical, the entered password is correct. You do not even need to store the passwords to authenticate users.

When the form is submitted, the response typed by the visitor, together with the visitor's IP address, are hashed, and the hash value is compared to the known hashed version of the correct answer. When the form is submitted, it passes through GET both the answer submitted by the visitor, and the hash value of the known correct answer:

```
http://localhost/seophp/comments.php?response=662&hash=
be3159ad04564bfb90db9e32851ebf9c
```

The IP address — retrieved using $_SERVER['SERVER_ADDR'] — was added to the mix, so that a potential attacker will not be able to take a known "good" URL, which has a matching answer and hash value, and use it to submit information.

Your comments.php script calls the check_answer() method of SimpleCAPTCHA to check if the hashed version of the provided answer is the same as the hashed version of the known correct answer:

```
// display answer
if (isset($_GET['response']) && isset($_GET['hash']))
{
  if(SimpleCAPTCHA::check_answer($_GET['response'], $_GET['hash']))
  {
    echo 'Correct!';
  }
  else
  {
    echo 'Wrong answer!';
  }
}
```

The code of check_answer() itself is pretty simple. It returns true if the hash value of the answer plus the visitor's IP address is equal to the known hash value of the correct answer:

```
// SimpleCAPTCHA library
class SimpleCAPTCHA
{
  // verify answer
  function check_answer($answer, $hash)
  {
    return (md5(trim($answer) . $_SERVER['SERVER_ADDR']) == $hash);
  }
```

Note that you use the MD5 (Message Digest 5) hashing algorithm, which is the most widely used hashing algorithm. Another popular hashing algorithm, which is generally agreed to be more secure (although a bit slower) is SHA (Secure Hash Algorithm).

301 Redirect Attacks

A legitimate site will often employ a script that redirects URLs, as part of an internal linking scheme, using URLs like this:

```
http://www.example.com/redirect.php?url=http://another.example.com
```

In this case, the redirect.php script would redirect to the URL specified by the url parameter. The problem comes when a 301 redirect is used. The fact that such a redirection link can be altered to point to any other URL is manifest from the URL itself. And a 301 redirect may be interpreted as a vote. Black hat SEOs will link to such a URL from many spam sites so as to acquire a vote.

You may want to revisit Chapter 4 for more details on the HTTP status codes and redirection.

For example, someone from http://too.much.spam/ may post links, on their site or others, to URLs such as http://www.example.com/redirect.php?url=http://too.much.spam/. If these links do

301 redirects to `http://too.much.spam/`, a search engine would interpret that the content at `http://www.example.com` was moved to `http://too.much.spam/`, effectively giving credit to the latter site.

> **This practice can also be applied to humans, and, in that case, is called "phishing."
> The attacker tries to suggest, to human visitors and to search engines, that your
> site (`http://www.example.com/`) is in some way is associated with `http://too.much.spam/`. Popular, old web sites should be particularly careful, because
> the potential benefits that can be achieved through phishing are significant.**
>
> **An example involving a previous *Google* "phishing" vulnerability is cited here:**
>
> `http://ha.ckers.org/blog/20060807/google-spam-redirects/`

If you use such a redirection script in your site, there are three possible solutions to prevent 301 attacks:

- ❏ Use a 302 redirect instead of 301
- ❏ Use `robots.txt` to exclude `redirect.php`
- ❏ Use a database-driven solution, so that `http://www.example.com` redirects only known links

Any of these solutions will suffice. The last is usually unnecessary for most sites, but it's mentioned here because, theoretically, leaving a script like that can be used by a social engineer to assert that your site advocates any other site to a non-sophisticated layman — phishing.

Using a 302 Redirect

As discussed in Chapter 4, 302 redirects do not transfer any link equity, and therefore have little value from a spammer's perspective. However, they may potentially have a use to "phishers," as mentioned later.

```php
<?php
$new_url = $_GET["url"];
header('HTTP/1.1 302 Found');
header("Location: $new_url");
?>
```

Using robots.txt to Exclude redirect.php

This technique can be used in addition to using a 302 redirect. It, however, does not prevent "phishing," either. Read Chapter 5, if you haven't already, for more details on the `robots.txt` file.

```
User-agent: *
Disallow: /redirect.php
```

Using a Database-Driven Solution

You could store the URL (either embedded in the script itself, or in a database), instead of embedding it visibly in the URL:

```php
<?php
// define URL lookup table
$lookup_table = array(
```

```
    0=>'http://www.example.com/0',
    1=>'http://www.example.com/1',
    2=>'http://www.example.com/2');

// perform redirect
header('HTTP/1.1 302 Found');
header('Location:'. $lookup_table[$_GET['url_id']]);
?>
```

Your URLs in this case would look like `http://www.example.com/redirect.php?redirect_id=` `[number]`, and eliminate problems.

With this solution, you're also free to use 301 redirects, which can be beneficial because 301 redirects count as votes. (However, never do 301 redirects when the URL can be freely modified.)

If you already have a web site that redirects to the URL specified as query string parameter, you could also simply verify that it's a known URL before performing the redirect, like this:

```
<?php
// define URL lookup table
$lookup_table = array(
    0=>'http://www.example.com/0',
    1=>'http://www.example.com/1',
    2=>'http://www.example.com/2');

// extract destination URL
if (isset($_GET['url']))
{
    $url = $_GET['url'];
}

// perform redirect only if the target URL is known
if (isset($url) && in_array($url, $lookup_table))
{
    header('HTTP/1.1 302 Found');
    header('Location: '.$url);
}
?>
```

Content Theft

This concept is detailed in Chapter 9, where the use of sitemaps is discussed. A black hat SEO may employ the use of scripts to lift part or even all of another site's content — using an RSS feed perhaps, or screen scraping. Many take various pieces of content from many sites and glue them together, leading to what Chris Boggs, director of online marketing of Cs Group terms as "Frankenstein content." The spammers who take a site's content verbatim are more of a concern, however, and using sitemaps may prevent, or at least reduce, the necessity of a cease and desist order.

If you know the IP address of a script on a web server scraping the content, it can also be blocked with the following `.htaccess` directives (where `xxx.xxx.xxx.xxx` is the IP address):

```
RewriteEngine on
RewriteCond %{REMOTE_HOST} ^xxx\.xxx\.xxx\.xxx$
RewriteRule .? - [F]
```

On Buying Links

As a result of the new focus on link-building to acquire relevant links, instead of the historical focus on on-page factors (discussed in Chapter 2), an entire industry of link-buying sprung up. This is expected, because it is a natural reaction by the search engine marketing industry to facilitate their jobs. It is Matt Cutts' (of Google) opinion that purchased links should include a `rel="nofollow"` attribute. However, in practice this has proven to be Matt Cutts' wishful thinking, because this policy has never been widely adopted for obvious reasons.

We consider buying links completely ethical, so long as the links are semantically related. Realistically, a content provider can reject placing your link on their site if it is not relevant, and if they consider it as relevant, there is no reason to include the `rel="nofollow"` attribute. Therefore, in our opinion Matt Cutts' argument doesn't approximate an analogy of traditional marketing. Therefore, buying links, when done properly, is not a black hat technique. When done aggressively and improperly, it may, however, be perceived as spamming by a search engine.

Digital Point Co-op, Link Vault

Both Digital Point Co-op (`http://www.digitalpoint.com/tools/ad-network/`) and Link Vault (`http://www.link-vault.com`) are advertising networks that operate on the premise that they are promoting sites on other semantically related sites. In reality, however, their real purpose is questioned by many. We will form no clear conclusion here, but using such techniques may be against the guidelines of search engines and can result in penalties when used in excess.

Link Vault is probably safe when used in small doses, but the other networks like Digital Point Co-op, which advertise their existence with an invisible one-pixel image in the ad copy (for tracking), are extremely dangerous in our opinion. And though it hasn't provably gotten anyone into major trouble yet, it may in the future. If we can write a regular expression with ease that detects Digital Point links, can anyone reasonably conclude that Google cannot detect it? Google can clearly proceed to at least *devalue* those links.

Summary

This chapter summarizes the black hat techniques that are requisite background material for every search engine marketer. We do not advocate the use of any of these techniques. Understanding them, however, may provide insight as to how a competitor is ranking. It may also serve as an education, in that it will prevent the inadvertent use of such questionable tactics in the future. Lastly, it prevents you from being the victim of certain black hat techniques that can be detrimental to your web site.

9

Sitemaps

A sitemap provides an easy way for both humans and search engines to reference pages of your web site from one central location. Usually, the sitemap enumerates all, or at least the important, pages of a site. This is beneficial for humans in that it can be a navigational aide, and for search engines, because it may help a web site get spidered more quickly and comprehensively.

In this chapter you learn about:

- ❑ The two types of sitemaps: traditional sitemaps and search engine sitemaps.
- ❑ The Google XML sitemaps standard.
- ❑ The Yahoo! plaintext sitemaps standard.
- ❑ The new sitemaps.org standard — soon to be implemented by all search engines.

You'll implement PHP code that generates both Google and Yahoo! search engine sitemaps programmatically. But first, this chapter starts at the beginning and talks about traditional sitemaps.

Traditional Sitemaps

A traditional sitemap is simply an HTML web page that contains links to the various pages of your web site. Typically the traditional sitemap breaks down the referenced pages into groupings for easy reading. This kind of sitemap is generally designed to assist humans in navigating, but search engine marketers realized early on that it had a beneficial side effect of helping spiders to crawl a site.

Historically, search engines did not crawl very deeply into a web site, and it helped to link pages located deeper in the site hierarchy (that is, one must traverse many pages to arrive there) from a sitemap page. Today, that particular problem is *mostly* squashed (search engines now do a much better job at crawling more deeply), but a sitemap may still assist in getting such pages spidered faster. It may also improve their rankings somewhat by providing an additional internal link.

Traditional sitemaps, as well as search engine sitemaps (discussed next), are especially useful to cite pages that are not linked anywhere else in a web site's navigation. Indeed, the Google sitemap help page says that *"sitemaps are particularly beneficial when users can't reach all areas of a website through a browseable interface."*

Creating a traditional sitemap is done as any other web page is. It can be created by hand, or generated dynamically using PHP. The sitemap page should be linked to in the navigation or footer of every web page in your web site — or at least on the home page. For larger sites, it may make sense to create a multiple page sitemap, partitioned into sections somehow, because we recommend not having too many links on a page. Please refer to Chapter 6, "SE-Friendly HTML and JavaScript," for recommendations regarding internal linking and pagination.

> *We used that unfortunate vague qualifier again — "too many." As usual, there really is no concrete definition for "too many," and it varies by search engine, but search engine marketers usually cite an upper limit of 50 to 100 links per page.*

Search Engine Sitemaps

Search engine sitemaps are not for human consumption. Rather, they are specifically designed to facilitate search engines to spider a web site. Especially if a site has added or modified content deep within its navigation, it may take many weeks before a search spider takes note of the changes without any assistance. Likewise, if a web page is referenced nowhere in a web site's navigational structure, it will not get spidered without any assistance, either.

> **We do question how well such an orphaned page would rank (that is, one that is referenced only by a search engine sitemap), and we would recommend using a traditional sitemap in any case, because it *does* provide an internal link whereas a search engine sitemap does not.**

Search engine sitemaps provide this assistance. Google and Yahoo! both have implementations in that vein. MSN search does not offer one at the time of writing. However, the end of this chapter points to a new unified standard that all search engines will eventually adhere to.

Search engine sitemaps do *not* replace the traditional spidering of a site, so a site will continue to get spidered normally. But if their systems notice changes via these sitemaps, a spider will visit the included URLs more quickly.

You can see how a traditional sitemap accomplishes some of the same things that a search engine sitemap does. Because the traditional sitemap is linked prominently on the web site, it is frequently spidered. Thus, by linking deep content on a traditional sitemap page, you can accomplish most of the same goals, but it is still advantageous to create a search engine sitemap.

For example, you can inform Google how often a page is likely to change, or that a change occurred with a later timestamp on a web page. You can also "ping" Google to inform it of changes within the actual sitemap.

> *By the same token, if the timestamps are out of date, providing a sitemap can actually be detrimental. If you do choose to provide timestamps, you must dutifully update it when changes occur!*

We recommend using both traditional and search engine sitemaps.

> Let's also note one lesser-known benefit of using sitemaps — mitigation of the damage as a result of content theft and scraper sites. Unfortunately, on the web there are unsavory characters who, without permission, lift content from your web site and place it on theirs.
>
> These sites are called *most* affectionately "scraper sites," but when it happens to you, they're called much less affectionate terms. One of the most difficult challenges search engines face is assigning the original author of content that is duplicated in several places. As discussed in Chapter 5, search engines aim to filter duplicate content from their indices. When you get filtered as a result of scrapers stealing your content, it can be particularly difficult to resolve. If a well-ranked scraper site (they do exist) gets spidered with your content before you do, *your web site content* may be deemed the duplicate! Because search engine sitemaps will get your new web pages spidered more quickly, they may help in avoiding some of these content-theft snafus.

The Yahoo! sitemap protocol is less popular than the Google protocol, but this chapter demonstrates code that allows both to be created with the same PHP code. Thus, it is worthwhile to support both formats, because it will require minimal effort. Because the Yahoo! sitemap protocol uses only a subset of the information that the Google sitemap protocol does, if provided, that information will simply be ignored when the Yahoo! sitemap is created.

Google and Yahoo! both also support reading news feeds in the formats of RSS and Atom. These formats may suffice for blogs and certain content management systems; often, they are provided by such applications by default. The problem with these implementations is that they usually only enumerate the newest content, and this is only really suitable for a blog. If you are doing search engine optimization for a blog, feel free to skip this chapter and use the feed functionality provided by your blog application instead. Also, theoretically it would be possible to create an RSS or Atom feed with all URLs as a sitemap for a site that is not a blog, but this is probably not what Yahoo! or Google expects, and we would not recommend it.

Using Google Sitemaps

Google has a very elaborate standard for providing a sitemap. It allows a webmaster to provide information in several formats, but the preferred format is an XML-based standard specified by Google. Google claims that using Google Sitemaps will result in "a smarter crawl because you can tell [them] when a page was last modified or how frequently a page changes." For more information regarding Google Sitemaps, visit http://www.google.com/webmasters/sitemaps/. There is also a Google-run Sitemaps blog at http://sitemaps.blogspot.com/.

However, according to Google, "using this protocol does not guarantee that your web pages will be included in search indexes," and "… using this protocol will not influence the way your pages are ranked by Google." Creating a sitemap for your site entails the following:

1. Creating a Google account, if you don't have one: https://www.google.com/accounts/NewAccount.

2. Creating a sitemap file.

3. Adding the sitemap to your account.

4. Verifying the site. This implies making a certain change to your site, so that Google will know you're a person authorized to modify the site. Doing so involves the addition of a randomly named file or meta-tag to your web site. To maintain Google sitemap functionality, these must not be removed once added.

Please see `http://www.google.com/support/webmasters/bin/answer.py?answer=34592&topic=8482` for more details about this procedure.

The Google Sitemaps service also allows you to see if there are any issues with the crawling of a site; these include errors returned by your server (404, 500, and so on), errors as a result of networking, and so on. It also gives you a list of URLs as restricted by `robots.txt` *and various statistics useful for analysis.*

As soon as you've finished the registration process, you can create the sitemap file named `sitemap.xml` in the root of your web site, and then submit this file using the Google Sitemaps page. `sitemap.xml` could look like this:

```xml
<?xml version="1.0" encoding="UTF-8"?>
<urlset xmlns="http://www.google.com/schemas/sitemap/0.84">
  <url>
    <loc>http://www.cristiandarie.ro/</loc>
    <lastmod>2006-09-17</lastmod>
    <changefreq>weekly</changefreq>
    <priority>0.5</priority>
  </url>
  <url>
    <loc>http://www.cristiandarie.ro/books/</loc>
    <lastmod>2006-09-17</lastmod>
    <changefreq>weekly</changefreq>
    <priority>0.8</priority>
  </url>
  <url>
    <loc>http://www.cristiandarie.ro/forthcoming/</loc>
    <lastmod>2006-09-17</lastmod>
    <changefreq>weekly</changefreq>
    <priority>0.2</priority>
  </url>
</urlset>
```

The file contains a `<url>` element for each URL that you need to include. The children of this element have these meanings:

❑ `<loc>` specifies the URL.

❑ `<lastmod>` specifies the last modification date for the URL. The date is written in ISO 8601 format, which is YYYY-MM-DD. The standard also supports a number of alternative notations, and also supports the inclusion of the time. ISO 8601 is very nicely described at http://www.iso.org/iso/en/prods-services/popstds/datesandtime.html.

❑ <changefreq> tells Google how often the page changes. The possible values are always (for pages that change with each request), hourly, daily, weekly, monthly, yearly, and never.

❑ <priority> lets you tell Google how you evaluate the importance of individual pages of your web site as compared to the others. The value is a number between 0.0 and 1.0. Please note that the <priority> element only has significance over the relative importance of pages *within* a web site, and it *does not* affect the overall ranking of a web site!

Using Yahoo! Sitemaps

Yahoo!'s sitemap protocol is considerably simpler than Google's protocol. It too supports several formats including news feeds, but the format discussed here is the flat URL list plaintext file. It does not utilize XML, nor does it ask for any information other than a list of URLs delimited by linefeeds. Yahoo! requires that a file named urllist.txt appear in the root directory of a web site, and that you register a Yahoo! account with them.

The site must then be added at http://submit.search.yahoo.com/free/request. Arguably, Yahoo! accomplishes some of what Google does with its simpler approach — though it does not accept information regarding last modified dates, estimates of update frequency, or the relative importance of the pages. Yahoo! also cannot be pinged regarding sitemap updates.

The Yahoo! sitemaps equivalent of the previously shown Google sitemap would be a file named urllist.txt in the root directory of a web site with the following contents:

```
http://www.cristiandarie.ro/
http://www.cristiandarie.ro/books/
http://www.cristiandarie.ro/forthcoming/
```

Like Google, using Yahoo!'s sitemap protocol will not influence a web site's rankings, but it may get a site spidered more quickly.

Generating Sitemaps Programmatically

It would be useful to have a library that can create Yahoo! and Google sitemaps programmatically using the same information. The exercise that follows demonstrates such a library.

You'll create a class named Sitemap, which can store a number of links from your site, and generate the associated Yahoo! and Google sitemap files for you. (The notion of *class*, as well as the basic notions of object-oriented programming with PHP, was explained in Chapter 7, when you used it for the first time in this book.)

Generating Sitemaps

1. In your `seophp/include` folder, create a new file named `sitemap.inc.php`, with this code:

```php
<?php

// sitemap generator class
class Sitemap
{
  // constructor receives the list of URLs to include in the sitemap
  function Sitemap($items = array())
  {
    $this->_items = $items;
  }

  // add a new sitemap item
  function addItem($url,
                   $lastmod = '',
                   $changefreq = '',
                   $priority = '',
                   $additional_fields = array())
  {
    $this->_items[] = array_merge(array('loc' => $url,
                                        'lastmod' => $lastmod,
                                        'changefreq' => $changefreq,
                                        'priority' => $priority),
                                  $additional_fields);
  }

  // get Google sitemap
  function getGoogle()
  {
    ob_start();
    header('Content-type: text/xml');
    echo '<?xml version="1.0" encoding="UTF-8"?>';
    echo '<urlset xmlns="http://www.google.com/schemas/sitemap/0.84">';
    foreach ($this->_items as $i)
    {
      echo '<url>';
      foreach ($i as $index => $_i)
      {
        if (!$_i) continue;
        echo "<$index>" . $this->_escapeXML($_i) . "</$index>";
      }
      echo '</url>';
    }
    echo '</urlset>';
    return ob_get_clean();
  }

  // get Yahoo sitemap
  function getYahoo()
  {
    ob_start();
```

```
    header('Content-type: text/plain');
    foreach ($this->_items as $i)
    {
      echo $i['loc'] . "\n";
    }
    return ob_get_clean();
  }

  // escape string characters for inclusion in XML structure
  function _escapeXML($str)
  {
    $translation = get_html_translation_table(HTML_ENTITIES, ENT_QUOTES);
    foreach ($translation as $key => $value)
    {
      $translation[$key] = '&#' . ord($key) . ';';
    }
    $translation[chr(38)] = '&';
    return preg_replace("/&(?![A-Za-z]{0,4}\w{2,3};|#[0-9]{2,3};)/","&#38;" ,
                        strtr($str, $translation));
  }
}
?>
```

2. You need to add the following two rewrite rules to the `.htaccess` file in `/seophp`. If you have other entries in the file from previous exercises, just add the new rules; otherwise, create the file from scratch. (If you haven't already, see Chapter 3 for details on mod_rewrite.)

```
RewriteEngine On

# Rewrite requests for sitemap.xml
RewriteRule ^sitemap.xml$ /sitemap.php?target=google [L]

# Rewrite requests for urllist.txt
RewriteRule ^urllist.txt$ /sitemap.php?target=yahoo [L]
```

3. You need to have `url_factory.inc.php` and `config.inc.php`, which you created in Chapter 3, in your `seophp/include` folder. Feel free to take them from the code download, if needed.

4. In the `seophp` folder, create a file named `sitemap.php` and type this code in it:

```php
<?php
// redirect requests to dynamic to their keyword rich versions
require_once 'include/sitemap.inc.php';
// load configuration
require_once 'include/config.inc.php';
// load URL factory
require_once 'include/url_factory.inc.php';

// create the Sitemap object
$s = new Sitemap();

// add sitemap items
$s->addItem(SITE_DOMAIN . '/catalog.html', '2006/10/27', 'weekly');
$s->addItem(make_category_product_url(
        "Carpenter's Tools", 12, "Belt Sander", 45), '2006/10/27', 'weekly');
```

```
$s->addItem(make_category_product_url(
        "SEO & Toolbox", 6, "Link Juice", 31), '2006/10/27', 'weekly');
$s->addItem(make_category_product_url(
        "Friends' Shed", 2, "AJAX PHP Book", 42), '2006/10/27', 'weekly');

// output sitemap
if (isset($_GET['target']))
{
  // generate Google sitemap
  if (($target = $_GET['target']) == 'google')
  {
    echo $s->getGoogle();
  }
  // generate Yahoo sitemap
  else if ($target == 'yahoo')
  {
    echo $s->getYahoo();
  }
}
?>
```

5. Load `http://seophp.example.com/sitemap.xml`. You should get a Google sitemap, as shown in Figure 9-1.

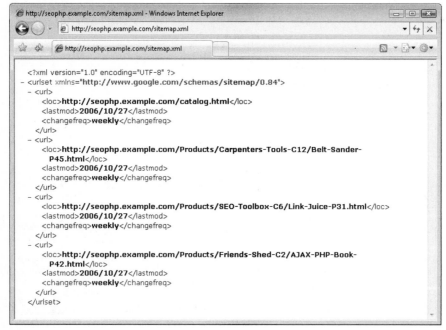

Figure 9-1

6. Load `http://seophp.example.com/urllist.txt`. You should get a Yahoo! sitemap, as shown in Figure 9-2.

Figure 9-2

The `Sitemap` class creates both Yahoo! and Google sitemap formats via the same class interface. To use it, you first create an object of the class `Sitemap`, then use the `addItem()` method to add each of your URLs. That's what you do in `sitemap.php`:

```
// create the Sitemap object
$s = new Sitemap();

// add sitemap items
$s->addItem(SITE_DOMAIN . '/catalog.html', '2006/10/27', 'weekly');
$s->addItem(make_category_product_url(
        "Carpenter's Tools", 12, "Belt Sander", 45), '2006/10/27', 'weekly');
$s->addItem(make_category_product_url(
        "SEO & Toolbox", 6, "Link Juice", 31), '2006/10/27', 'weekly');
$s->addItem(make_category_product_url(
        "Friends' Shed", 2, "AJAX PHP Book", 42), '2006/10/27', 'weekly');
```

Note that you use the `make_category_product_url()` function from the URL factory to obtain proper URLs. In a real example, the information provided to this function would be pulled from records in a database, and not specified directly in application code. But this example again illustrates how using the URL factory eases programming and enhances consistency.

The last modified date, change frequency, and priority should be provided in the formats elicited by Google sitemaps. These fields are not included in the Yahoo! sitemap. To create the sitemaps, simply call the `getGoogle()` or `getYahoo()` methods of the `Sitemap` class, respectively. Your `sitemap.php` script calls one of these methods depending on the value of the `target` query string parameter:

```
// output sitemap
if (isset($_GET['target']))
{
```

```
    // generate Google sitemap
    if (($target = $_GET['target']) == 'google')
    {
      echo $s->getGoogle();
    }
    // generate Yahoo sitemap
    else if ($target == 'yahoo')
    {
      echo $s->getYahoo();
    }
  }
```

However, the `sitemap.php` script will not be referenced directly, but through rewritten URLs. You added two entries in `.htaccess` that use mod_rewrite to rewrite requests to the Yahoo! sitemap file (`urllist.txt`) to `sitemap.php?target=yahoo`, and requests to the Google sitemap file (`sitemap.xml`) to `sitemap.php?target=google`. Here are the rewrite rules:

```
RewriteRule ^sitemap.xml$ /sitemap.php?target=google [L]
RewriteRule ^urllist.txt$ /sitemap.php?target=yahoo [L]
```

The case study in Chapter 14 demonstrates all types of sitemaps.

Informing Google about Updates

In general, Google does a pretty good job at reading your sitemap at intervals and taking note of any updates; however, you can tell Google that your sitemap has changed by making a request to this URL:

```
http://www.google.com/webmasters/sitemaps/ping?sitemap=http://seophp.example.com/
sitemap.xml
```

If you load this URL with a web browser you'll simply be informed that your sitemap has been added to the queue, and that you should register your sitemap through `http://www.google.com/webmasters/sitemaps` if you haven't already (see Figure 9-3).

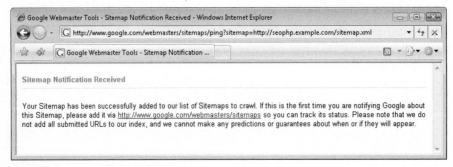

Figure 9-3

Creating such a request programmatically is simple. For example, using the cURL library, the following code would do the trick:

```
$sitemapUrl = SITE_DOMAIN . SITE_FOLDER . '/sitemap.xml';
$pingUrl = "http://www.google.com/webmasters/sitemaps/ping?sitemap=" .
urlencode($sitemapUrl);
$ch = curl_init();
curl_setopt($ch, CURLOPT_URL, $pingUrl);
curl_setopt($ch, CURLOPT_RETURNTRANSFER,1);
$result = curl_exec($ch);
```

Program logic can be implemented that executes the preceding code whenever changes occur to your Google sitemap, such as whenever a product or content page is modified.

The Sitemaps.org Standard Protocol

At the time of writing, there is a brand new initiative in the works standardizing a search engine sitemaps protocol for all search engine vendors. The standard and information is available at http:// www.sitemaps.org/. It adheres mostly to the Google standard, but its XML namespace is different:

```
<urlset xmlns="http://www.google.com/schemas/sitemap/0.84">
```

becomes:

```
<urlset xmlns="http://www.sitemaps.org/schemas/sitemap/0.9">
```

Also, using this sitemaps protocol does not require creating any account with the particular search engine vendors. Rather, you must simply "ping" a URL in the following format with the location of the sitemap at least once (and optionally more when there are updates):

```
<searchengine_URL>/ping?sitemap=sitemap_url
```

At this time, the only search vendor adhering to this standard is Google — recognizing requests such as:

```
http://www.google.com/webmasters/sitemaps/ping?sitemap=www.example.com/sitemap.xml
```

MSN hasn't implemented this functionality yet, but Yahoo! supports sitemap notification using this (non-standard) request:

```
http://search.yahooapis.com/SiteExplorerService/V1/updateNotification?appid=[YOUR_Y
AHOO_APPLICATION_ID]&url=http://www.example.com/sitemap.xml
```

> **To get a Yahoo Application ID visit** http://api.search.yahoo.com/webservices/
> register_application.

For more current information on this subject, we encourage you to visit the book's updates page maintained by Jaimie Sirovich at `http://www.seoegghead.com/seo-with-php-updates.html`.

Summary

In this chapter you learned about the two forms of sitemaps — traditional and search engine based. Search engine sitemaps, read only by search engines, help a web site get spidered more quickly and comprehensively. Traditional sitemaps are designed for human consumption, but they are beneficial to the same end as well.

There is no conflict in creating both forms of sitemaps. A properly designed traditional sitemap also benefits human usability in ways a search engine sitemap cannot. We recommend creating both in the interest of usability as well as speedy and comprehensive indexing.

10

Link Bait

Link bait is any content or feature within a web site that is designed to bait viewers to place links to it from other web sites. Matt Cutts defines link bait as "something interesting enough to catch people's attention." Typically, users on bulletin boards, newsgroups, social bookmarking sites, or blogs will place a link to a web site in some copy that further entices a fellow member or visitor to click. It is an extremely powerful form of marketing because it is viral in nature, and links like these are exactly what a search engine algorithm wants to see — that is, votes for a particular web site.

Soliciting links via link-exchanging is less effective than it once was to the end of improving rankings, as discussed in Chapter 2. Link bait creation is one of the newer popularized concepts in link building. In the article at `http://www.seomoz.org/blogdetail.php?ID=703`, Rand Fishkin of SEOmoz states "… I'd guess that if Matt (from Google) or Tim (from Yahoo!) had their druthers, this would be the type of tactic they'd prefer were used to achieve rankings." It is frequently, with a lot of luck and some skill, an economical and ethical way to get links to a web site; it is considered to be a white hat search engine optimization technique universally.

This chapter introduces the link bait concept, then shows an example of what we term "interactive link bait," which is an *application* that garners links naturally and virally.

> *As discussed in Chapter 2, building links is a crucial part of any search engine optimization campaign. In general, a site that earns links over time will be seen as valuable by a search engine. Link bait, in reality, is not a new concept. People have been linking to things that they like since the inception of the World Wide Web. It is just a concise term that describes an extremely effective technique — "provide something useful or interesting in order to entice people to link to your web site."*

Hooking Links

Link bait is a hit-or-miss technique. Do not expect success with every attempt. However, one clever idea, when implemented, may yield thousands of links. Andy Hagans of BizNicheMedia launched a contest in January 2006, which perhaps is link bait itself, that offers $1,000.00 for what they assess as the best link baiting idea (`http://www.biznichemedia.com/2006/01/biznichemedia_1.html`). Good ideas are seemingly made of gold.

Link bait will be generated as a matter of course on any web site with quality content. However, learning to recognize content as such is useful in itself. Social bookmarking sites such as the famed `http://del.icio.us` and `http://www.digg.com` can help to promote content. Including hooks to such services may provide an easy "call to action" for users to promote you. This is a popular technique especially used to promote blogs. This topic was discussed at length in Chapter 7.

There are myriad ways to "hook" a link. There are many examples, but there are a few basic categories of hooks that they tend to fall into. They are:

- ❑ Informational hooks
- ❑ News story hooks
- ❑ Humor/fun hooks
- ❑ "Evil" hooks

Informational Hooks

These are resources that people will tend to link to by virtue of the fact that they provide useful information. For example, posting a "how-to" article for how to set up a web server is an informational hook. A user will read the article one day, it will help him, and then the user will post a link to it somewhere indicating that it was helpful. As time progresses, this may happen several times, and many links will accumulate.

News Story Hooks

The early bird catches the worm — and perhaps the links, too. Being the first web site to report a pertinent news story will typically get your web site cited as a source via links as the news spreads. Posting an op-ed with a different and refreshing opinion on news may also get some attention. Debate always encourages dialogue, and it is viral in nature.

Humor/Fun Hooks

People love to laugh, and humorous content is very viral in nature. A good joke is always going to spread. Alexa often highlights this when a blog with a funny post appears in the "Movers and Shakers" section with an increase in traffic of quadruple-digit percents. Traffic increases like that are almost always accompanied by links as a lasting effect. Fun games also work, because people send those around as well.

Evil Hooks

Saying something unpopular or mean will likely get links and attention, but it may be the wrong type of attention. Be careful with this technique.

Traditional Examples of Link Bait

One typical baiting scheme is a prank — or something otherwise extremely funny and/or controversial. Typically, if a certain amount of momentum is created, that is, a few users see it and post it, the rest becomes automatic, as hundreds or thousands of users spread the link about the Internet. One fine example is Zug's "Viagra Prank." Viagra, one of the most queried key phrases in the search engine landscape, is also extremely competitive.

In Zug's "Viagra Prank," `http://www.zug.com/pranks/viagra/`, the author writes about a man who attempts to order Viagra from a Viagra spam site, and reflects on his experience. It's actually rather funny. So funny, in fact, that we've decided to place it in this book. After reading this book, you may choose to tell your friend and place it on your blog. And the cycle continues. That particular page has been in Google's top 10 for "viagra" for many months (at the time of writing), because there are many hundreds of high-quality links linking to it.

Another example of link bait is Burger King's "Subservient Chicken," a funny game where you can tell a man dressed up as a chicken what to do; and a more narcissistic example is a blog entry on the SEO Egghead blog, `http://www.seoegghead.com/blog/seo/mattcuttsarama-a-summary-of-useful-stuff-matt-cutts-has-said-p112.html`). Other traditionally successful examples of link bait include contests, funny pictures, and cartoons.

Unfortunately, some of these link bait examples are not well-suited to straight-edge sites. A particular scheme may look funny and hook links on a personal web site, but may simply look too unprofessional in the context of a commercial site. One form of link bait that can be adapted to any kind of site — even the more conservative ones — is the interactive *web tool*. These tools provide free, useful functionality to users, but usually require at least some programming on the part of the web developer.

Lastly, do not forget that extremely valuable or insightful content is the original link bait. High-quality content is important for many other reasons. Matt Cutts affirms this when he states "if everything you ever say is controversial, it can be entertaining, but it's harder to maintain credibility over the long haul." We could not agree more. And for some sites, being controversial is simply not an option.

Interactive Link Bait: Put on Your Programming Hardhat!

Interactive link bait is an interactive application that attracts links. It's typically useful, or at least cute. Common examples of electronic link bait are RustyBrick's *Future Page Rank Predictor* (`http://www.rustybrick.com/pagerank-prediction.php`), which purports to be a tool to foretell your page rank on the next update (but also notes that it's entirely fictitious), and Text-Link-Ads' Link Calculator (`http://www.text-link-ads.com/link_calculator.php`).

The latter is an example of a useful tool. A tool to approximate the value of a link on a page should attract many relevant links from the search engine marketing community. And, in our opinion, it does usually manage to calculate reasonable ballpark estimations.

The former is an example of a cute tool. PageRank, more recently, is widely regarded as less important than it used to be. However, in a time when the green bar in the toolbar meant everything to search engine marketers, the idea of predicting PageRank was extremely appealing, and, despite the fact that the tool itself stated it was fictitious, many people used and linked to it. According to Yahoo!, as of June 2006, the page has more than 3,000 links (Yahoo! reports backlinks the most accurately of all search engines; see: http://www.seroundtable.com/archives/002473.html).

Other traditional examples of interactive link bait include calorie counters, mortgage calculators, and currency converters.

Case Study: Fortune Cookies

Because the sample e-commerce catalog will sell cookies, this example will be a cute graphical fortune cookie tool that tells a site visitor his or her fortune. This tool may be included by other web sites, so that they too can provide their visitors with fortunes. It can include a logo for branding, and it contains a link to your store in order to hook your links and encourage more users to use the tool. The fortunes are stored in a list and returned randomly. A few sample fortunes are in the sample database script. The fortune cookie image looks like Figure 10-1.

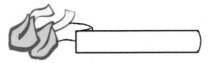

Figure 10-1

A page is placed on your site to showcase the tool, and you link to that page from your site menu with the anchor text "free fortune cookies." This affects some click-throughs. You show users how to add the fortune cookie to their sites on the page, and the HTML to do so, in turn, is linked to your free fortune cookie page. You also may place a link to another part of your site below that says, "Get your free cookies at Cookie Ogre's Warehouse." The following is a quick exercise that demonstrates the technique.

Building the Fortune Cookie

1. In this exercise you'll make use of the GD function imagecreatefromgif. This function is supported in GD versions prior to version 1.6, or more recent than 2.0.28, as explained in the documentation at http://www.php.net/imagecreatefromgif. You've already learned how to enable the GD2 module in Chapter 6 — but if you haven't here's a quick refresher. To enable GD2, you need to edit the php.ini configuration file, and uncomment the following line by removing the leading semicolon. Afterwards, you need to restart the Apache server.

```
extension=php_gd2.dll
```

2. Create a folder named images under your seophp folder, and copy the fortune_cookie.gif file from the book's code download to the images folder.

3. You need a font that will be used to write the text to the fortune cookie. For legal reasons, we can't provide you with a font, but you should have plenty to choose from on your machine.

On a Windows machine, you can find the font files in the hidden `\Windows\Fonts` folder, or via the Fonts applet that you can find in Control Panel. Create a folder named `fonts` under your `seophp` folder, and copy `comic.ttf` (or another font) to the `fonts` folder you've just created.

4. Create `fortune_cookie.php` in the `seophp` folder, with this code:

```php
<?php

class Fortunes
{
  // Array with possible fortune predictions
  var $_fortunes = array(
    "Jaimie Sirovich will become your\r\nfavorite author.",
    "You will recommend this book to\r\nall your friends.",
    "Tomorrow you will make \r\nyour first million.",
    "You will read AJAX and PHP: \r\nBuilding Responsive Web Applications."
  );

  // Member that will the generated image
  var $_image_resource;

  // Generate fortune cookie image
  function MakeFortune()
  {
    $text = $this->_fortunes[rand(0, sizeof($this->_fortunes) - 1)];
    $this->_image_resource = imagecreatefromgif('images/fortune_cookie.gif');
    imagettftext($this->_image_resource, 9, 0, 135, 64,
                 imagecolorallocate($this->_image_resource, 0, 0, 0),
                 'fonts/comic.ttf', $text);
    imagegif($this->_image_resource);
  }
}

// Set proper content type for GIF image
header('Content-type: image/gif');

// Generate the GIF image
$f = new Fortunes();
$f->MakeFortune();

?>
```

5. Load `http://seophp.example.com/fortune_cookie.php`. The result should look like Figure 10-2.

6. To be used as link bait, the fortune cookie needs to be easily placed in other pages. Assume that one of your visitors has a page named `linkbait.html`, and that he or she wants to add your fortune cookie to that page. Create a new file named `linkbait.html` in your `seophp` folder, and type the following code. The highlighted piece of code is what you need to give your visitors so that they can use your fortune cookie:

```html
<!DOCTYPE html PUBLIC "-//W3C//DTD XHTML 1.1//EN"
  "http://www.w3.org/TR/xhtml11/DTD/xhtml11.dtd">
<html>
  <head>
```

```
    <title>Professional Search Engine Optimization with PHP: LinkBait
Example</title>
  </head>
  <body>
    <h1>Professional Search Engine Optimization with PHP: LinkBait Example</h1>
```

```
<a href="http://seophp.example.com">
  <img src="http://seophp.example.com/fortune_cookie.php" border="0">
</a>
<br />Get your free
<a href="http://seophp.example.com">cookies at Cookie Ogre's Warehouse</a>.
```

```
  </body>
</html>
```

7. After adding the highlighted code, your visitor can load `http://seophp.example.com/linkbait.html` to admire his or her new fortune cookie, as shown in Figure 10-3.

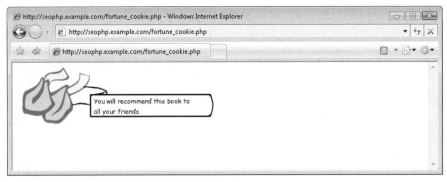

Figure 10-2

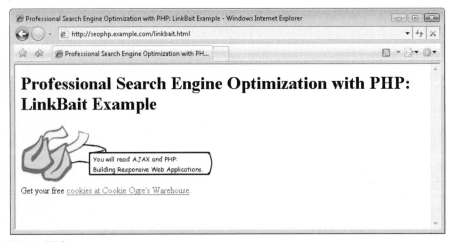

Figure 10-3

The basic idea is very simple. You need to tell your visitors that if they paste the following code into their HTML pages, they get a free fortune cookie:

```
<a href="http://seophp.example.com">
  <img src="http://seophp.example.com/fortune_cookie.php" border="0">
</a>
<br />Get your free
<a href="http://seophp.example.com">cookies at Cookie Ogre's Warehouse</a>.
```

What's interesting about this code is that it not only delivers the fortune cookie, but it also includes a link to your web site (and the tool, so others may get fortunes). A small amount of users may remove the link, but a significant amount will leave the link around the image. You're providing your visitor with a free service, in exchange for some publicity.

The code of the fortune cookie generator itself is simple. It simply takes a random text from an array, and displays it over the cookie image contained in `fortune_cookie.gif`. If you had more entries, it would make more sense to use a database, but for simplicity's sake you store the possible fortune phrases into an array:

```
class Fortunes
{
  // Array with possible fortune predictions
  var $_fortunes = array(
    "Jaimie Sirovich will become your\r\nfavorite author.",
    "You will recommend this book to\r\nall your friends.",
    "Tomorrow you will make \r\nyour first million.",
    "You will read AJAX and PHP: \r\nBuilding Responsive Web Applications."
  );
```

The code that adds the text over the .gif image template is very simple as well. You used the `image-createfromgif`, `imagettftext`, and `imagegif` functions of the GD2 library to generate and output the fortune cookie image:

```
// Generate fortune cookie image
function MakeFortune()
{
  $text = $this->_fortunes[rand(0, sizeof($this->_fortunes) - 1)];
  $this->_image_resource = imagecreatefromgif('images/fortune_cookie.gif');
  imagettftext($this->_image_resource, 9, 0, 135, 64,
               imagecolorallocate($this->_image_resource, 0, 0, 0),
               'fonts/comic.ttf', $text);
  imagegif($this->_image_resource);
}
```

Keep in mind that this is just one hypothetical example of link bait. Because we cannot possibly assist readers with all of their ideas for link bait, we will suggest that if you do have a great idea, but cannot implement it yourself, that you can use a service like eLance (http://www.elance.com/), which can assist you in finding a freelance programmer. For simple projects this can be very effective.

Summary

Link bait is not a new concept; it is just a concise term that describes an effective search engine marketing technique. Although some search engine marketers shun the term as just another word for viral marketing, we think the term and concept is quite useful. Deliberately creating link bait can provide a large return on investment, and even learning to recognize link bait when it is created as a matter of course is useful, because it can prompt a search engine marketer to provide hooks to services such as social bookmarking services to aid in the propagation of the bait.

11

Cloaking, Geo-Targeting, and IP Delivery

Cloaking is defined as the practice of providing different content to a search engine spider than is provided to a human user. It is an extremely controversial technique in the realm of search engine optimization. And like most things controversial, cloaking can be used for both good and evil. It is discussed in depth in this chapter, along with a discussion of the controversy surrounding its use. Geo-targeting is a similar practice, but it provides different content to both spiders and users on the basis of their respective geographical regions — its use is far less controversial. Both practices are typically implemented using a technology called IP delivery.

In this chapter, you:

❑   Learn the fundamentals of cloaking, geo-targeting, and IP delivery.

❑   Implement IP delivery–based cloaking and geo-targeting in step-by-step exercises.

Cloaking, Geo-Targeting, and IP Delivery

Before writing any code, make sure you understand these important definitions:

❑   **Cloaking** refers to the practice of delivering different content to a search engine than to human visitors browsing a web site. In practice, cloaking is implemented through IP delivery. See `http://en.wikipedia.org/wiki/Cloaking` for more details.

❑   **Geo-targeting** is similar to cloaking in that it provides different content depending on the type of visitor — but this time by their physical location on Earth. Search engine spiders are not treated any differently than human visitors. This technique is useful when you want to show different content to a user from France than to a user from the United States, for example.

Both cloaking and geo-targeting are covered in this same chapter because they're usually implemented in practice using the same technique — IP delivery.

❑ **IP delivery** is the practice of using the IP, the network address of the connecting computer, whether robot or human, and sending different content based on that. A database is used to assist with the process. In the case of cloaking, the database stores the IP addresses of the various spiders that may hit your site. The cloaking script implementation scans the list to see if the current IP is a spider, and the programmer can use this information to effect changes in presentation or logic. In the case of geo-targeting, the database stores various ranges of IP addresses, and indicates where these ranges of IPs are in the world. A geo-targeting script scans the list to see in which country the current IP is located, and the programmer can use this value to effect changes in presentation or logic.

Usually, implementations of IP delivery cloaking also look at the `User-Agent` header of the request. The user agent header is a header sent by both browsers and spiders. It, however, is not regarded as authoritative, because both users and spiders may not tell the truth about who they really are. In the former case, spiders indicate that they are humans in order to detect spamming employing cloaking as a means to provide optimized spam content to the spiders, while providing different content to the users. In the latter case, users (usually competitors) may actually set the user agent in their browser to see if a site is cloaking on the basis of user agent. It provides a convenient method for people to see if your site employs cloaking by *spoofing* their user agent. This is why many implementations of cloaking do not use it as a determining factor.

To change your user agent in your browser, see `http://johnbokma.com/mexit/2004/04/24/changinguseragent.html` *(in Firefox) or* `http://winguides.com/registry/display.php/799/` *(for Internet Explorer).*

More on Geo-Targeting

Geo-targeting is related to foreign search engine optimization in that it allows a site to tailor content to various regions. For example, Google uses geo-targeting to redirect users of `www.google.com` to country-specific domains, which is an implied approval of IP delivery as an ethical practice. This is a stark contrast to Google's current stated stance on cloaking.

Geo-targeting is regarded as ethical by all search engines. Matt Cutts of Google states (`http://www.mattcutts.com/blog/boston-pubcon-2006-day-1/#comment-22227`) that "*IP delivery [for Geo-targeting] is fine, but don't do anything special for Googlebot. Just treat it like a typical user visiting the site.*" However, because Google may use the actual physical location of *your web server* in the ranking algorithms, it may be wise to use this technique to redirect your users to a server located in their region, instead of simply changing the content. That is one example that is featured in this chapter.

One obvious caveat with regard to geo-targeting is that it can be misled by VPNs and strange network configurations in general that span multiple countries. This may be a concern, but it's likely to affect a small minority of users.

A Few Words on JavaScript Redirect Cloaking

JavaScript cloaking is the (usually deceptive) use of redirecting a user to a different page with Java-Script. Because spiders do not execute JavaScript, this used to be an effective method to feed spam to search engines. Most notoriously, BMW of Germany was briefly removed from the German Google search engine index. Matt Cutts states in his blog (http://www.mattcutts.com/blog/ramping-up-on-international-webspam/) that "... *our webspam team continued ramping up our anti-spam efforts by removing bmw.de from our index ...*" And, although search engines do not generally execute JavaScript, they do look for this technique.

Using JavaScript to implement cloaking is not advisable in our opinion, because it is really only useful for spamming — in contrast to IP delivery–based cloaking. It also requires a totally new page to be implemented, whereas IP delivery–based cloaking can effect small changes in presentation, as you'll see in the examples.

The most trivial implementation of Java redirect cloaking is one that simply changes the location of a page via JavaScript. Following is an example of JavaScript redirect cloaking code:

```
<script language='javascript'>
<!--
document.location = 'http://www.example.com/new_location.html';
-->
</script>
```

In practice, different methods are used to obscure this code from a search engine's view to make it more difficult to detect. Because this method is almost always used for spamming, it is not discussed further.

The Ethical Debate on Cloaking

Very few areas of search engine optimization evoke as much debate as cloaking. Dan Thies states that "*cloaking is a very risky technique.*" He also states that "*... the intent of cloaking is to deceive search engines.*" This is a statement with which we do not entirely agree. In the opinion of many, there are legitimate uses of cloaking. In practice, Yahoo! and MSN are relatively ambivalent regarding cloaking for non-deceptive purposes.

Google, at the time of writing this text, states unequivocally in its terms of service that cloaking is not within its guidelines regardless of intent. In its webmaster guidelines at http://www.google.com/support/webmasters/bin/answer.py?answer=40052 Google says that "*... cloaking ... may result in removal from our index.*"

Dan Thies states that "we do not consider IP cloaking to be an acceptable technique for professionals to associate themselves with." We take a milder view, especially in light of recent developments.

Recently, Google has also shown some ambivalence in actual enforcement of this principle. In particular, the *New York Times* cloaks content. In short, it shows a search engine spider the entirety of a news article, but only shows the abstract to a regular user. Human users must pay to be able to see the same content a search engine can read. The *New York Times* uses IP delivery–based cloaking to do this.

The New York Times *clearly uses IP delivery–based cloaking, and does not pay attention to the user agent. If that were not the case, users could spoof their user agent and get a free subscription. We tried it. It doesn't work.*

Meanwhile, Matt Cutts of Google states "*Googlebot and other search engine bots can only crawl the free portions that non-subscribed users can access. So, make sure that the free section includes meaty content that offers value.*" Danny Sullivan, editor of SearchEngineWatch, states with regard to the *New York Times*:

"*Do I think the NYT is spamming Google? No. Do I think they are cloaking? Yes. Do I think they should be banned because Google itself warns against cloaking? No. I've long written that Google guidelines on that are outdated. To be honest, it's a pretty boring issue to revisit, very 2004. The NYT is just the latest in a string of big companies showing that cloaking in and of itself isn't necessarily bad.*"

We don't necessarily agree with this statement. Clicking a link in a SERP that gets you to a subscription page *is deceiving* to users. Results of a search engine query are supposed to contain data relevant to what the user has searched for. We leave the assessment to you.

Cloaking may be becoming more normatively acceptable recently, but it should still be avoided as the first choice for solving a problem. Solutions that do not involve cloaking should be applied instead. Some of this was previously discussed in Chapter 8. Cloaking is often suggested as a solution to preexisting sites that use Flash or AJAX, and it is also the only way to implement indexed subscription-based content, as in the *New York Times* example.

Examples of legitimate uses of cloaking — in our opinion — are demonstrated in this chapter.

Cloaking Dangers

Clearly, despite the fact that certain uses of cloaking are becoming accepted, it is still a risk, and it is likely that if you are caught by Google for doing cloaking that it deems as unethical, your site will be banned. Therefore, if you do not own an extremely popular site whose ban would elicit a public response, and you're not willing to take a risk, cloaking should be avoided — at least for Google. Minor changes are probably safe, especially for Yahoo! and MSN, as implemented in the exercise that follows, where you replace a figure with text.

It is, however, very difficult to define the meaning of "minor change," and a ban may still occur in the worst case. As aforementioned, `http://bmw.de` was reincluded in the index in a matter of days; however, in practice, for a smaller business, it would likely be much more devastating and take more time to get reincluded after such a ban. The cloaking toolkit provided in this chapter allows you to cloak for some search engines and not others. We cannot comment further, because it is a very complex set of decisions. Use your own judgment.

Using the Meta Noarchive Tag

One problem that arises with cloaking is that the cache feature provided by most major search engines would display the cloaked version to human visitors, instead of the version they are intended to see. Needless to say, this is probably not what you want for several reasons — among them, that it conveniently indicates to your competitors that you are cloaking.

To prevent this, the following meta tag should be added to the `<head>` section of all cloaked documents:

```
<meta name="robots" content="noarchive" />
```

If you are cloaking only for a specific spider, you can use a tag like the following. (This can also be applied for `noindex`, `nofollow`, as shown in Chapter 5.)

```
<meta name="googlebot" content="noarchive" />
```

This prevents the cache from being stored or displayed to users. The *New York Times* also notably uses this tag to prevent people from reading its content through the search engines' cache.

Implementing Cloaking

In the following exercise you implement a simple cloaking library, in the form of a class named `SimpleCloak`. This class will have two functions that you can access from your web applications:

❑   `updateAll()` updates your cloaking database with search engine IP and user agent data

❑   `ipSpider()` indicates if the visitor is a search engine spider

The cloaking data is retrieved from Dan Kramer's `iplists.com`. Kudos to Dan to providing such a useful set of data for everyone to use!

To test the `SimpleCloak` library, you'll create a script named `cloaking_test.php`, which will present the output shown in Figure 11-1 if read by a "normal" visitor, and the output shown in Figure 11-2 when read by a search engine.

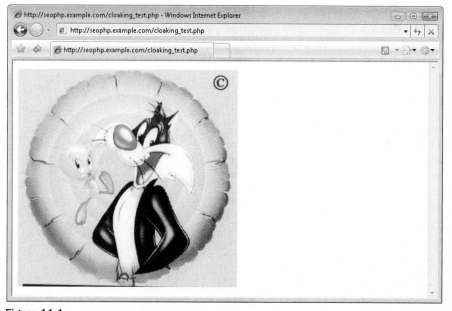

Figure 11-1

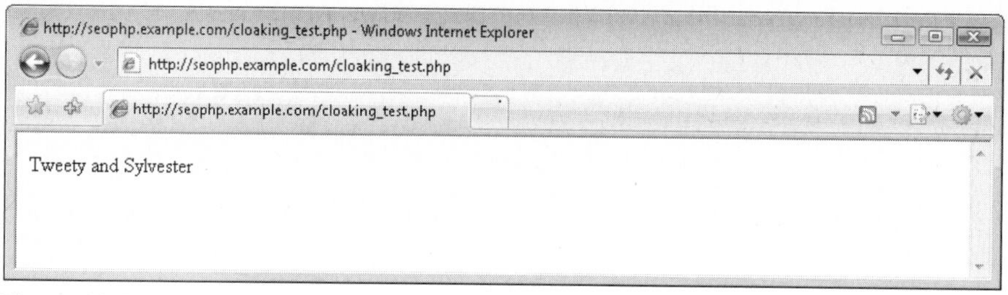

Figure 11-2

Let's write some code, then!

Implementing Cloaking

1. This example uses the cURL library. If you've prepared Apache and PHP as instructed in Chapter 1, you should have cURL installed, otherwise it may not be enabled. To enable cURL, open the `php.ini` configuration file (located by default in `\xampp\apache\bin`), uncomment the following line by removing the leading semicolon, and then restart Apache:

```
extension=php_curl.dll
```

2. You need to prepare the `simple_cloak` database table, which still store the search engine IPs. Make sure you've configured your MySQL database as described in Chapter 1. Then open a Command Prompt window, and navigate to the `mysql\bin` folder using a command like this:

```
cd \Program Files\xampp\mysql\bin
```

3. Connect to your MySQL server using the following command, and type the `seomaster` password when asked. (If you chose another password when creating the user, type that password instead.)

```
mysql -u seouser -p
```

Note that you can use your tool of choice to connect to the database server, instead of the command-line utility. For example, you can use phpMyAdmin, which in a default XAMPP installation is accessible via `http://localhost/phpmyadmin/`. *The following steps will have the same effect no matter how you've connected to MySQL.*

4. Type the following command to connect to the `seophp` database:

```
use seophp;
```

5. Create the `cloak_data` and `cloak_update` tables by typing the following SQL command:

```
CREATE TABLE `cloak_data` (
  `id` int(11) NOT NULL AUTO_INCREMENT,
  `spider_name` VARCHAR(255) NOT NULL DEFAULT '',
  `record_type` ENUM('UA','IP') NOT NULL DEFAULT 'UA',
  `value` varchar(255) NOT NULL DEFAULT '',
  PRIMARY KEY  (`id`),
  KEY `value` (`value`)
```

```
);
CREATE TABLE `cloak_update` (
  `version` VARCHAR(255) NOT NULL,
  `updated_on` DATETIME NOT NULL
);
```

6. Type exit to exit the MySql console. After executing these commands, your console should look like shown in Figure 11-3.

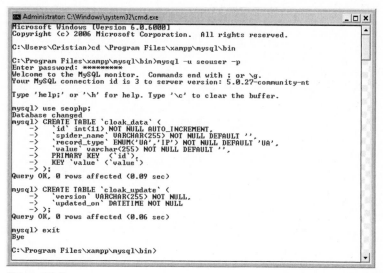

Figure 11-3

7. Add the following highlighted constants to your seophp/include/config.inc.php file. (If you don't have the file from the previous exercises in this book, create it now with these contents.)

```php
<?php
// defines database connection data
define("DB_HOST", "localhost");
define("DB_USER", "seouser");
define("DB_PASSWORD", "seomaster");
define("DB_DATABASE", "seophp");
?>
```

8. Create a new file named simple_cloak.inc.php in your seophp/include folder, and type the following code:

```php
<?php

/*
// +-----------------------------------------------------------------+
// | SimpleCloak                                                     |
// | Class for cloaking content                                     |
// | http://www.SEOEgghead.com                                      |
// +-----------------------------------------------------------------+
```

```php
// | Copyright (c) 2005-2006 Jaimie Sirovich and Cristian Darie        |
// +------------------------------------------------------------------+
*/

// load configuration file
require_once('config.inc.php');

class SimpleCloak
{
  // returns the confidence level
  function isSpider($spider_name = '', $check_uas = true, $check_ips = true)
  {
    // default confidence level to 0
    $confidence = 0;

    // matching user agent?
    if ($check_uas)
      if (SimpleCloak::_get(0, $spider_name, 'UA', $_SERVER['HTTP_USER_AGENT']))
        $confidence += 2;

    // matching IP?
    if ($check_ips)
      if (SimpleCloak::_get(0, $spider_name, 'IP', '', $_SERVER['REMOTE_ADDR']))
        $confidence += 3;

    // return confidence level
    return $confidence;
  }

  // retrieve cloaking data filtered by the supplied parameters
  function _get($id = 0, $spider_name = '', $record_type = '',
               $value = '', $wildcard_value = '')
  {
    // by default, retrieve all records
    $q = " SELECT cloak_data.* FROM cloak_data WHERE TRUE ";

    // add filters
    if ($id) {
      $id = (int) $id;
      $q .= " AND id = $id ";
    }
    if ($spider_name) {
      $spider_name = mysql_escape_string($spider_name);
      $q .= " AND spider_name = '$spider_name' ";
    }
    if ($record_type) {
      $record_type = mysql_escape_string($record_type);
      $q .= " AND record_type = '$record_type' ";
    }
    if ($value) {
      $value = mysql_escape_string($value);
      $q .= " AND value = '$value' ";
    }
```

```php
if ($wildcard_value) {
  $wildcard_value = mysql_escape_string($wildcard_value);
  $q .= " AND ( '$wildcard_value' = value OR '$wildcard_value' LIKE
  CONCAT(value, '.%') ) ";
}

// Connect to MySQL server
$dbLink = mysql_connect(DB_HOST, DB_USER, DB_PASSWORD)
             or die("Could not connect: " . mysql_error());

// Connect to the seophp database
mysql_select_db(DB_DATABASE) or die("Could not select database");

// execute the query
$tmp = mysql_query($q);

// close database connection
mysql_close($dbLink);

// return the results as an associative array
$rows = array();
while ($_x = mysql_fetch_assoc($tmp)) {
  $rows[] = $_x;
}
return $rows;
}

// updates the entire database with fresh spider data, but only if our data is
// more than 7 days old, and if the online version from iplists.org has changed
function updateAll()
{
  // Connect to MySQL server
  $dbLink = mysql_connect(DB_HOST, DB_USER, DB_PASSWORD)
               or die("Could not connect: " . mysql_error());

  // Connect to the seophp database
  mysql_select_db(DB_DATABASE) or die("Could not select database");

  // retrieve last update information from database
  $q = "SELECT cloak_update.* FROM cloak_update";
  $tmp = mysql_query($q);
  $updated = mysql_fetch_assoc($tmp);
  $db_version = $updated['version'];
  $updated_on = $updated ['updated_on'];

  // get the latest update more recent than 7 days, don't attempt an update
  if (isset($updated_on) &&
      (strtotime($updated_on) > strtotime("-604800 seconds")))
  {
    // close database connection
    mysql_close($dbLink);
    // return false to indicate an update wasn't performed
    return false;
  }
```

```php
      // read the latest iplists version
      $version_url = 'http://www.iplists.com/nw/version.php';
      $latest_version = mysql_escape_string(file_get_contents($version_url));

      // if no updated version information was retrieved, abort
      if (!$latest_version)
      {
        // return false to indicate an update wasn't performed
        return false;
      }

      // save the update data
      $q = "DELETE FROM cloak_update";
      mysql_query($q);
      $q = "INSERT INTO cloak_update (version, updated_on) " .
          "VALUES('$latest_version', NOW())";
      mysql_query($q);

      // if we already have the current data, don't attempt an update
      if ($latest_version == $db_version)
      {
        // close database connection
        mysql_close($dbLink);
        // return false to indicate an update wasn't performed
        return false;
      }

      // update the database
      SimpleCloak::_updateCloakingDB('google',
                                'http://www.iplists.com/nw/google.txt');
      SimpleCloak::_updateCloakingDB('yahoo',
                                'http://www.iplists.com/nw/inktomi.txt');
      SimpleCloak::_updateCloakingDB('msn',
                                'http://www.iplists.com/nw/msn.txt');
      SimpleCloak::_updateCloakingDB('ask',
                                'http://www.iplists.com/nw/askjeeves.txt');
      SimpleCloak::_updateCloakingDB('altavista',
                                'http://www.iplists.com/nw/altavista.txt');
      SimpleCloak::_updateCloakingDB('lycos',
                                'http://www.iplists.com/nw/lycos.txt');
      SimpleCloak::_updateCloakingDB('wisenut',
                                'http://www.iplists.com/nw/wisenut.txt');

      // close connection
      mysql_close($dbLink);

      // return true to indicate a successful update
      return true;
    }

    // update the database for the mentioned spider, by reading the provided URL
    function _updateCloakingDB($spider_name, $url,
        $ua_regex = '/^# UA "(.*)"$/m', $ip_regex = '/^([0-9.]+)$/m')
```

```
{
  // use cURL to read the data from $url
  // NOTE: additional settings are required when accessing the web through a proxy
  $ch = curl_init();
  curl_setopt ($ch, CURLOPT_URL, $url);
  curl_setopt ($ch, CURLOPT_HEADER, 1);
  curl_setopt ($ch, CURLOPT_RETURNTRANSFER, 1);
  curl_setopt ($ch, CURLOPT_FOLLOWLOCATION, 1);
  curl_setopt ($ch, CURLOPT_TIMEOUT, 60);
  $result = curl_exec($ch);
  curl_close($ch);

  // use _parseListURL to parse the list of IPs and user agents
  $lists = SimpleCloak::_parseListURL($result, $ua_regex, $ip_regex);

  // if the user agents and IPs weren't retrieved, we cancel the update
  if (!$lists['ua_list'] || !$lists['ip_list']) return;

  // lock the cloack_data table to avoid concurrency problems
  mysql_query('LOCK TABLES cloak_data WRITE');

  // delete all the existing data for $spider_name
  SimpleCloak::_deleteSpiderData($spider_name);

  // insert the list of user agents for the spider
  foreach ($lists['ua_list'] as $ua) {
    SimpleCloak::_insertSpiderData($spider_name, 'UA', $ua);
  }

  // insert the list of IPs for the spider
  foreach ($lists['ip_list'] as $ip) {
    SimpleCloak::_insertSpiderData($spider_name, 'IP', $ip);
  }

  // release the table lock
  mysql_query('UNLOCK TABLES');
}

// helper function used to parse lists of user agents and IPs
function _parseListURL($data, $ua_regex, $ip_regex)
{
  $ua_list_ret = preg_match_all($ua_regex, $data, $ua_list);
  $ip_list_ret = preg_match_all($ip_regex, $data, $ip_list);
  return array('ua_list' => $ua_list[1], 'ip_list' => $ip_list[1]);
}

// inserts a new row of data to the cloaking table
function _insertSpiderData($spider_name, $record_type, $value)
{
  // escape input data
  $spider_name = mysql_escape_string($spider_name);
  $record_type = mysql_escape_string($record_type);
  $value = mysql_escape_string($value);
```

```
     // build and execute the INSERT query
     $q  = "INSERT INTO cloak_data (spider_name, record_type, value) " .
           "VALUES ('$spider_name', '$record_type', '$value')";
     mysql_query($q);
   }

   // delete the cloaking data for the mentioned spider
   function _deleteSpiderData($spider_name)
   {
     // escape input data
     $spider_name = mysql_escape_string($spider_name);

     // build and execute the DELETE query
     $q = "DELETE FROM cloak_data WHERE spider_name='$spider_name'";
     mysql_query($q);
   }
 }
 ?>
```

9. Create a file named `cloaking_prepare.php` in your `seophp` folder, and type the following code. This script only tests the functionality of `SimpleCloak::updateAll()`, which updates the database with fresh data:

```php
<?php

// load the SimpleCloak library
require_once 'include/simple_cloak.inc.php';

// update cloaking data and indicate the success status
if (SimpleCloak::updateAll())
{
  echo "Cloaking database updated!";
}
else
{
  echo "Cloaking database was already up to date, or the update failed.";
}

?>
```

10. Load `http://seophp.example.com/cloaking_prepare.php`. If everything works okay, the page will not simply output "Cloaking database updated!" On any subsequent requests (before a week elapses), the message should read "Cloaking database was already up to date, or the update failed."

11. However, your `simple_cloak` table from the `seophp` database should be populated with search engine data. To view the contents of your `simple_cloak` table, you can use the phpMyAdmin utility that ships with XAMPP. Load the utility through `http://localhost/phpmyadmin/`, select the `seophp` database from the left pane, and click the Browse button for the `simple_cloak` table. If everything worked alright, you should see the list of IPs in your table, as shown in Figure 11-4.

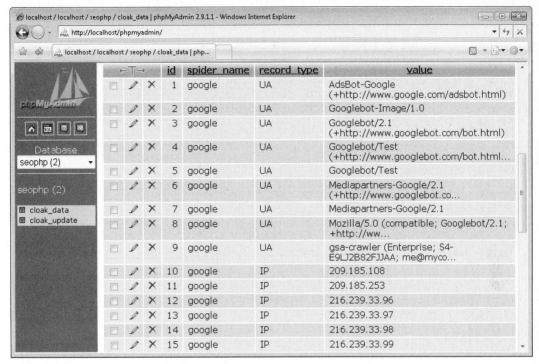

Figure 11-4

12. Now, to make effective use of your cloaking library, create a new file in your `seophp` folder, named `cloaking_test.php`, and type this code in it:

```php
<?php

// load the SimpleCloak library
require_once 'include/simple_cloak.inc.php';

// Use cloaking to render text instead of images
if (SimpleCloak::isSpider() >= 3)
{
  echo 'Tweety and Sylvester';
}
else
{
  echo '<img src="http://seophp.example.com/Images/tweety.jpg" />';
}

?>
```

13. Create a folder named `images` in your `seophp` folder, and copy the `tweety.jpg` image from the code download of the book to this folder.

14. Load `http://seophp.example.com/cloaking_test.php`. Because you're not a search engine, you will be shown the picture of Tweety and Sylvester, as shown in Figure 11-1.

15. The simplest way to test what happens if you're a search engine is to add your local IP to the `simple_cloak` table. Use either the MySQL console or phpMyAdmin to connect to the `seophp` database, and execute this query:

```
INSERT INTO cloak_data (spider_name, record_type, value)
VALUES ('localtest', 'IP', '127.0.0.1')
```

16. Load `http://seophp.example.com/cloaking_test.php` again. This time the script will think you're a search engine, and will output the text "Tweety and Sylvester" instead of the picture, as shown in Figure 11-2.

Implementing cloaking is basically a three-step process.

First, you needed to prepare the cloaking database and the cloaking library. The `cloak_data` table stores data about search engine IPs and user agents, and the `cloak_update` table stores data about the last database update. You use this latter table to store the time and version of your last update.

The `SimpleCloak` class contains two methods that you can use in your programs: `updateAll()` and `isSpider()`. The `updateAll()` method retrieves data from `www.iplists.com` and saves it into the local database — but not more often than once a week, and only when the version information retrieved from `www.iplists.com` is different than that stored in your `cloak_update` table.

In the pages that need to implement cloaking, you use `SimpleCloak::isSpider()`, which returns a positive number representing the "confidence" it has in the request being that of a spider. The confidence has one of these values:

❏ 0 if neither the user agent nor the IP match that of a spider

❏ 2 if the user agent is that of a spider

❏ 3 if the IP address is that of a spider

❏ 5 if both the IP address and the user agent are that of a spider

In this example, you verified that the value is greater or equal than 3 to ensure that the IP address is from a spider. Also, note that `isSpider()` may optionally receive a number of optional parameters, which you can use to have it verify if the visitor is a particular spider, and/or check only the user agent or the IP address.

Cloaking Case Studies

Following are a few typical scenarios where cloaking could be used:

❏ Rendering text images as text

❏ Redirecting excluded content to a non-excluded equivalent

❑ Feeding subscription-based content only to the spider (*New York Times* example)

❑ Using cloaking to disable URL-based session handling (trans_sid) for spiders

Rendering Images as Text

Unfortunately, as discussed in Chapter 6, the use of graphics containing text is detrimental to search engine optimization. The reasoning is simple — search engines cannot read the graphics contained by text. So one obvious ethical use of cloaking would be to detect if a user agent is a spider, and replace the images with the text included by the said image. Using the cloaking toolkit in this chapter, it would be implemented as follows:

```
require_once('include/simple_cloak.inc.php');
if (SimpleCloak::isSpider())
{
  echo 'Wacky Widget Model XX';
}
else
{
  echo '<img src="/images/wacky-widget-model-xx.gif">';
}
```

We will note, however, that sIFR is likely a better solution to this problem for text headings, because it does not entail the same risk. sIFR is discussed in detail in Chapter 6.

Redirecting Excluded Content

As discussed in Chapter 5, if you have, for example, a product in three categories, it will usually result in two almost identical pages with three different URLs. This is a fundamental duplicate content problem. In Chapter 3 we suggested the concept of a "primary category," and then proceeded to exclude the non-primary pages using robots.txt or meta-exclusion. The cloaking variation is to simply 301 redirect all non-primary pages to the primary page if the user agent is a spider.

This example is demonstrated in Chapter 14 in the sample e-commerce store catalog.

Feeding Subscription-Based Content Only to Spiders

This is the *New York Times* example. In this case, the code would detect if a user agent is a spider, then echo either a substring of the content if the user agent is human, or the entire content if it is a spider. Using the cloaking toolkit in this chapter, it would be implemented as follows:

```
if (SimpleCloak::isSpider())
{
  echo $content;
}
else
{
  echo substr($content, 0, 100);
}
```

Disabling URL-Based Session Handling for Spiders

As discussed in Chapter 5, PHP's trans_sid feature, which performs automatic modification of URLs and forms to include session variables, is used to preserve session state for those users who do not accept cookies. However, this has the side effect of sending spiders a potentially infinite amount of duplicate content. For this reason, nowadays many web sites turn this feature off altogether.

However, because this feature can be turned on and off dynamically in PHP code, cloaking can be employed to dynamically turn it on and off based on whether the visitor is a human or a search engine spider. This allows the site to both accommodate users, but not confuse a spider when it visits with an infinite number of semantically meaningless URL-variations containing different session IDs. Using the cloaking toolkit in this chapter, it would be implemented as follows:

> This code should be placed at the top of a PHP script, and before any headers or output is sent to the client.

```
if (SimpleCloak::isSpider())
{
  ini_set ('session.use_trans_sid', 0);
}
else
{
  ini_set ('session.use_trans_sid', 1);
}
session_start();
```

Obviously, your site must also not require a session to be functional either — because search engines will not accept cookies regardless.

Other Cloaking Implementations

The preceding implementation of cloaking works if you have the source code to your application and you are willing and able to modify it. If not, there are cloaking toolkits that allow you to easily and dynamically serve different content to various user agents. One such toolkit is KloakIt from Volatile Graphix, Inc. You can find it at http://www.kloakit.com. It is written by and utilizes the same cloaking data used as provided by Dan Kramer.

Implementing Geo-Targeting

Geo-targeting isn't very different than cloaking — so you'll probably feel a little déjà vu as you read this section. After creating the database table geo_target_data, you'll create a class named SimpleGeoTarget that includes the necessary geo-targeting features.

The SimpleGeoTarget class contains three methods to be used by an application:

❑ getRegion() receives an optional IP address, and returns the country code of that IP. If no IP is specified, the method returns the region of the current visitor.

❑ isRegion() receives a region code and an optional IP address. It returns true if the region code corresponds to the region of the IP address, or false otherwise. If no IP address is provided, the address of the current visitor is used.

❑ importGeoTargetingData() loads MaxMind's geo-targeting file into your geo_target_data database table.

Because the geo-targeting database isn't likely to change as frequently as search engine spider data, in this case you won't implement an automatic update feature. Instead, the exercise assumes that you'll populate your database with geo-targeting data once, and then update periodically.

You'll use the free geo-target database provided by MaxMind (http://www.maxmind.com/).

At the end of the exercise you'll test your geo-targeting library by displaying a geo-targeted welcome message to your visitor. A person from the United States would get the greeting that's shown in Figure 11-5, and a person from Romania would be shown the message that appears in Figure 11-6.

Put this to work in the following exercise.

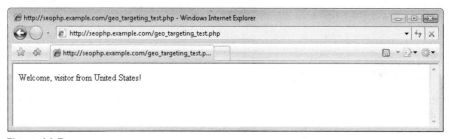

Figure 11-5

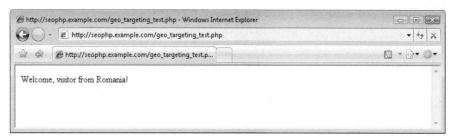

Figure 11-6

Implementing Geo-Targeting

1. Connect to your `seophp` database, as you did in the previous exercise, and execute the following SQL command. It will create the `geo_target_data` table:

```
CREATE TABLE `geo_target_data` (
  `id` int(11) NOT NULL auto_increment,
  `start_ip_text` varchar(15) NOT NULL default '',
  `end_ip_text` varchar(15) NOT NULL default '',
  `start_ip_numeric` bigint(20) NOT NULL default '0',
  `end_ip_numeric` bigint(20) NOT NULL default '0',
  `country_code` char(2) NOT NULL default '',
  `country_name` varchar(50) NOT NULL default '',
  PRIMARY KEY  (`id`),
  KEY `start_ip_numeric` (`start_ip_numeric`,`end_ip_numeric`),
  KEY `country_code` (`country_code`)
);
```

2. Create a folder named `geo_target_data` in your `seophp` folder. Then download `http://www.maxmind.com/download/geoip/database/GeoIPCountryCSV.zip`, and unzip the file in the `geo_target_data` folder you've just created. You should end up with a file named `GeoIPCountryWhois.csv` in your `geo_target_data` folder.

    Note that we're not including the `GeoIPCountryWhois.csv` file in the book's code download. You need to download and unzip that file for yourself even when using the code download.

3. Add the following constant definitions to your `include/config.inc.php` file:

```php
<?php
// defines database connection data
define("DB_HOST", "localhost");
define("DB_USER", "seouser");
define("DB_PASSWORD", "seomaster");
define("DB_DATABASE", "seophp");

// the geo-targeting file name
define('GEO_TARGETING_CSV', 'geo_target_data/GeoIPCountryWhois.csv');
?>
```

4. Create a new file named `simple_geo_target.inc.php` in your `include` folder, and type this code:

```php
<?php

/*
// +---------------------------------------------------------------+
// | SimpleGeoTarget                                               |
// | Class for targeting content for specific geographical regions |
// | http://www.SEOEgghead.com                                     |
// +---------------------------------------------------------------+
// | Copyright (c) 2004-2006 Jaimie Sirovich <jsirovic@gmail.com>  |
// +---------------------------------------------------------------+
*/
```

```php
// load configuration file
require_once('config.inc.php');

// simple geo-targeting class
class SimpleGeoTarget
{

  // returns true if the specified ip is located in $country_code, false otherwise
  function getRegion($ip = '')
  {
    // retrieve the IP of the visitor if one wasn't provided
    $ip = ($ip) ? $ip : $_SERVER['REMOTE_ADDR'];

    // transform the IP into its long version
    $ip = sprintf("%u", ip2long($ip));

    // build the SQL query that obtains the country code of the specified IP
    $q = "SELECT geo_target_data.* FROM geo_target_data WHERE " .
        "start_ip_numeric <= $ip AND end_ip_numeric >= $ip";

    // connect to MySQL server
    $dbLink = mysql_connect(DB_HOST, DB_USER, DB_PASSWORD)
                  or die("Could not connect: " . mysql_error());

    // connect to the seophp database
    mysql_select_db(DB_DATABASE) or die("Could not select database");

    // execute the query
    $tmp = mysql_query($q);
    $result = mysql_fetch_assoc($tmp);

    // close database connection
    mysql_close($dbLink);

    // return false if no database records for that IP were found
    if (!$result) return false;

    // return the region
    return ($result['country_code']);
  }

  // returns true if the specified IP is located in $country_code, false otherwise
  function isRegion($country_code, $ip = '')
  {
    // retrieve the region
    $visitor_country_code = SimpleGeoTarget::getRegion($ip);

    // return false if the region code couldn't be found
    if (!$visitor_country_code) return false;

    // return true if the IP and the country code match, false otherwise
    return ($country_code == $visitor_country_code);
  }
```

```php
/* methods used for importing the geo-targeting database */

// imports MaxMind's geo-targeting database into the geo_target_data table
function importGeoTargetingData()
{
  // open the geo-targeting file
  $csv_file_handle = fopen(GEO_TARGETING_CSV, 'r');

  // continue only if the geo db file was opened successfully
  if (!$csv_file_handle)
  {
    echo "Could not open the geodb file.";
    return;
  }

  // Connect to MySQL server
  $dbLink = mysql_connect(DB_HOST, DB_USER, DB_PASSWORD)
                  or die("Could not connect: " . mysql_error());

  // Connect to the seophp database
  mysql_select_db(DB_DATABASE) or die("Could not select database");

  // lock the simple_geo_target file for writing
  mysql_query('LOCK TABLES simple_geo_target WRITE');

  // remove all existing entries from the table
  $q = "DELETE FROM geo_target_data";
  mysql_query($q);

  // parse each record from the geo-targeting file and save it to the database
  while (($data = fgetcsv($csv_file_handle, 10000, ",")) !== false)
  {
    SimpleGeoTarget::_insert($data[0], $data[1], $data[2],
                         $data[3], $data[4], $data[5]);
  }

  // unlock the tables
  mysql_query('UNLOCK TABLES');

  // close database connection
  mysql_close($dbLink);

  // close the file handler
  fclose($csv_file_handle);
}

function _insert($start_ip_text, $end_ip_text, $start_ip_numeric,
                 $end_ip_numeric, $country_code, $country_name)
{
  // escape input data
  $start_ip_text = mysql_escape_string($start_ip_text);
  $end_ip_text = mysql_escape_string($end_ip_text);
  $start_ip_numeric = mysql_escape_string($start_ip_numeric);
  $end_ip_numeric = mysql_escape_string($end_ip_numeric);
```

```
    $country_code = mysql_escape_string($country_code);
    $country_name = mysql_escape_string($country_name);

    // build and execute the INSERT query
    $q = "INSERT INTO geo_target_data (start_ip_text, end_ip_text " .
        ", start_ip_numeric, end_ip_numeric, country_code, country_name)" .
        "VALUES ('$start_ip_text', '$end_ip_text', '$start_ip_numeric', " .
        "'$end_ip_numeric', '$country_code', '$country_name')";
    mysql_query($q);
  }
}
?>
```

5. Create a file named `geo_targeting_prepare.php` in your `seophp` folder, and type this code:

```php
<?php

// load the geo-targeting library
require_once 'include/simple_geo_target.inc.php';

// update the geo-targeting database
SimpleGeoTarget::importGeoTargetingData();
echo "Geo-targeting database updated!"

?>
```

6. Load `http://seophp.example.com/geo_targeting_prepare.php`. It will take a while until the geo-targeting database is copied into your database, so be patient. At the moment of writing, there are approximately 60,000 records in the database. Once the process is finished, you should get a message saying "Geo-targeting database updated!"

Note that the sample script simply deletes the old data and refreshes it with new data whenever it is run.

To test that the `geo_target_data` table was populated correctly, you can open it for browsing using phpMyAdmin, as shown in Figure 11-7.

7. Test the geo-targeting library now with a real example! Create a file named `get_targeting_test.php` in your `seophp` folder, and type this code in:

```php
<?php

// load the SimpleGeoTarget library
require_once 'include/simple_geo_target.inc.php';

// display geo-targeted welcome message
if (SimpleGeoTarget::isRegion("RO"))
{
  echo "Welcome, visitor from Romania!";
}
else if (SimpleGeoTarget::isRegion("US"))
{
  echo "Welcome, visitor from United States!";
}
else if (!SimpleGeoTarget::getRegion())
```

```
{
  echo "Welcome, visitor! We couldn't find your country code!" ;
}
else
{
  echo "Welcome, visitor! Your country code is: " . SimpleGeoTarget::getRegion();
}

?>
```

8. Now, if Jaimie from the United States loaded this script, he would get the output shown in Figure 11-5. If Cristian loaded the same script, he would get the output shown in Figure 11-6.

> Note that when loading the script from your local machine, your IP is 127.0.0.1, which doesn't belong to any country — so the message you'd get is "Welcome, visitor! We couldn't find your country code!" To test your region, you need to supply your network IP address as the second parameter of SimpleGeoTarget::isRegion(), or as the first parameter to SimpleGeoTarget::getRegion().

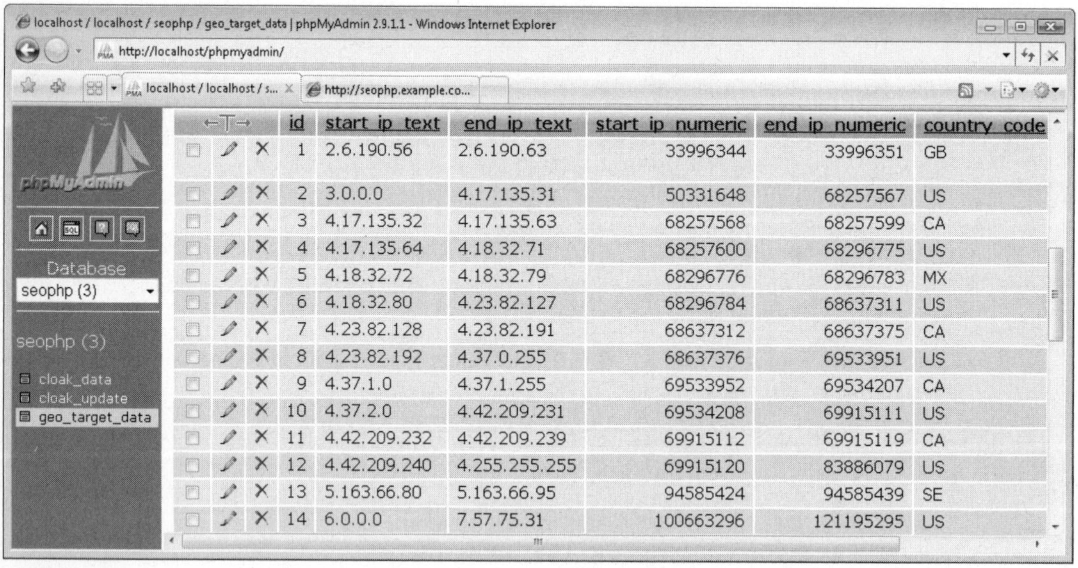

id	start_ip_text	end_ip_text	start_ip_numeric	end_ip_numeric	country_code
1	2.6.190.56	2.6.190.63	33996344	33996351	GB
2	3.0.0.0	4.17.135.31	50331648	68257567	US
3	4.17.135.32	4.17.135.63	68257568	68257599	CA
4	4.17.135.64	4.18.32.71	68257600	68296775	US
5	4.18.32.72	4.18.32.79	68296776	68296783	MX
6	4.18.32.80	4.23.82.127	68296784	68637311	US
7	4.23.82.128	4.23.82.191	68637312	68637375	CA
8	4.23.82.192	4.37.0.255	68637376	69533951	US
9	4.37.1.0	4.37.1.255	69533952	69534207	CA
10	4.37.2.0	4.42.209.231	69534208	69915111	US
11	4.42.209.232	4.42.209.239	69915112	69915119	CA
12	4.42.209.240	4.255.255.255	69915120	83886079	US
13	5.163.66.80	5.163.66.95	94585424	94585439	SE
14	6.0.0.0	7.57.75.31	100663296	121195295	US

Figure 11-7

In this exercise you presented different output depending on the country the visitor is from. Another popular use of geo-targeting involves redirecting visitors to localized web sites depending on their region. This example is analogous to the example of Google's practice of redirecting visitors from foreign countries from www.google.com to their respective local version of Google.

Here is an example of implementing this feature, using your simple geo-targeting library. To redirect French users to `http://fr.example.com`, you'd need to do something like this:

```
if (SimpleGeoTarget::isRegion('FR')) {
    header('Location: http://fr.example.com');
    exit();
}
```

Summary

We hope you've had fun going through the exercises in this chapter! Although cloaking is a potential minefield in search engine optimization, we have shown some of its relevant uses. Geo-targeting, on the other hand, is a unanimously accepted practice that you can use to offer a more pleasant browsing experience to your international visitors. Both, in turn, rely on IP-delivery technology to function.

12

Foreign Language SEO

Incidentally, the authors of this book are from two different countries. Jaimie is from the United States and speaks English, along with some Hebrew and Spanish. Cristian is from Romania and speaks Romanian, English, and some French. Why does this matter? There are concerns — both from a language angle, as well as some interesting technical caveats — when one decides to target foreign users with search engine marketing. This section reviews some of the most pertinent factors in foreign search engine optimization.

> *As far as this book is concerned, "foreign" refers to anything other than the United States because this book is published in the United States. We consider the UK to be foreign as well; and UK English is a different language dialect, at least academically.*

The Internet is a globalized economy. Web sites can be hosted and contain anything that the author would like. Users are free to peruse pages or order items from any country. Regardless, for the most part, a user residing in the United States would like to see widgets from the United States. And a user in Romania would like to see widgets from Romania. It is also likely that a user in England would prefer to see products from England, not the United States — regardless of the language being substantially the same. There are some exceptions, but in general, to enhance user experience, a search engine may treat web sites from the same region in the same language as the user preferentially.

Foreign Language Optimization Tips

Needless to say, Internet marketing presents many opportunities; and nothing stops a search engine marketer from targeting customers from other countries and/or languages. However, he or she should be aware of a few things, and use all applicable cues to indicate properly to the search engine which language and region a site is focused on.

First of all, if you aim at a foreign market, it is essential to employ a competent copywriting service to author or translate your content to a particular foreign language. He or she should know how to translate for the *specific* market you are targeting. American Spanish, for example, is somewhat different than Argentine Spanish. Even proper translation may be riddled with problems. Foreign language search behavior often differs by dialect, and using the common terminology is key.

Indicating Language and Region

A webmaster should use the `lang` attribute in a meta tag, or inside an enclosing `span` or `div` tag in HTML. Search engines may be able to detect language reasonably accurately, but this tag also provides additional geographical information. The language codes `es-mx`, `es-us`, and `es-es` represent Spanish from Mexico, the United States, and Spain, respectively. This is helpful, because a language dialect and region cannot be detected easily, if at all, just by examining the actual copy. Here's an example:

```
Use '<span lang="es-us">CONTENT</span>' to indicate language in a particular text
region.
```

Or:

```
Use '<meta lang="es-us"> in the header ("<head>") section of the page to indicate
language of the entire page.
```

Table 12-1 lists a few examples of languages and region modifiers.

Table 12-1

Language	Dialects
English	en-AU (Australia), en-CA (Canada), en-GB (UK), en-US (United States), en-HK (Hong Kong)
German	de-AT (Austria), de-BE (Belgium), de-CH (Switzerland), de-DE (Germany)
French	fr-CA (Canada), fr-CH (Switzerland), fr-FR (France), fr-MC (Monaco)
Spanish	es-AR (Argentina), es-CU (Cuba), es-ES (Spain), es-MX (Mexico), es-US (United States)
Japanese	ja (Japan)

You can find a complete list at `http://www.i18nguy.com/unicode/language-identifiers.html`.

Server Location and Domain Name

Search engines sometimes also use the actual geographic location of a web server as a cue in target market identification, and hence determining rankings in that region. Therefore, it is desirable to locate your web server in the same geographic region as is targeted. It is also desirable to use the country-code domain applicable to your target country, but that is not necessary if a `.com` or `.net` domain is used.

The original domain suffixes — .com, .net, and so on — are not strictly U.S. domains and are somewhat region-agnostic. For that reason, especially if the site is in English targeting UK individuals, it becomes very important to use other cues to indicate what region the site targets. Using something other than a .com or .net should be avoided for a differing region; that is, a .co.uk should probably not be used for a Japanese site, despite the obvious language cues, and it certainly should not be used for an American site, which would normally lack such cues.

A server's physical location can be derived by IP using a database of IP range locations. You used such a database in the geo-targeting example from Chapter 11. In the case of a UK site hosted on a .com domain, it is important to check that the server is located in the UK, not just that the company has a presence in the UK. You can check the location of a netblock using the tool at http://www.dnsstuff.com/tools/ipall.ch?domain=xxx.xxx.xxx.xxx, where xxx.xxx.xxx.xxx is the IP address of your web server. Many hosting companies in the UK actually locate their servers elsewhere in Europe due to high overhead in the UK.

> Subdomains can be used on a .com or a .net domain name as a means to locate hosting elsewhere. So instead of http://www.example.com/uk, http://uk.example.com could be used, and a separate server with a UK IP address could be employed. This is the only way to accomplish this, because subfolders on a web server must be delivered by the same IP address/network.

Include the Address of the Foreign Location if Possible

This is an obvious factor that search engines are known to use for local search. Ideally, a web site would have the address in the footer of every page.

Dealing with Accented Letters (Diacritics)

Many languages, including Spanish and most other European languages, have accented letters. In practice, especially on American keyboards, which lack the keys necessary to generate these characters, users do not use the accented characters (that is, é vs. e). Yet some search engines, including Google, do distinguish, and they represent different words in an index, effectively.

Figure 12-1 shows a Google search on Mexico. You can access this page through http://www.google.com/search?hl=en&q=Mexico. Figure 12-2 shows a search for México, through http://www.google.com/search?hl=en&lr=&q=M%C3%A9xico. As you can see, the results are very different.

Google Trends also makes it clear that the two keywords have entirely different quantities of traffic, with the unaccented version winning by a landslide. This is probably because Mexico itself is also an American word, but it is clear that not all Spanish speakers use the accented spelling as well. Figure 12-3 shows the Google Trends comparison between Mexico and México, which you can reach yourself at http://www.google.com/trends?q=Mexico%2C+M%C3%A9xico.

URLs are particularly appropriate because it actually looks more professional to remove the accented characters, because they are encoded in the URL and look confusing — that is, /Mexico.html versus /M%C3%A9xico.html.

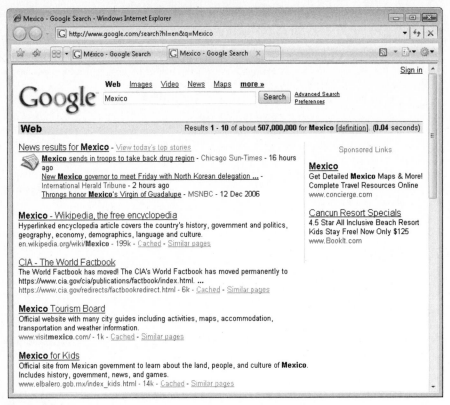

Figure 12-1

It may also be possible to use the unaccented characters in a misspelling in a heading, because that is normatively acceptable in some languages. The following function normalizes accented characters in Western European languages to their non-accented equivalents. It can be applied anywhere in code, including to URL functions and code at the presentation level. You will apply it in the example e-commerce store for URLs, both to make them more aesthetically pleasing, as well as to optimize for non-accent misspellings. Following is a function that replaces accented characters with their non-accented equivalents. This function was originally found on `http://us3.php.net/strtr`:

```
function normalizeExtendedCharacters($str)
{
  return strtr($str,
  "\xe1\xc1\xe0\xc0\xe2\xc2\xe4\xc4\xe3\xc3\xe5\xc5".
  "\xaa\xe7\xc7\xe9\xc9\xe8\xc8\xea\xca\xeb\xcb\xed".
  "\xcd\xec\xcc\xee\xce\xef\xcf\xf1\xd1\xf3\xd3\xf2".
  "\xd2\xf4\xd4\xf6\xd6\xf5\xd5\x8\xd8\xba\xf0\xfa".
  "\xda\xf9\xd9\xfb\xdb\xfc\xdc\xfd\xdd\xff\xe6\xc6\xdf",
  "aAaAaAaAaAaAaAacCeEeEeEeEiIiIiIiInNoOoOoOoOoOoouUuUuUuUyYyaAs");
}
```

Figure 12-2

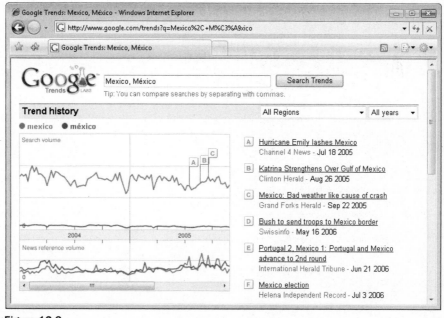

Figure 12-3

Foreign Language Spamming

Google in particular has begun to focus more of its efforts on combating the foreign language spamming that has been going on, mostly with impunity. Matt Cutts states in his blog at `http://www.mattcutts.com/blog/seo-mistakes-spam-in-other-languages/` that "In 2006, I expect Google to pay a lot more attention to spam in other languages, whether it be German, French, Italian, Spanish, Chinese, or any other language. For example, I have no patience for keyword-stuffed doorway pages that do JavaScript redirects, no matter what the language."

We expect all search engines to follow. Spanish, in particular, is the next front for search engine marketing, as well as Chinese; it would be wise, therefore, to avoid any spamming techniques in any language, tempting though it may be. It may work now, but it will definitely be less successful in the future.

Summary

Ironically, one of the effects of globalization is the need for better localization efforts. The search engine optimization strategies when dealing with foreign language web sites aren't much different than with dealing with .coms. Still, there are a few specific issues to keep in mind, and this chapter introduced you to the most important of them.

13

Coping with Technical Issues

This chapter deals with a few common technical issues that relate to SEO efforts:

❑   Unreliable hosting or DNS

❑   Changing hosting providers

❑   Cross-linking

❑   Split testing

❑   Broken links (and how to detect them)

Unreliable Web Hosting or DNS

It is common sense that if a web site is down it cannot get spidered, but we'll state it regardless: *When a site is down, it cannot get spidered*. And when your domain's designated DNS is down, your site cannot get spidered either — even if your web server is up. Reliable hosting and DNS, then, is critical to your web site's well-being. A web site that is down will irritate users and result directly in fewer users visiting your web site. It may also reflect badly on your business, and users may not be back. Likewise, if a search engine spider visits your web site and it does not respond after quite a few unsuccessful attempts, it may result in your web site getting dropped from the index. For this reason we recommend cutting costs elsewhere.

This underscores the need to find reliable hosting. In a field that is ultra-competitive, many web hosting providers choose to provide large amounts of bandwidth and features while compromising service and support. Two dollars per month for hosting will likely get you just that — two dollars worth of web hosting. A lot can be gleaned from the list compiled by NetCraft of "Hosting Providers' Network

Performance." You can find this information at `http://uptime.netcraft.com/perf/reports/Hosters`. There is also an abundance of specific information, including praises and gripes, at Web-HostingTalk — `http://www.webhostingtalk.com`.

> *Most of the time, users opt to use a web hosting provider's DNS. This may be wise, because they may need to alter DNS records in order to move you to another server with another IP if the server your web site is located on fails. However, domain providers (Network Solutions, GoDaddy, and so on) have more recently begun to offer free managed DNS services as well. If you use managed DNS, the hosting provider will not be able to change your domain's records to reflect the new IP, and your site will be down as a result. For this reason, we do not recommend using managed DNS unless your provider is aware of it, and knows to notify you, so that you can change the records yourself to reflect the new IP.*

Changing Hosting Providers

Should the need exist to change hosting providers, the process must be completed in the proper order. Not doing so may result in a time window where your site is unreachable; and this is clearly not desirable, from both a general *and* SEO perspective. The focus of this elaborate process is to prevent both users and search engines from perceiving that the site is gone — or in the case of virtual hosting, possibly seeing the wrong site.

> ***Virtual hosting*** *means that more than one web site is hosted on one IP. This is commonplace, because the world would run out of IPs very quickly if every web site had its own IP. The problem arises when you cancel service at your old web hosting provider and a spider still thinks your site is located at the old IP. In this case, it may see the wrong site or get a 404 error; and as you suspect, this is not desirable.*

The proper approach involves having your site hosted at both hosting providers for a little while. When your site is 100% functional at the new hosting provider, DNS records should then be updated. If you are using a managed DNS service, simply change the "A" records to reflect the new web server's IP address. This change should be reflected almost instantly, and you can cancel the web hosting service at the old provider shortly thereafter. If you are using your old web hosting provider's DNS, you should change to the new hosting provider's DNS. This change may take up to 48 hours to be fully reflected throughout the Internet. Once 48 hours have passed, you can cancel your service at the old hosting provider.

> *You do not have to follow these procedures exactly; the basic underlying concept is that there is a window of time where both users and spiders may still think your site is located at the old hosting provider's IP address. For this reason, you should only cancel after you are certain that that window of time has elapsed.*

One helpful hint to ease the process of moving your domain to a new web hosting provider is to edit your `hosts` file to reflect the new IP on your local machine. This causes your operating system to use the value provided in the file instead of using a DNS to get an IP address for the specified domains.

This functionality was also used to set up the `seophp.example.com` domain. On Windows machines, the file is located in `C:\WINDOWS\system32\drivers\etc\hosts`. Add the following lines, where `xxx.xxx.xxx.xxx` is the IP address of your web server:

```
xxx.xxx.xxx.xxx www.yourdomain.com
xxx.xxx.xxx.xxx yourdomain.com
```

This will let you access your web site at the new provider as if the DNS changes were already reflected. Simply remove the lines after you are done setting up the site on the new web hosting provider's server to verify the changes have actually propagated.

If you have concerns about this procedure, or you need help, you may want to contact your new hosting provider and ask for assistance. Explain your concerns, and hopefully they will be able to accommodate you and put your mind at ease. If they are willing to work with you, it is a good indication that they are a good hosting provider.

Cross-Linking

A typical spammer's accoutrement consists of several thousand cross-linked web sites. These sites collectively drive ad revenue from the aggregate of many usually obscure, but nevertheless queried search terms. Many sites containing many key phrases have to be created to make his spam enterprise worthwhile. Originally, many spammers hosted all of the sites from one web hosting company, and, hence, the same or similar IP addresses. Search engines caught on, and may have applied filters that devalue links exchanged between the web sites within similar IP ranges. This made it much harder to spam, because a spammer would need to host things at different ISPs to continue.

Similarly, it has been speculated that Google in particular, because it is a registrar that does not actually sell domain names, looks at the records associated with domains. Yahoo! is also a registrar, so it may follow suit; but it actually sells domains, so the intent is less clear.

In both cases, even if you are not a spammer, and you want to cross-link, it may be advisable to obscure the relationship. Many larger web hosting companies have diverse ranges of IPs, and can satisfy your explicit request for a different range. The information that is provided to a domain registrar is up to you, but if the name and address do vary, the information must also be correct regardless. Otherwise you risk losing the domain according to ICANN policies. There is also an option for private registration, which prevents Google or Yahoo! from using an automated process to find relationships, at least. To check the registration information for a domain, use a WHOIS tool such as the one at `http://www.seoegghead.com/tools/whois-search.php`. Figure 13-1 shows the tool displaying the data for `www.yahoo.com`.

MSN Search has a useful feature that allows you to see all virtual hosts on one IP by the syntax of `IP:xxx.xxx.xxx.xxx`. Multiple statements can be separated by OR to request a list of a range of IPs. This lets you see who else is hosting in a range. Spam tends to travel in packs. Search engine algorithms are also aware of this. The fact that the operator exists may be a tacit admission by Microsoft that it does examine the sites in an IP range for some reason. See Figure 13-2 for an example, where we examined the sites located at `66.39.117.78`.

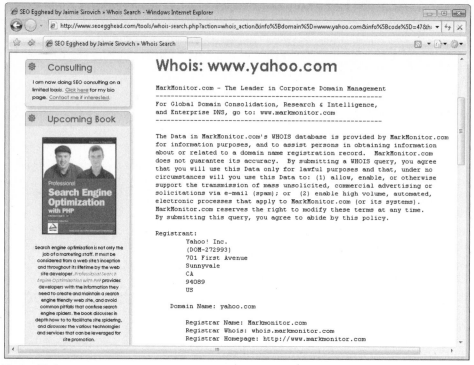

Figure 13-1

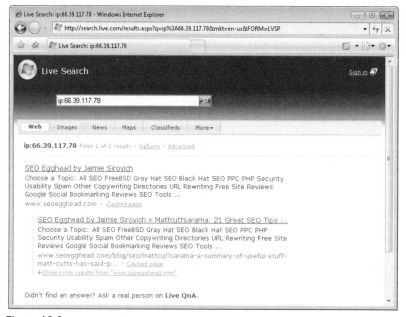

Figure 13-2

SEO-Aware Split Testing

Often, marketers want to create several variations on content for a particular URL in the interest of observing which one converts the best. It is typically an ongoing optimization process, and many different variations may be served over time to that end. This is called *split testing*.

The problem with split testing is that, if it isn't implemented correctly, it may result in complex problems. When implementing changes on a page, there are actually three important effects to analyze:

1. The variation of the performance of the page in search results.
2. The variation in the page CTR.
3. The variation in the conversion rate for visitors that land on your page (the primary purpose of split testing).

You don't necessarily want to sacrifice CTR or rankings for higher conversion rates. But if you do split testing, it's good to be aware of these possible consequences.

This complicates matters, because it introduces other factors into the performance equation. For example, if a page converts *twice* as well, but doesn't rank at all, it may be a net loss for a web site that is driven by organic search. Therefore, you must consider search engine optimization principles when making any changes for split testing.

Ideally, all changes would be purely aesthetic. In most cases doing so would not affect the rankings or CTR of the page — which would make it easier to analyze your results. If the changes are more profound, such as changing the on-page content, the page search engine rankings can be influenced, and this must also be taken into consideration as a performance factor.

One method employed to collect data for split testing is to randomly show page A or page B and track conversion rates for each. Unfortunately, when done incorrectly, this practice can confuse search engines or raise red flags. This is the other problem with split testing. At worst, implementing this will be perceived as spamming and/or cloaking.

There are three different approaches to implement split testing:

1. Redirect requests for a page to other pages with variations randomly
2. Use internal program logic to display the variations randomly
3. Implement temporal split testing

The first two methods are similar in that they randomly display variations of a page. However, redirects are not ideal in this situation because they may confuse search engines, and they should be avoided. Therefore, we recommend using internal program logic. This is consistent with Matt Cutts' recommendation in his video http://video.google.com/videoplay?docid=1156145545372854697.

That implies some light programming. For example, if you have five versions of a web page, page[1..5].php, you can use include() to display its variations, like this:

```
$id = rand(1,5);
include('page' . $id . '.php');
// performance tracking code here
```

The problem, regardless, is that if the pages are significantly different and served randomly, it might actually be perceived as cloaking. Matt Cutts hinted at that in the aforementioned video.

Cloaking may be used to show only one version to a particular search engine. This eliminates the problem whereby a certain version ranks better in search engines than others. It also eliminates the possibility that it will be perceived as spam *academically* (so long as you're not detected!). Yes, cloaking is being used to prevent the perception of cloaking! However, we recommend doing this with a caution that Google frowns upon it.

Either way, if you're detected, you might be sent to the corner. For more information on cloaking, read Chapter 11.

The last method, "temporal split testing," is also safe, and extremely easy to implement. Simply collect data for one timespan for A (perhaps a week), and again for B. However, doing so may be less accurate and requires more time to make determinations.

So, in summary:

1. Don't ignore the organic, possibly detrimental, effects of split testing.

2. Use internal program logic or temporal-based split testing. Do not use redirects.

3. You can use cloaking to show only one version to search engines, but Google frowns upon this approach.

Detecting Broken Links

Broken links are telltale sign of a poorly designed site. The Google Webmaster Guidelines advise webmasters to "Check for broken links and correct HTML." There are a number of online tools that you can use for checking links, such as the one at `http://www.webmaster-toolkit.com/link-checker.shtml`.

However, in many cases you'll want to create your own tools for internal verification. To help you with this task, in the following exercise you build a simple library in the form of a class named LinkChecker, which verifies a given link for validity and provides additional information about that URL. The library probably does more than would be strictly necessary for detecting broken links, but the extra functionality may come in handy for other administrative purposes.

Because there's quite a bit of code to write, the functionality is demonstrated through an exercise, and how things work is explained afterwards.

Detecting Broken Links

1. Create a new file named `link_checker.inc.php` in the `seophp/include` folder. This file contains the `LinkChecker` helper class. Type this code into the file:

```php
<?php

$LINKCHECKER_total_str = '';
```

```php
// +------------------------------------------------------------------+
// | LinkChecker                                                      |
// | Gets URL header data using cURL                                  |
// +------------------------------------------------------------------+
// | Copyright (c) 2003 Jaimie Sirovich                               |
// +------------------------------------------------------------------+
// | Author: Jaimie Sirovich <jsirovic@gmail.com>                     |
// +------------------------------------------------------------------+

class LinkChecker
{
  // helper function for the cURL request
  function CURLOPT_WRITEFUNCTION($ch, $str)
  {
    global $LINKCHECKER_total_str;
    $LINKCHECKER_total_str .= $str;
    if (preg_match('/^(.*?)\r\n\r\n/s', $LINKCHECKER_total_str, $matches))
    {
      echo $matches[1];
      return -1;
    }
    else
    {
      return strlen($str);
    }
  }

  // return the header data
  function getHeader($url, $userAgent = "Mozilla/4.0")
  {
    global $LINKCHECKER_total_str;
    $LINKCHECKER_total_str = "";
    ob_start();
    $ch = curl_init();
    curl_setopt ($ch, CURLOPT_URL, $url);
    curl_setopt ($ch, CURLOPT_USERAGENT, $userAgent);
    curl_setopt ($ch, CURLOPT_HEADER, 1);
    curl_setopt ($ch, CURLOPT_RETURNTRANSFER, 1);
    curl_setopt ($ch, CURLOPT_FOLLOWLOCATION, 1);
    curl_setopt ($ch, CURLOPT_TIMEOUT, 60);
    curl_setopt ($ch, CURLOPT_WRITEFUNCTION,
                 array("LinkChecker", "CURLOPT_WRITEFUNCTION"));

    $result = curl_exec($ch);
    curl_close($ch);
    return ob_get_clean();
  }

  // return response code
  function parseResponseCode($str)
  {
    preg_match('/^HTTP\/\d\.\d (.{3})/', $str, $matches);
    return (isset($matches[1]) ? $matches[1] : '(not available)');
  }
```

```php
// return the MIME type
function parseMimeType($str)
{
  preg_match('/Content-Type: (.*)/', $str, $matches);
  return (isset($matches[1]) ? $matches[1] : '(not available)');
}

// return the Content-Length
function parseContentLength($str)
{
  preg_match('/Content-Length: (.*)/', $str, $matches);
  return (isset($matches[1]) ? $matches[1] : '(not available)');
}

// return the Location
function parseLocation($str)
{
  preg_match('/Location: ?([^\r\n]*)/i', $str, $matches);
  return (isset($matches[1]) ? $matches[1] : '(not available)');
}

// return the path to the destination URL
function getPath($url, &$_response_code, $userAgent = 'Mozilla/4.0')
{
  $_url = $url;
  $path = array();
  $path[] = 'Initial destination ' . $_url;
  $iterations = 0;

  do
  {
    $_buffer = LinkChecker::getHeader($_url);
    if (!$_buffer)
    {
      $path[] = 'ERROR: Maximum number of redirections exceeded; aborting.';
      break;
    }
    $_url = LinkChecker::parseLocation($_buffer) ?
            LinkChecker::parseLocation($_buffer) : $_url;
    $_response_code = LinkChecker::parseResponseCode($_buffer);
    $path[] = ($_response_code != 200 && $_response_code != 404) ?
              ('Redirect (' . $_response_code . ') to => ' . $_url) :
              ('Final destination (' . $_response_code . ') ' . $_url );
    $iterations++;
    if ($iterations > 10)
    {
      $path[] = 'ERROR: Maximum number of redirections exceeded; aborting.';
      break;
    }
  }
  while ($_response_code != '200' && $_response_code != '404');
```

```
      return $path;
    }
}
?>
```

2. In the seophp folder, create a file named check_links.php with the following code. This is a simple script created to demonstrate the functionality of the LinkChecker class:

```php
<?php
// include link checker library
require_once 'include/link_checker.inc.php';
?>

<!DOCTYPE html PUBLIC "-//W3C//DTD XHTML 1.1//EN"
 "http://www.w3.org/TR/xhtml11/DTD/xhtml11.dtd">
<html>
  <head>
    <title>Professional Search Engine Optimization with PHP: Link Checker</title>
  </head>
  <body>
    <h1>Professional Search Engine Optimization with PHP: Link Checker</h1>

<?php

// stablish the URL to analyze
$url = "http://www.cristiandarie.ro/pages/seophp.aspx";

// retrieve URL data
$responseHeader = LinkChecker::getHeader($url);
$statusCode = LinkChecker::parseResponseCode($responseHeader);
$mimeType = LinkChecker::parseMimeType($responseHeader);
$contentLength = LinkChecker::parseContentLength($responseHeader);
$location = LinkChecker::parseLocation($responseHeader);
$path = LinkChecker::getPath($url, $responseCode);

// display URL request data
echo 'URL: ' . $url . '<br />';
echo 'Response header: ' . $responseHeader . '<br />';
echo 'Response status code: ' . $statusCode . '<br />';
echo 'Response MIME type: ' . $mimeType . '<br />';
echo 'Response content length: ' . $contentLength . '<br />';
echo 'Response location: ' . $location . '<br />';

// display the redirection path
echo 'Path: <br />';
for ($i = 0; $i < count($path); $i++)
{
  echo '  ' . $path[$i] . '<br />';
}

// display the HTTP status code of the last request
echo 'Final status code: ' . $responseCode . '<br />';
```

```
?>

  </body>
</html>
```

3. It's showtime! Feel free to change the value of the `$url` variable in `check_links.php` if you want to check another URL, then load `http://seophp.example.com/check_links.php`. The output should look like the one in Figure 13-3.

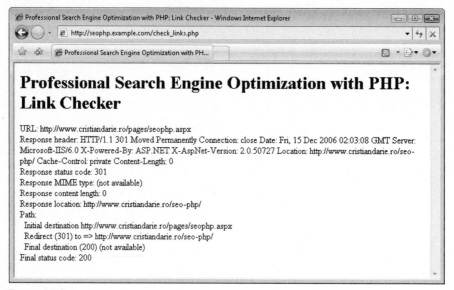

Figure 13-3

Figure 13-3 shows various data that the link library could provide about the input URL, `http://www.cristiandarie.ro/pages/seophp.aspx`. As you can see, this URL does a 301 redirect to `http://www.cristiandarie.ro/seo-php/`.

Basically, all you're usually interested in is the final status code reached by this page. If it's 200, then the link is valid. This is the code that retrieves the last status code:

```
// stablish the URL to analyze
$url = "http://www.cristiandarie.ro/pages/seophp.aspx";

// obtain redirection path
$path = LinkChecker::getPath($url, $responseCode);

// display the HTTP status code of the last request
echo 'Final status code: ' . $responseCode . '<br />';
```

The `getPath()` method traces the path of a request and sets the second parameter to the final result code subject to a limit of 10 redirections. You can use this class to audit lists of links around your site or in a database and remove or flag dead links.

Apart from `getPath()`, the `LinkChecker` class has other useful methods as well, and the `check_links.php` script uses them all. For example, the `getHeader()` method retrieves the header of the URL sent as parameter. The result of this can be fed as parameter to `parseResponseCode()`, which reads the header data and returns the HTTP status code by reading it from the header. Depending on your requirements, an answer of 200, or a 301 or 302 that eventually leads to a 200 response, may be acceptable.

Summary

This chapter talked about a few common technical problems that you may encounter when maintaining your web sites. You've learned about the detrimental effects of unreliable web hosting providers (and how to safely switch!), as well as the dangers of having cross-linked web sites in the same C class. You've explored safe approaches to split-testing. At the end of the chapter you had your share of geek-fun, building the `LinkChecker` library. This chapter has finished covering all necessary background material. In the next chapter you build a search engine–optimized cookie catalog. We hope you are hungry!

14

Case Study: Building an E-Commerce Store

You've come a long way in learning how to properly construct a web site with regard to search engine optimization. Now it is time to demonstrate and tie together what you have learned. This chapter demonstrates an e-commerce store called "Cookie Ogre's Warehouse." This store sells all sorts of cookies and pastries. You implement only what relates to search engine optimization; the store will not have a functional shopping cart or checkout process.

In this chapter you:

❑ Develop a set of requirements for a simple product catalog

❑ Implement the product catalog with search engine–friendly architecture

You'll notice that the site you're building in this chapter is very basic, but highlights the most important SEO-related principles taught in this book. The simplicity is necessary for the purposes of this demonstration, because a complex implementation could easily be extended throughout an entire book itself.

> To learn how to build a real-world search engine–optimized product catalog from scratch, and learn how to design its database and architectural foundations to allow for future growth, see Cristian's *Beginning PHP and MySQL E-Commerce: From Novice to Professional*, 2nd edition (Apress, 2007).

Establishing the Requirements

As with any other development project, you design your site based on a set of requirements. For Cookie Ogre's Warehouse, we've come up with this short list:

- ❏ The catalog contains products that are grouped into categories.

- ❏ A product can belong to any number of categories, and a category can contain many products.

- ❏ The properties of a product are name, price, description, the primary category that it is part of, and an associated search engine brand.

- ❏ The properties of a category are: name.

- ❏ The properties of a brand are: name.

- ❏ The first page of the catalog contains links to the category pages. The page title should contain the site name.

- ❏ A category page displays the category name, the site name, a link to the home page, and links to the pages of the products in that category. The page title should contain the site name and the category name.

- ❏ Category pages should have a maximum number of products they can display, and use a search engine-friendly paging feature to allow the visitors to browse the products on multiple pages.

- ❏ A product page must display the product name, price and a link to the home page, a link to its category, the product's description, and the associated brand name and picture.

- ❏ All catalog pages must be accessible through keyword-rich URLs.

- ❏ If a catalog page is accessed through a URL other than the proper version, it should be automatically 301 redirected to the proper version.

- ❏ Requests for `index.php` and `index.html` should be automatically 301 redirected to `/`.

- ❏ Canadian users should see the product price in CAD currency. All the other visitors should see the price in USD.

- ❏ Because a product that is in multiple categories can be reached through more than one category link, all the links except the one associated with its primary category must be excluded through `robots.txt`.

Implementing the Product Catalog

Starting from the list of requirements enumerated above, you implement three catalog pages, whose functionality is sustained by a few helper scripts. The first catalog page is `index.php`, and it looks as shown in Figure 14-1.

Clicking one of the category links gets you to `category.php`, which displays the details of the category, including links to its products. The script is accessed — obviously — through a keyword-rich URL, so the user will never know it's a script named `category.php` that does all the work. Figure 14-2 shows this script at work.

Clicking a product link in the category page loads the details page of that product, which looks like Figure 14-3.

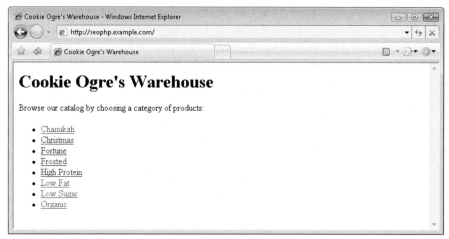

Figure 14-1

Figure 14-2

Figure 14-3

Now you see what we're up to. Follow the steps of the exercise to implement it.

Creating Cookie Ogre's Warehouse

1. In order to display different prices for Canadian users, you need geo-targeting functionality, which was covered in Chapter 11. Because the exercise is quite long, the steps are not repeated here. If you haven't already, please follow the geo-targeting exercise in Chapter 11 to create and populate the `geo_target_data` table, and create the `simple_geo_target.inc.php` library.

2. Inside your `seophp` folder, create a folder named `media`. This folder needs to contain four files named 1, 2, 3, and 4, which are the pictures of the search engine company logos — Google, Yahoo!, Microsoft, and Ask. Then take these files from the code download of this book, and copy them to your `media` folder.

3. Now create the new necessary database structures. Connect to your database using either phpMyAdmin or the MySQL console, like you did in the other database exercises in this book. Then execute the following SQL commands, which create and populate with data from the `brands` table:

```
CREATE TABLE `brands` (
  `id` int(11) NOT NULL auto_increment,
  `name` varchar(50) NOT NULL default '',
  PRIMARY KEY  (`id`)
);

INSERT INTO `brands` (`id`, `name`) VALUES (1, 'Google');
INSERT INTO `brands` (`id`, `name`) VALUES (2, 'Yahoo');
INSERT INTO `brands` (`id`, `name`) VALUES (3, 'Microsoft');
INSERT INTO `brands` (`id`, `name`) VALUES (4, 'Ask');
```

4. Continue by executing these SQL commands, which create and populate the `categories` data table:

```
CREATE TABLE `categories` (
  `id` int(11) NOT NULL auto_increment,
  `name` varchar(50) NOT NULL default '',
  PRIMARY KEY  (`id`)
);

INSERT INTO `categories` (`id`, `name`) VALUES (1, 'Chanukah');
INSERT INTO `categories` (`id`, `name`) VALUES (2, 'Christmas');
INSERT INTO `categories` (`id`, `name`) VALUES (3, 'Frosted');
INSERT INTO `categories` (`id`, `name`) VALUES (4, 'Low Sugar');
INSERT INTO `categories` (`id`, `name`) VALUES (5, 'Low Fat');
INSERT INTO `categories` (`id`, `name`) VALUES (6, 'High Protein');
INSERT INTO `categories` (`id`, `name`) VALUES (7, 'Fortune');
INSERT INTO `categories` (`id`, `name`) VALUES (8, 'Organic');
```

5. Next you're creating and populating the `product_categories` table, which contains associations between products and categories. Each record is formed of a product ID and a category ID:

```
CREATE TABLE `product_categories` (
  `product_id` int(11) NOT NULL default '0',
  `category_id` int(11) NOT NULL default '0',
  PRIMARY KEY (product_id, category_id)
);
```

```
INSERT INTO `product_categories` (product_id, category_id) VALUES (1, 3);
INSERT INTO `product_categories` (product_id, category_id) VALUES (2, 4);
INSERT INTO `product_categories` (product_id, category_id) VALUES (2, 5);
INSERT INTO `product_categories` (product_id, category_id) VALUES (3, 6);
INSERT INTO `product_categories` (product_id, category_id) VALUES (4, 2);
INSERT INTO `product_categories` (product_id, category_id) VALUES (4, 3);
INSERT INTO `product_categories` (product_id, category_id) VALUES (5, 1);
INSERT INTO `product_categories` (product_id, category_id) VALUES (6, 7);
INSERT INTO `product_categories` (product_id, category_id) VALUES (6, 8);
INSERT INTO `product_categories` (product_id, category_id) VALUES (6, 3);
```

6. The last table you're creating is `products`. This contains data about each product sold by the Cookie Ogre's Warehouse:

```
CREATE TABLE `products` (
  `id` int(11) NOT NULL auto_increment,
  `brand_id` int(11) NOT NULL default '0',
  `name` varchar(255) NOT NULL default '',
  `price` double(8,2) NOT NULL default '0.00',
  `desc` text NOT NULL,
  `primary_category_id` int(11) NOT NULL default '0',
  PRIMARY KEY  (`id`)
);

INSERT INTO `products` VALUES (1, 1, 'Matt Cutts'' Spam Flavored Cookie', 2.00,
'This delicious cookie tastes exactly like spam.', 3);

INSERT INTO `products` VALUES (2, 2, 'Jeremy Zawodny''s Snickerdoodles', 3.00,
'These cookies are the Zawodny Family secret recipe, passed down throughout the
generations. They are low fat and low sugar.', 4);

INSERT INTO `products` VALUES (3, 3, 'Bill Gates'' Cookie', 999999.99, 'These
cookies taste like... a million bucks. Note: before consuming, these cookies must
be activated by Microsoft.', 6);

INSERT INTO `products` VALUES (4, 4, 'Jeeve''s Favorite Frosted Cookie', 2.00,
'Shaped like a butler, sugar coated. Now in Christmas holiday colors.', 3);

INSERT INTO `products` VALUES (5, 1, 'Google Menorah Cookies', 3.00, 'Snatched from
one of the famed snack bars at Google while all of the employees were home. ', 1);

INSERT INTO `products` VALUES (6, 2, 'Frosted Fortune Cookie', 2.00, 'Dipped
 organic sugar.', 7);
```

7. Now you need to create a file named `config.inc.php`, in your `seophp/include` folder, with the following code. You should already have this file from the geo-targeting exercise; make sure it contains the following constant definitions:

```php
<?php
// site domain; no trailing '/' !
define('SITE_DOMAIN', 'http://seophp.example.com');

// defines database connection data
define('DB_HOST', 'localhost');
```

```
define('DB_USER', 'seouser');
define('DB_PASSWORD', 'seomaster');
define('DB_DATABASE', 'seophp');

// defines the number of products for paging
define('PRODUCTS_PER_PAGE', 1);

// the geo-targeting file name
define('GEO_TARGETING_CSV', 'geo_target_data/GeoIPCountryWhois.csv');
?>
```

8. Add the following mod_rewrite rules to the `.htaccess` file in your `seophp` folder:

```
RewriteEngine On

# Redirect to correct domain if incorrect to avoid canonicalization problems
RewriteCond %{HTTP_HOST} !^seophp\.example\.com
RewriteRule ^(.*)$ http://seophp.example.com/$1 [R=301,L]

# Redirect URLs ending in /index.php or /index.html to /
RewriteCond %{THE_REQUEST} ^GET\ .*/index\.(php|html)\ HTTP
RewriteRule ^(.*)index\.(php|html)$ /$1 [R=301,L]

# Rewrite keyword-rich URLs for paged category pages
RewriteRule ^Products/.*-C([0-9]+)/Page-([0-9]+)/?$ category.php?category_id=$1&↵
page=$2 [L]

# Rewrite keyword-rich URLs for category pages
RewriteRule ^Products/.*-C([0-9]+)/?$ category.php?category_id=$1&page=1 [L]

# Rewrite keyword-rich URLs for product pages
RewriteRule ^Products/.*-C([0-9]+)/.*-P([0-9]+)\.html$ /product.php?category_id=$1&↵
product_id=$2&%{QUERY_STRING} [L]

# Rewrite media files
RewriteRule ^.*-M([0-9]+)\..*$ /media/$1 [L]

# Rewrite robots.txt
RewriteRule ^robots.txt$ /robots.php
```

9. Create `include/url_factory.inc.php` and add the following code. This file contains helper functions that create links to product pages, category pages, and media files. You can also find a function that does 301 redirects to the proper version of a URL if the visitor isn't already there.

```
<?php
// include config file
require_once 'config.inc.php';

// redirects to proper category URL if not already there
function fix_url($proper_url)
{
  // 301 redirect to the proper URL if necessary
  if (SITE_DOMAIN . $_SERVER['REQUEST_URI'] != $proper_url)
  {
```

```php
        header('HTTP/1.1 301 Moved Permanently');
        header('Location: ' . $proper_url);
        exit();
    }
}

// prepares a string to be included in an URL
function _prepare_url_text($string)
{
    // remove all characters that aren't a-z, 0-9, dash, underscore or space
    $NOT_acceptable_characters_regex = '#[^-a-zA-Z0-9_ ]#';
    $string = preg_replace($NOT_acceptable_characters_regex, '', $string);

    // remove all leading and trailing spaces
    $string = trim($string);

    // change all dashes, underscores and spaces to dashes
    $string = preg_replace('#[-_ ]+#', '-', $string);

    // return the modified string
    return $string;
}

// builds a category link
function make_category_url($category_name, $category_id, $page = 1)
{
    // prepare the category name for inclusion in URL
    $clean_category_name = _prepare_url_text($category_name);

    // build the keyword-rich URL
    $url = SITE_DOMAIN . '/Products/' .
        $clean_category_name . '-C' . $category_id . '/';

    // add page number if page is different than 1
    $url = ($page == 1) ? $url : $url . 'Page-' . $page . '/';

    // return the URL
    return $url;
}

// builds a product link
function make_category_product_url($category_name, $category_id,
                                  $product_name, $product_id)
{
    // prepare the product name and category name for inclusion in URL
    $clean_category_name = _prepare_url_text($category_name);
    $clean_product_name = _prepare_url_text($product_name);

    // build the keyword-rich URL
    $url = SITE_DOMAIN . '/Products/' .
        $clean_category_name . '-C' . $category_id . '/' .
        $clean_product_name . '-P' . $product_id . '.html';
```

```
    // return the URL
    return $url;
}


// builds a link to a media file
function make_media_url($id, $name, $extension)
{
    // prepare the medium name for inclusion in URL
    $clean_name = _prepare_url_text ($name);

    // build the keyword-rich URL
    $url = SITE_DOMAIN . '/' . $clean_name . '-M' . $id . '.' . $extension;

    // return the URL
    return $url;
}
?>
```

10.   Create `include/database_tools.inc.php`, and type the following code. This file contains a class named DatabaseTools, which includes common database functionality, such as opening and closing database connections. These functions are called from other classes that need to read data from the database.

```
<?php
// load configuration file
require_once('config.inc.php');

// database related tools
class DatabaseTools
{
    // helper function used to filter data for the database
    function dbIdentifier($str)
    {
        $stripped = preg_replace('/[^A-Z0-9_.]/i', '', $str);
        $tmp = preg_replace('/(.+?)(\.|$)/', '`\\1`\\2', $stripped);
        return $tmp;
    }

    // connect to the database and return the connection handler
    function getConnection()
    {
        // connect to MySQL server
        $db_link = mysql_connect(DB_HOST, DB_USER, DB_PASSWORD);

        // throw a 500 error if the database couldn't be reached
        if ($db_link === false)
        {
            header('HTTP/1.0 500 Internal Server Error');
            echo 'Sorry, the Cookie Ogre lost his beloved Cookie Ogress, went bingeing
and ate all of our cookies; consequentially, we will be closed until Friday.';
        }

        // Connect to the seophp database
        mysql_select_db(DB_DATABASE) or die("Could not select database");
```

```
      // return the connection handler
      return $db_link;
    }

    // close the database connection
    function closeConnection($db_handler)
    {
      mysql_close($db_handler);
    }
  }
?>
```

11. Save the following code in `include/catalog.inc.php`. This file contains three classes: `Brands`, `Categories`, and `Products`, which contain the functionality to read brand, category, and product data from the database:

```php
<?php
// load configuration file
require_once('config.inc.php');
// load database tools
require_once('database_tools.inc.php');

// Database class for handling brands
class Brands
{

  // retrieve cloaking data filtered by the supplied parameters
  function get($id = 0, $name = '', $order_by = '', $order_dir = '')
  {
    // by default, retrieve all records
    $q = " SELECT brands.* FROM brands WHERE TRUE ";

    // filter by brand ID
    if ($id) {
      $id = (int) $id;
      $q .= " AND id = $id ";
    }

    // filter by brand name
    if ($name) {
      $name = mysql_escape_string($name);
      $q .= " AND name = '$name' ";
    }

    // add sorting options
    if ($order_by) {
      if ($order_dir !== '' && !$order_dir) {
        $order_q = ' DESC ';
      } else {
        $order_q = ' ';
      }
      $q .= " ORDER BY " . db_identifier($order) . $order_q;
    }
```

```php
    // get a database connection
    $db_link = DatabaseTools::getConnection();

    // execute the query
    $query_results = mysql_query($q);

    // close database connection
    DatabaseTools::closeConnection($db_link);

    // return the results as an associative array
    $rows = array();
    while ($result = mysql_fetch_assoc($query_results)) {
      $rows[] = $result;
    }
    return $rows;
  }

}

// Database class for handling categories
class Categories
{
  // retrieves categories data filtered by the supplied parameters
  function get($id = 0, $name = '', $order_by = '', $order_dir = '')
  {
    // by default, retrieve all records
    $q = " SELECT categories.* FROM categories WHERE TRUE ";

    // filter by category id
    if ($id) {
      $id = (int) $id;
      $q .= " AND id = $id ";
    }

    // filter by category name
    if ($name) {
      $name = mysql_escape_string($name);
      $q .= " AND name = '$name' ";
    }

    // add sorting options
    if ($order_by) {
      if ($order_dir !== '' && !$order_dir) {
        $order_q = ' DESC ';
      } else {
        $order_q = ' ';
      }
      $q .= " ORDER BY " . DatabaseTools::dbIdentifier($order_by) . $order_q;
    }

    // get a database connection
    $db_link = DatabaseTools::getConnection();
```

```
    // execute the query
    $query_results = mysql_query($q);

    // close database connection
    DatabaseTools::closeConnection($db_link);

    // return the results as an associative array
    $rows = array();
    while ($result = mysql_fetch_assoc($query_results)) {
      $rows[] = $result;
    }
    return $rows;
  }
}

// Database class for handling products
class Products
{
  // retrieves products data filtered by the supplied parameters
  function get($id = 0, $category_id = 0, $brand_id = 0, $name = '')
  {
    // by default, retrieve all records
    $q = "SELECT products.* FROM products WHERE TRUE ";

    // filter by ID if the $id parameter was provided
    if ($id) {
      $id = (int) $id;
      $q .= " AND id = $id ";
    }

    // filter by product name if the $name parameter was provided
    if ($name) {
      $name = mysql_escape_string($name);
      $q .= " AND name = '$name' ";
    }

    // filter by category ID if the category_id parameter was provided
    if ($category_id) {
      $category_id = (int) $category_id;
      $q .= " AND (SELECT COUNT(*) FROM product_categories " .
            " WHERE product_categories.product_id = products.id " .
            " AND product_categories.category_id = $category_id) ";
    }

    // filter by brand ID if the $brand_id parameter was provided
    if ($brand_id) {
      $brand_id = (int) $brand_id;
      $q .= " AND brand_id = $brand_id ";
    }

    // get a database connection
    $db_link = DatabaseTools::getConnection();
```

```php
    // execute the query
    $query_results = mysql_query($q);

    // close database connection
    DatabaseTools::closeConnection($db_link);

    // return the results as an associative array
    $rows = array();
    while ($result = mysql_fetch_assoc($query_results)) {
      $rows[] = $result;
    }
    return $rows;
  }
}
?>
```

12. Create a new file named `simple_pager.inc.php` in your `include` folder. Then write the following code, which contains the `SimplePager` class. This class includes the functionality to generate pager text and links:

```php
<?php

// generates pager links
class SimplePager
{
  var $_rows;
  var $_limit;
  var $_function_callback;
  var $_page_number_parameter_index;
  var $_max_listed_pages;
  var $_previous_prompt;
  var $_next_prompt;
  var $_show_disabled_links;

  // constructor
  function SimplePager($rows, $limit, $function_callback,
                       $page_number_parameter_index = 1)
  {
    $this->_rows = $rows;
    $this->_limit = $limit;
    $this->_function_callback = $function_callback;
    $this->_page_number_parameter_index = $page_number_parameter_index;
    $this->_max_listed_pages = 10;
    $this->_previous_prompt = '<< back';
    $this->_next_prompt = 'next >>';
  }

  // displays the pager links
  function display($page_number = 1, &$rows, $additional_parameters = '')
  {
    $offset = ($page_number - 1) * $this->_limit;
    $row_count = sizeof($this->_rows);
    $total_pages = ceil($row_count / $this->_limit);
    $rows = array_slice($this->_rows, $offset, $this->_limit);
```

```php
// will contain the pager links
$links = array();

// display the "<< back" link
if ($page_number > 1)
{
  $prev_page = $page_number - 1;
  $links[] =
    "<a href='" .
    call_user_func_array($this->_function_callback,
      array_merge($additional_parameters,
      array($this->_page_number_parameter_index => $prev_page))) .
    "'>$this->_previous_prompt</a>";
}
else
{
  // no "<< back" link if the visitor is on the first page
  $links[] = $this->_previous_prompt;
}

// calculate the first and last listed pages
$start = floor($page_number / ($this->_max_listed_pages))
        * $this->_max_listed_pages;
if (!$start) $start = 1;
$end = ($total_pages < $start + $this->_max_listed_pages - 1) ?
        $total_pages : $start + $this->_max_listed_pages - 1;

// display pager links
for ($i = $start; $i <= $end; $i++)
{
  // display links for all pages except the current one
  if ($i != $page_number)
  {
    $links[] =
      "<a href='" .
      call_user_func_array($this->_function_callback,
        array_merge($additional_parameters,
        array($this->_page_number_parameter_index => $i))) .
      "'>$i</a>";
  }
  else
  {
    // no link for the current page
    $links[] = $i;
  }
}

// display "next >>" link
if ($page_number < $total_pages)
{
  $next_page = $page_number + 1;
  $links[] =
    "<a href='" .
    call_user_func_array($this->_function_callback,
      array_merge($additional_parameters,
```

```
            array($this->_page_number_parameter_index => $next_page))) .
        "'>$this->_next_prompt</a>";
  }
  else
  {
    // no "next >>" link if the visitor is on the last page
    $links[] = $this->_next_prompt;
  }

    // return the pager text
    return implode(' | ', $links);
  }
}
?>
```

13. It's time to create `index.php` in your `seophp` folder, with the following code. This file generates the first page of the catalog, displaying all the existing categories of the catalog:

```
<?php
// load the catalog library
require_once 'include/catalog.inc.php';
// load the URL factory
require_once 'include/url_factory.inc.php';

// retrieve the list of categories ordered by name
$categories = Categories::get(0, '', 'name');
?>

<!DOCTYPE html PUBLIC "-//W3C//DTD XHTML 1.0 Transitional//EN"
"http://www.w3.org/TR/xhtml1/DTD/xhtml1-transitional.dtd">
<html>
  <head>
    <title>Cookie Ogre's Warehouse</title>
  </head>
  <body>
    <h1>Cookie Ogre's Warehouse</h1>
    Browse our catalog by choosing a category of products:

<?php
// display each category
echo "<ul>";
foreach ($categories as $category)
{
  $url = make_category_url($category['name'], $category['id']);
  echo '<li>' .
       '<a href="' . $url . '"' . '>' . $category['name'] . '</a>' .
       '</li>';
}
echo "</ul>"
?>

  </body>
</html>
```

14. Now create `category.php` in your `seophp` folder. This script displays category details:

```php
<?php
// load the catalog library
require_once 'include/catalog.inc.php';
// load the URL factory library
require_once 'include/url_factory.inc.php';
// load pager library
require_once 'include/simple_pager.inc.php';

// retrieve the category details
$category_id = $_GET['category_id'];
$categories = Categories::get($category_id);
$category = $categories[0];
$category_name = $category['name'];

// retrieve the page number; if none is provided, assume 1
$page = isset($_GET['page']) ? $_GET['page'] : 1;

// redirect to the proper URL if necessary
$proper_url = make_category_url($category['name'], $category_id, $page);
fix_url($proper_url);

// retrieve the products in the category
$products = Products::get(0, $category_id);

// send a 404 if the category does not exist.
if (!$products) {
  header("HTTP/1.0 404 Not Found");
  exit();
}
?>

<!DOCTYPE html PUBLIC "-//W3C//DTD XHTML 1.0 Transitional//EN"
"http://www.w3.org/TR/xhtml1/DTD/xhtml1-transitional.dtd">
<html>
  <head>
    <title><?php echo $category_name ?> - Cookie Ogre's Warehouse</title>
  </head>
  <body>
    <h1>
      <?php echo $category_name ?> -
      <a href="/">Cookie Ogre's Warehouse</a>
    </h1>
    Find these extraordinary products in our
    <b><?php echo $category_name ?></b> category:

<?php
// load the URL factory
require_once 'include/url_factory.inc.php';

// display each product
echo "<ul>";
```

```php
// calculate which products to display on this page
$start = ($page - 1) * PRODUCTS_PER_PAGE;
$end = min ($start + PRODUCTS_PER_PAGE, count($products));

// display the products for the current page
for ($i = $start; $i < $end; $i++ )
{
  $url = make_category_product_url($category_name, $category_id,
                                   $products[$i]['name'], $products[$i]['id']);
  echo '<li>' .
       '<a href="' . $url . '"' . '>' . $products[$i]['name'] . '</a>' .
       '</li>';
}
echo "</ul>";

// use the SimplePager library to display the pager
$simple_pager = new SimplePager($products, PRODUCTS_PER_PAGE, 'make_category_url');
echo $simple_pager->display($page, $products, array($category_name, $category_id));
?>

  </body>
</html>
```

15. Finally, create `product.php` in your `seophp` folder. This is the page that individual products appear on:

```php
<?php
// load the catalog library
require_once 'include/catalog.inc.php';
// load the URL factory
require_once 'include/url_factory.inc.php';
// load the SimpleGeoTarget library
require_once 'include/simple_geo_target.inc.php';

// retrieve the product details
$product_id = $_GET['product_id'];
$products = Products::get($product_id);
$product = $products[0];

// retrieve the category details and create the category link
$category_id = $_GET['category_id'];
$categories = Categories::get($category_id);
$category = $categories[0];
$category_url = make_category_url($category['name'], $category['id']);

// redirect to the proper URL if necessary
$proper_url = make_category_product_url($category['name'], $category_id,
                                        $product['name'], $product_id);
fix_url($proper_url);

// retrieve the brand details
$brand_id = $product['brand_id'];
$brands = Brands::get($brand_id);
$brand = $brands[0];
```

```php
$brand_image_url = make_media_url($brand_id, $brand['name'], 'jpg');

// send a 404 if the product or category does not exist
if  (!$product || !$category) {
  header("HTTP/1.0 404 Not Found");
  exit();
}
?>

<!DOCTYPE html PUBLIC "-//W3C//DTD XHTML 1.0 Transitional//EN"
"http://www.w3.org/TR/xhtml1/DTD/xhtml1-transitional.dtd">
<html>
  <head>
    <title><?php echo $product['name'] ?> - Cookie Ogre Warehouse</title>
  </head>
  <body>
    <!-- Display title, which includes link to the home page -->
    <h1>
      <?php echo $product['name'] ?> -
      <a href="/">Cookie Ogre Warehouse</a>
    </h1>

    <!-- Display the product description -->
    <p><?php echo $product['desc'];?></p>

    <!-- Display the brand logo -->
    <p>
      This cookie is brought to you by <?php echo $brand['name']; ?>.
      <br /><img src="<?php echo $brand_image_url; ?>"/>
    </p>

    <!-- Display the product price -->
    <p>Price:
<?php
// display price in CAD for canadian visitors, or in USD otherwise
if (SimpleGeoTarget::isRegion("CA"))
  echo $product['price'] * 1.17 . ' CAD';
else
  echo $product['price'] . ' USD';
?>
    </p>

    View more products in our
    <a href="<?php echo $category_url; ?>">
      <?php echo $category['name']; ?></a>
    category.
  </body>
</html>
```

16. The final step is to exclude the product links that aren't in the primary category. Obtaining this data isn't extremely complicated, but it does involve a longer-than-usual SQL query. Also, although you do not have a shopping cart, assume that you do and deliberately exclude it using `robots.txt`. Otherwise, assuming your add-to-cart URLs look like `/cart.php?action=add&product_id=5`,

you will create a duplicate shopping cart page per product. Create the following `robots.php` file in your `seophp` folder. This file is already mapped to handle `robots.txt` requests using a mod_rewrite rule:

```php
<?php
// set propert content type
header('Content-type: text/plain');

// include config file
require_once 'include/config.inc.php';
// load database tools
require_once('include/database_tools.inc.php');
// load the URL factory
require_once 'include/url_factory.inc.php';

// this query returns product_id and secondary_category_id data which needs to be
// excluded using robots.txt
$q = 'SELECT products.*, ' .
     'product_categories.category_id AS secondary_category_id, ' .
     'categories.name AS secondary_category_name ' .
     'FROM products LEFT JOIN product_categories ' .
     'ON (product_categories.product_id = products.id) ' .
     'LEFT JOIN categories ' .
     'ON (product_categories.category_id = categories.id) ' .
     'WHERE products.primary_category_id <> product_categories.category_id';

// get a database connection
$db_link = DatabaseTools::getConnection();

// execute the query
$query_results = mysql_query($q);

// close database connection
DatabaseTools::closeConnection($db_link);

// create an associative array with the results
$rows = array();
while ($result = mysql_fetch_assoc($query_results)) {
  $rows[] = $result;
}

// User agent
echo "User-agent: * \r\n";

// display the links that need to be excluded
foreach ($rows as $row)
{
  // get the category and product IDs
  $product_id = $row['id'];
  $category_id = $row['secondary_category_id'];
  $product_name = $row['name'];
  $category_name = $row['secondary_category_name'];
```

```
    // create disallow definition
    $url = make_category_product_url($category_name, $category_id,
                                      $product_name, $product_id);

    $disallow = str_replace(SITE_DOMAIN, '', $url);
    echo "Disallow: " . $disallow . "\r\n";
}


?>
Disallow: /cart.php
```

17. That's it! Load `http://seophp.example.com` and expect to see the page shown in Figure 14-1. Play around with your site a little bit to understand it works. Also verify that loading `http://seophp.example.com/robots.txt` yields the results shown in Figure 14-4.

Figure 14-4

Next, analyze how you made this work, and what design decisions you have made to implement the set of requirements. To understand such an application, even a simple one, you need to start with the database. You need to understand how the database works and how the data is organized.

Your database is comprised of four data tables:

- ❑ `brands` — Contains search engine company names.

- ❑ `categories` — Contains the categories in which your products are grouped.

- ❑ `products` — Contains data about the products in your catalog.

- ❑ `product_categories` — Contains associations between products and categories. This table is required because a category is allowed to contain more products, so that multiple associations can be created for each product, and for each category. (If each of your products belonged to a single category, you could have referenced that category through a separate column in the `products` table, instead of creating the `product_categories` table — just like you're now using the `primary_category_id` column in `products`.)

To visualize the relationship between these tables, see the diagram in Figure 14-5.

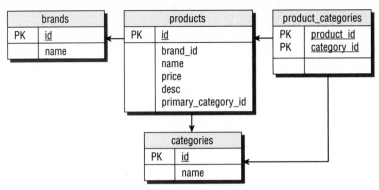

Figure 14-5

When it comes to the code, you'll find most of it familiar from the previous chapters. This section focuses only on the new details.

The functions you're using to display catalog data are located in the `catalog.inc.php` file. There you can find the `Brands`, `Categories`, and `Products` classes — each of these classes have a method called `get()`. The various parameters of `get()` allow you to either retrieve the complete list of brands, categories, and products, or to filter the results according to various criteria.

The `get()` methods return an associate array with the query results. If you're expecting a single result, then you need to read the first element of the returned array. Take the following example, which uses `Products::get()` to retrieve the details of a single product:

```
// retrieve the product details
$product_id = $_GET['product_id'];
$products = Products::get($product_id);
$product = $products[0];
```

You can see the same function called in `category.php` to retrieve all the products in a category, like this:

```
// retrieve the products in the category
$products = Products::get(0, $category_id);
```

The other new material in this chapter is the implementation of the pager library. This library, located in `simple_pager.inc.php`, contains the basic functionality for displaying a pager. You use this functionality in the category pages, where you want to display a limited number of products per page. You can set the number of products by editing the `PRODUCTS_PER_PAGE` constant in `config.inc.php`. For the purposes of this test this value is set to 1, but feel free to change it to any value:

```
// defines the number of products for paging
define('PRODUCTS_PER_PAGE', 1);
```

A number of settings related to the pager are hard-coded in the constructor of the `SimplePager` class — depending on how flexible you want this functionality to be, you may want to make these configurable. Also, in a professional implementation you would need to add support for including CSS styles in the pager output.

```
// constructor
function SimplePager($rows, $limit, $function_callback,
                    $page_number_parameter_index = 1)
{
  $this->_rows = $rows;
  $this->_limit = $limit;
  $this->_function_callback = $function_callback;
  $this->_page_number_parameter_index = $page_number_parameter_index;
  $this->_max_listed_pages = 10;
  $this->_previous_prompt = '<< back';
  $this->_next_prompt = 'next >>';
}
```

Once this library is in place, it's fairly easy to use it, provided that the other parts of your web site are aware of your paging feature. For example, you have a mod_rewrite rule in .htaccess to handle category URLs that contain a pager parameter. The make_category_url() function of the URL factory also takes an optional $page parameter, and uses it to add the page to the category link if $page is not equal to 1.

The place where you use the pager is category.php:

```
// use the SimplePager library to display the pager
$simple_pager = new SimplePager($products, PRODUCTS_PER_PAGE, 'make_category_url');
echo $simple_pager->display($page, $products, array($category_name, $category_id));
```

As you see, first you need to create a SimplePager instance, providing as parameters the complete list of items the page needs to display, the number of items per page, and the function that creates links to the individual pages (in this case, that is make_category_url).

After creating the instance, you call its display() function, providing as parameters the current page, the list of items, and the parameters to send to the function specified when creating the SimplePager instance. In this case, make_category_url() needs to know the $category_name and $category_id in order to create the category links. The page number parameter is added by your library.

The final technical aspect we need to highlight is the fact that your catalog can contain the same product in more categories, and you can view its details with different URLs for each of those categories. As you know, this generates duplicate content. To avoid duplicate content problems each product has a primary category (identified by the primary_category_id column in the products table), and you eliminate all the product URLs except the one associated with the primary category, in robots.txt. For example, if you look at Figure 14-4, you'll see that two Frosted Fortune Cookie URLs are mentioned. The third one, which doesn't appear there, is that of the primary category.

Summary

We hope you've had fun developing Cookie Ogre's Warehouse! Even though the implemented functionality is very simplistic, it did demonstrate how to tie together the bits and pieces of code you met in the previous chapters of the book. At this point your journey into the world of technical search engine optimization is almost complete. In the next chapter you'll meet a checklist of details to look after when examining the search engine friendliness of an existing site.

15

Site Clinic: So You Have a Web Site?

Although we recommend otherwise, many web sites are initially built without any regard for search engines. Consequently, they often have a myriad of architectural problems. These problems comprise the primary focus of this book. Unfortunately, it is impossible to exhaustively and generally cover the solutions to all web site architectural problems in one short chapter. But thankfully, there is quite a bit of common ground involved.

Likewise, there are many feature enhancements that web sites may benefit from. Some only apply to blogs or forums, whereas others apply generally to all sites. Here, too, there is quite a bit of common ground involved. Furthermore, many such enhancements are easy to implement, and may even offer instant results.

This chapter aims to be a useful list of common fixes and enhancements that many web sites would benefit from. This list comprises two general kinds of fixes or enhancements:

❑ Items 1 through 9 in the checklist can be performed without disturbing site architecture. These items are worthwhile for most web sites and should be tasked without concern for detrimental effects.

❑ Items 10 through 15 come with caveats when implemented and should therefore be completed with caution — or not at all.

This chapter is not intended to be used alone. Rather, it is a sort of "alternative navigation" scheme that one with a preexisting web site can use to quickly surf *some* of the core content of this book. Appropriate references to the various chapters in this book are included with a brief description. Eventually, we hope that you read the book from cover to cover. But until then, let's dive in to some information that you can use right away!

1. Creating Sitemaps

There are two types of sitemaps — traditional and search engine site maps. Both are relatively easy to add to a web site. A traditional sitemap is created as any other HTML web page, whereas a search engine sitemap is formatted specifically according to a search engine's specifications. Creating either will typically increase the rate that your content gets indexed, as well as get deeper or otherwise unreferenced content indexed. The former is important, not only because it gets you indexed faster in the first place, but it may mitigate content theft. A well-organized traditional sitemap is also useful for the human user.

Both types of sitemaps are covered in detail in Chapter 9, "Sitemaps."

2. Creating News Feeds

News feeds are a great way to streamline the process of content distribution. You can create news feeds so that others can conveniently read or syndicate a web site's content. Or you can programmatically use news feeds to publish information provided by others.

Read more on this topic, and learn how to optimize your web site for social search in Chapter 7, "Web Feeds and Social Bookmarking."

3. Fixing Duplication in Titles and Meta Tags

Using the same titles or meta tags on many pages of a web site can be detrimental to rankings. This may be, in part, because a search engine does not want such redundant-looking results to be displayed in its SERPs, as a user's perceived relevance is consequentially lowered. Furthermore, a generic-looking title will usually not prompt a user to click. This is usually a minor fix to an oversight made by a programmer.

More such commonly encountered SEO-related problems are mentioned in Chapter 2, "A Primer in Basic SEO." Duplicate content is discussed at length in Chapter 5, "Duplicate Content."

4. Getting Listed in Reputable Directories

Getting back links from reputable directories can provide a boost in the rankings — or at least get a new web site indexed to start. Best of the Web (http://botw.org), DMOZ (http://dmoz.org), Joe Ant (http://joeant.com), and Yahoo! Directory (http://dir.yahoo.com) are the web site directories we recommend.

DMOZ is free, but also notoriously difficult to get into. Though we will not espouse our opinion as to why, we invite you to use Google to search for "get into DMOZ" and interpret the results.

5. Soliciting and Exchanging Relevant Links

Sending a few friendly emails to get a link from a neighbor may result in a few high-quality links. Exchanging links in *moderation* with various related *relevant* web sites may also help with search engine rankings. "Moderation," as usual, is difficult to define. However, a good metric is whether you believe that the link could realistically appear on its own regardless. If not, or it's on a "directory" page referenced at the bottom of the page with a sea of other random links, probably not!

6. Buying Links

Because relevant links are a major factor in search engine rankings, they have an equity — a "link equity." Predictably, individuals and businesses are now in the business of selling links. There is some disagreement, however, as to whether this is against the terms of service of the various search engines.

> *This topic is discussed in Chapter 8, "Black Hat SEO," although we do* not *consider buying relevant links a black hat practice. Several reputable companies are in the business of selling or brokering links.*

We strongly recommend only buying relevant links. This is not only because it is definitely against the terms of service of many search engines to buy irrelevant links, but also because such irrelevant links do not work as well in the first place. Some reputable link brokers are listed here:

- ❑ Text Link Ads (`http://www.text-link-ads.com`)
- ❑ Text Link Brokers (`http://www.textlinkbrokers.com`)
- ❑ LinkAdage (`http://www.linkadage.com/`)

Text Link Ads also estimates the value of a link on a given web site. The tool is located at `http://www.text-link-ads.com/link_calculator.php`.

> *Chapter 2, "A Primer in Basic SEO," discusses the essentials of link building and related concepts at length.*

7. Creating Link Bait

Although link bait can be difficult and hit-or-miss as far as results, it can frequently be an extremely economical way to build links. Link bait can vary from useful information and humor to intricate site tools and browser toolbars. For example, the link value calculator cited in section 6 is a great example of link bait.

> *Link bait is discussed in Chapter 10, "Link Bait."*

8. Adding Social Bookmarking Functionality

Social bookmarking web sites allow users to bookmark and tag content with keywords and commentary. The aggregate of this information is used both to cite popular content within certain timeframes and niches, as well as by query. Popular content may be featured on the home page of such a site or ranked well for relevant keywords. Adding icons and buttons to web pages that facilitate the process of bookmarking will likely increase the number of users who bookmark your content.

Social bookmarking is discussed in Chapter 7, "Web Feeds and Social Bookmarking."

9. Starting a Blog and/or Forum

Blogs and forums both may attract traffic and links in droves if approached correctly. Bloggers readily exchange links amongst themselves, and a blog may also afford a company a more casual place to post less mundane, fun content. Whereas a humorous comment would not fit in a corporate site proper, it may be more appropriate for a blog. Blogs work quite well in harmony with social bookmarking functionality.

Forums, once they gain momentum, also attract many links. The trick to a forum is building such momentum. Once started, much of the content is generated by the users. If a web site does not already have many thousands of unique visitors per day, though, a forum is most likely not going to be a success.

Chapter 16, "WordPress: Creating an SE-Friendly Blog," shows you how to install and optimize WordPress, a popular PHP-based blog application.

10. Dealing with a Pure Flash or AJAX Site

Flash sites present many problems from a search engine optimization perspective. There is really no way to approach this problem, except to design a site that replaces or supplements the Flash design that is *not* Flash-based. There are other less onerous "solutions," but they are less than ideal.

Flash sites are discussed in Chapter 6, "SE-Friendly HTML and JavaScript."

11. Preventing Black Hat Victimization

Black hat SEOs are always on the lookout for places to inject links, JavaScript redirects, and spam content. Properly sanitizing and/or escaping foreign data can prevent or mitigate such attacks. Where links are appropriate to post, if they are unaudited, they should be "nofollowed." Known, problematic anonymous proxies should be blocked. Vulnerabilities to such attacks are typically found in comments, guestbooks, and forums.

This material is covered in detail in Chapter 8, "Black Hat SEO."

12. Examining Your URLs for Problems

URLs with too many parameters or redirects can confuse a search engine. You should construct URLs with both users and search engines in mind.

URLs are discussed in Chapter 3, "Provocative SE-Friendly URLs." Redirects are discussed in Chapter 4, "Content Relocation and HTTP Status Codes." In Chapter 13, "Coping with Technical Issues," you learn how to build your own library that verifies the links within your web site are functional.

13. Looking for Duplicate Content

Having many pages with the same or similar content in excess can result in poorer rankings. And though it is a matter of contention as to whether an explicit *penalty* exists for having duplicate content, it is undesirable for many reasons. Duplicate content is, however, not a simple problem with a single cause. Rather, it is a complex problem with myriad causes.

Duplicate content is the subject of Chapter 5, "Duplicate Content" (aptly named).

14. Eliminating Session IDs

Use of URL-based session management may allow users with cookies turned off to use a web site that requires session-related information, but it may also wreak havoc for the web site in search engines. For this reason URL-based sessions should either be completely turned off, or cloaking should be employed to turn off the URL-based session management if the user-agent is a spider.

Session IDs and their associated problems are discussed at length in Chapter 2, "A Primer in Basic SEO." This particular technique is discussed in Chapter 11,"Cloaking, Geo-Targeting, and IP Delivery."

15. Tweaking On-page Factors

On-page factors may have diminished in effect over the years, but it is still advantageous to author HTML that employs elements that mean something semantically. Especially if you author HTML using a WYSIWYG editor, or use a content management system with a WYSIWYG editor, this may not be occurring. Other problems may involve having a large navigation element physically before the content.

Chapter 6 discusses the aforementioned topics as well as many other HTML and JavaScript-related issues at length.

Summary

Wow, so much to do! And this chapter is only a guide covering *some* of the important points for those who already have a preexisting web site. There is much more information throughout this book than the 15 sections touched upon here. But covering these bases should go a long way in getting you started. So grab that can of Red Bull and dive in!

16

WordPress: Creating an SE-Friendly Blog

WordPress is a very feature-rich and extensible blogging application that, with a bit of tweaking, can be search engine–friendly. It is entirely written in PHP, and it can be modified and extended in the same. Duplicating even its core functionality in a custom application would take a lot of time — so why reinvent the wheel? Furthermore, many plugins are readily available that extend and enhance its functionality.

Because the blog has been mentioned as a vehicle for search engine marketing so many times in this book, it seems fitting to document the process of setting up a blog with WordPress. You will also install quite a few WordPress plugins on the way.

Please note that this is not a comprehensive WordPress tutorial: although we present step-by-step installation and configuration instructions for the specific topics that we cover, we assume that you will do your own additional research regarding additional customization and other plugins you may require.

> *Note that we encountered a few problems with some of the presented plugins during our tests in **certain** server configurations.*

> **At the time of this writing, WordPress 2.0 is the current generally available release. WordPress 2.1 is on the way (in beta), and certain of these directions and plugins will be obsolete or in error for version 2.1. Please visit** `http://www.seoegghead.com/seo-with-php-updates.html` **for information regarding updated procedures for WordPress 2.1.**

In this chapter, you learn how to:

❑   Install WordPress 2.0

❑   Turn on permalinks

❑   Prevent comment spam with the Akismet plugin

❑   Add social bookmarking icons with the Sociable plugin

❑   Implement "Email a friend" functionality with the WP-Email plugin

❑   Add "chicklets" with the Chicklet Creator plugin

❑   Generate a traditional sitemap with the Sitemap Generator plugin

❑   Generate a Google sitemap with the Google Sitemap plugin

❑   Create a Digg button plugin

❑   Create a "Pagerfix" plugin, to add links to individual pages in the blog's pagination

❑   Add a `robots.txt` file to your blog and exclude some content that should not be indexed

❑   Make the blog your home page and redirect `/blog` to `/` (if desired)

Much of these are optional, but you'll want to implement at least *some* of them. This chapter tackles them one by one.

Installing WordPress

To install WordPress, you need to create a database and extract its files to the web server directory. You will use the `seophp` database you created in Chapter 1, but creating a separate database would suffice as well.

Following these steps, you'll create a WordPress blog in the `/blog/` folder of your `seophp` directory. This will make your blog accessible via the URL `http://seophp.example.com/blog/`.

1.   Download WordPress 2.0 from `http://wordpress.org/download/`, and unpack the archive in your `seophp` folder.

2.   The WordPress archive contains a folder named `wordpress`. Rename that folder to `blog`, so that your WordPress installation will reside in `/seophp/blog`.

3.   Open the `blog` folder, and copy the `wp-config-sample.php` file to `wp-config.php`.

4.   Open `wp-config.php`, and change it to reflect the database connection data:

```php
<?php
// ** MySQL settings ** //
define('DB_NAME', 'seophp');     // The name of the database
define('DB_USER', 'seouser');    // Your MySQL username
define('DB_PASSWORD', 'seomaster'); // ...and password
define('DB_HOST', 'localhost');  // 99% chance you won't need to change this value

// You can have multiple installations in one database if you give each a unique ↵
prefix
$table_prefix  = 'wp_';    // Only numbers, letters, and underscores please!
```

```
// Change this to localize WordPress.  A corresponding MO file for the
// chosen language must be installed to wp-includes/languages.
// For example, install de.mo to wp-includes/languages and set WPLANG to 'de'
// to enable German language support.
define ('WPLANG', '');

/* That's all, stop editing! Happy blogging. */

define('ABSPATH', dirname(__FILE__).'/');
require_once(ABSPATH.'wp-settings.php');
?>
```

5. You're now ready to run the installation script, which configures the database for your WordPress blog. The installation script is `wp-admin/install.php`. Loading `http://seophp.example.com/blog/wp-admin/install.php` should open a page such as the one in Figure 16-1.

6. Go through the single installation step that follows, and write down the password WordPress generates for your WordPress admin account.

7. To test your login data, load `http://seophp.example.com/blog/wp-admin/`, and supply the username admin and the generated password. You'll be taken to the welcome screen, which looks like Figure 16-2.

8. WordPress was friendly enough to write a first blog post for you. You can view it by loading the `http://seophp.example.com/blog/` folder — see Figure 16-3.

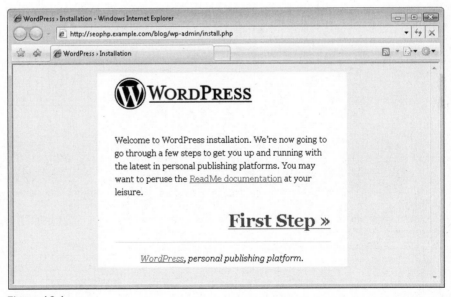

Figure 16-1

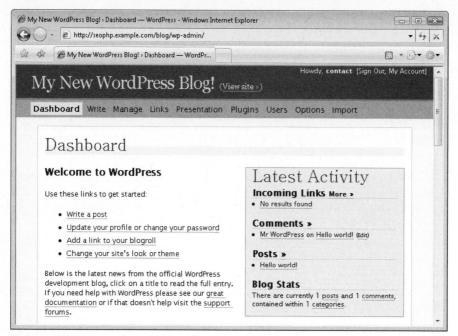

Figure 16-2

Figure 16-3

Turning On Permalinks

Next, you turn on permalinks. This changes the dynamic URLs to rewritten static URLs (that is, `/this-is-a-post/`) in your blog.

1. Load the admin page (`http://seophp.example.com/blog/wp-admin/`), click the Options link in the top menu, and select Permalinks. Choose the "Date and name based" entry, as shown in Figure 16-4. This enables keyword-rich URLs for your blog.

Alternatively, you can choose to have only the post name and post ID in the link — without the date, in which case you would type `/%postname%/%post_id%/` in the Custom box.

2. After making your choice, verify that the `.htaccess` file in the `blog` folder (*not* in the root `seophp` folder) is writable, and click the Update Permalink Structure button. This writes the mod_rewrite rules necessary for the rewritten URLs to `.htaccess`. The rules for your particular configuration are listed here:

```
# BEGIN WordPress
<IfModule mod_rewrite.c>
```

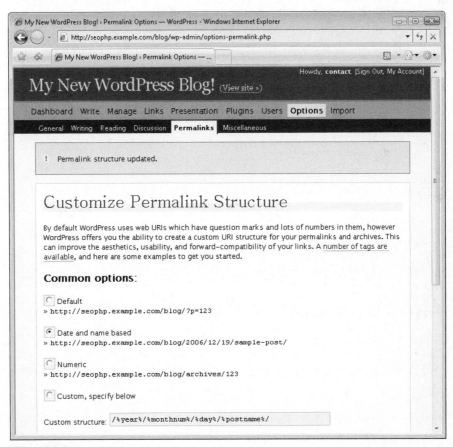

Figure 16-4

```
RewriteEngine On
RewriteBase /blog/
RewriteCond %{REQUEST_FILENAME} !-f
RewriteCond %{REQUEST_FILENAME} !-d
RewriteRule . /blog/index.php [L]
</IfModule>

# END WordPress
```

3. Now you can visit your blog again, and notice the link for your first post changed to `http://seophp.example.com/blog/2006/12/19/hello-world/`. Loading it would successfully load the page shown in Figure 16-5.

Figure 16-5

Akismet: Preventing Comment Spam

As your blog becomes more popular, it will become more popular with spammers too. Thankfully, WordPress comes with a plugin called Akismet — but you must configure it. The Akismet plugin filters out most comment spam, so you do not have to do so manually. To enable it, follow these steps:

1. Load `http://seophp.example.com/blog/wp-admin/`.

2. Click the Plugins item from the menu.

3. Click the Activate link for Akismet.

4. After activating the plugin, a message will appear on the top of the window that reads "Akismet is not active. You must enter your WordPress.com API key for it to work." as shown in Figure 16-6. Get your API key from `http://wordpress.com/api-keys/`.

5. After activating your WordPress account, you'll receive the API key by email. Click the "enter your WordPress.com API key" link at the top of the page, which sends you to a page where you can enter the API key. Enter it. At that point, your plugin is enabled and ready for use! For more information on using Akismet, visit `http://codex.wordpress.org/Akismet`.

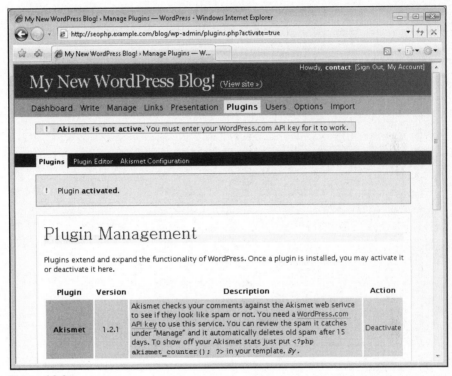

Figure 16-6

Sociable: Social Bookmarking Icons

The Sociable plugin generates social bookmaking icons for your blog posts. Social bookmarking is discussed at length in Chapter 7.

> This plugin does not support adding icons to web feeds. If you want to do so, you can apply the Sociable patch described at `http://www.seoegghead.com/blog/seo/patched-sociable-code-to-enable-feed-icons-p155.html`.

Sociable can be installed using the following steps:

1. Download Sociable from `http://push.cx/sociable`. Unzip the archive, and copy the `sociable` folder to the `blog/wp-content/plugins` folder.

2. Load the WordPress administration page, select Plugins, and click Activate for the Sociable plugin.

3. After enabling Sociable, you can configure it by clicking the Options menu item, then selecting Sociable. We recommend turning on at least del.icio.us and Reddit for most sites, and Digg, in addition, for technical sites.

4. After you select your options, don't forget to click the Save Changes button. If you now visit a blog entry, you should see the new social bookmarking links, as shown in Figure 16-7.

Figure 16-7

WP-Email: Email a Friend

The WP-Email plugin adds "email a friend" functionality to your blog. You can read more about the plugin at `http://www.lesterchan.net/wordpress/readme/wp-email.html`. You can install WP-Email by following these steps:

1. Download the latest version of WP-Email from `http://dev.wp-plugins.org/wiki/wp-email`.

2. Copy the `email` folder from the archive to your `blog/wp-content/plugins` folder.

3. In WordPress, go to the plugins administration page, and activate the WP-Email plugin. Then click the e-mail tab, select e-mail options, and set up your mail options as desired.

4. Now you need to alter the theme you're using to include this new feature. For example, assuming you're using the default theme, open the `blog/wp-content/themes/default/index.php`, and find the line that starts with:

```
<p class="postmetadata">Posted in <?php the_category(', ') ?>
```

This is the line that generates, by default, the links that follow each post. You can add the following code to include an "e-mail this link" link:

```php
<?php
  if(function_exists('wp_email'))
  {
    email_link('e-mail this link', 'e-mail this page');
  }
?> |
```

5. Reloading the page displays a link as shown in Figure 16-8.

Figure 16-8

Chicklet Creator Plugin

To have feed reader buttons generated for you as shown in Figure 16-10, install and configure the Chicklet Creator plugin.

1. Download the plugin from `http://www.twistermc.com/shake/wordpress-chicklet.php`, and unpack the archive into a new folder named `Chicklet-Creator`. Then copy (or move) this folder to your `blog/wp-content/plugins` folder.

2. Go to the Plugins section of your blog admin page, and activate the Chicklet Creator plugin.

3. In the same page, click the Config Instructions link to configure the plugin (you can also reach the configuration page by going to Options ⇨ Chicklet Creator). We recommend turning on the XML chicklet if not already prominently advertised, as well as Google, My Yahoo!, and Bloglines. The icon selection page looks like that shown in Figure 16-9; after making your selection, don't forget to click the Update Feed Buttons button.

4. Finally, update your pages by adding the following piece of code where you want your new buttons to show up:

```php
<?php if (function_exists('chicklet_creator')) { chicklet_creator(); } ?>
```

For example, I'm adding this line to my `blog/wp-content/themes/Default/sidebar.php` file. You can see the result using the default plugin options in Figure 16-10. You can use the plugin configuration page to fine-tune the icons and their layout.

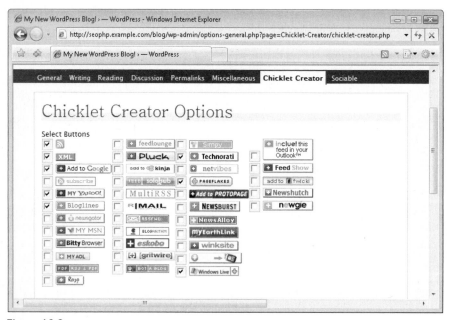

Figure 16-9

Figure 16-10

Sitemap Generator Plugin

The Sitemap Generator plugin does exactly what its name implies — it generates a sitemap for your blog as shown in Figure 16-11. See the official sitemap demo page at http://www.dagondesign.com/sitemap/. To install this plugin:

1. Go to http://www.dagondesign.com/articles/sitemap-generator-plugin-for-wordpress/. Download dd-sitemap-gen.txt from the main page, and save it as dd-sitemap-gen.php to your /blog/wp-content/plugins folder.

2. If you now load the Plugins section in the admin page, you'll see the new entry named Dagon Design Sitemap Generator. Click Activate to activate the plugin.

3. After activating the plugin, go to Options ⇨ DDSitemapGen to configure the sitemap generator. Set a permalink, sitemap, for the sitemap. Next, set "Items per page" to 0 so all items are on one page. After you select your options, don't forget to click the Update button.

4. To add the sitemap to your blog, navigate to the Write ⇨ Write Page section to create a new page for it. Set the page title to the value "Sitemap." Add <!-- ddsitemapgen --> as shown in Figure 16-12. (Note that when editing the page, the markup will not show up because it is an HTML comment. To edit the markup or an existing page, you must edit the page in HTML mode by clicking the HTML button of the editor.)

5. Visit the Sitemap page of your blog to see your new sitemap in action — see Figure 16-13.

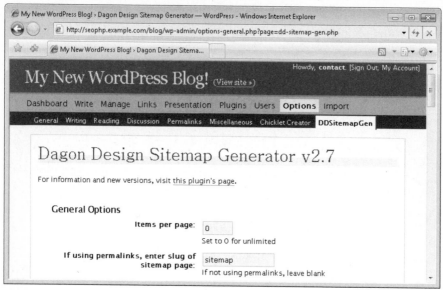

Figure 16-11

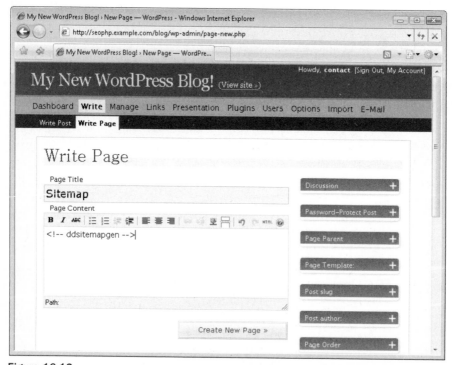

Figure 16-12

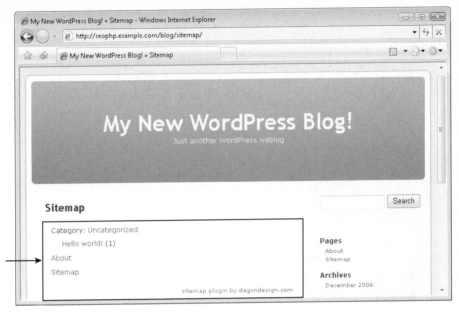

Figure 16-13

Google Sitemaps Plugin

This plugin generates a Google sitemap for your blog. Download the plugin from `http://www.arnebrachhold.de/2006/01/07/google-sitemap-generator-for-wordpress-3-beta`. Unzip the archive, and copy `sitemap.php` to your `/blog/wp-content/plugins` folder.

Load the administration page, and activate the Google Sitemaps plugin from the Plugins page. Then click the Configuration Page link to open the configuration page. Here you find a plethora of options that let you configure your sitemap with many of the options that were described in Chapter 9. The configuration options are grouped in nine sections (see Table 16-1).

Table 16-1

Configuration Group	Description
Manual rebuild / Log	Here you find a button that lets you manually rebuild the sitemap. Note that this is not normally necessary, because by default the sitemap is re-created automatically when you add new posts or modify old ones.
Additional pages	The Google Sitemaps plugin can include all the pages in your blog automatically. In the case that your web site has content that is not administered by WordPress, you can add those pages manually in this section.

Table continued on following page

Configuration Group	Description
Basic options	Here you can check or uncheck a number of options regarding your sitemap. The default settings are appropriate for most blogs.
Post priority	As you learned in Chapter 9, you can give each page a priority. You can set the plugin to calculate the priority automatically depending on the Comment Count or Comment Average, or you can define the priorities manually from the Priorities configuration section.
Location of the sitemap file	By default the sitemap location is the root of your blog, but you can change it here if you wish.
Sitemap content	Here you can choose which pages of your blog should be included in the sitemap.
Change frequencies	As you learned in Chapter 9, you can assign an update frequency for each sitemap item.
Priorities	In case you decide to establish priorities manually rather than have the plugin calculate them for you depending on the number of comments, here you can customize the manual priority for each page type.
XML-Sitemap button	This option shows you the code that generates an "XML Sitemap" button. You can place this button on your blog if you want to advertise the existence of a sitemap in your web site.

Remember to click the Update Options button if you make changes to options in this page. If you want to test the functionality of this plugin, simply click the Rebuild Sitemap button. You will be shown a message such as that in Figure 16-14, containing the sitemap generation report.

Figure 16-14

Checking the `sitemap.xml` file in your `seophp/blog` folder, you will find a sitemap generated using the options you've chosen in the configuration page. In my case, with a new WordPress blog, I can see these contents:

```xml
<?xml version="1.0" encoding="UTF-8"?>
<!-- generator="wordpress/2.0.5" -->
<!-- sitemap-generator-url="http://www.arnebrachhold.de"
sitemap-generator-version="3.0b4" -->
<!-- generated-on="December 30, 2006 8:09 pm" -->
<urlset xmlns:xsi="http://www.w3.org/2001/XMLSchema-instance"
xsi:schemaLocation="http://www.sitemaps.org/schemas/sitemap/0.9
http://www.sitemaps.org/schemas/sitemap/09/sitemap.xsd"
xmlns="http://www.sitemaps.org/schemas/sitemap/0.9">
    <url>
        <loc>http://seophp.example.com/blog/</loc>
        <lastmod>2006-12-19T03:56:13+00:00</lastmod>
        <changefreq>daily</changefreq>
        <priority>1</priority>
    </url>

    <url>
        <loc>http://seophp.example.com/blog/sitemap/</loc>
        <lastmod>2006-12-29T21:03:32+00:00</lastmod>
        <changefreq>weekly</changefreq>
        <priority>0.6</priority>
    </url>

    <url>
        <loc>http://seophp.example.com/blog/about/</loc>
        <lastmod>2006-12-21T02:55:29+00:00</lastmod>
        <changefreq>weekly</changefreq>
        <priority>0.6</priority>
    </url>

    <url>
        <loc>http://seophp.example.com/blog/2006/12/19/hello-world/</loc>
        <lastmod>2006-12-19T05:56:13+00:00</lastmod>
        <changefreq>monthly</changefreq>
        <priority>1</priority>
    </url>

    <url>
        <loc>http://seophp.example.com/blog/category/uncategorized/</loc>
        <lastmod>2006-12-19T05:56:13+00:00</lastmod>
        <changefreq>weekly</changefreq>
        <priority>0.5</priority>
    </url>

    <url>
        <loc>http://seophp.example.com/blog/2006/12/</loc>
        <lastmod>2006-12-19T05:56:13+00:00</lastmod>
        <changefreq>daily</changefreq>
        <priority>0.5</priority>
    </url>

</urlset>
```

Digg Button Plugin

Adding a Digg button to your site can encourage visitors to digg an article that has already been dugg. This plugin has been presented at http://www.seoegghead.com/blog/seo/how-to-get-dugg-digg-for-wordpress-plugin-p113.html. There you can also see how the Digg button looks in practice — see Figure 16-15.

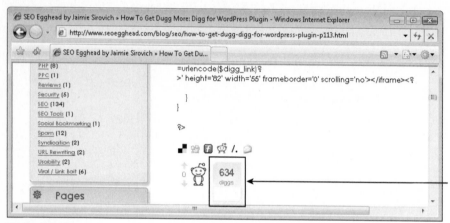

Figure 16-15

To add the Digg button to your blog, follow these steps:

1. Create a file named digg-button.php in your /blog/wp-content/plugins folder, and type the following code. Alternatively, you can pick up the code from the book's code download.

```php
<?php
/*
Plugin Name: Digg
Plugin URI: http://www.seoegghead.com/
Description: Creates an interactive Digg button.
Author: Jaimie Sirovich
Version: 1.0
Author URI: http://www.seoegghead.com/
*/
function _scrape_check_digg($digg_link, $the_permalink)
{
    $ch = curl_init();
    curl_setopt($ch, CURLOPT_URL, $digg_link);
    curl_setopt($ch, CURLOPT_RETURNTRANSFER, 1);
    $http_result = curl_exec($ch);
```

```
    curl_close($ch);
    $_ = preg_match('#<h3 id="title"><a href="(.*?)">#is', $http_result, $cap
tures);
    return ($captures[1] == $the_permalink);
}
function digg_this()
{
    global $id;
    $digg_link = get_post_meta($id, 'DIGG_CLASS_digg_link', true);

    if (is_single() && !$digg_link && preg_match('#^http://(www\.)?digg\.com/
.+#i', $_SERVER['HTTP_REFERER']) && !preg_match('#^http://(www\.)?digg\.com/(
view|users)#i', $_SERVER['HTTP_REFERER']) && _scrape_check_digg($_SERVER['HTT
P_REFERER'], get_permalink()))) {
        add_post_meta($id, 'DIGG_CLASS_digg_link', $_SERVER['HTTP_REFERER']);
        $digg_link = $_SERVER['HTTP_REFERER'];
    }
    if ($digg_link) {
        ?><iframe src='http://digg.com/api/diggthis.php?u=<?php echo
urlencode($digg_link)?>' height='82' width='55' frameborder='0' scrolling='no
'></iframe><?php
    }
}
?>
```

2.   Load the admin page (http://seophp.example.com/blog/wp-admin/), go to the Plugins section, and activate the Digg plugin.

3.   Call the digg_this() function from your templates, in the place where you want your Digg button to show up. For example, you can place this code in the index.php file of your template, at the place you want the Digg button to show up:

```
<?php digg_this(); ?>
```

> Note that the Digg button will only start to appear if a user visits a *permalink post page* from a Digg page that refers to it in HTTP_REFERER.

Pagerfix Plugin

In Chapter 2 you learned about the problems that pages deeply buried within your web site may present — and one cause of this problem is pagination. You can implement a plugin that fixes the default pagination links, that is, "< prev" and "next >" to link to the individual pages as well. Figure 16-16 shows this in action at http://www.seoegghead.com.

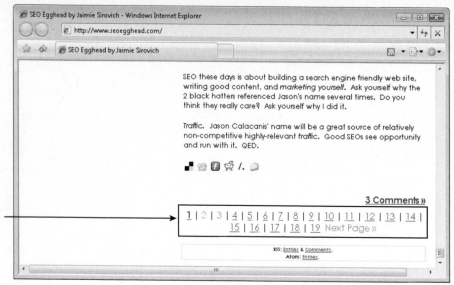

Figure 16-16

The following plugin does the trick. Save it as `pagerfix.php` in your `blog/wp-content/plugins` folder, then activate it from the WordPress administration page:

```php
<?php
/*
Plugin Name: PagerFix
Plugin URI: http://www.seoegghead.com/
Description: Makes the paging in WP more SE-friendly.
Author: Jaimie Sirovich
Version: 1.0
Author URI: http://www.seoegghead.com/
*/
function pager_fix($separator = ' | ',
                   $after_previous = '  ',
                   $before_next = '  ',
                   $prelabel='&laquo; Previous Page',
                   $nxtlabel='Next Page &raquo;',
                   $current_page_tag = 'b')
{
  global $request, $posts_per_page, $wpdb, $paged;

  posts_nav_link('',$prelabel,'');
  echo $after_previous;
  preg_match('#FROM (.*) GROUP BY#', $request, $matches);
  $fromwhere = $matches[1];
  $numposts = $wpdb->get_var("SELECT COUNT(ID) FROM $fromwhere");
  $max_num_pages = ceil($numposts / $posts_per_page);
  if ($max_num_pages > 1)
  {
```

```
      for ($cnt = 1; $cnt <= $max_num_pages; $cnt++)
      {
        if ($current_page_tag && $paged == $cnt)
        {
          $begin_link = "<$current_page_tag>"; $end_link = "</$current_page_tag>";
        }
        else
        {
          $begin_link = ''; $end_link = '';
        }

        $x[] = $begin_link .
               '<a href="' . get_pagenum_link($cnt) . '">' .
               $cnt . '</a>' . $end_link;
      }

      echo join($separator, $x);

    }
    echo $before_next;
    posts_nav_link('','',$nxtlabel);

  }
?>
```

After creating and activating this plugin, you need to call the function `pager_fix()` in your template somewhere. For example, in the `index.php` file of your default template you can find this code (with perhaps slightly different formatting):

```
<div class="navigation">
  <div class="alignleft">
    <?php next_posts_link('&laquo; Previous Entries') ?>
  </div>
  <div class="alignright">
    <?php previous_posts_link('Next Entries &raquo;') ?>
  </div>
</div>
```

To use the "pagerfix" version of the pager, you'd need to replace the highlighted code like this:

```
<div class="navigation">
  <?php pager_fix() ?>
</div>
```

Eliminating Duplicate Content

A common problem with blogs — WordPress blogs included — is that they often generate quite a bit of duplicate content by showing an article in more than one place on the blog. For example, a certain article may be shown on the home page, on the page of the category it's part of, as well as the archives. That is a lot of duplication! This section examines and fixes some of these problems.

Pull-downs and Excluding Category Links

If you plan to use a pull-down list of categories in your interface, add the following to your robots.txt file. This list does not use the permalinks (because it is a form, and cannot by design), and Google is capable of crawling simple forms like these. Add the following lines to your robots.txt file:

```
User-agent: Googlebot
Disallow: /blog/*?cat=
```

This pull-down is generated using `<?php dropdown_cats(); ?>`, as shown in Figure 16-17.

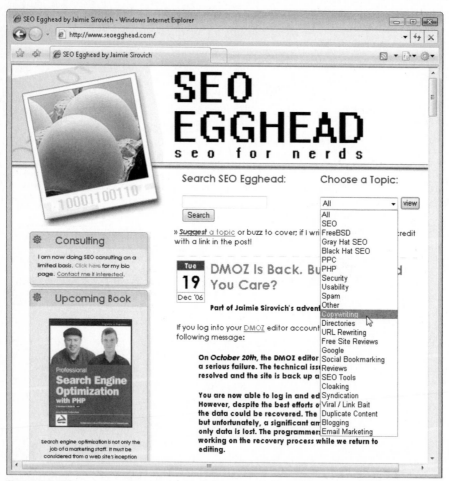

Figure 16-17

Excerpting Article Content

Another potential duplicate content problem occurs when you display the entire article in multiple pages that enumerate articles — such as the home page, the category pages, and so on. A workaround that we suggest is to show the full content only on the actual permalink page (the article's page), and on the home page for the most recent posts on the home page. All other pages will only show titles and excerpts.

There are many possible implementation solutions. One suggested method is to modify the `index.php` file of your WordPress template — this is located in `/wp-content/themes/{your-theme}/`. There, you have to look after the code that displays the post's content, which is basically a call to the `the_content()` function, like this:

```
<?php the_content('Read the rest of this entry &raquo;'); ?>
</div>
```

To display the entire content of posts only on the first page, and on the post's permalink page, and excerpts everywhere else, modify the code highlighted earlier like this:

```
<?php if (is_home() && (!$paged || $paged == 1)
    || is_search() || is_single() || is_page()): ?>
  <div class="entry">
  <?php the_content() ?>
<?php else: ?>
  <small>Archived; click post to view. <br />
  <b>Excerpt:</b> <?php echo substr(strip_tags($post->post_content), 0, 300); ?>
...
  </small>
<?php endif; ?>
```

This code makes the excerpts 300 characters long, but this feature is easy to customize to your liking.

Making the Blog Your Home Page

If you want the home page to also be the blog, follow the next steps. This will make / output the same as /blog, and will redirect all the requests for /blog to /. This avoids the problem of having two duplicate home pages, / and /blog/.

1. Copy this file to the seophp directory as `index.php`:

```
<?php

/* Short and sweet */
define('WP_USE_THEMES', true);
define('WP_IN_ROOTDIR', true);
require('.//blog/wp-blog-header.php');

?>
```

2. Save the following code as `blog301fix.php`, and copy it to your `/blog/wp-content/plugins` folder:

```php
<?php

/*
Plugin Name: Blog301Fix
Plugin URI: http://www.seoegghead.com/
Description: Redirects /blog to /.
Author: Jaimie Sirovich
Version: 1.0
Author URI: http://www.seoegghead.com/
*/

if ($_SERVER['REQUEST_URI'] == '/blog/') {
  header("HTTP/1.1 301 Moved Permanently");
  header('Location: ' . preg_replace('#blog#', '', get_bloginfo('url'), 1));
  exit();
}

?>
```

3. Enable the plugin from the Plugins area of your WordPress admin page. Now, loading `http://seophp.example.com/` will display your blog, and loading `http://seophp.example.com/blog/` will 301 redirect you to `http://seophp.example.com`.

Summary

This chapter has shown you how to use WordPress as a basis for a successful blog by making some modifications and installing some plugins to the end of search engine optimization. Creating such an application from scratch would be a task the size of — well, WordPress. Plugins are available to implement much of the concerns discussed in this book. Therefore, using WordPress is a viable option if you decide to launch a blog as part of your search engine marketing efforts. Please see `http://www.seoegghead.com/seo-with-php-updates.html` for updates to this chapter, especially with regard to updated WordPress releases.

Simple Regular Expressions

This appendix examines some basic aspects of constructing regular expressions. One reason for working through the simple examples presented in this appendix is to illuminate the regular expressions used in Chapter 3 and further extend your knowledge of them.

The following exercises use OpenOffice.org Writer — a free document editor that makes it easy to apply regular expressions to text, and verify that they do what you expected. You can download this tool from `http://www.openoffice.org`.

> This appendix has been "borrowed" from the Wrox title *Beginning Regular Expressions* (Wiley, 2005) by Andrew Watt. We recommend this book for further (and more comprehensive) reference into the world of regular expressions.

The examples used are necessarily simple, but by using regular expressions to match fairly simple text patterns, you should become increasingly familiar and comfortable with the use of foundational regular expression constructs that can be used to form part of more complex regular expressions.

One of the issues this appendix explores in some detail is the situation where you want to match occurrences of characters other than those characters simply occurring once.

This appendix looks at the following:

- ❑ How to match single characters
- ❑ How to match optional characters

- ❑ How to match characters that can occur an unbounded number of times, whether the characters of interest are optional or required
- ❑ How to match characters that can occur a specified number of times

First, look at the simplest situation: matching single characters.

Matching Single Characters

The simplest regular expression involves matching a single character. If you want to match a single, specified alphabetic character or numeric digit, you simply use a pattern that consists of that character or digit. So, for example, to match the uppercase letter L, you would use the following pattern:

```
L
```

The pattern matches any occurrence of the uppercase L. You have not qualified the pattern in any way to limit matching, so expect it to match any occurrence of uppercase L. Of course, if matching is being carried out in a case-insensitive manner, both uppercase L and lowercase l will be matched.

Matching a Single Character

You can apply this pattern to the sample document UpperL.txt, which is shown here:

```
Excel had XLM macros. They were replaced by Visual Basic for Applications in later
versions of the spreadsheet software.

CMLIII

Leoni could swim like a fish.

Legal difficulties plagued the Clinton administration. Lewinski was the source of
some of the former president's difficulties.
```

1. Open OpenOffice.org Writer, and open the file UpperL.txt.

2. Use the Ctrl+F keyboard shortcut to open the Find And Replace dialog box, and check the Regular Expressions check box and the Match Case check box in the Options section.

3. Enter the regular expression pattern L in the Search For text box at the top of the Find And Replace dialog box, and click the Find All button.

If all has gone well, each occurrence of an uppercase L should be highlighted.

Figure A-1 shows the matching of the pattern L in OpenOffice.org Writer against the sample document UpperL.txt. Notice that there are five matches contained in the sequences of characters XLM, CMLIII, Leoni, Legal, and Lewinski.

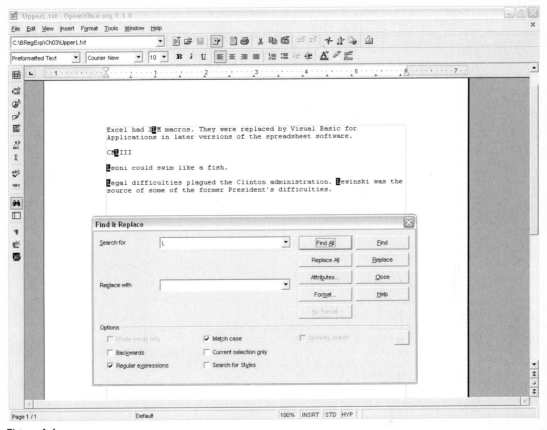

Figure A-1

The default behavior of OpenOffice.org Writer is to carry out a case-insensitive match. As you can see in Figure A-1, the Match Case check box is checked so that only the same case as specified in the regular expression is matched.

For each character in the document, OpenOffice.org Writer checks whether that character is an upper-case L. If it is, the regular expression pattern is matched. In OpenOffice.org Writer, a match is indicated by highlighting of the character(s) — in this case, a single character — for each match, assuming that the Find All button has been clicked.

How can you match a single character using JavaScript?

Appendix A: Simple Regular Expressions

Matching a Single Character in JavaScript

You want to find all occurrences of uppercase L. You can express the simple task that you want to use regular expressions to do as follows:

Match any occurrence of uppercase L.

You can see, using JavaScript as a sample technology, how most regular expression engines will match the pattern L using the XHTML file UpperL.html, shown here:

```
<html>
<head>
<title>Check for Upper Case L</title>
<script language="javascript" type="text/javascript">
var myRegExp = /L/;

function Validate(entry){
return myRegExp.test(entry);
} // end function Validate()

function ShowPrompt(){
var entry = prompt("This script tests for matches for the regular expression
pattern: " + myRegExp + ".\nType in a string and click on the OK button.", "Type
your text here.");
if (Validate(entry)){
alert("There is a match!\nThe regular expression pattern is: " + myRegExp + ".\n
The string that you entered was: '" + entry + "'.");
} // end if
else{
 alert("There is no match in the string you entered.\n" + "The regular expression
pattern is " + myRegExp + "\n" + "You entered the string: '" + entry + "'." );
} // end else

} // end function ShowPrompt()

</script>
</head>
<body>
<form name="myForm">
<br />
<button type="Button" onclick="ShowPrompt()">Click here to enter text.</button>
</form>
</body>
</html>
```

1. Navigate in Windows Explorer to the directory that contains the file UpperL.html, and double-click the file. It should open in your default browser.

2. Click the button labeled Click Here To Enter Text. A prompt window is shown, as you can see in Figure A-2.

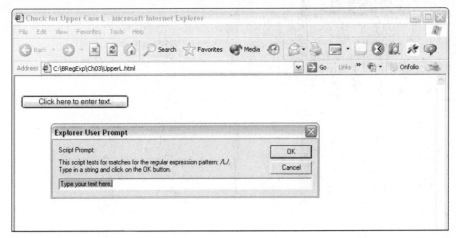

Figure A-2

3.   Type a character or a string in the text box that contains the default text *Type your text here*, and the JavaScript code will test whether or not there is a match for the regular expression pattern, in this case L. Click the OK button.

4.   Inspect the alert box that is displayed to assess whether or not a match is present in the string that you entered. Figure A-3 shows the message when a successful match is made. Figure A-4 shows the message displayed when the string that you enter does not match the regular expression pattern.

Figure A-3

Figure A-4

Appendix A: Simple Regular Expressions

The simple web page contains JavaScript code.

The JavaScript variable myRegExp is assigned the literal regular expression pattern L, using the following declaration and assignment statement:

```
var myRegExp = /L/;
```

In JavaScript, the forward slash is used to delimit a regular expression pattern in a way similar to how paired quotes are used to delimit a string. There is an alternate syntax, which is not discussed here.

When you click the button labeled Click Here to Enter Text, the ShowPrompt() function is called.

The entry variable is used to collect the string you enter in the prompt box:

```
var entry = prompt("This script tests for matches for the regular expression
pattern: " + myRegExp + ".\nType in a string and click on the OK button.", "Type
your text here.");
```

The output created depends on whether or not the text you entered contains a match for the regular expression pattern. Once the text has been entered and the OK button clicked, an if statement is executed, which checks whether or not the text you entered (and which is stored in the entry variable) contains a match for the regular expression pattern stored in the variable myRegExp:

```
if (Validate(entry)){
```

The if statement causes the Validate function to be called:

```
function Validate(entry){
return myRegExp.test(entry);
} // end function Validate()
```

The test() method of the myRegExp variable is used to determine whether or not a match is present.

If the if statement

```
if (Validate(entry))
```

returns the Boolean value true, the following code is executed

```
alert("There is a match!\nThe regular expression pattern is: " + myRegExp + ".\n
The string that you entered was: '" + entry + "'.");
```

and uses the myRegExp and entry variables to display the regular expression pattern and the string that you entered, together with explanatory text.

If there is no match, the following code is executed, because it is contained in the else clause of the if statement:

```
alert("There is no match in the string you entered.\n" + "The regular expression
pattern is " + myRegExp + "\n" + "You entered the string: '" + entry + "'." );
```

Again, the myRegExp and entry variables are used to give feedback to the user about what is to be matched and the string that he or she entered.

Of course, in practice, you typically want to match a sequence of characters rather than a single character.

Matching Sequences of Characters That Each Occur Once

When the regular expression pattern L was matched, you made use of the default behavior of the regular expression engine, meaning that when there is no indication of how often a character (or sequence of characters) is allowed to occur, the regular expression engine assumes that the character(s) in the pattern occur exactly once, except when you include a quantifier in the regular expression pattern that specifies an occurrence other than exactly once. This behavior also allows the matching of sequences of the same character.

To match two characters that are the same character and occur twice without any intervening characters (including whitespace), you can simply use a pattern with the desired character written twice in the pattern.

Matching Doubled Characters

As an example, look at how you can match sequences of characters where a character occurs exactly twice — for example, the doubled r that can occur in words such as arrow and narrative.

A problem definition for the desired match can be expressed as follows:

Match any occurrence of the lowercase character r immediately followed by another lowercase r.

An example file, DoubledR.txt, is shown here:

```
The arrow flew through the air at great speed.

This is a narrative of great interest to many readers.

Apples and oranges are both types of fruit.

Asses and donkeys are both four-legged mammals.

Several million barrels of oil are produced daily.
```

The following pattern will match all occurrences of rr in the sample file:

```
rr
```

1. Open OpenOffice.org Writer, and open the sample file DoubledR.txt.
2. Use the keyboard shortcut Ctrl+F to open the Find And Replace dialog box.
3. Check the Regular Expressions check box and the Match Case check box.
4. Enter the pattern rr in the Search For text box, and click the Find All button.

Figure A-5 shows DoubledR.txt opened in OpenOffice.org Writer, as previously described. Notice that all occurrences of rr are matched, but single occurrences of r are not matched.

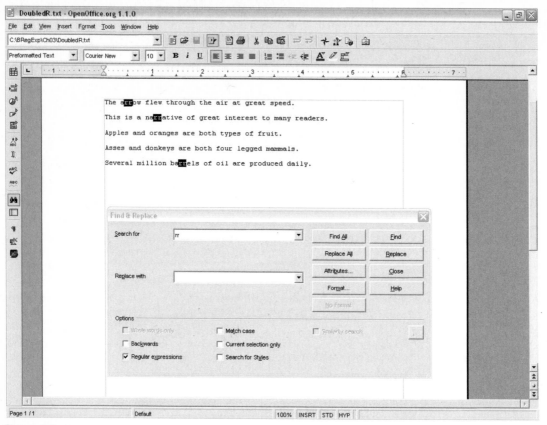

Figure A-5

The pattern `rr` indicates to the regular expression engine that an attempt should be made to match the lowercase alphabetic character `r`; then, if that first match is successful, an attempt should be made to match the next character. The entire match is successful if the second character is also a lowercase `r`.

If the attempt to match the first character fails, the next character is tested to see if it is a lowercase `r`. If it is not a lowercase `r`, the match fails, and a new attempt is made to match the following character against the first `r` of the regular expression pattern.

You can also try this out in the Komodo Regular Expression Toolkit, as shown in Figure A-6, which matches successive lowercase ms. You can download the latest trial version of the Komodo IDE, which includes the Regular Expression Toolkit, from `http://activestate.com/Products/Komodo`. Komodo version 2.5 is used in this appendix. Clear the regular expression and the test text from the Komodo Toolkit. Enter **mammals** in the area for the string to be matched, and type **m** in the area for the regular expression. At that point, the initial m of `mammals` is matched. Then type a second **m** in the area for the regular expression, and the highlight indicating a match moves to the mm in the middle of `mammals`, as you can see in Figure A-6.

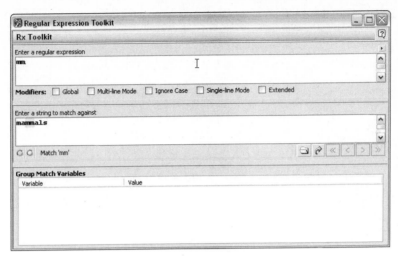

Figure A-6

These two examples have shown how you can match doubled characters using one of the syntax options that are available. Later in this appendix, you will look at an alternative syntax that can match an exact number of successive occurrences of a desired character, which can be exactly two or can be a larger number. The alternative syntax uses curly braces and, in addition to allowing matches of an exact number of occurrences, allows variable numbers of occurrences to be matched.

Introducing Metacharacters

To match three characters, you can simply write the character three times in a row to form a pattern. For example, to match part numbers that take the form ABC123 (in other words, three alphabetic characters followed by three numeric digits, which will match the alphabetic characters AAA), simply use the following pattern:

```
AAA
```

To match the other part of such part numbers, you need to introduce the concept of a *metacharacter*. The patterns you have seen so far include characters that stand, literally, for the same character. A metacharacter can be a single character or a pair of characters (the first is typically a backslash) that has a meaning other than the literal characters it contains.

There are several ways in which you can match the 123 part of a part number of the form ABC123. One is to write the following:

```
\d\d\d
```

Each \d is a metacharacter that stands for a numeric digit 0 through 9, inclusive. The \d metacharacter does *not* stand for a backslash followed by a lowercase d.

Notice that the \d metacharacter differs significantly in meaning from the literal characters used in patterns so far. The character L in a pattern could match only an uppercase L, but the metacharacter \d can match *any* of the numeric digits 0, 1, 2, 3, 4, 5, 6, 7, 8, or 9.

A metacharacter often matches a *class* of characters. In this case, the metacharacter \d matches the class of characters that are numeric digits.

When you have the pattern \d\d\d, you know that it matches three successive numeric digits, but it will match 012, 234, 345, 999 and hundreds of other numbers.

Matching Triple Numeric Digits

Suppose that you want to match a sequence of three numeric digits. In plain English, you might say that you want to match a three-digit number. A slightly more formal way to express what you want to do is this: Match a numeric digit. If the first character is a numeric digit, attempt to match the next character as a numeric digit. If both the characters are numeric digits, attempt to match a third successive numeric digit.

The metacharacter \d matches a single numeric digit; therefore, as described a little earlier, you could use the pattern

```
\d\d\d
```

to match three successive numeric digits.

If all three matches are successful, a match for the regular expression pattern has been found.

The test file, ABC123.txt, is shown here:

```
ABC123

A234BC

A23BCD4

Part Number DRC22

Part Number XFA221

Part Number RRG417
```

For the moment, aim to match only the numeric digits using the pattern \d\d\d shown earlier.

This example uses JavaScript, for reasons that will be explained in a moment.

1. Navigate to the directory that contains the file ABC123.txt and ThreeDigits.html. Open ThreeDigits.html in a web browser.

2. Click the button labeled Click Here To Enter Text.

3. When the prompt box opens, enter a string to test. Enter a string copied from ABC123.txt.

4. Click the OK button and inspect the alert box to see if the string that you entered contained a match for the pattern \d\d\d.

Figure A-7 shows the result after entering the string Part Number RRG417.

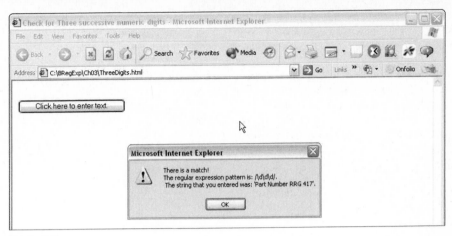

Figure A-7

Try each of the strings from `ABC123.txt`. You can also create your own test string. Notice that the pattern `\d\d\d` will match any sequence of three successive numeric digits, but single numeric digits or pairs of numeric digits are not matched.

The regular expression engine looks for a numeric digit. If the first character that it tests is not a numeric digit, it moves one character through the test string and then tests whether that character matches a numeric digit. If not, it moves one character further and tests again.

If a match is found for the first occurrence of `\d`, the regular expression engine tests if the next character is also a numeric digit. If that matches, a third character is tested to determine if it matches the `\d` metacharacter for a numeric digit. If three successive characters are each a numeric digit, there is a match for the regular expression pattern `\d\d\d`.

You can see this matching process in action by using the Komodo Regular Expressions Toolkit. Open the Komodo Regular Expression Toolkit, and clear any existing regular expression and test string. Enter the test string **A234BC**; then, in the area for the regular expression pattern, enter the pattern `\d`. You will see that the first numeric digit, 2, is highlighted as a match. Add a second `\d` to the regular expression area, and you will see that 23 is highlighted as a match. Finally, add a third **\d** to give a final regular expression pattern `\d\d\d`, and you will see that 234 is highlighted as a match. See Figure A-8.

You can try this with other test text from `ABC123.txt`. I suggest that you also try this out with your own test text that includes numeric digits and see which test strings match. You may find that you need to add a space character after the test string for matching to work correctly in the Komodo Regular Expression Toolkit.

Why was JavaScript used for the preceding example? Because you can't use OpenOffice.org Writer to test matches for the `\d` metacharacter.

Matching numeric digits can pose difficulties. Figure A-9 shows the result of an attempted match in `ABC123.txt` when using OpenOffice.org Writer with the pattern `\d\d\d`.

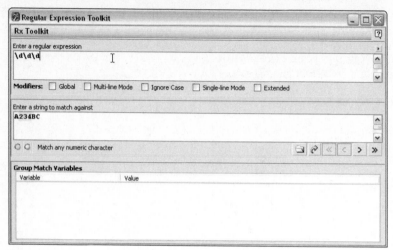

Figure A-8

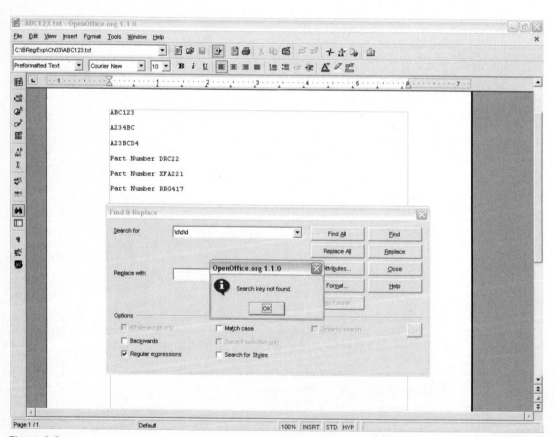

Figure A-9

As you can see in Figure A-9, no match is found in OpenOffice.org Writer. Numeric digits in OpenOffice.org Writer use nonstandard syntax in that OpenOffice.org Writer lacks support for the \d metacharacter.

One solution to this type of problem in OpenOffice.org Writer is to use character classes. For now, it is sufficient to note that the regular expression pattern

```
[0-9][0-9][0-9]
```

gives the same results as the pattern \d\d\d, because the meaning of [0-9][0-9][0-9] is the same as \d\d\d. The use of that character class to match three successive numeric digits in the file ABC123.txt is shown in Figure A-10.

Another syntax in OpenOffice.org Writer uses POSIX metacharacters.

The findstr utility also lacks the \d metacharacter, so if you want to use it to find matches, you must use the preceding character class shown in the command line, as follows:

```
findstr /N [0-9][0-9][0-9] ABC123.txt
```

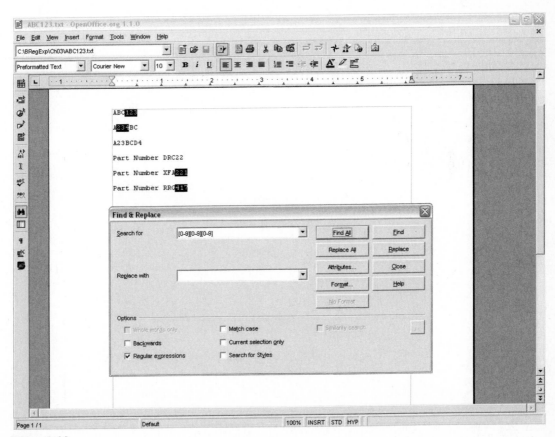

Figure A-10

You will find matches on four lines, as shown in Figure A-11. The preceding command line will work correctly only if the ABC123.txt file is in the current directory. If it is in a different directory, you will need to reflect that in the path for the file that you enter at the command line.

The next section combines the techniques that you have seen so far to find a combination of literally expressed characters and a sequence of characters.

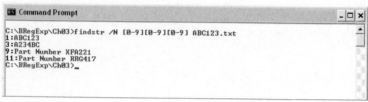

Figure A-11

Matching Sequences of Different Characters

A common task in simple regular expressions is to find a combination of literally specified single characters plus a sequence of characters.

There is an almost infinite number of possibilities in terms of characters that you could test. This section focuses on a very simple list of part numbers and look for part numbers with the code DOR followed by three numeric digits. In this case, the regular expression should do the following:

Look for a match for uppercase D. *If a match is found, check if the next character matches uppercase* O. *If that matches, next check if the following character matches uppercase* R. *If those three matches are present, check if the next three characters are numeric digits.*

Finding Literal Characters and Sequences of Characters

The file PartNumbers.txt is the sample file for this example:

```
BEF123

RRG417

DOR234

DOR123

CCG991
```

First, try it in OpenOffice.org Writer, remembering that you need to use the regular expression pattern [0-9] instead of \d.

1. Open the file PartNumbers.txt in OpenOffice.org Writer, and open the Find And Replace Dialog box by pressing Ctrl+F.

2. Check the Regular Expression check box and the Match Case check box.

3. Enter the pattern **DOR[0-9][0-9][0-9]** in the Search For text box and click the Find All button.

The text DOR234 and DOR123 is highlighted, indicating that those are matches for the regular expression.

The regular expression engine first looks for the literal character uppercase D. Each character is examined in turn to determine if there is or is not a match.

If a match is found, the regular expression engine then looks at the next character to determine if the following character is an uppercase O. If that too matches, it looks to see if the third character is an uppercase R. If all three of those characters match, the engine next checks to see if the fourth character is a numeric digit. If so, it checks if the fifth character is a numeric digit. If that too matches, it checks if the sixth character is a numeric digit. If that too matches, the entire regular expression pattern is matched. Each match is displayed in OpenOffice.org Writer as a highlighted sequence of characters.

You can check the PartNumbers.txt file for lines that contain a match for the pattern

```
DOR[0-9][0-9][0-9]
```

using the findstr utility from the command line, as follows:

```
findstr /N DOR[0-9][0-9][0-9] PartNumbers.txt
```

As you can see in Figure A-12, lines containing the same two matching sequences of characters, DOR234 and DOR123, are matched. If the directory that contains the file PartNumbers.txt is not the current directory in the command window, you will need to adjust the path to the file accordingly.

The Komodo Regular Expression Toolkit can also be used to test the pattern DOR\d\d\d. As you can see in Figure A-13, the test text DOR123 matches.

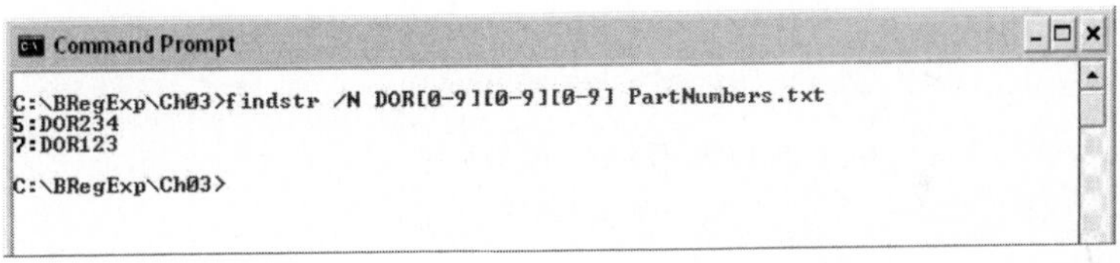

Figure A-12

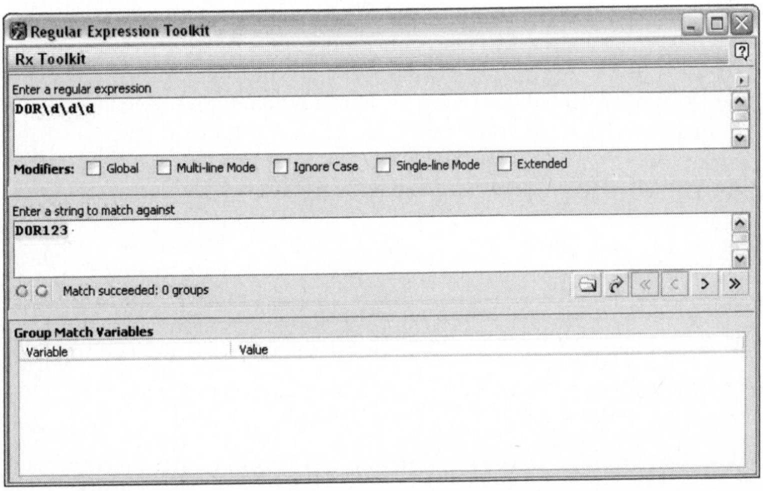

Figure A-13

Now that you have looked at how to match sequences of characters, each of which occur exactly once, the next section moves on to look at matching characters that can occur a variable number of times.

Matching Optional Characters

Matching literal characters is straightforward, particularly when you are aiming to match exactly one literal character for each corresponding literal character that you include in a regular expression pattern. The next step up from that basic situation is where a single literal character may occur zero times or one time. In other words, a character is optional. Most regular expression dialects use the question mark (?) character to indicate that the preceding chunk is optional. I am using the term "chunk" loosely here to mean the thing that precedes the question mark. That chunk can be a single character or various, more complex regular expression constructs. For the moment, you will deal with the case of the single, optional character.

For example, suppose you are dealing with a group of documents that contain both U.S. English and British English.

You may find that words such as `color` (in U.S. English) appear as `colour` (British English) in some documents. You can express a pattern to match both words like this:

```
colou?r
```

You may want to standardize the documents so that all the spellings are U.S. English spellings.

Matching an Optional Character

Try this out using the Komodo Regular Expression Toolkit:

1. Open the Komodo Regular Expression Toolkit and clear any regular expression pattern or text that may have been retained.

2. Insert the text `colour` into the area for the text to be matched.

3. Enter the regular expression pattern `colou?r` into the area for the regular expression pattern. The text `colour` is matched, as shown in Figure A-14.

Try this regular expression pattern with text such as that shown in the sample file `Colors.txt`:

```
Red is a color.

His collar is too tight or too colouuuurful.

These are bright colours.

These are bright colors.

Calorific is a scientific term.

"Your life is very colorful," she said.
```

The word `color` in the line `Red is a color.` will match the pattern `colou?r`.

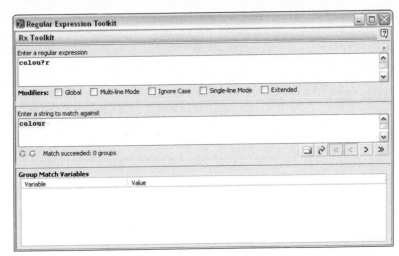

Figure A-14

When the regular expression engine reaches a position just before the c of color, it attempts to match a lowercase c. This match succeeds. It next attempts to match a lowercase o. That too matches. It next attempts to match a lowercase l and a lowercase o. They match as well. It then attempts to match the pattern u?, which means zero or one lowercase u characters. Because there are exactly zero lowercase u characters following the lowercase o, there is a match. The pattern u? matches zero characters. Finally, it attempts to match the final character in the pattern — that is, the lowercase r. Because the next character in the string color does match a lowercase r, the whole pattern is matched.

There is no match in the line His collar is too tight or too colouuuurful. The only possible match might be in the sequence of characters colouuuurful. The failure to match occurs when the regular expression engine attempts to match the pattern u?. Because the pattern u? means "match zero or one lowercase u characters," there is a match on the first u of colouuuurful. After that successful match, the regular expression engine attempts to match the final character of the pattern colou?r against the second lowercase u in colouuuurful. That attempt to match fails, so the attempt to match the whole pattern colou?r against the sequence of characters colouuuurful also fails.

What happens when the regular expression engine attempts to find a match in the line These are bright colours.?

When the regular expression engine reaches a position just before the c of colours, it attempts to match a lowercase c. That match succeeds. It next attempts to match a lowercase o, a lowercase l, and another lowercase o. These also match. It next attempts to match the pattern u?, which means zero or one lowercase u characters. Because exactly one lowercase u character follows the lowercase o in colours, there is a match. Finally, the regular expression engine attempts to match the final character in the pattern, the lowercase r. Because the next character in the string colours does match a lowercase r, the whole pattern is matched.

The findstr utility can also be used to test for the occurrence of the sequence of characters color and colour, but the regular expression engine in the findstr utility has a limitation in that it lacks a metacharacter to signify an optional character. For many purposes, the * metacharacter, which matches zero, one, or more occurrences of the preceding character, will work successfully.

To look for lines that contain matches for `colour` and `color` using the `findstr` utility, enter the following at the command line:

```
findstr /N colo*r Colors.txt
```

The preceding command line assumes that the file `Colors.txt` is in the current directory.

Figure A-15 shows the result from using the `findstr` utility on `Colors.txt`.

Notice that lines that contain the sequences of characters `color` and `colour` are successfully matched, whether as whole words or parts of longer words. However, notice, too, that the slightly strange "word" `colouuuurful` is also matched due to the * metacharacter's allowing multiple occurrences of the lower-case letter u. In most practical situations, such bizarre "words" won't be an issue for you, and the * quanti-fier will be an appropriate substitute for the ? quantifier when using the `findstr` utility. In some situations, where you want to match precisely zero or one specific characters, the `findstr` utility may not provide the functionality that you need, because it would also match a character sequence such as `colonifier`.

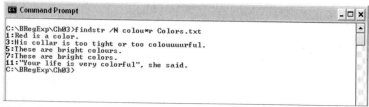

Figure A-15

Having seen how you can use a single optional character in a regular expression pattern, take a look at how you can use multiple optional characters in a single regular expression pattern.

Matching Multiple Optional Characters

Many English words have multiple forms. Sometimes, it may be necessary to match all of the forms of a word. Matching all those forms can require using multiple optional characters in a regular expression pattern.

Consider the various forms of the word `color` (U.S. English) and `colour` (British English). They include the following:

```
color (U.S. English, singular noun)

colour (British English, singular noun)

colors (U.S. English, plural noun)
```

```
colours (British English, plural noun)

color's (U.S. English, possessive singular)

colour's (British English, possessive singular)

colors' (U.S. English, possessive plural)

colours' (British English, possessive plural)
```

The following regular expression pattern, which includes three optional characters, can match all eight of these word forms:

```
colou?r'?s?'?
```

If you tried to express this in a semiformal way, you might have the following problem definition:

Match the U.S. English and British English forms of color *(*colour*), including the singular noun, the plural noun, and the singular possessive and the plural possessive.*

Try it out, and then I will explain why it works and what limitations it potentially has.

Matching Multiple Optional Characters

Use the sample file Colors2.txt to explore this example:

```
These colors are bright.

Some colors feel warm. Other colours feel cold.

A color's temperature can be important in creating reaction to an image.

These colours' temperatures are important in this discussion.

Red is a vivid colour.
```

To test the regular expression, follow these steps:

1. Open OpenOffice.org Writer, and open the file Colors2.txt.
2. Use the keyboard shortcut Ctrl+F to open the Find And Replace dialog box.
3. Check the Regular Expressions check box and the Match Case check box.
4. In the Search For text box, enter the regular expression pattern **colou?r'?s?'?**, and click the Find All button. If all has gone well, you should see the matches shown in Figure A-16.

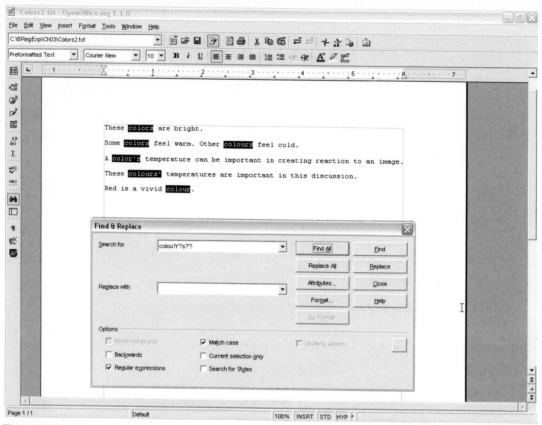

Figure A-16

As you can see, all the sample forms of the word of interest have been matched.

This description focuses initially on matching of the forms of the word `colour/color`.

How does the pattern `colou?r'?s?'?` match the word `color`? Assume that the regular expression engine is at the position immediately before the first letter of `color`. It first attempts to match lowercase c, because one lowercase c must be matched. That matches. Attempts are then made to match a subsequent lowercase o, l, and o. These all also match. Then an attempt is made to match an optional lowercase u. In other words, zero or one occurrences of the lowercase character u is needed. Because there are zero occurrences of lowercase u, there is a match. Next, an attempt is made to match lowercase r. The lowercase r in `color` matches. Then an attempt is made to match an optional apostrophe. Because there is no occurrence of an apostrophe, there is a match. Next, the regular expression engine attempts to match an optional lowercase s — in other words, to match zero or one occurrence of lower-case s. Because there is no occurrence of lowercase s, again, there is a match. Finally, an attempt is made to match an optional apostrophe. Because there is no occurrence of an apostrophe, another match is found. Because a match exists for all the components of the regular expression pattern, there is a match for the whole regular expression pattern `colour?r'?s?'?`.

Now, how does the pattern `colou?r'?s?'?` match the word `colour`? Assume that the regular expression engine is at the position immediately before the first letter of `colour`. It first attempts to match lowercase c, because one lowercase c must be matched. That matches. Next, attempts are made to match a subse-quent lowercase o, l, and another o. These also match. Then an attempt is made to match an optional lowercase u. In other words, zero or one occurrences of the lowercase character u are needed. Because there is one occurrence of lowercase u, there is a match. Next, an attempt is made to match lowercase r. The lowercase r in `colour` matches. Next, the engine attempts to match an optional apostrophe. Because there is no occurrence of an apostrophe, there is a match. Next, the regular expression engine attempts to match an optional lowercase s — in other words, to match zero or one occurrences of lowercase s. Because there is no occurrence of lowercase s, a match exists. Finally, an attempt is made to match an optional apostrophe. Because there is no occurrence of an apostrophe, there is a match. All the compo-nents of the regular expression pattern have a match; therefore, the entire regular expression pattern `colour?r'?s?'?` matches.

Work through the other six word forms shown earlier, and you'll find that each of the word forms does, in fact, match the regular expression pattern.

The pattern `colou?r'?s?'?` matches all eight of the word forms that were listed earlier, but will the pattern match the following sequence of characters?

```
colour's'
```

Can you see that it does match? Can you see why it matches the pattern? If each of the three optional characters in the regular expression is present, the preceding sequence of characters matches. That rather odd sequence of characters likely won't exist in your sample document, so the possibility of false matches (reduced specificity) won't be an issue for you.

How can you avoid the problem caused by such odd sequences of characters as `colour's'`? You want to be able to express it something like this:

> *Match a lowercase c. If a match is present, attempt to match a lowercase o. If that match is present, attempt to match a lowercase l. If there is a match, attempt to match a lowercase o. If a match exists, attempt to match an optional lowercase u. If there is a match, attempt to match a lowercase r. If there is a match, attempt to match an optional apostrophe. And if a match exists here, attempt to match an optional lowercase s. If the earlier optional apostrophe was not present, attempt to match an optional apostrophe.*

> *With the techniques that you have seen so far, you aren't able to express ideas such as "match something only if it is not preceded by something else." That sort of approach might help achieve higher specificity at the expense of increased complexity.*

Other Cardinality Operators

Testing for matches only for optional characters can be very useful, as you saw in the `colors` example, but it would be pretty limiting if that were the only quantifier available to a developer. Most regular expression implementations provide two other cardinality operators (also called *quantifiers*): the * operator and the + operator, which are described in the following sections.

The * Quantifier

The * operator refers to zero or more occurrences of the pattern to which it is related. In other words, a character or group of characters is optional but may occur more than once. Zero occurrences of the chunk that precedes the * quantifier should match. A single occurrence of that chunk should also match. So should two occurrences, three occurrences, and ten occurrences. In principle, an unlimited number of occurrences will also match.

Try this out in an example using OpenOffice.org Writer.

Matching Zero or More Occurrences

The sample file, `Parts.txt`, contains a listing of part numbers that have two alphabetic characters followed by zero or more numeric digits. In the simple sample file, the maximum number of numeric digits is three, but because the * quantifier will match three occurrences, you can use it to match the sample part numbers. If there is a good reason why it is important that a maximum of three numeric digits can occur, you can express that notion by using an alternative syntax, which is discussed a little later in this appendix. Each of the part numbers in this example consists of the sequence of uppercase characters ABC followed by zero or more numeric digits:

```
ABC

ABC123

ABC12

ABC889

ABC8899

ABC34
```

You can express what you want to do as follows:

Match an uppercase A. *If there is a match, attempt to match an uppercase* B. *If there is a match, attempt to match an uppercase* C. *If all three uppercase characters match, attempt to match zero or more numeric digits.*

Because all the part numbers begin with the literal characters ABC, you can use the pattern

```
ABC[0-9]*
```

to match part numbers that correspond to the description in the problem definition.

1. Open OpenOffice.org Writer and open the sample file, `Parts.txt`.

2. Use Ctrl+F to open the Find And Replace dialog box.

3. Check the Regular Expression check box and the Match Case check box.

4. Enter the regular expression pattern ABC[0-9]* in the Search For text box.

5. Click the Find All button, and inspect the matches that are highlighted.

Figure A-17 shows the matches in OpenOffice.org Writer. As you can see, all of the part numbers match the pattern.

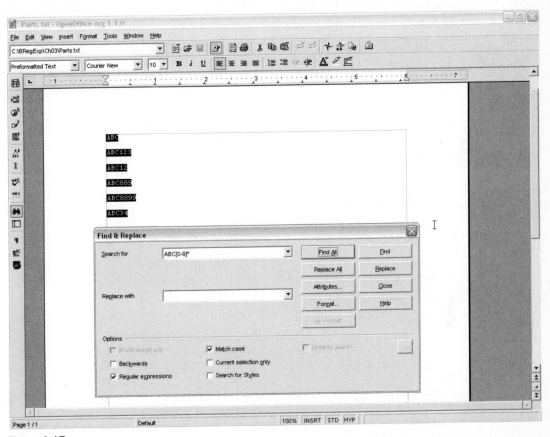

Figure A-17

Before working through a couple of the matches, briefly look at part of the regular expression pattern, [0-9]*. The asterisk applies to the character class [0-9], which I call a *chunk*.

Why does the first part number ABC match? When the regular expression engine is at the position immediately before the A of ABC, it attempts to match the next character in the part number with an uppercase A. Because the first character of the part number ABC is an uppercase A, there is a match. Next, an attempt is made to match an uppercase B. That too matches, as does an attempt to match an uppercase C. At that stage, the first three characters in the regular expression pattern have been matched. Finally, an attempt is made to match the pattern [0-9]*, which means "Match zero or more numeric characters." Because the character after C is a newline character, there are no numeric digits. Because there are exactly zero numeric digits after the uppercase C of ABC, there is a match (of zero numeric digits). Because all components of the pattern match, the whole pattern matches.

Why does the part number ABC8899 also match? When the regular expression engine is at the position immediately before the A of ABC8899, it attempts to match the next character in the part number with an uppercase A. Because the first character of the part number ABC8899 is an uppercase A, there is a match. Next, attempts are made to match an uppercase B and an uppercase C. These too match. At that stage, the first three characters in the regular expression pattern have been matched. Finally, an attempt is made to match the pattern [0-9]*, which means "Match zero or more numeric characters." Four numeric digits follow the uppercase C. Because there are exactly four numeric digits after the uppercase C of ABC, there is a match (of four numeric digits, which meets the criterion "zero or more numeric digits"). Because all components of the pattern match, the whole pattern matches.

Work through the other part numbers step by step, and you'll find that each ought to match the pattern ABC[0-9]*.

The + Quantifier

There are many situations where you will want to be certain that a character or group of characters is present at least once but also allow for the possibility that the character occurs more than once. The + cardinality operator is designed for that situation. The + operator means "Match one or more occurrences of the chunk that precedes me."

Take a look at the example with Parts.txt, but look for matches that include at least one numeric digit. You want to find part numbers that begin with the uppercase characters ABC and then have one or more numeric digits.

You can express the problem definition like this:

Match an uppercase A. If there is a match, attempt to match an uppercase B. If there is a match, attempt to match an uppercase C. If all three uppercase characters match, attempt to match one or more numeric digits.

Use the following pattern to express that problem definition:

```
ABC[0-9]+
```

Matching One or More Numeric Digits

1. Open OpenOffice.org Writer, and open the sample file Parts.txt.

2. Use Ctrl+F to open the Find And Replace dialog box.

3. Check the Regular Expressions and Match Case check boxes.

4. Enter the pattern ABC[0-9]+ in the Search For text box; click the Find All button, and inspect the matching part numbers that are highlighted, as shown in Figure A-18.

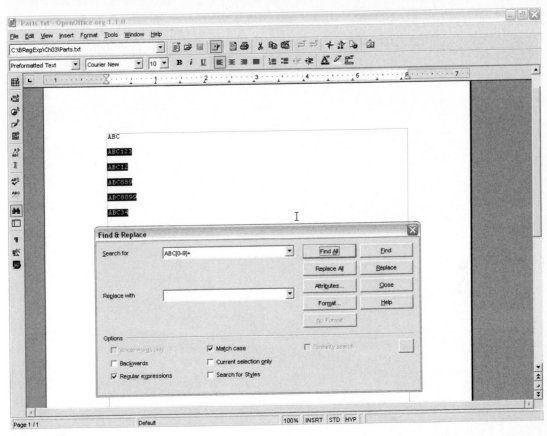

Figure A-18

As you can see, the only change from the result of using the pattern ABC[0-9]* is that the pattern ABC[0-9]+ fails to match the part number ABC.

When the regular expression engine is at the position immediately before the uppercase A of the part number ABC, it attempts to match an uppercase A. That matches. Next, subsequent attempts are made to match an uppercase B and an uppercase C. They too match. At that stage, the first three characters in the regular expression pattern have been matched. Finally, an attempt is made to match the pattern [0-9]+, which means "Match one or more numeric characters." There are zero numeric digits following the uppercase C. Because there are exactly zero numeric digits after the uppercase C of ABC, there is no match (zero numeric digits fails to match the criterion "one or more numeric digits," specified by the + quantifier). Because the final component of the pattern fails to match, the whole pattern fails to match.

Why does the part number ABC8899 match? When the regular expression engine is at the position immediately before the A of ABC8899, it attempts to match the next character in the part number with an uppercase A. Because the first character of the part number ABC8899 is an uppercase A, there is a match. Next, attempts are made to match an uppercase B and an uppercase C. They too match. At that stage, the first three characters in the regular expression pattern have been matched. Finally, an attempt is made to match the pattern [0-9]+, which means "Match one or more numeric characters." Four numeric digits follow the uppercase C of ABC, so there is a match (of four numeric digits, which meets the criterion "one or more numeric digits"). Because all components of the pattern match, the whole pattern matches.

Before moving on to look at the curly-brace quantifier syntax, here's a brief review of the quantifiers already discussed, as listed in Table A-1.

Table A-1

Quantifier	Definition
?	0 or 1 occurrences
*	0 or more occurrences
+	1 or more occurrences

These quantifiers can often be useful, but there are times when you will want to express ideas such as "Match something that occurs at least twice but can occur an unlimited number of times" or "Match something that can occur at least three times but no more than six times."

You also saw earlier that you can express a repeating character by simply repeating the character in a regular expression pattern.

The Curly-Brace Syntax

If you want to specify large numbers of occurrences, you can use a curly-brace syntax to specify an exact number of occurrences.

The {n} Syntax

Suppose that you want to match part numbers with sequences of characters that have exactly three numeric digits. You can write the pattern as

```
ABC[0-9][0-9][0-9]
```

by simply repeating the character class for a numeric digit. Alternatively, you can use the curly-brace syntax and write

```
ABC[0-9]{3}
```

to achieve the same result.

Most regular expression engines support a syntax that can express ideas like that. The syntax uses curly braces to specify minimum and maximum numbers of occurrences.

The {n,m} Syntax

The * operator that was described a little earlier in this appendix effectively means "Match a minimum of zero occurrences and a maximum occurrence, which is unbounded." Similarly, the + quantifier means "Match a minimum of one occurrence and a maximum occurrence, which is unbounded."

Using curly braces and numbers inside them allows the developer to create occurrence quantifiers that cannot be specified when using the ?, *, or + quantifiers.

The following subsections look at three variants that use the curly-brace syntax. First, look at the syntax that specifies "Match zero or up to [a specified number] of occurrences."

{0,m}

The {0,m} syntax allows you to specify that a minimum of zero occurrences can be matched (specified by the first numeric digit after the opening curly brace) and that a maximum of m occurrences can be matched (specified by the second numeric digit, which is separated from the minimum occurrence indicator by a comma and which precedes the closing curly brace).

To match a minimum of zero occurrences and a maximum of one occurrence, you would use the pattern

```
{0,1}
```

which has the same meaning as the ? quantifier.

To specify matching of a minimum of zero occurrences and a maximum of three occurrences, you would use the pattern

```
{0,3}
```

which you couldn't express using the ?, *, or + quantifiers.

Suppose that you want to specify that you want to match the sequence of characters ABC followed by a minimum of zero numeric digits or a maximum of two numeric digits.

You can semiformally express that as the following problem definition:

> Match an uppercase A. If there is a match, attempt to match an uppercase B. If there is a match, attempt to match an uppercase C. If all three uppercase characters match, attempt to match a minimum of zero or a maximum of two numeric digits.

The following pattern does what you need:

```
ABC[0-9]{0,2}
```

The ABC simply matches a sequence of the corresponding literal characters. The [0-9] indicates that a numeric digit is to be matched, and the {0,2} is a quantifier that indicates a minimum of zero occurrences of the preceding chunk (which is [0-9], representing a numeric digit) and a maximum of two occurrences of the preceding chunk is to be matched.

Match Zero to Two Occurrences

1. Open OpenOffice.org Writer, and open the sample file `Parts.txt`.

2. Use Ctrl+F to open the Find And Replace dialog box.

3. Check the Regular Expressions and Match Case check boxes.

4. Enter the regular expression pattern **ABC[0-9]{0,2}** in the Search For text box; click the Find All button, and inspect the matches that are displayed in highlighted text, as shown in Figure A-19.

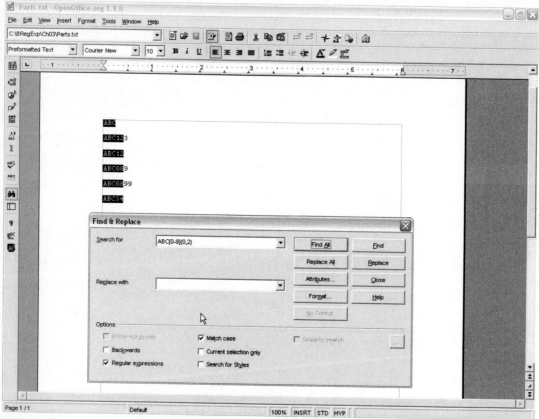

Figure A-19

Notice that on some lines, only parts of a part number are matched. If you are puzzled as to why that is, refer back to the problem definition. You are to match a specified sequence of characters. You haven't specified that you want to match a part number, simply a sequence of characters.

How does it work with the match for the part number ABC? When the regular expression engine is at the position immediately before the uppercase A of the part number ABC, it attempts to match an uppercase A. That matches. Next, an attempt is made to match an uppercase B. That too matches. Next, an attempt is made to match an uppercase C. That too matches. At that stage, the first three characters in the regular expression pattern have been matched. Finally, an attempt is made to match the pattern [0-9]{0,2}, which means "Match a minimum of zero and a maximum of two numeric characters." Zero numeric digits follow the uppercase C in ABC. Because there are exactly zero numeric digits after the uppercase C of ABC, there is a match (zero numeric digits matches the criterion "a minimum of zero numeric digits" specified by the minimum-occurrence specifier of the {0,2} quantifier). Because the final component of the pattern matches, the whole pattern matches.

What happens when matching is attempted on the line that contains the part number ABC8899? Why do the first five characters of the part number ABC8899 match? When the regular expression engine is at the position immediately before the A of ABC8899, it attempts to match the next character in the part number with an uppercase A and finds it is a match. Next, an attempt is made to match an uppercase B. That too matches. Then an attempt is made to match an uppercase C, which also matches. At that stage, the first three characters in the regular expression pattern have been matched. Finally, an attempt is made to match the pattern [0-9]{0,2}, which means "Match a minimum of zero and a maximum of two numeric characters." Four numeric digits follow the uppercase C. Only two of those numeric digits are needed for a successful match. Because there are four numeric digits after the uppercase C of ABC, there is a match (of two numeric digits, which meets the criterion "a maximum of two numeric digits"), but the final two numeric digits of ABC8899 are not needed to form a match, so they are not highlighted. Because all components of the pattern match, the whole pattern matches.

{n,m}

The minimum-occurrence specifier in the curly-brace syntax doesn't have to be 0. It can be any number you like, provided it is not larger than the maximum-occurrence specifier.

Look for one to three occurrences of a numeric digit. You can specify this in a problem definition as follows:

> *Match an uppercase A. If there is a match, attempt to match an uppercase B. If there is a match, attempt to match an uppercase C. If all three uppercase characters match, attempt to match a minimum of one and a maximum of three numeric digits.*

So if you wanted to match one to three occurrences of a numeric digit in Parts.txt, you would use the following pattern:

```
ABC[0-9]{1,3}
```

Figure A-20 shows the matches in OpenOffice.org Writer. Notice that the part number ABC does not match, because it has zero numeric digits, and you are looking for matches that have one through three numeric digits. Notice, too, that only the first three numeric digits of ABC8899 form part of the match.

> *The explanation in the preceding section for the {0,m} syntax should be sufficient to help you understand what is happening in this example.*

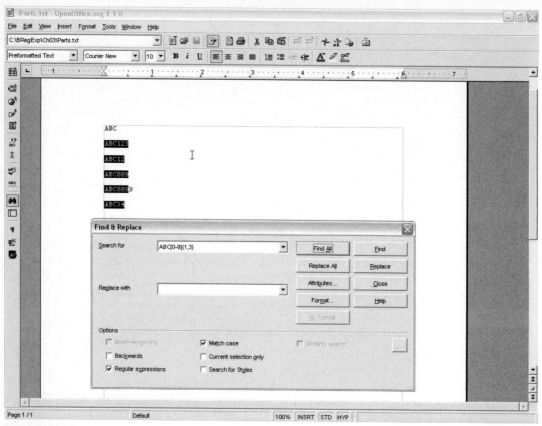

Figure A-20

{n,}

Sometimes, you will want there to be an unlimited number of occurrences. You can specify an unlimited maximum number of occurrences by omitting the maximum-occurrence specifier inside the curly braces.

To specify at least two occurrences and an unlimited maximum, you could use the following problem definition:

Match an uppercase A. *If there is a match, attempt to match an uppercase* B. *If there is a match, attempt to match an uppercase* C. *If all three uppercase characters match, attempt to match a minimum of two occurrences and an unlimited maximum occurrence of three numeric digits.*

You can express that using the following pattern:

```
ABC[0-9]{2,}
```

Figure A-21 shows the appearance in OpenOffice.org Writer. Notice that now all four numeric digits in ABC8899 form part of the match, because the maximum occurrences that can form part of a match are unlimited.

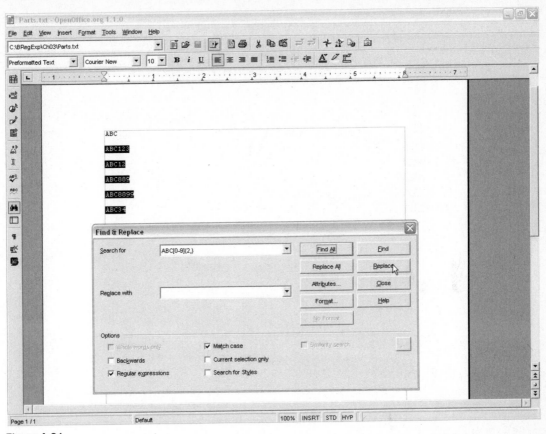

Figure A-21

Glossary

This glossary contains a list of terms that may be useful to a web developer or search engine marketer reading this book. Glossary entries contained within other entries are presented in *italics*.

200   A web server *status code* that indicates the requested URL has been retrieved successfully. See Chapter 4 for more details.

301   A type of *redirect* sent by a web server that indicates the content of a URL has been relocated permanently. See Chapter 4 for more details.

302   A type of *redirect* sent by a web server that indicates the content of a URL has been relocated temporarily. See Chapter 4 for more details.

404   A web server *status code* returned when the requested URL does not exist on the server. See Chapter 4 for more details.

500   A web server *status code* returned when the server is encountering temporary technical problems. See Chapter 4 for more details.

Accessibility   The ease of use exhibited by a web site with regard to users who have disabilities or impairments.

Ad-hoc query   A search request that retrieves information without knowledge of the underlying storage structures of the database.

Aggregator   See *feed reader*.

AJAX   An acronym for *Asynchronous JavaScript and XML*. It is a technology that uses *DOM*, *JavaScript*, and the `XMLHttpRequest` object to create interactive web applications within a web page. With an AJAX application, users do not navigate through different pages of content — instead, the application executes (and displays updated content when necessary) inside a single web page. For a practical tutorial, we recommend Cristian Darie's *AJAX and PHP: Building Responsive Web Applications* (Packt Publishing, 2006). SEO implications of AJAX are discussed in Chapter 6.

Glossary

Algorithm   A set of instructions that directs a computer to complete a task or solve a problem; in search engines, a series of such algorithms is used to create the list of search results for a particular user query, ranking the results in order of relevance.

Anchor text   The text a user clicks when he or she follows a link; in HTML it is the text contained by `<a>...</a>`.

Apache   A popular open-source web server; it is the web server used in this book.

Application programming interface (API)   Functions of a computer program that can be accessed and used by other programs. For example, many shipping companies use application programming interfaces to allow applications to query shipping prices over the Internet.

ASP.NET   A development framework created by Microsoft for creating dynamic web applications and web services. It is part of Microsoft's .NET platform and shares very little with "classic" ASP. See the companion Wrox title *Professional Search Engine Optimization with ASP.NET: A Developer's Guide to SEO* (Wiley, 2007) for details on optimizing ASP.NET web sites.

Asynchronous JavaScript and XML   See *AJAX*.

Atom   A *web feed* standard based on *XML*. For more details, see Chapter 7.

BigDaddy   An update to Google's ranking algorithms for web sites that occurred in early 2006. It is similar in scope to the *Florida* update.

Black hat   The use of techniques that to varying degrees do not follow the guidelines of search engines and may also exploit the work or property of others. For more details, see Chapter 8.

Blog   A content management system that presents articles in reverse chronological order. Blogs are explored in Chapter 16 when you set one up using *WordPress*.

Bot   See *spider*.

Breadcrumb navigation   Navigational links appearing on a web page that show the path taken to reach that particular page; for example, "home ⇨ products ⇨ cookies."

Cascading Style Sheets   A language that defines the presentation and aesthetics of a markup language such as HTML.

Class   A blueprint for an object in object-oriented programming.

Click through   The act of a user clicking a particular ad or *SERP*.

Click through rate   The ratio of click-throughs per number of visitors who view the advertisement or *SERP*.

Cloaking   The (sometimes deceptive) practice of delivering different content to a search engine than to human visitors browsing a web site.

Content theft   The practice of stealing another individual's web content.

Conversion rate   The ratio of conversions or sales per the number of visitors.

CSS   See *Cascading Style Sheets*.

CTR   See *click through rate*.

Data escaping   Altering the text and other data received from a non-trusted source, such as a comment added with a form on your web site, so that it doesn't cause any unwanted side effects when that data is further processed by your application.

Delist   To remove a web site from a search engine's index.

Directory   A human-edited catalog of web sites organized into categories; examples include the Yahoo! directory and DMOZ.

DNS   Acronym for Domain Name Server.

Document Object Model   The representation of a hierarchical structure such as that of an *XML* or HTML document. Most programming languages provide a Document Object Model (DOM) object that allows loading and manipulating such structures. In particular, *AJAX* web applications use DOM to create web applications inside of a web page.

DOM   See *Document Object Model*.

Domain Name Server   A server that stores various data about domain names and translates them to their designated IP addresses.

Duplicate content   Substantially identical content located on different web pages.

Extensible Markup Language   Better known as XML, this is a general-purpose text-based document structure that facilitates the sharing of data across diverse applications. See http://en.wikipedia.org/wiki/Xml for more information.

Feed   See *web feed*.

Feed reader   An application that reads and displays web feeds for human consumption.

.FLA   A source script file used to generate Flash .SWF files.

Flash   A technology developed by Adobe that can be used to add animation and interactive content to web pages using vector graphics.

Florida   An update to Google's ranking *algorithms* for web sites that occurred in late 2003.

Geo-targeting   The practice of providing different content depending on a user's or spider's physical location on Earth.

Glossary

Google Sandbox   The virtual "purgatory" that many newly launched sites must pass through in order to rank well in Google. This concept is described in Chapter 2.

HTTP status codes   Numeric codes that provide information regarding the state of an HTTP request. You can use them, for example, to indicate that the information requested is not available or has been moved.

Inbound link   A link to your web site from an external web site.

IP address   The unique numerical address of a particular computer or network device on the Internet; it can be analogized to a phone number in purpose.

IP delivery   The practice of using the IP address of the connecting computer, whether robot or human, and sending different content based on that. It is the technology behind both *geo-targeting* and *cloaking*.

JavaScript   A scripting language implemented by all modern web browsers, best known for its use as a client-side programming language embedded within web pages. Some common uses of JavaScript are to open popup windows, validate data on web forms, and more recently to create *AJAX* applications.

Link bait   Any content or feature within a web site that is designed to bait viewers to place links to it from other web sites.

Link equity   The equity, or value, transferred to another URL by a particular link. This concept is discussed in Chapter 2.

Link farm   A web page or set of web pages that is contrived for the express purpose of manipulating link popularity by strategically interlinking web sites.

Keyword density   A metric that calculates how frequently a certain keyword appears in web page copy to calculate relevance to a query.

Keyword stuffing   Excessive and contrived keyword repetition for the purpose of manipulating search results.

Matt Cutts   An outspoken Google engineer who runs a *blog* at http://www.mattcutts.com/blog.

mod_rewrite   An *Apache* module that performs *URL rewriting*. See Chapter 3 for more details.

MySQL   A free open-source relational database that uses *SQL* to specify requests or queries for data contained therein.

Natural   See *organic*.

Nofollow   An attribute that can be applied to links to specify that search engines shouldn't count them as a vote, with regard to *link equity*, for the specified URL. The concept is discussed in Chapter 8.

Object-oriented programming (OOP)   A feature implemented by modern programming languages (including PHP) that allows the programmer to create data types that are modeled after real-world behavior — objects; the object is a self-contained entity that has state and behavior, just like a real-world object. The concept of *OOP* is introduced in Chapter 7, when using this feature in PHP for the first time in the book.

Organic   An adjective that describes the results from unpaid results in a search engine.

Outbound link   A link from a web page to an external web site.

PageRank (PR)   An algorithm patented by Google that measures a particular page's importance relative to other pages included in the search engine's index. It was invented in the late 1990s by Larry Page and Sergey Brin.

Pay Per Click (PPC)   An advertising method whereby advertisers competitively bid for clicks resulting particular keywords or contextually placed advertisement blocks. These advertisements are called "sponsored ads" and appear above or next to the organic results in *SERPs*.

PHP   A programming language designed primarily for producing dynamic web pages, originally written by Rasmus Lerdorf. PHP is a recursive acronym of "PHP: Hypertext Preprocessor."

Redirect   The process of redirecting requests for a web page to another page. Redirecting is discussed in Chapter 4.

REFERER   A header sent by a web browser indicating where it arrived from — or where it was referred from. Our misspelling of "referer" is deliberate and in the specification.

Regex   See *regular expression*.

Regular expression   A string written in a special language that matches text patterns. Regular expressions are used in text manipulation and are discussed in Chapter 3 and Appendix A.

Return on investment (ROI)   A metric for the benefit attained by a particular investment.

Robot   In the context of this book, a robot refers to a *spider*.

robots.txt   A text file located in the root directory of a web site that adheres to the `robots.txt` standard, described at `http://www.robotstxt.org`. The standard specifies files that should not be accessed by a search engine *spider*.

ROI   Acronym for *return on investment*.

RSS   A *web feed* standard based on *XML*. For more details, see Chapter 7.

Screen scraping   The practice of using a program to parse out information from an HTML document.

Search engine optimization   The subset of search engine marketing that aims to improve the *organic* rankings of a web site for relevant keywords.

SEM   An acronym for search engine marketing or search engine marketer.

SEO   An acronym for search engine optimization.

Glossary

SEO copywriting The practice of authoring content in such a way that it not only reads well for the surfer, but additionally targets specific search terms in search engines.

SERP An acronym for search engine results page.

Sitemap A file that provides an easy way for both humans and search engines to reference pages of your web site from one central location. Sitemaps are covered in Chapter 9.

Social bookmarking Offers users convenient storage of their bookmarks remotely for access from any location. Examples of web sites that offer this service include del.icio.us, Digg, Reddit, and so on. Social bookmarking is covered in Chapter 7.

Spam (search engine) Web page(s) that are contrived to rank well in search engines but actually contain no valuable content.

Spider A computer program that performs the process of *spidering*.

Spider trap A set of web pages that cause a web spider to make an infinite number of requests without providing any substantial content and/or cause it to crash.

Spidering The process of traversing and storing the content of a web site performed by the *spider*.

Spoofing Sending of incorrect information deliberately.

SQL An acronym for *Structured Query Language*.

Status code See *HTTP status codes*.

Structured Query Language A computer language used to create, update, select, and delete data from (relational) databases.

Supplemental index A secondary index provided by Google that is widely believed to contain content that it regards as less important. See more details in Chapter 2.

Supplemental result A result in the *supplemental index*.

.SWF A vector graphics format created by Macromedia (now owned by Adobe) used to publish animations and interactive applications on the web. Although technically incorrect, SWF files are frequently referred to as "Flash movies."

URL rewriting The practice that translates incoming URL requests to requests for other URLs. You use URL rewriting to serve pages with search-engine friendly URLs from dynamic scripts written in PHP (or another programming language). This topic is discussed in Chapter 3.

Usability The ease of use exhibited by a web site.

User agent Any user or web spider accessing a web site; also refers to the string sent by a user's web browser or a web spider indicating what or who it is, that is, "Mozilla/5.0 (Windows; U; Windows NT 5.1; en-US; rv:1.8.1) Gecko/20061010 Firefox/2.0."

Viral marketing   Marketing techniques that use social phenomena to spread a message through self-replicating viral processes — not unlike those of computer viruses.

Web analytics   A software package that tracks various web site data and statistics used for analyzing and interpreting results of marketing efforts.

Web feed   Provides automated access to content contained by a web site via some sort of software application. *XML* is typically used to transport the information in a structured format.

Web log   See *blog*.

Web spider   See *spider*.

Web syndication   Permits and facilitates other web sites to publish your web content.

White hat   Describes the use of techniques that follow the guidelines of a search engine.

WordPress   A popular open-source blogging application written in *PHP*.

XML   See Extensible Markup Language.

Index

CONTENTS

HOW TO USE THIS BOOK

IT'S AN AGE OF ENDLESS INFORMATION, AND STUDENTS ARE OVERWHELMED. FURTHERMORE, THEY HAVE A HARD TIME UNDERSTANDING HOW—AND EVEN *IF*—ALL THAT THEY KNOW FITS TOGETHER. THEY ARE DROWNING IN THE FLOOD OF DATA THAT POURS FORTH FROM THEIR MEDIA-RICH YET WISDOM-POOR WORLD.

Help them make a significant connection between the Bible and culture with **40 Instant Studies: Old Testament**. Each two-page study is easy to prepare, yet rich with true-to-life relevance and biblical depth.

This book is designed as a resource for those in student ministry. In this volume you will find 40 easy-to-prepare lessons that can be used in a pinch or as a part of a larger strategy you have in mind. Each lesson contains:

A REAL STORY

Each lesson is contained on the front and back sides of a single sheet. Remove a lesson by tearing on the handy perforations and head to the copy machine. Make a copy of the introductory story and discussion questions for each student. Start your lesson with high student interest and involvement.

AN EASY-TO-FOLLOW LESSON PLAN

Keep the back page of the lesson to help you guide your group through a Bible study that addresses the questions raised by the introductory article. At your fingertips you have probing discussion questions and clear Scripture commentary.

A CLOSING CHALLENGE

A good Bible study should inspire one to action. At the end of each lesson is a simple activity designed to give your students something concrete to do as a result of the study. These challenges use a variety of teaching methods, but are always focused and memorable.

In addition, find a quick summary of each lesson in the table of contents. Search the Scripture index for specific Bible references used, the story index for the topics covered in the introductory activity, or the topic index to find how specific scriptural themes are handled. You will find a wealth of teaching resources at your fingertips.

In an age of information glut, you need a way to grab the attention of your students and help them apply God's Word to the world around them. Do exactly that with **40 Instant Studies: Old Testament**.

Adam and Eve—Problems in the Beginning

The Cost of "Free" Music

Andrew Johnson was looking forward to having the summer off after he completed his freshman year in college. But he found himself having to work three summer jobs because of an unexpected debt. He had to pay the recording industry $3,000 to avoid being sued for music piracy.

Johnson had used his university's network to download one hundred songs with a program called *LimeWire*. During the second semester of his freshman year, the eighteen-year-old was one of more than 400 college students to receive a pre-litigation letter from the Recording Industry Association of America (RIAA). The RIAA represents the major recording companies. The letters informed Johnson and the others who received them that they could settle out of court for $3,000 each or the cases would go to trial. Were the college students to lose in court, they could be liable for damages of $750 per song that they had downloaded.

A recent survey by *Student Monitor* found that more than half of college students download music and movies illegally. College students alone are responsible for more than 1.3 billion illegal music downloads a year. College students surveyed admitted that more than two-thirds of all their music was acquired illegally.

Sophomore Sarah Barg also settled with the RIAA. She had downloaded 381 songs with the university computers and another file sharing program called *Ares*. "Obviously I knew it [downloading music] was illegal, but no one got in trouble for it," Barg said. Andrew Johnson had a similar complaint when he was caught. "It's not like I downloaded millions of songs and sold them to people," Johnson said.

Barg was angry about having to borrow money from her parents to pay for the settlement. "Without their help, I don't know what I would have done. I'm only twenty years old," she said. Barg agrees that sharing music is common and that other students don't understand the consequences. She believes the university should warn students that the recording industry will not look the other way when someone is caught.

RIAA spokesperson Jenni Engebretsen agreed. "Any student on any campus in the country who is illegally downloading music may receive one of these letters in the coming months, [and] . . . just one song can bring a lawsuit."

QUESTIONS TO CONSIDER:

■ How common is illegal downloading of music among your friends? Why do you think music piracy is so common? What should be done about it, in your opinion?

■ What lines from this article indicate that these students did not imagine the consequences of their actions when downloading music illegally? Have you ever made a single bad decision that led to a flood of negative consequences? Tell about that time.

■ The students mentioned in this article learned the hard way that illegal actions have consequences. Some people in the Bible seriously underestimated the consequences of disobeying a command of God. Let's learn about one of those incidents.

BIBLE TRUTHS

BIBLE**TRUTH** 1

The sin of Adam and Eve separated human beings from God. GENESIS 3:8-10, 21-24

■ **What was Adam and Eve's first reaction after sinning? Why do you think that was?**

INSIDE STORY: Before they sinned, the first couple communed with God "in the cool of the day" (Genesis 3:8). They stood before him unashamed, being totally open and honest with their creator.

After they sinned, however, Adam and Eve lost that intimacy and transparency. Their first reaction was to cover themselves and hide from God's sight.

Note that God replaced the fig leaf garments the couple fashioned for themselves with garments of animal skins (v. 21). Some speculate that God demonstrated the need for a blood sacrifice at this time. Animals were killed and blood was spilled in order to form a covering for sinful humankind (Hebrews 9:22).

BIBLE**TRUTH** 2

The sin of Adam and Eve separated human beings from each other. GENESIS 3:7, 12, 16

■ **When Adam and Eve rebelled against God, they had become partners in crime. Give evidence that their joint lawbreaking created separation, not togetherness.**

INSIDE STORY: After the fall, that unity was replaced by one of the greatest relational flaws of all time—"blame-storming." They became adversaries rather than partners. Adam quickly blamed his God-created partner for his problems (Genesis 3:12).

Note that even their pure and holy sexual relationship was corrupted. Sexual desire would remain, but it would result in painful childbirth and an inequity between husband and wife that was not present before (v. 16).

BIBLE**TRUTH** 3

The sin of Adam and Eve separated them from the rest of the natural world. GENESIS 3:17-19

■ **Compare the world before sin (Genesis 2:8-16) with the world after sin (Genesis 3:17-19).**

INSIDE STORY: Adam and those of us who follow would have to fight a fertility-impaired earth just to survive, deal with thorny weeds, sweat to earn a living, wrestle the elements of nature and many sorrows of life, and eventually face the failing of our bodies and death. Our conflict with the natural world is obvious to this day. Our attempts to overcome the infertility of the earth with fertilizers, pesticides, and herbicides have caused us to create cancer-causing agents and pollution that shorten the lives we were trying to sustain. The waste created by us may even alter the environment, contributing to floods and disruption of weather patterns. New diseases and epidemics replace ones we believe modern medicines have been able to eradicate.

CHALLENGE Ask your students: "What 'weeds' has sin caused in your life? How can you go about pulling those weeds, reversing the consequences of your own sin?"

INSTANT**STUDY 01** . . . CONTINUED

8

Abraham— Unshaken Faith

And Other Duties as Assigned

Both the U.S. Constitution and American history have defined the duties required of the president of the United States. Yet on a radio call-in program during a presidential campaign, a candidate learned that the job just might include a duty no one has ever considered!

While on the campaign, Senator Hillary Clinton took calls from listeners of WOKQ-FM in Portsmouth, New Hampshire. While other listeners asked the senator about controversial political issues, one caller had something else in mind. While on the air, Clinton was asked what the United States could do to remove Sanjaya Malakar from competition in TV's *American Idol*.

For those not familiar with that particular season of *American Idol*, seventeen-year-old Malakar was a controversial finalist on the program. *Idol* judges questioned Malakar's talent week after week, yet viewers continued to vote for him, allowing arguably more talented contestants to be eliminated. Acerbic *Idol* judge Simon Cowell went so far as to say that he would violate his contract and quit the show should Malakar win. Some TV critics predicted that a win for Malakar would have spelled the end for the popular program.

There were orchestrated campaigns to discredit the popular program by getting viewers to vote for poorer performers. Radio shock-jock Howard Stern and Web site votefortheworst.com were among those who did so.

Senator Clinton seemed unfazed when asked this unusual question. "That's the best question I've been asked in a long time," Clinton said. "Well, you know, people can vote for whomever they want. That's true in my election, and it's true on *American Idol*." While Democratic Party candidates tend to support more government regulation than their opponents, no one seriously believed that any candidate would suggest government intervention in such a case!

While the radio station that aired the call-in program did not take a position on whether or not monitoring TV reality shows should be a presidential duty, WOKQ-FM encouraged listeners to oust Sanjaya Malakar. Visitors to the station's Web site were able to download free "Make Sanjaya Go Bye-Bye-Ah!" posters for display at their workplaces. (Malakar was voted off of the program shortly thereafter.)

QUESTIONS TO CONSIDER:

■ Are you an *American Idol* fan? What would have been your position on the Sanjaya Malakar controversy? Do you think it should be a duty of the president of the United States to solve such an issue? Why or why not? What do you think of Senator Clinton's response to the radio caller?

■ What are some duties that you have been asked to perform? Has there ever been a time when you have been asked to do something that did not make sense to you at the time? Tell about it.

■ This lesson is about Abraham. While Abraham was determined to obey God, God asked Abraham to do some things that must not have made sense to him at the time. Let's examine Abraham's attitude and responses to such requests.

9

BIBLE TRUTHS

BIBLE**TRUTH** 1

Abraham knew that God could do anything. GENESIS 17:17-19

■ **List problems in life that may seem almost impossible to overcome at the time.**

INSIDE STORY: When Abraham was ninety-nine years old, God assured him that he would become a father and his descendants would become a whole nation (Genesis 17:1-8). This promise seemed impossible. Abraham's wife Sarai could not conceive. Added to this was the fact that Abraham was ninety-nine years old. Why should Abraham think anything would change now? When Sarah heard this, she fell down and laughed. When the baby was born, they were to name him Isaac, which means "he laughs" (v. 19).

Even though it seemed impossible, Abraham still believed God. Against all hope he became the father of many nations. He did not waver in his faith, being completely confident that God had power to do the impossible (Romans 4:18-21; Hebrews 11:11).

BIBLE**TRUTH** 2

Abraham knew that he owed God everything. GENESIS 22:1-3

■ **We may claim to believe that everything we own comes from God, but sometimes we struggle with this. Name a possession you would hate to give up.**

INSIDE STORY: Some years later, Abraham faced another test of his faith. God commanded him to take Isaac and sacrifice him as a burnt offering! However stunned and shaken Abraham must have been by this command, he set about to obey what God said. Abraham and Isaac traveled to Mount Moriah, the mount at Jerusalem on which the temple was later built (2 Chronicles 3:1). Isaac carried the wood; Abraham carried the fire container and the knife. Then came the heart-wrenching question from Isaac: "Where is the lamb for the burnt offering?" (Genesis 22:7). Even though it could not have made sense to him, Abraham was prepared to do whatever God said.

BIBLE**TRUTH** 3

Abraham knew that a promise from God meant something. GENESIS 22:7-12

■ **Think of some promises God makes in the Bible to all believers. Which of these is hardest for you to believe? Why?**

INSIDE STORY: Even in this dark moment, Abraham believed that God would provide the lamb (Genesis 22:8). Somehow God would surely preserve Abraham's son, through whom all his promises were to be fulfilled. Abraham knew that God could raise Isaac from the dead, if necessary, to keep that promise (Hebrews 11:19). In the meantime, Abraham would proceed to obey God's instructions. Just then the angel of the Lord stepped in (Genesis 22:11, 12). God provided a ram as a substitute sacrifice. Abraham's trust was not misplaced; God did not let him down. His descendants would become a nation and live in the Promised Land, a land that God himself would give them. More importantly, all nations on earth would one day be blessed through a single descendant of Abraham, Jesus Christ.

CHALLENGE

Close by using art to aid prayer. Ask students to write or draw a picture of something in their life that seems impossible to overcome. Then they should pray about that situation, asking God to help that situation since he can do anything. Then ask them to write or draw something that they have a hard time giving up. Again, they should pray, placing that thing in God's hands since they owe him everything. Finally, they should write down a promise from the Bible that they have a hard time believing, praying that they would take a step of faith and believe it since God's promises mean something.

Moses—God's Reluctant Servant

Feeling Insecure

Sometimes it appears that celebrities have it all together. But many stars confess that they sometimes lack self-confidence. Look at these quotes:

"My self-image, it still isn't that all right. No matter how famous I am, no matter how many people go to see my movies, I still have the idea that I'm that pale no-hoper that I used to be . . . Tomorrow it'll be all over, then I'll have to go back to selling pens again." – Johnny Depp, actor

"I look at myself as that same scared kid growing up trying to fit in, just trying to make it." – Mia Hamm, professional soccer player

"When I was younger, my whole sense of self-worth was based on whether or not I was working. When I wasn't the flavor of the week, the month, or day, those were hard times." – Kiefer Sutherland, actor

"I was 102 pounds, and people at the record label were telling me that I needed to lose weight." – Jessica Simpson, singer

"I know I'm not ugly, but I don't think I'm a pretty girl. I'm very critical of myself, definitely." – Drew Barrymore, actress

"Growing up, I never heard 'I love you' from my mother, my grandmother, my father. I heard it from my mom the first time two years ago, and it still seems awkward. There's hesitance." – Terrell Owens, NFL player

"There definitely must be an insecurity that lies beneath someone who wants to be successful and adored by other people." – Melanie C (formerly Sporty Spice), singer

"I always feel like I'm the butler when I'm with famous people." – Ashton Kutcher, actor

"Certainly, I was lost at times in my life. I'd like to think I was never a bad person, but I certainly went through times where I was not clear about who I was . . . where I never had a sense of purpose, never felt useful as a person." – Angelina Jolie, actress

QUESTIONS TO CONSIDER:

■ Are you surprised to see that these celebrities have felt or currently feel insecure? Why or why not? Do you think celebrities have more or fewer problems with self-esteem than non-famous people?

■ How does it make you feel knowing that celebrities have self-esteem issues just like you? Don't we sometimes imagine that being famous would take away such insecurities? Why can't fame do that?

■ Which of the quotes do you identify with? What things cause you or your friends to feel insecure? What things make you feel confident about yourself?

■ We're going to look at the life of Moses and discover what causes bad self-esteem and what can offer lasting good self-esteem.

BIBLE TRUTHS

BIBLE**TRUTH** 1

Poor self-esteem results when we see only our own imperfections. EXODUS 4:10, 13

■ **Tell about a time when you talked yourself out of doing something because you felt unqualified.**

INSIDE STORY: Once Moses had been a big shot. Raised as the son of Pharaoh's daughter in Egypt, he was highly educated, rich, and important. But that was forty years earlier. In the third chapter of Exodus things had changed—Moses was just a shepherd, with little thought of ever leading anything more than a flock of sheep.

Then one day at a burning bush God spoke to Moses. "I am sending you," God said, "to bring my people the Israelites out of Egypt" (Exodus 3:4-10). Moses was afraid to tackle the job. But each time he protested, God brushed away his excuse. Then Moses raised his final objections (4:10-16). "I have never been eloquent... I am slow of speech and tongue . . . please send someone else to do it." Moses felt incapable of performing this task alone. Seeing only his own abilities in the esteem equation led Moses into fear, doubt, and self-loathing. Looking inward to find reason for self-worth is a losing proposition.

BIBLE**TRUTH** 2

Healthy self-esteem results when we look at God's power available to us. EXODUS 4:11, 14-16

■ **How would your behavior change if you really believed God could help you do almost anything?**

INSIDE STORY: God would have none of Moses' excuses. It was God who had made Moses' mouth, so God could very well help Moses use it. In fact, all the human faculties were designed and given by God. Since God was the designer of all these abilities, he knew exactly what Moses was capable of. "Now go," God insisted, "I will help you speak and will teach you what to say" (v. 12). When Moses tried to shift

the mission to someone else (v. 13), God was angry. He told Moses to get his brother Aaron, who could speak very well (v. 14). With Aaron as his spokesman, and with God empowering both of them, Moses could do the job God demanded.

Moses would put words in Aaron's mouth (v. 15), and Aaron would speak to the people for Moses (v. 16). Interestingly, Aaron was a useful spokesman in the first meetings with Pharaoh (5:1), but later Moses himself found the courage to speak for God (8:9).

Our self-esteem and self-confidence are not derived from what comes from within ourselves, but from God! Paul taught this same lesson in 2 Corinthians 3:5. Though Paul himself sometimes shook with fear when he spoke for God (1 Corinthians 2:3), he had great confidence. He knew that the Lord had taken feeble men with glaring weaknesses and had made them into powerful apostles. God made them competent as ministers of the New Covenant (2 Corinthians 3:6). All of us can take pride in what we do when Christ is living in us (Galatians 2:20) and working through us (Galatians 5:22-24). Healthy self-esteem, then, does not come from thinking highly of ourselves—it comes from thinking rightly of God.

CHALLENGE

Lead your students in this visualized prayer activity: Moses met God while he was going about his normal, day-to-day activities. Imagine yourself going about some part of your daily life. What are you doing? Tell God what you are thinking about yourself. Imagine that a burning bush appears nearby. How does that make you feel? Tell God. From that bush, the voice of God speaks to you. What tasks is he calling you to perform? You begin to make excuses to God, telling him you are not qualified to do what he asks of you. What are you saying? Listen for God's response. What is he saying?

INSTANT**STUDY** 03 ... CONTINUED

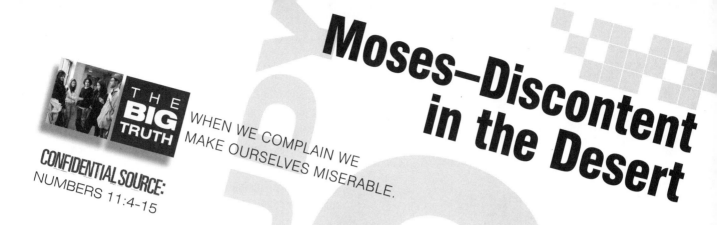

THE BIG TRUTH

WHEN WE COMPLAIN WE MAKE OURSELVES MISERABLE.

CONFIDENTIAL SOURCE:
NUMBERS 11:4-15

Moses—Discontent in the Desert

Sing It

While taking a walk on a bitterly cold winter's day in Finland, Tellervo Kalleinen and Oliver Kochta-Kalleinen had an idea. There is a unique Finnish word, *Valituskuoro*, used to describe situations where a lot of people are complaining simultaneously. Since the word literally means *complaints choir*, they asked one another, "Wouldn't it be fantastic to take this expression literally and organize a real complaints choir?"

The Kalleinens, both of whom are artists, formed a makeshift complaints choir in Birmingham, England. This group of college students sang in public squares and bars. Although this was meant to be a one-time-only project, the idea turned into a worldwide movement of griping in song. While complaining seems to be universal, the things people find to complain about seem to vary all over the world. Here are a few lyrics from a variety of complaints choirs:

Penn State University—"Tuition is through the roof, and I can't even get a 3.0" "Computer lab is full, and everyone is checking their Facebook."

Birmingham, England—"I want to complain about fat women driving in yellow sports cars like they own the world." "People eat my biscuits when we have a pot of tea. They never share their biscuits; no one appreciates me."

Jerusalem, Israel—"My bags don't open and there's passion fruit on everything." "And my fork is crooked, so crooked."

Helsinki, Finland—"In the public sauna they never ask if it's okay to throw water on the stove." "And why is the cord of the vacuum cleaner too short—like summer?"

St. Petersburg, Russia—"Bus Number 9 goes every five minutes to Vasilievsky but it never comes back." "When my cat eats Wiskas it withers away."

Budapest, Hungary—"Krishna people give me books but never stickers." "My neighbor holds folk dance classes right above my place."

QUESTIONS TO CONSIDER:

■ Have you ever heard of the complaints choir movement? Why do you think it has grown worldwide so quickly? What complaints in the above article make you laugh? Why? What would you complain about if you were singing in such a choir?

■ Why do you think people complain so much? Contrast how you feel when you complain to others to how you feel when others complain to you. What does that tell us about the dangers of complaining?

■ Complaint choirs are nothing new. In fact, the Bible tells us that after the Israelites were freed from Egypt, they formed such a choir in the wilderness. Let's look at the results of their complaining.

INSTANT **STUDY 04** ■ OLD **TESTAMENT**

BIBLE TRUTHS

BIBLE**TRUTH** 1

When we are discontent, we become more like the rest of the world. NUMBERS 11:4-6

■ **What is it like to be around people who are always complaining? How does that affect your actions and attitude?**

INSIDE STORY: Just three days after the escape from Egypt and the miracle at the Red Sea, the Israelites grumbled about the lack of drinkable water (Exodus 15:22-24). Then, just three days after setting out from Mount Sinai, they began grumbling again (Numbers 10:33–11:1). All they thought about were their hardships. Stirred up by "the rabble with them" (non-Israelites who had fled Egypt with them), God's people wailed, "If only we had meat! " (11:4). Fondly they misremembered Egypt as a place of free fish and flavorful vegetables. Here in the desert, however, all they had was manna.

This is the first problem that occurs when we complain—we follow the crowd, not God. Jesus warned those who would be his disciples not to worry about food and clothing. "The pagans run after all these things," but disciples of Jesus trust that our "heavenly Father knows that [we] need them" (Matthew 6:31, 32).

BIBLE**TRUTH** 2

When we are discontent we cease to be grateful for what we have. NUMBERS 11:7-9

■ **What is the silliest thing you ever complained about? Why do you consider that complaint to have been foolish?**

INSIDE STORY: The word *manna* meant "What is it?" There was never anything like it. It was a special provision from Heaven unknown before that time and a phenomenon yet to be repeated. Manna had been supplied faithfully by God since Exodus 16:14, 15. Appearing every morning except the Sabbath, the manna was remarkably versatile. It was gathered and ground into flour. Then it was cooked like hot

cereal or baked into pancakes. It was flavorful and tasted like something made with olive oil. There was always enough, and people did not have to do the work of planting, harvesting, and preparing grain. But the people were not content. This is another problem of discontent. When we complain, we forget to be thankful for what we have. Although the Israelites were the recipients of a unique miracle, they did not appreciate it.

BIBLE**TRUTH** 3

When we are discontent we make life difficult for those who care for us. NUMBERS 11:10-15

■ **Have you ever tried to do something nice but only got complaints for doing it? Tell about that time.**

INSIDE STORY: The Lord was understandably angry (v. 10) at this ingratitude. Likewise, Moses was frustrated. (vv. 11-15). This is the third fruit of discontent. Those that love us the most are grieved. Solomon wrote, "A foolish son brings grief to his father and bitterness to the one who bore him" (Proverbs 17:25). Complaining also frustrates our Christian leaders. "Obey your leaders and submit to their authority. . . . Obey them so that their work will be a joy, not a burden, for that would be of no advantage to you" (Hebrews 13:17). The work of Christian leadership, which should bring joy, becomes a burden when those being led bubble with discontent. Finally, complaining grieves the Holy Spirit who lives in us (Ephesians 4:29, 30).

CHALLENGE

Ask your students: When was the last time you told God thank you? In our study we have talked about how God provides for our needs daily. What are some needs that God provides that we sometimes take for granted? Continue by telling your students to write a thank-you note to God for providing such blessings.

Joshua and Caleb—Trusting God

Furry Landlord

Deborah and John Herrin had a concern about their home. A pond that was shared by them and the neighboring property was having problems, and it was caused by their neighbor's dam. The Herrins took the matter to the town board and were told that the board would have to look into the matter further before stepping in to do anything about it. They said for now it was a concern that must be handled between the two property owners. The problem? "How do you have a property dispute with a cat?" John asked.

Yes, you heard that right. Teddy Bear, a cat, was the owner of the property known as the Kirby house in Charlton, New York. In 1996, former homeowner Dorothy Corbin died. In her will she made a provision that her animals be allowed to live out the rest of their lives on the property—this included a horse, a dog, and two cats. The other pets have died, and now Teddy Bear, who is about ten years old, is the only one that remains. Dorothy left $500,000 to care for the pets, and with the money the Trustco Bank hired a caretaker to watch over the animals.

The property has historic value, first established by Revolutionary War veteran Seth Kirby in 1785. His son was a major in the War of 1812. Relatives who inherited the property built the current house in the 1850s and changed the original home into a barn that still stands. Neighbors Deborah and John, as well as other members of the community, hope that the barn and property are restored and kept up after Teddy Bear passes on. They'd like to see it put on the list of the National Registry of Historic Places.

But Dorothy stated in her will that after the animals die, she wanted the house to be rented out on a yearly basis and all the proceeds to go to an animal welfare organization. Currently Trustco Bank is not even sure what exactly will happen once Teddy Bear dies. Bob Leonard, the bank's vice president, is not talking. "It's a customer, and we can't talk about customers like that," he said.

QUESTIONS
TO CONSIDER:

■ Can you imagine having a cat own an entire piece of property? What would you do if you were the neighbors, Deborah and John, who have to live next door and have problems with the property? What would you do if you were the bank in charge of the house that must care for Teddy Bear? How would you handle the property once the cat dies?

■ The bank has several seemingly odd roles in this situation. The bank had to hire a caretaker for the animals, it has to decide how to handle disputes such as the one the neighbors brought up, it has a cat for a client, and it has to decide what to do once the cat dies. We all have different roles we play in life and different duties we are expected to perform. What roles do you play and what duties do you have to fulfill in those roles? (Ex: one role might be as a son or daughter; duties expected from that role might be to participate in household chores)

■ As you mature, you are given more responsibility. As your character becomes known, people around you learn that you can be trusted to complete those tasks. We'll read today that as Joshua and Caleb grew to know God more, they saw that God could be trusted to do what he promised.

BIBLE TRUTHS

BIBLE**TRUTH** 1

God will provide us with knowledge if we seek it.
NUMBERS 13:1-3

■ **What sort of knowledge should faithful Christians seek today?**

INSIDE STORY: God commanded Moses to send men into enemy territory to determine their military strength, what the land was like, and if the cities were well fortified (Numbers 13:1-3, 17-20). Joshua and Caleb took on that task, confident that God would give them the knowledge that they sought. As David would say years later, they knew that "those who seek the LORD lack no good thing" (Psalm 34:10). Solomon, David's son, agreed when he said, "Those who seek me [God] find me" (Proverbs 8:17). The writer of the book of Hebrews observed that the person of faith must "believe that he [God] exists and that he rewards those who earnestly seek him" (Hebrews 11:6). Joshua and Caleb trusted God to provide answers, so they intensely searched the land, looking for what God wanted them to find there.

BIBLE**TRUTH** 2

God will do the impossible if we let him. NUMBERS 13:26-30

■ **What seemingly impossible tasks do you face in your life sometimes?**

INSIDE STORY: All the spies recognized that the promised land was a wonderful place but agreed that the inhabitants of the land were big, powerful, scary, and well armed. Joshua and Caleb had seen the same enemy, but they had the eyes of faith. By faith they knew God was going to deliver on his promise (Numbers 13:30).

Joshua and Caleb, like David who would achieve many military victories in his day, knew that success was a gift from the Lord, not just the product of their knowledge and skills (Psalm 21:1, 5). These daring two spies did not know

how God would provide victory, but knew that his blessings, in the words of Paul, were "immeasurably more than all we ask or imagine, according to his power that is at work within us" (Ephesians 3:20). The finest warrior will eventually meet someone with superior skills; the one empowered by God "overcomes the world" (1 John 5:4).

BIBLE**TRUTH** 3

God will allow us to stand against the world if we stand with him. NUMBERS 13:31; 14:6-10A

■ **How easy is it for you to stand up against your peers? What would it take for you to take such a stand?**

INSIDE STORY: The Israelites chose to listen to the unbelieving spies rather than Joshua and Caleb. They actually discussed rebelling against Moses and returning to slavery in Egypt (14:2-4)! Yet Joshua and Caleb bravely stood their ground, even though the crowd wanted to kill them (14:6-10a). Joshua and Caleb did not fear being in the minority. Being right is more important than agreeing with the popular culture (Matthew 7:13, 14). They stood unafraid in "the valley of the shadow of death" (Psalm 23:4), facing the physical power of the Canaanites. They also did not fear literally sitting at dinner in "the presence of [their] enemies" (v. 5), their own countrymen, because they knew that the Lord would protect them from both. Our world needs Christians like Joshua and Caleb.

CHALLENGE

Write the words of these five verses about trusting God on the board: 2 Samuel 7:28; Psalm 9:10; Psalm 20:6, 7; Psalm 22:3-5; and Isaiah 12:2. Have each student pick one verse and write it on a note card. Encourage each student to keep that card handy and try to internalize that verse this week.

INSTANT **STUDY 05** . . . CONTINUED

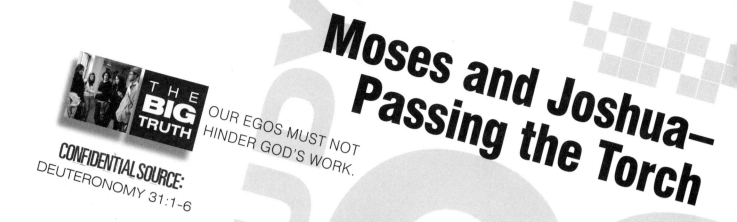

THE BIG TRUTH — OUR EGOS MUST NOT HINDER GOD'S WORK.

CONFIDENTIAL SOURCE: DEUTERONOMY 31:1-6

U R Fired

After hearing John Eid's story, people may think twice when they receive text messages on their cell phones. Some time ago John received a text message saying that he was fired from his job as a traffic controller in Sydney, Australia. He decided to sue his former employer for unfair dismissal.

John received this SMS (short message service) message on his cell phone from a director in his company: "Its official, you no longer work for JNI Traffic Control & u have forfided any arrangements made." (sic)

"There was no justification. The lack of procedural fairness culminated in the undignified process of being terminated via an SMS message," said Tom Earls, John's lawyer.

However, JNI Traffic Control said that John had been the one who quit. Kathryn Dent, the company's lawyer said that John "stated he would not work for JNI ever again and swore in colorful language, at length. The SMS message that was sent the next day was an acceptance of a resignation."

Another spokesperson said, "I had been trying to get hold of him to confirm he was no longer working for us, but he wouldn't come into the office and he said he didn't want me to ring him anymore, so I sent him an SMS. . . . It isn't one of our normal practices. I shouldn't have done it."

Commissioner Elizabeth Bishop who presided over the case said that the text message should not have been sent, even if John had been the one to quit. "What happened to the old-fashioned letter or talking to someone in person?" she asked. She ordered JNI and John Eid to attempt to reconcile the matter privately.

QUESTIONS TO CONSIDER:

■ Do you think it was fair of JNI to fire John via text message? Explain. If that happened to you, how would you feel? Have you ever been rejected by text message? by e-mail? How did you handle it? Did you confront the person who rejected you? Did you talk to him or her in person?

■ What do people do when they are rejected? (feel bitter, get revenge, etc.) How does rejection affect people's self-confidence?

■ We've all been rejected at one time or another—even Moses experienced rejection. From his experiences recorded in Deuteronomy 31:1-6, we can learn three secrets for trusting God when we feel rejected.

17

BIBLE TRUTHS

BIBLE**TRUTH** 1

Recognize your limitations. DEUTERONOMY 31:1, 2

■ **What makes you envious of someone else? Give an example.**

INSIDE STORY: After leading the Israelites through the wilderness for forty years, Moses would not be able to finish the course (Deuteronomy 31:2). This rejection was a result of an incident that took place years before. The Israelites had settled in a desert and the whole nation was grumbling about the lack of water. God directed Moses to speak to a rock and bring forth water. But instead of speaking to the rock as commanded, he and Aaron boasted to the people: "Listen, you rebels, must *we* bring you water out of this rock?" (Numbers 20:10). After taking credit for God's glorious work, Moses was corrected by God. To demonstrate that the work was done by God, not man, God would use someone other than Moses to complete the mission (v. 12).

BIBLE**TRUTH** 2

Allow the Lord to work through others.
DEUTERONOMY 31:3

■ **Name someone who has a talent you wish you had. How does that make you feel?**

INSIDE STORY: Out of around two million people, Moses chose twelve of his best to explore the land of Canaan. Only two of those trusted God (Numbers 13, 14). Moses changed this young spy's name from Hoshea, meaning "salvation," to Joshua, meaning "Jehovah is salvation" (Numbers 13:16). Moses continued to distinguish between human leadership and divine leadership. Moses told Israel that "the LORD your God himself will cross over ahead of you" and complete the conquest of Canaan (Deuteronomy 31:3). Joshua would be the deputy of God. Moses gladly resigned from his position and allowed another to be used by God to do his work.

BIBLE**TRUTH** 3

Express encouragement rather than disappointment. DEUTERONOMY 31:4-6

■ **Whom have you cheered on lately? Who else could use your encouragement?**

INSIDE STORY: Moses was surely saddened for himself, yet his heart was ever with the people. Moses expressed genuine confidence in Joshua, and blessed him (Deuteronomy 31:4-6). We'd all like to think we're indispensable. But Moses *was*. He was the greatest of the great, mentioned in half the books of the Bible and transfigured with Jesus and Elijah (Matthew 17:3). Revelation 15:3 tells us that victorious believers will sing his song in Heaven. Yet Moses knew that God's work would not cease without his leadership. He gladly encouraged the Israelites by predicting an even brighter future under Joshua's watch.

CHALLENGE

Have students get together with a partner or two. Ask all students to share some situation where they've recently felt rejected. Partners should then encourage each other to overcome the rejection and come up with strategies on how to do that.

The First Commandment— No Other Gods

Hanging Up

Could you live without your cell phone? Most school districts across the country say students have to live without cell phones during the school day. But several states have repealed statewide laws against cell phones in class and now allow individual school districts to make their own policies concerning phones. The Newport News, Virginia, school district is one that decided to allow cell phones in class once again.

At one time Newport News students were required to leave their cell phones in their cars or at home. But parents were complaining. They wanted to know that they could get ahold of their kids at all times, especially in light of school shootings and terrorist threats. Some Virginia districts compromised and allowed middle school and high school students to bring in cell phones—but students had to leave phones in the school's office. Nevertheless, many parents weren't satisfied.

"Parents feel better knowing that they can get in touch with their child," said Gene Jones, the principal at Warwick High School and co-chairperson of the committee that changed the Newport News policy.

Cell phones can be a problem in class when students play games on their phones instead of listening to the teacher or if they use text-messaging capabilities to cheat on tests. Other drawbacks go beyond classroom concerns. Kenneth Trump, spokesman for National School Safety and Security Services, said that students could phone in false bomb threats; or there could be so many calls to parents in a real emergency that phone lines jam and parents panic over exaggerated rumors.

Newport News said the positive uses of cell phones outweighed the negatives. "As long as it's not abused, I think parents and students should be able to use the technology because it could possibly save a life," said Mike Wagner, a school board member and a lieutenant with the Newport News Sheriff's Department.

QUESTIONS
TO CONSIDER:

■ Does your school allow cell phones in class? If so, how have you seen students abuse this privilege? If not, how do you imagine this privilege would be abused? What are some other positives and negatives about having cell phones in schools?

■ Some of your friends would probably say that they couldn't live without their cell phones. Do you feel that way? Why or why not? Name something you couldn't imagine living without. How would you feel if that thing were taken away from you?

■ We're going to look at Deuteronomy 5:6, 7 and 1 Corinthians 8:4-6 to learn how we can keep from putting the things we enjoy before God.

BIBLE TRUTHS

BIBLE**TRUTH** 1

All gods except Jehovah are illusions.
1 CORINTHIANS 8:4

■ **Consider Monopoly® money. What good is it? What would happen if you tried to spend it?**

INSIDE STORY: Recall the games you played as a child. If you are a guy, you may remember taking a large tree branch as your horse and a smaller twig as your gun. If you are a girl, perhaps you held tea parties with invisible tea and cookies made of modeling clay. Were you to continue to keep your imaginary substitutes as you grew older, you would be considered strange indeed! But this is just the picture the Bible paints of those who place anything else before God. Substitute gods are of no more help to people than are twig six-shooters or mud pies. "We know that an idol is nothing at all in the world," as the apostle Paul wrote, "and that there is no God but one" (1 Corinthians 8:4). False gods have no power. They are literally "senseless"—they do not have the five senses of a living creature, being unable to see, hear, or communicate (Psalm 115:3-7). Jehovah God, in contrast, is able to sense and to act. While our false gods are mere toys, Jehovah is truly present (Habakkuk 2:18-20).

BIBLE**TRUTH** 2

Jehovah God has a claim on us because he made us and sustains us. 1 CORINTHIANS 8:5, 6

■ **Name your prized possession. Imagine that you loaned it to someone else and they sold it. Explain your feelings about that.**

INSIDE STORY: Think about a time you loaned an item to someone and it was returned damaged. A situation like that may make us a bit angry. We expect someone to give special care to an item that belongs to us that has been entrusted to him or her. This leads us to another biblical argument against false gods. We don't belong to them. Our

money, entertainment, sexuality, or any of the host of other modern gods has not created us. A common argument says, "It's my body, I can do whatever I want with it." But that is untrue. We have nothing to do with our creation, so we have no claim of ownership (1 Corinthians 8:6). The God who "made the heavens" (Psalm 96:5) and "who made us" and to whom we belong is the only one who has a claim on us. Putting anyone or anything else before God is giving our life, which belongs only to God, to someone or something else.

BIBLE**TRUTH** 3

Jehovah God has shown his faithfulness by saving his people throughout history.
DEUTERONOMY 5:6, 7

■ **Imagine that you have been given a brand new car. How would you protect it? How could someone tell that it was valuable to you?**

INSIDE STORY: When numbering the Ten Commandments, Jews count Deuteronomy 5:6 as a separate first commandment: "I am the LORD your God, who brought you out of Egypt, out of the land of slavery." The fact that God has a unique claim on his people is shown in his efforts to keep them safe and unspoiled. Therefore, he has a right to demand that his people follow no other master (v. 7). In Psalm 106:7-10, the psalmist describes the heroic actions of God in leading his people out of Egypt. He brought his people out of slavery "for his name's sake." In other words, God saves his people because he alone has his stamp of ownership on them.

CHALLENGE Give each student a packet of sugar and a packet of artificial sweetener to take with them. Let this be a reminder to accept no substitutes for the real God of the universe.

THE BIG TRUTH

IDOLATRY CAUSES US TO LOSE THE RICH LIFE GOD HAS FOR US.

CONFIDENTIAL SOURCE:
DEUTERONOMY 5:8-10;
ROMANS 1:21-23

Trust, but Verify

Some things you've just got to see to believe.

When Henry and Roma Gerbus took their computer to the local Best Buy electronics store in Cincinnati, Ohio, to have its hard drive replaced, they were told that their old hard drive would be destroyed. Because a hard drive may contain a great amount of personal data of its owners, it is important that the device be rendered ineffective so that no one gets a hold of such information.

"[A store employee] said, 'Rest assured.' They drill holes in it so it's useless," Henry explained. He and his wife trusted the store to complete this process. They wished that they would have requested to watch and verify the destruction after they received a fateful phone call.

"[The caller] said, 'My name is Ed. I just bought your hard drive for $25 at a flea market in Chicago,'" Henry recalled. Henry was overwhelmed that something like this could have happened. "I thought my world was coming down," Henry said. With their hard drive in his hands, Ed now had such information as Henry and Roma's social security numbers, bank statements, and investment records. In fact, because such information was on the hard drive, Ed was able to find out where the Gerbus couple lived and call them.

"He said, 'Do you want me to wipe it clean or send it to you?'" Henry said. But he was not going to trust a stranger again to do a process he couldn't watch. "I told him to send it to me. I wanted it in my hands." Henry and Roma aren't sure what Ed will do with the information he has about them.

They called their credit card companies and others to warn them that their information might be used improperly. "I don't know if we're going to have a problem. I just don't know," said Henry.

When a Cincinnati reporter contacted the Best Buy store that was supposed to destroy the hard drive, the company gave the following statement: "Our company values and places the utmost importance on maintaining the privacy of our customers. We will fully investigate these allegations."

QUESTIONS TO CONSIDER:

■ Are you generally a trusting person? Would you have trusted the store to destroy your personal information? If you were in the Gerbus family's situation, would you trust Ed not to improperly use the information he discovered about you? Explain your answers.

■ Sometimes we don't fully trust people to do what they say they will do unless we see it happen. Name some other things that you have trouble believing unless you see them.

■ Sometimes it's easier to believe something when you can see it. But God asks us to believe in him without seeing him. When we try to create an image to represent God, we can run into trouble. God warns us through the Bible of the consequences of making him into an image that he's not. He calls it idolatry. Let's look at God's commandment against idolatry.

INSTANT**STUDY 08** ■ OLD**TESTAMENT**

BIBLE**TRUTH** 1

Idolatry is counting on created things rather than the Creator to save us. DEUTERONOMY 5:8; ROMANS 1:21-23

■ **What is meant by the term *vicarious experience*? Why might one choose a vicarious experience over a real one**

INSIDE STORY: Imagine a guy who likes a girl. He approaches her, and instead of talking, he takes her picture. He enlarges the photo into a life-size poster. He spends time with the poster and talks to it daily. Meanwhile, the girl is wondering why the guy never calls or talks to *her!*

Yes, it's a ridiculous story. But it can show us much about what idolatry is. Instead of dealing with God directly, the idolater creates an image in the shape of a creature on earth or a mythical spiritual being (Deuteronomy 5:8). Paul said that idolaters rejected "the immortal God for images made to look like mortal man and birds and animals and reptiles" (Romans 1:23).

Why would someone make such a trade? Why would someone stop worshiping a living invisible God and exchange him for lifeless statues? Paul makes it clear that this is *not* done out of ignorance—"they knew God" (Romans 1:21). For example, the Israelites demanded Aaron make idols for them in Moses' absence (Exodus 32:1). Their problem certainly was not ignorance, because they had an experience unequalled in history. They had been camped around Mount Sinai when the law was given (Exodus 19:16-19). They were given stone tablets inscribed by the very finger of God! (Exodus 31:18).

In fact, people exchange worship of God for idols for similar reasons. That fictitious photographer might have traded a relationship with a real girl for her picture. Images are controllable. God is not. Idols make no demands and offer no objection when ignored or mistreated.

BIBLE**TRUTH** 2

Idolatry causes us to lose the rich life God intends for us. DEUTERONOMY 5:9, 10; ROMANS 1:21, 22

■ Imagine that a friend invited you to come along on vacation, but you turn down the offer, asking that your friend share pictures of the trip. How might that request change your friendship? Why?

INSIDE STORY: Let's return to our fictitious photographer. Sure, he has a very safe relationship with an image of a girl. The picture makes no demands on him. But what is he missing in this relationship? Remember, the girl liked this guy and was flattered when he took her photograph. She would have been happy to go out with him and get to know him better. He would have been able to have a real friendship with a real person. It would have been a friendship that would have challenged him to grow. It would have been a friendship that would have kept him from being lonely and would have given him encouragement and support. But he missed out on all of this.

Furthermore, the friendship that the girl offered would eventually turn to wrath. At first she might simply be perplexed when he ignored her. But this snubbing would soon anger her. And when she found out that he was idolizing her picture but ignoring her, she probably would have considered the boy to be a real creep!

Idolatry comes with a similar price tag. Sure, the idol makes no demands. But the idol also offers no benefits. God wants to show "love to a thousand generations of those who love [him] and keep [his] commandments" (Deuteronomy 5:10). Idolatry cheats the idolater out of a relationship with God that empowers and blesses and brings about personal growth. What a tragedy.

Like the jilted girl, God reacts to rejection with wrath and jealousy (Deuteronomy 5:9). Rejection of God has serious and lasting consequences. The idolater not only misses out in sharing God's wisdom and goodness, but his own intelligence is dulled and his own morality is corrupted (Romans 1:21). In fact, idolaters become so deluded that they are unaware of their corrupted state (v. 22). Finally, without God's guidance, the idolater makes moral choices that are increasingly corrupt and perverted. The cost of idolatry is high indeed.

CHALLENGE

Read Hebrews 12:28, 29 aloud and ask students to explain what is meant that God is a "consuming fire." Ask them to think of things that "insulate" them from God's all consuming and cleansing love.

INSTANT **STUDY** 08 . . . CONTINUED

22

THE BIG TRUTH

USE GOD'S NAME WITH CARE AND REVERENCE.

CONFIDENTIAL SOURCE:
DEUTERONOMY 5:11;
LEVITICUS 24:10, 11;
MATTHEW 5:33-37; 6:7

Lame Name Lanes

"What's in a name?" asked Juliet in William Shakespeare's *Romeo and Juliet*.
"That which we call a rose /
By any other word would smell as sweet."

John Trichak of Riverside County in California would disagree. Names matter very much to him. In fact, he has a lengthy list of rules for selecting street names in his county.

Riverside is the fastest-growing county in the country. Every week, Trichak receives up to fifty maps of new housing tracks. His job is to approve the names of the new streets. The job is not as easy as it would seem. Trichak is quick to reject names that do not meet his criteria.

First of all, Trichak eliminates names he can't pronounce or spell easily. "If I can't pronounce it, you can't have it," he says. "It's as simple as that." Furthermore, common street names such as Oak or Elm or Washington or Jefferson are out, because they could be confused with streets in nearby counties. Names that won't fit on a standard street sign, such as the recently-rejected Bird of Paradise Street, won't make the cut. In addition, if a street is a cul-de-sac, the name must be properly labeled as a "Court" or "Circle."

Names should not cause confusion for police and firefighters. With that in mind, Trichak gave thumbs down to Merriman Drive, since a Merrimac Court already existed. Overly-cute names such as Thata Way, Whicha Way, Goa Way, Keepa Way, and Staya Way are nixed for the same reason. (Imagine a 911 call when the operator asks for an address!)

Nevertheless, drivers looking for whimsical street names can still find them in other parts of the country. One may visit the corner of Grinn and Barrett in West Chester, Ohio, or the corner of Eaton/Cereal in neighboring Hamilton, Ohio. Patriotic Harrisville, Wisconsin, boasts streets named Yankee, Doodle, *and* Dandy. Unintentional political commentary may be found in Ann Arbor, Michigan at the corner of Nixon/Bluett or at the corner of Clinton and Fidelity in Houston, Texas.

Mitsubishi Motors recently polled drivers for unusual street names, including the only road to Constipation Ridge, Tennessee, aptly named Farfrompoopen Road. At the top of the list were Divorce Court in Heather Highlands, Pennsylvania, and Psycho Path in Traverse City, Michigan.

QUESTIONS TO CONSIDER:

■ Why did you find some of these names to be humorous? What examples of humorous street or city names have you seen?

■ Do you see a negative side to any of these funny names? Why might someone be unwilling to buy a house on Psycho Path or Divorce Court? What might happen if people like Mr. Trichak did not take their jobs seriously and allow virtually any name to be used for a street?

■ Think about your own name. Has it ever been mispronounced or purposely misused? Tell about it.

■ Names are important to us. We like our names to be used correctly and not used to make fun of us. It's not hard to understand that God feels the same way about his name. Let's see what the Bible teaches about misusing the name of God.

BIBLE TRUTHS

BIBLETRUTH 1

We dishonor God's name when we declare that he is our enemy. DEUTERONOMY 5:11; LEVITICUS 24:10, 11

■ **Have you heard anyone say, "Those are fighting words?" What is meant by that?**

INSIDE STORY: Calling someone a name is similar to declaring a personal war on that person. God commanded that his name should never be misused in that way (Deuteronomy 5:11). The first recorded violation of that commandment is found in Leviticus 24:10, 11. There was a young man in the camp who had a Jewish mother and an Egyptian father. When fighting with an Israelite, the man cursed the name of God. This was not a minor matter. It was the equivalent of saying that he was loyal to the Pharaoh rather than the King of the Jews, God himself. Sometimes the people of God can blaspheme the name of God in another way. Instead of showing our contempt for God with our words, we do so by boldly showing that we defy him by our actions. We preach God's standards of morality to others, but openly break them (Romans 2:19-23). In doing so we take God's name in vain and also cause others to blaspheme him (v. 24).

BIBLETRUTH 2

We dishonor God's name when we claim his authority as our own. DEUTERONOMY 5:11; MATTHEW 5:33-37

■ **What does it mean to be a *namedropper*? Why might a person be a namedropper?**

INSIDE STORY: Another way of misusing God's name is to claim to have his authority for our actions. A minor bureaucrat in Washington who dared to make demands in the name of the president would be reprimanded for his arrogance. Likewise, we violate the third Commandment when we make promises, expecting God to fulfill them, or state personal opinions, claiming God's support for them. In the Sermon on the Mount, Jesus addressed this issue (Matthew 5:33-37). When someone promises to accomplish a goal "by the authority of Heaven," he is making executive

decisions that are only to be made at the throne of God (v. 34). To seal similar promises by invoking the power of the earth or Jerusalem is similarly vain, because we have no more claim to this real estate than we do to Heaven! (v. 35). We do not even have the right to swear by our own lives, since it is God, not us, who sustains life (v. 36). It is wise simply to follow through on our promises and let our record for honesty speak for itself (v. 37).

BIBLETRUTH 3

We dishonor God's name when we use empty religious speech. DEUTERONOMY 5:11; MATTHEW 6:7

■ **A radio host used to say, "Words mean things." What do you think he meant?**

INSIDE STORY: The word *awesome*, properly used to describe that which is deserving of worship, was once dreadfully overused. When it became common to talk of awesome cheeseburgers and awesome athletic shoes, the true meaning of the word was lost. When a word is overused, it becomes empty and devoid of meaning.

In the same way, we can misuse God's name by using it too casually or too much. This is what happens when the name of the Father or the Son is simply used as an interjection to denote strong feeling—what is commonly referred to as "taking the Lord's name in vain." When believers speak "Christianese," reducing talk about our God to buzzwords, we commit a similar transgression.

CHALLENGE

Give a tongue depressor to each student and have permanent markers available to all. Ask your students to consider a time when either their words or actions did not bring honor to God's name. Have them write the words of the Third Commandment on the tongue depressor and keep it as a reminder of this study.

THE BIG TRUTH

A DAY OF WORSHIP IS A PRECIOUS GIFT.

CONFIDENTIAL SOURCE:
DEUTERONOMY 5:12-15;
ISAIAH 58:13, 14;
HEBREWS 10:25

The Fourth Commandment— Take Time For God

Health Hazard

Does work cause health problems? Sure, that sounds like an excuse that you may give to your parents to get out of responsibilities! Nevertheless, one study suggests that it may be true—stressful working conditions, such as an overbearing boss, can cause high blood pressure.

A study in the United Kingdom discovered that employees who work for bosses they dislike end up having increased blood pressure throughout the day. Having consistently high blood pressure increases the risk of a heart attack or a stroke.

The UK study by Dr. Nadia Wager was done on women who were healthcare assistants. Dr. Wager and her team monitored twenty-eight healthcare assistants for three days, recording their blood pressure every thirty minutes. On days when the healthcare workers were working under supervisors whom they considered fair and who treated them with respect, their blood pressure stayed low. But days working for supervisors who didn't trust the assistants and who showed favoritism caused the women's blood pressure to increase.

Dr. Wager tried to offer solutions to the healthcare employees for the days working in stressful conditions. She suggested talking to the boss about the problem or taking assertiveness training, which research has shown to improve employer/employee relationships. Finally, a great way to help deal with the high blood pressure is to relax outside of work, through exercise or other restful hobbies.

QUESTIONS TO CONSIDER:

■ Have you ever worked in a stressful situation, or have you had someone in authority over you who treated you unfairly? Describe your situation. How did your environment affect your productivity? How did it affect your physical health? How did you try to remedy the situation? Did you do any of the things Dr. Wager suggested? Which ones?

■ The easiest tip Dr. Wager gave the healthcare assistants was to relax outside of work. What things do you do to relax? How often do you take time to do those relaxing activities? What benefits do you find from taking time to relax?

■ God knows how rest benefits our physical, mental, and spiritual health. He even included the principle of rest in the Ten Commandments. Today we're going to look at Deuteronomy 5:12-15; Isaiah 58:13, 14; and Hebrews 10:25 to examine why God implemented a day of worship and rest.

BIBLE**TRUTH** 1

Setting time aside for God allows us to renew our strength. DEUTERONOMY 5:12-15

■ **What is you favorite holiday? What is its significance? Why is a special day called a *holy day* (holiday)?**

INSIDE STORY: God told his people to "observe the Sabbath day by keeping it holy" (v. 12). There are three key words in this command. To "observe" means to "keep as a memorial." The word *Sabbath* means a day of "ceasing from one's work." The word *holy* means that something is "set apart as special." Six days were for work (v. 13), but the seventh day was for rest and worship (v. 14). This day belonged to God. This was a principle that God put into place from the time of Creation (Genesis 2:3; Exodus 20:11). Back in Egypt the people of Israel had been slaves, worked hard, and shown no mercy. Therefore, keeping the Sabbath would also be a reminder of how God had given them rest from their grievous servitude (v. 15). The Sabbath was not a task to be performed. Rather it illustrated that the benevolent boss of the universe loved them enough to give them a day off!

BIBLE**TRUTH** 2

Setting time aside for God demonstrates our dedication to him. ISAIAH 58:13, 14

■ **Think of a friend who will drop everything he or she is doing just to hang out with you. What does that say about that friend?**

INSIDE STORY: God's people did not do a very good job of keeping God's commandments. Because of their repeated disobedience, they were often punished by foreign enemies. The prophet Isaiah warned the people about the Babylonian Captivity, but also promised a future age that would bring the blessings of the Messiah. If they would only keep God's commands, they could rebuild the kingdom and enjoy the future glory of Zion. (See Isaiah 52:1ff.) In that coming era of blessing they were told to honor the Sabbath by not continuing to conduct business as usual (Isaiah 58:13). The Sabbath was God's; he claimed it as "my holy day." A day of rest was not only given for the physical wellbeing of God's people. It was also a spiritual discipline that recognized God as the giver of the other six days as well.

BIBLE**TRUTH** 3

Setting time aside for God allows us to meet and encourage other believers. HEBREWS 10:25

■ **To which clubs or organizations do you belong? Why do you think people join clubs?**

INSIDE STORY: God has always intended the Sabbath to be a blessing, not a ritual. In the New Testament the same principle holds true, although the specific day of rest is not commanded. In honor of Jesus' resurrection on the first day of the week, the early church quickly adopted Sunday as the day they devoted to God. (See John 20:1, 19, 26; 1 Corinthians 16:2; Revelation 1:10.) It was also a Sunday when the church was born. The Day of Pentecost was fifty days after the Sabbath of Firstfruits. (See Acts 2:1 and Leviticus 23:15, 16.) From that very first Sunday, Christians met together to worship God and to encourage each other (Acts 2:42, 20:7). Certain Christians, however, were beginning to forsake the assembly of God's people (Hebrews 10:25). Because of persecution they were abandoning Jesus and returning to Judaism. Therefore the writer of Hebrews says, "Let us not give up meeting together." Instead, his readers were to come together and use the occasion to "encourage one another" and "consider how we may spur one another on toward love and good deeds" (v. 24).

CHALLENGE

Before class, gather some stickers small enough to fit on the face of a watch. Give your students a sticker and ask them to place it on their watch or cell phone (if they use it to check the time) as a reminder to set time aside for God.

26

THE BIG TRUTH

PARENTS ARE IMPORTANT IN GOD'S PLAN.

CONFIDENTIAL SOURCE:
DEUTERONOMY 5:16;
EPHESIANS 6:1-3

Responsibility of Privilege

What do you do if you were the second-richest person in the world, having a fortune of $44 billion? If you were Warren Buffett, the answer would be to give 80 percent of it away.

Some time ago, Warren Buffett, the world's second-richest person, announced that he was donating about $37 billion to charitable foundations run by his friend Bill Gates and by the Buffett family. This was the largest charitable donation ever made by a single donor at that time.

Buffett is chief executive of Berkshire Hathaway, a corporation that owns a variety of about fifty well-known businesses, including Geico auto insurance, Benjamin Moore paint, and Dairy Queen ice cream. When Buffett took over Berkshire Hathaway in 1965, it was a struggling textile maker. The corporation is now worth in excess of $141 billion.

Buffett's decision came a few days after Bill Gates announced that he would step away from the day-to-day operations of the software giant Microsoft and become more involved in charity work. Bill Gates, who has a fortune of about $50 billion, is the only person in the world richer than Buffett.

The Bill & Melinda Gates Foundation was founded in 2000 upon the idea that "every life has equal value" and that the Gates fortune should be used "to help reduce inequities in the United States and around the world." In the past six years the foundation has committed millions of dollars to fighting diseases such as malaria and tuberculosis in developing countries. It has also given funds to education and library technology in the United States.

In a letter to Gates and his wife, Buffett wrote: "You have committed yourselves to a few extraordinarily important but underfunded issues, a policy that I believe offers the highest probability of your achieving goals of great consequence."

Gates and his wife responded by writing: "We are awed by our friend Warren Buffett's decision to use his fortune to address the world's most challenging inequities, and we are humbled that he has chosen to direct a large portion of it to the Bill & Melinda Gates Foundation."

QUESTIONS TO CONSIDER:

■ What are some attitudes many people have about rich people? How does this news story challenge some of those attitudes? How do you feel about the decision of Warren Buffett to give away so much money? What would you have done if you were him? Why?

■ Some people believe that they can do anything they want with their money. But Jesus once said, "From everyone who has been given much, much will be demanded; and from the one who has been entrusted with much, much more will be asked" (Luke 12:48). Which of these attitudes is displayed in this article? Defend your response.

■ Being a very rich person is a position of great responsibility. Another position of great responsibility is being a parent. But sometimes parents get very little respect. Let's learn why we should honor our parents and the benefits we get from doing so.

INSTANT **STUDY 11** ■ OLDTESTAMENT

BIBLE TRUTHS

BIBLETRUTH 1

God has given parents a standing worthy of respect. DEUTERONOMY 5:16a; EPHESIANS 6:1

■ **What does showing honor to one's parents mean to you? How can you show honor to someone even if that person is imperfect?**

INSIDE STORY: Parents are to be honored because "the LORD your God has commanded you" (Deuteronomy 5:16a) and "for this is right" (Ephesians 6:1). The Hebrew word for *honor* comes from a word meaning *weight* and refers to people who are heavy with importance. The word is translated other places in the Bible as *glorify* (Psalm 86:12), *highly respect* (1 Samuel 9:6), *reward* (Numbers 24:11), and even *make wealthy* (Habakkuk 2:6)! God's command to honor parents is echoed throughout the Old Testament (Proverbs 1:8, 23:22; Malachi 4:6).

To *dishonor* would be to treat parents as lightweight, to brush them off as irrelevant, paying no attention to their needs or feelings. It would be to disregard their advice and instructions, to disobey their orders. Finally, in their old age it would be to shove them out of our lives and neglect them. The Bible does not expect children to submit unquestioningly to abusive parents, of course. But the position of parenthood is worthy of respect, even when the person is not.

Although parents described in the Bible were far from perfect, they took their jobs seriously. Jacob failed God often, but when his father-in-law Laban made it difficult for Jacob to support his family (Genesis 31:4-7), Jacob left his oppressive job, confident in God's promise to be with him (vv. 3, 14-18). Moses' parents, Amram and Jochebed, acted honorably as parents, even when it meant disobeying an unjust law of the land. When Pharaoh commanded the Israelites to kill their newborn babies, they hid the baby Moses in their house as long as possible, then they hid him outside in a floating basket under the care of his older sister (Exodus 2:1-4). King David made more than his share of mistakes. But he demonstrated a life of dependence on the Spirit of God. David allowed God to speak through him (2 Samuel 23:2) and counted on God, not his own strength, to see that his family was "arranged and secured in every part" (v. 5).

BIBLETRUTH 2

God rewards children who rightly give that respect. DEUTERONOMY 5:16b; EPHESIANS 6:2, 3

■ **Imagine someone your age who defied his parents every chance he got. How are you better off than he would be?**

INSIDE STORY: In Deuteronomy 5:16b and Ephesians 6:2, 3 we see the same two results of honoring our parents—safety and prosperity. People who grow up obeying good parents generally live longer than those who don't. Children who ignore parental advice may suffer an early death due to accident or a shortened life due to bad habits. These verses are not a guarantee that people who honor their parents will never die young. It is, however, a broad promise in which the percentages hold true. Furthermore, things will "go well" with God's people when they honor their parents. Because parents and grandparents have been around longer than their children, they often have a storehouse of wisdom. Besides gaining the benefits of wise parental guidance, respectful children can expect God to step in and bless their lives.

We see these two results in the lives of biblical characters who honored their parents. Joseph, though a victim of a plot by his brothers, thrived in the most difficult of circumstances (Genesis 39:1, 2, 20, 21). Amram and Jochebed saved Moses from the Egyptians by trusting God when they placed him in the water. How ironic that when Moses led Israel out of Egypt, God again used water to defeat his enemies (Exodus 15:1-15)! David's dependence upon the spirit of wisdom with which he was anointed paid off in the life of his son Solomon. When Solomon became king, he placed the spiritual wisdom given to his father as a higher priority in his own life than riches and honor (1 Kings 3:7-14).

CHALLENGE Help your students plan to hold a parent reception sometime in the near future for the purpose of showing honor to them.

THE **BIG** TRUTH

HUMAN LIFE MUST BE VALUED.

CONFIDENTIAL SOURCE:
DEUTERONOMY 5:17;
GENESIS 9:5, 6;
1 JOHN 3:15

The Sixth Commandment— Do Not Murder

Make Cents?

"A penny saved is a penny earned." "Just want to put my two cents in." "Penny for your thoughts?" The one-cent coin has been a part of our lives and even a part of our language for centuries. But does the penny have any real value any more? Some say no, but others are afraid of what might happen if the copper-colored coin is done away with.

Rising costs of metals have lowered the value of the penny. A penny now costs more than one cent for the government to manufacture. The rising cost of copper caused the government to make the coins mostly from zinc rather than copper in 1982, but the cost of zinc is again making the penny too expensive to produce. "I'm very surprised they haven't gone to plastic," quips Bill Johnson, the owner of a company that still sells "penny candy."

Many Americans agree that pennies have little value. "They weigh down our wallets, rattle around in our vacuum cleaners, and are summarily dismissed by most vending machines . . . their value is so inconsequential that store clerks leave bowls of them by the checkout counter completely unguarded," argues columnist Dayana Yochim. Credit union teller Ashley Guy complains, "Pennies by far [cause] the most problems in the [coin] machine. They've got crud or gum on them . . . We've told people to go home and wash [their pennies]." Groups such as Citizens to Retire the Penny (CRP) have even been founded to educate the public on the advantages of retiring the penny from general circulation.

But others fear dire consequences if the penny is removed from circulation. Professor Raymond Lombra of Pennsylvania State University testified before Congress in 1990 that rounding prices to the nearest five cents could cost Americans $600 million each year. Others predict that taking away the penny will hurt charities. Organizations like Ronald McDonald House Charities and the Salvation Army rely heavily on donations from the collection of pennies. Teddy Gross, founder of the Penny Harvest charity drive in New York City schools, reports that last year his drive brought in 55 million pennies—over half a million dollars. Citizens for Common Cents, a group founded to save the penny, also predict that elimination of the coin would erode consumer confidence in the economy, hurt the poor and the elderly, and increase the federal deficit.

Still, some say that the value of the small copper coin is more than monetary. "Pennies are like baseball and apple pie," says Valerie Huebsch of Pennsylvania. "Think of all the kids around the world who would be sad not to pick up pennies. It's fun to have a jar of pennies."

QUESTIONS TO CONSIDER:

■ Do you think the penny should be retired? Does the penny no longer have any real value? Why or why not?

■ Is monetary value the only kind of value there is? What are some things that you find valuable even though they have little monetary value?

■ In a materialistic culture, making decisions based on cash value is done all the time. The penny may be an unimportant example of this, but there are others. The most controversial is trying to assign a value to human life. Let's look at what the Bible says about the value of life in the eyes of God.

BIBLE TRUTHS

BIBLE**TRUTH** 1

Murder is the sum of acts and attitudes that result in hostility toward innocent human beings.
DEUTERONOMY 5:17; 1 JOHN 3:15

■ **What do people mean when they say, "I could just kill [a certain person]"? What might cause this feeling?**

INSIDE STORY: The Hebrew word *ratsach* is best translated as *murder* (Exodus 20:13; Deuteronomy 5:17), killing a human being on purpose, without the legal authority of government. Jesus made it clear that murder is rooted in anger and hatred that treats another human being as worthless (Matthew 5:21, 22). These words of Christ were in the mind of the apostle John when he referred to the murder of Abel by his brother Cain (1 John 3:12-15). Abel had brought an acceptable blood sacrifice to God, but Cain brought a sacrifice of vegetables, violating God's requirements. As a result, Cain became angry and murdered Abel in a jealous rage (Genesis 4:3-8).

The sixth commandment is not a prohibition of slaughtering an animal, or even the taking of human life in self-defense or in a legal execution or just war. What God does condemn, however, is the demonic hatred that causes a person to devalue another person to the extent that he or she feels justified in taking that innocent life.

BIBLE**TRUTH** 2

Murder takes what God considers his greatest treasure. GENESIS 9:5

■ **Tell of a time you did something as a part of a crowd that violated your personal value system. What do you think social commentators mean when they talk about creating a culture of death?**

INSIDE STORY: The Law of Moses taught, "bloodshed pollutes the land" (Numbers 35:33a). After Cain murdered Abel, God told Cain, "Your brother's blood cries out to me from the ground" (Genesis 4:10). When human life is considered to be of little worth, everyone in that culture suffers. The reason for the seriousness of murder was given to Noah after the flood. God had destroyed the entire human race, with the exception of Noah's family, because "all the people on earth had corrupted their ways" (Genesis 6:12). In starting over again, God made a covenant with Noah. In this new world, human life would have to be treated as valuable. God would "demand an accounting" from anyone who took a human life "for in the image of God has God made man" (Genesis 9:5, 6). Only human beings are created in God's image and can be "murdered."

BIBLE**TRUTH** 3

Murder must be punished severely. GENESIS 9:6

■ **Tell about a time that you were punished more strictly than you should have been. Then tell of a time when you were punished more leniently than you should have been. Why is it important that punishment be just?**

INSIDE STORY: Because of the heinous nature of the crime, the Bible demands that murderers be punished severely. In the early days of humanity, the relatives of the murdered individual would avenge the murder by executing the murderer. For that reason, Cain believed that he would have to spend the rest of his life as a fugitive, trying to evade those who would take his life (Genesis 4:13, 14). Years later, after the flood, God required capital punishment as a part of his covenant with Noah and his descendants (Genesis 9:6). The Law of Moses also prescribed capital punishment as the only way a nation polluted by murder can keep from descending into savagery (Numbers 35:33).

CHALLENGE

Begin planning a class project that promotes life. You might choose to collect items for a local pregnancy care center that helps women choose life instead of abortion. You might also choose to call an organization that works with mentally or physically disabled people. Contact your local agencies to determine needs. These activities will help your students get to know people that society often devalues.

INSTANT**STUDY 12** ... CONTINUED

30

THE BIG TRUTH

ADULTERY IS AN ATTRACTIVE SIN WITH UGLY CONSEQUENCES.

CONFIDENTIAL SOURCE:
DEUTERONOMY 5:18;
PROVERBS 5:20-24; 6:32

Trading Up

Kyle MacDonald described himself as "a guy in Montreal who has an Internet connection and one red paper clip." One year later he was an international celebrity and a homeowner.

Twenty-six-year-old MacDonald had no job, but he had an Internet blog and a dream. MacDonald wanted to trade his red paper clip for a house. As outrageous as trading something so insignificant for a major asset might seem, MacDonald worked to accomplish that goal. He did so one step at a time.

The response of fellow-bloggers was phenomenal. "It went from a hobby, where I played it on a whim, to the point where thousands of people were showing up on a Web site," MacDonald said. He and his friends played "bigger and better" when he was a child. In that game, participants try to keep trading an object for something of greater value. So while MacDonald traveled and held odd jobs for a year, a childhood game became a full-time occupation and an Internet cult.

In fourteen trades and one year, MacDonald achieved his dream. In his first trade, two women from Vancouver traded a pen shaped like a fish for the paperclip. That same day, a sculptor from Seattle, Washington, offered a custom-made doorknob for the pen. Eleven days later the doorknob went to a Massachusetts man for a camp stove, which was in turn traded for an electrical generator in California in September. A man in New York City traded a neon beer sign and a keg of beer for the generator on November 9, 2005. On December 1 this became a snowmobile from Quebec that was swapped for an all-expenses-paid trip to Yahk, British Columbia, shortly thereafter. In January, MacDonald traded for a van, which he exchanged for a recording contract in February. The contract bought the price of a rent-free apartment in Arizona for a year and then became an afternoon with rock legend Alice Cooper in April. In May, MacDonald traveled to the Cincinnati, Ohio, area to trade one music icon for another—a KISS snow globe. In about a week, this trinket was traded to actor and snow globe collector Corbin Bernsen for a role in an upcoming Hollywood movie. A small town in Canada then traded the movie role for the house that stands at 503 Main Street in the town of Kipling, Saskatchewan.

MacDonald believed that his adventure inspired others. "There's people all over the world that . . . have paper-clips clipped to the top of their computer . . . and it proves that anything is possible."

QUESTIONS
TO CONSIDER:

■ What is the most surprising part of this story for you? Do you think MacDonald put a lot of thought into his trades? Defend your answer. How might this story have ended differently if MacDonald thought that his trades were "no big deal?"

■ Most people think that something like a paper clip is insignificant. Why is it logical to believe that? What lessons can one learn from this story? How might this story make you rethink your values? Explain.

■ Most people might say that a paper clip is "no big deal." But Kyle MacDonald proved them wrong. One thing led to another, resulting in remarkable consequences. Similarly, some argue that sexual morality is "no big deal." But God teaches that, like Kyle's now-famous paper clip, the "trades" we make with our sexuality might bring unexpected (but in this case, very unpleasant) results.

INSTANT **STUDY 13** ■ **OLD**TESTAMENT

31

BIBLE TRUTHS

BIBLE**TRUTH** 1

Adultery is never a private matter. DEUTERONOMY 5:18; PROVERBS 5:21; MATTHEW 5:27, 28

■ **Some people believe they can hide their sexual sins. Why do you think that is difficult to do?**

INSIDE STORY: Adultery is when a husband or wife breaks his or her wedding vows by having sex with someone else (Deuteronomy 5:18). From the beginning God ordained that a man and woman should "be united" and "become one flesh" (Genesis 2:24). In the sexual act one joins with another person not only physically, but also emotionally and spiritually. To please God we must avoid adultery as well as any sexual immorality.

Though people try to hide their sexual sins, "a man's ways are in full view of the LORD" (Proverbs 5:21). God even knows when a person fantasizes about committing adultery (Matthew 5:27, 28). In a society in which people insist that their bodies are their own, this idea seems like an invasion of privacy. But the fact is, "the body is not meant for sexual immorality" (1 Corinthians 6:13). God created us to be united with him through Christ. Committing sexual immorality is taking God's property and giving it away (vv. 15, 16).

BIBLE**TRUTH** 2

Adultery robs its victims. DEUTERONOMY 5:18; PROVERBS 5:20

■ **Why would people not buy a used toothbrush or pre-chewed gum? Why do you have the expectation that those products (and others like them) belong only to you?**

INSIDE STORY: Sexual immorality is not only done in full view of God, it also victimizes others. While our bodies belong to God, in marriage, partners also give their bodies to each other (1 Corinthians 7:4). For that reason, adultery steals the wife or husband of another person (Proverbs 5:20). Adulterers have no right to give their bodies to another or to take the spouse of another. When that happens,

the consequences can be great. It is not uncommon for the wronged spouse to seek revenge against the adulterer. With that in mind, Solomon described adultery as playing with fire (Proverbs 6:28, 29). A jealous spouse will certainly become furious when an affair is discovered and want justice (vv. 33, 34). Although sexual immorality outside of marriage is not technically adultery, fornication still robs someone of that which is rightfully his or hers. When a person is active sexually before marriage, he or she robs a future spouse of a gift that should be his or hers alone.

BIBLE**TRUTH** 3

Adultery destroys its participants. DEUTERONOMY 5:18; PROVERBS 5:22, 23; 6:32

■ **List some long-term consequences of sexual sin.**

INSIDE STORY: Adultery is also a deadly trap for the people who participate (Proverbs 5:22). The adulterer becomes entangled in a web of guilt, cover-up lies, and eventual public embarrassment. He may eventually lose his family, his friends, his self-respect—"shame [that] will never be wiped away" (Proverbs 6:33). Sexual immorality can also bring grave physical harm. The adulterer "will die for lack of discipline" (Proverbs 5:23). Adultery causes a person to literally destroy himself (Proverbs 6:32). Does the adulterer really think he can get away with it? Doesn't he know the fury of the outraged husband or parents? Doesn't he know how many sexually transmitted diseases he can get? Hasn't he read how often a jealous lover kills his rival? Disease and death are not just remote possibilities—they are very real dangers!

CHALLENGE Invite your students to write letters to their future husbands or wives sharing their commitment to remain pure for God, themselves, and their future marriage.

INSTANT**STUDY 13** ... CONTINUED

32

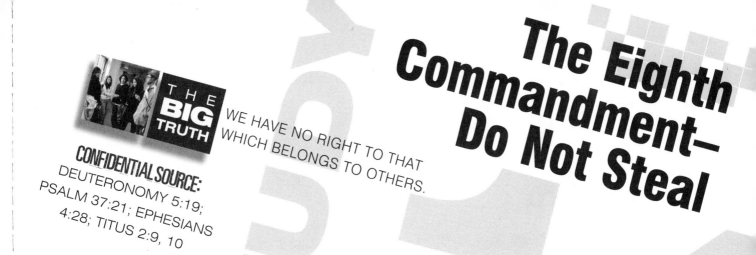

WE HAVE NO RIGHT TO THAT WHICH BELONGS TO OTHERS.

CONFIDENTIAL SOURCE:
DEUTERONOMY 5:19;
PSALM 37:21; EPHESIANS
4:28; TITUS 2:9, 10

The Eighth Commandment— Do Not Steal

Money Meeting

G8? What's that? A model of sports car? A vegetable juice cocktail? A vitamin? A space on a bingo card? Actually, G8 is something different and much more important than any of these.

The Group of Eight, or G8, is composed of the eight most industrialized countries in the world. Each year, the heads of these countries meet together to discuss world problems and how to solve them. This international organization began in 1975. The French president invited the heads of six major industrialized democracies (France, Germany, Italy, Japan, the United Kingdom, and the United States) to meet to discuss the oil crisis and global recession of that time. The group grew to seven when Present Gerald Ford asked that Canada be allowed to join in 1976. In 1997, Russia was added to the elite group.

The topics discussed by G8 leaders are often diverse. In these meetings nations have reaffirmed commitments to fight HIV/AIDS, tuberculosis, and malaria worldwide. Statements have been adopted on fighting piracy and counterfeiting, political corruption, and drug trafficking. The G8 has asked rogue nations to curb their nuclear capabilities. Economic and social development of Africa has been considered a high priority, as have availability of energy, bringing peace to the Middle East, and fighting terrorism.

This list of topics seems staggering. But, the reasoning goes, if the leaders of the most prosperous nations in the world will not take some responsibility in dealing with world problems, who will? It seems logical that these leaders are qualified to deal with such tasks and offer advice to the rest of the world. Others object, referring to the G8 as an unofficial, self-appointed world government. Critics of the G8 say that

these nations are really the cause of world problems and should not be trusted to provide solutions to them. Allowing the wealthiest nations to make rules for others, they reason, places too much emphasis on personal property. That emphasis leads, they argue, to global warming, poverty, disease, and the other problems that the G8 claims to want to solve. Therefore, the summits are often the scene of protests. Despite the enormity of the task and the criticism the group receives, the G8 continues to meet annually.

QUESTIONS TO CONSIDER:

■ How much do you know about the G8? In your opinion, how important are these annual meetings? Defend your answer. Do you think that it is fair that the richest nations of the world take responsibility for world problems? Why or why not?

■ In what other ways do people with a great deal of property exercise a great deal of control over society? Why is this good? Why is this bad? Do you think that the world as a whole places too much emphasis on personal property, not enough emphasis, or about the right amount of emphasis? Explain why you feel the way you do.

■ When we own things, we feel protective of our own property. We feel that we have some say in how that property is used and whether others *should* use that property. We do not want others to steal or misuse what we have worked hard for. That is understandable, but what does God say about the rights and responsibilities of property owners? The eighth commandment is about property. Let's see what the Bible has to say about stealing, its consequences, and its cure.

BIBLE TRUTHS

BIBLETRUTH 1

Theft can be active or passive. DEUTERONOMY 5:19; PSALM 37:21

■ **List as many ways you can think of that people rob one another.**

INSIDE STORY: The eighth Commandment forbids theft (Exodus 20:15; Deuteronomy 5:19). Elsewhere, the Bible differentiates between different kinds of theft. Burglary, the act of breaking and entering a residence at night to commit a crime, is distinguished from daytime theft (Exodus 22:2, 3). Causing loss of property through negligence is addressed (Exodus 22:6, 14, 15), as is embezzlement (Exodus 22:7, 8). The thieves who were crucified on either side of Jesus were *lestas*, the Greek word for armed robbers not unwilling to take the life of their victims (Mark 15:27). On the other hand, John described the thieving Judas a mere *kleptes* (where we get the English word *kleptomaniac*), the Greek word for embezzler or sneak thief (John 12:6). The Bible regularly condemns fraud, theft through trickery (Proverbs 11:1; Amos 8:5). King David wrote that it was wicked to steal by default, the failure to meet a financial obligation (Psalm 37:21). Punishment for all of these crimes differed from one another. But all of these crimes are theft and forbidden by God's law.

BIBLETRUTH 2

Theft can be counteracted by commitment to hard work. DEUTERONOMY 5:19; EPHESIANS 4:28

■ **An old saying goes, "Idle hands are the devil's workshop." What does that mean to you? Is it still true today?**

INSIDE STORY: In our legal system, theft is viewed as a crime against the government. The defendant, if found guilty, must surrender his or her freedom for a period of time in a state-run prison. The Bible, however, generally views theft as a crime against a person. Under the Law of Moses, if a thief stole a sheep and sold it, he would have to

pay the victim four sheep in return (Exodus 22:1). In the New Testament, that law was obviously still practiced. When Zacchaeus, a tax collector guilty of cheating his clients out of money, decided to follow Jesus, he knew the right way to reconcile with his victims (Luke 19:8).

In order to make restitution, the thief would have to stop stealing and earn an honest wage. Although this was a Jewish law, it is exactly what Paul demanded of Gentile Christians (Ephesians 4:28). Paul knew that people without constructive work were apt to be troublemakers. When some Christians in Thessalonica were living off of the income of others and stealing other's time with gossip and rumors, Paul demanded that they "earn the bread they eat" (2 Thessalonians 3:11, 12). The antidote for theft of all sorts is hard work.

BIBLETRUTH 3

Theft destroys the credibility of a Christian. DEUTERONOMY 5:19; TITUS 2:9, 10

■ **Have you ever loaned something to someone, only to have it returned damaged? How did you react?**

INSIDE STORY: Theft of any sort wrecks relationships. For that reason, Christians must make sure that they protect a reputation for honesty. Dishonesty on our part will not only cause others to be wary of us, but also to distrust God (Romans 2:21). But if we show respect for the property of others and consistently prove that we are trustworthy, we "will make the teaching about God our Savior attractive" (Titus 2:9, 10).

CHALLENGE Help students think of other types of theft: stealing from an employer by goofing off, stealing joy by having a bad attitude, stealing a good reputation with gossip.

INSTANT **STUDY** 14 … CONTINUED

34

LIES ARE ANYTHING BUT HARMLESS.

CONFIDENTIAL SOURCE:
DEUTERONOMY 5:20;
PROVERBS 6:16-19; 19:9;
1 PETER 3:10

The Ninth Commandment— Do Not Lie

Archeol-LIE-gy

He was arrested for the crime of forgery. If he had gotten away with it, he would've earned $1 million to $2 million for his artifact.

Oded Golan, antiquities dealer, was in possession of a burial box that had the inscription "James, the brother of Jesus." This was a startling concept to many because it could be physical proof that Jesus of Nazareth lived and had a brother. The box was controversial and was tested for authenticity. The other forged artifact Oded had was a tablet that had instructions on it about caring for the Jewish temple.

After examining the artifact, Israel Antiquities Authority announced that the burial box was fake. "The inscription appears new, written in modernity by someone attempting to reproduce ancient written characters," said officials. The box is probably from that era, they continued, but the inscriptions are false. However, at the time Oded said he believed these pieces bought from another dealer were real.

When Oded was arrested and taken to a Jerusalem court, police showed evidence that was confiscated from Oded's house: stencils, stones, and partially finished forgeries.

"It's breaking my heart to see such things," said Uzi Dahari, a member of the committee that had tried to verify the burial box of James. He said a crime such as this taints archeological science.

QUESTIONS TO CONSIDER:

■ How would you feel if an artifact confirming an incident in the Bible was historical? How would you feel later if you found out that it was a forgery? Describe the damage such a lie could cause.

■ Describe a time when you were caught in a lie. How did you feel? Describe a time when you caught someone else lying. How did that affect your relationship? Why do you think people lie? Is there ever a time when lying is OK?

■ Today we'll look in Deuteronomy, Proverbs, and 1 Peter to find what God says about lying and see some of the consequences of this sin.

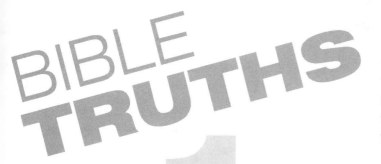

BIBLE TRUTHS

people what they want to hear allows those we say we love to remain immature. A false view of truth that is harsh and unloving is simply a way to put someone else down. Loving truth is the cornerstone of happy homes and lasting friendships.

BIBLE**TRUTH** 1

Truth is necessary for a just society.
DEUTERONOMY 5:20; PROVERBS 19:9

■ **Think about our court system. Why is honesty essential for justice?**

INSIDE STORY: The ninth Commandment specifically forbids perjury, giving testimony in court that is knowingly false (Exodus 20:16; Deuteronomy 5:20). The Jewish legal system had the important safeguard of not convicting a person of a crime based on the testimony of one person alone. Two or three witnesses were required (Deuteronomy 19:15). But it was essential that all witnesses could be counted on to be truthful. Therefore, the punishment for perjury was severe and could even include the death penalty (Proverbs 19:9). The perjurer would get the penalty for the crime for which he was trying to frame another with his testimony. This had to be done to ensure the integrity of the justice system (Deuteronomy 19:15-21). Unless there are strong penalties for doing so, any testimony in court would be suspect. Unless one can trust the integrity of the witnesses, how could anyone make a judgment as to the guilt of a defendant?

BIBLE**TRUTH** 2

Truth is necessary for successful relationships.
PROVERBS 6:16-19

■ **List some ways that you have been hurt because a person lied to you or about you.**

INSIDE STORY: In Proverbs 6:16-19, Solomon provides a checklist of dishonest characteristics. A dishonest person might be haughty, thinking that the rules that apply to others do not apply to him. Those with a "lying tongue" tell untruths for personal gain, even if it means innocent people suffer. On the other hand, the apostle Paul gives a simple phrase that describes what is essential for successful relationships. Even in a dangerous and deceitful world, we can build one another up if we are "speaking the truth in love" (Ephesians 4:15). A false view of love that simply tells

BIBLE**TRUTH** 3

Truth is necessary for personal peace. 1 PETER 3:10

■ **Tell about a time when you felt guilt because of a lie you told.**

INSIDE STORY: The apostle Peter knew the bitter fruit of deception. Lying to others after Jesus' arrest caused him to break down and cry (Matthew 26:75). With that in mind, Peter wrote that integrity allows us to "love life and see good days" (1 Peter 3:10). We can live life to the fullest when we do not have to avoid running into those we have betrayed with our lies. Truth is necessary for our personal mental health!

Also, the more we lie, the more guilt is suppressed to the point that it virtually disappears. Paul described people like this as those "whose consciences have been seared as with a hot iron" (1 Timothy 4:2). When we have a bad burn, the skin may heal, but a scar that is calloused and unfeeling remains. Jesus told the Pharisees that their lies made them unreceptive to him and made them the children of the father of lies (John 8:42-47).

CHALLENGE Illustrate how hard it is to be freed from a web of lies by tying the end of a ball of yarn to a fixed point and having a student walk among the class trailing a "web" behind. Talk about ways to be free from dishonesty.

The Tenth Commandment— Do Not Covet

AN UNGODLY DESIRE FOR MORE LEAVES EVERYONE WITH LESS.

CONFIDENTIAL SOURCE:
DEUTERONOMY 5:21;
1 KINGS 21:3-11, 14

Star Stuff

How far would you go to own something once used by your favorite celebrity? A fan in Beijing paid about $340 for the sheets and pajamas used by world-famous soccer star David Beckham. The *Beijing Morning Post* said the auctioneer described them as "still bearing the stink of Beckham's sweat."

David Beckham became famous playing for British soccer team Manchester United and was later traded to Spain's club team, Real Madrid for over $40 million. The Spanish team was in China to train and play an exhibition game against the China Dragons Select XI.

Chinese fans went crazy to see the famous star in his debut match for Real. Over 45,000 people watched the event live, paying as much as a month's wage for a ticket. It was estimated that over a billion people in China watched the game on TV. The Xu Kai hair salon said it was packed with people requesting the twin ponytail style of hair Beckham had been wearing during his training time.

Back at the Beijing hotel auction, another person bid $340 to stay in the hotel room where Beckham had just slept. A soccer ball signed by Beckham and other Real Madrid players was sold for $2,500. The money raised went to a fund to help children of nurses and doctors who died after being exposed to deadly diseases they treated.

QUESTIONS TO CONSIDER:

■ Do you think the fans got their money's worth when they paid lots of money to see David Beckham and own things he had used? Explain.

■ Who is your favorite celebrity? How much would you pay to own something by that person?

■ The people in China were obviously very excited over the soccer match. What event would make you and your friends go crazy? What would you do to make sure you attended such an event?

■ People go to a lot of trouble to meet celebrities. We may laugh at times, but we all go to a lot of trouble for things that we really want. Name something that you really, really want. What would you do to get that item? Why can it be a problem to want things that we don't have?

■ We all want things we don't have. But constantly desiring something that isn't ours can be dangerous. The Bible calls that greed coveting. We're going to look in 1 Kings 21 to learn more about coveting and what can happen as a result of this sin.

INSTANT**STUDY 16** ■ OLD**TESTAMENT**

BIBLE TRUTHS

Even today, some office holders have even been rumored to have political "hit lists." Supposedly, persons on that list are investigated in order to find information that can be used to taint his or her name. Like Ahab and Jezebel, some unscrupulous politicians are willing to trash a person's reputation in their lust for power.

BIBLE**TRUTH** 1

A covetous person feels entitled to the property of another. DEUTERONOMY 5:21; 1 KINGS 21:3-6

■ **How much is "enough"? Tell about a time when you got what you wanted but then wanted even more.**

INSIDE STORY: God's people were about to enter the promised land and would own their own houses, land, and animals. At that point, Moses reminded them that God forbade his people wanting wealth so badly that they would take it from others (Deuteronomy 5:21). The craving for stuff can grow so strong that it replaces a longing for God (Deuteronomy 6:10-12). During Jesus' ministry, he warned against greed, saying, "A man's life does not consist in the abundance of his possessions" (Luke 12:15). Ahab, a king of Israel, had made a lucrative deal with a conquered nation (1 Kings 20:34). Ahab lacked for nothing, but that did not stop him from desiring the small vineyard of a man named Naboth. When Naboth refused to sell it, Ahab pouted like a child (1 Kings 21:3-6). Covetousness makes one believe that without enough stuff, life is not worth living.

BIBLE**TRUTH** 2

A covetous person is willing to damage the reputation of another. DEUTERONOMY 5:21; 1 KINGS 21:7-10a

■ **Tell about a time when you were jealous. Why did you feel like that? How did jealousy affect your actions and attitude?**

INSIDE STORY: Seeing Ahab's distress, Queen Jezebel took matters into her own hands. She plotted to use false witnesses to frame Naboth for blasphemy and treason (1 Kings 21:7-10a). Because of Ahab's covetousness, the couple stole something even more valuable than Naboth's land—Naboth's good name. Solomon was a king much wealthier than Ahab. He knew, however, that "A good name is more desirable than great riches; to be esteemed is better than silver or gold" (Proverbs 22:1) and that "a good name is better than fine perfume" (Ecclesiastes 7:1).

BIBLE**TRUTH** 3

A covetous person eventually feels justified in taking the life of another. DEUTERONOMY 5:21; 1 KINGS 21:10b-15

■ **Name a person in history you would describe as *heartless*. Why do you say that? What made that person act that way?**

INSIDE STORY: But the plot for the vineyard does not stop there. As a result of the false charge, Naboth was executed. The deed was done and duly reported to Jezebel, who, in turn, directed her husband to confiscate the desired property (1 Kings 21:10b-15). The whole matter was cold, cruel, and calculated.

Ahab wasn't the first biblical king to take an innocent life to fulfill a personal lust. Years before, David was similarly heartless when he schemed to kill Uriah the Hittite. David even involved a trusted general who set Uriah up to be killed in battle. After receiving the news, David showed no remorse, but completed his plan to marry the dead man's wife (2 Samuel 11:14-27).

Even today the sin of coveting leads people to willfully take the life of another. In March of 2005, seventeen-year-old Steve Terret was shot in the back in an alley and died at a local hospital. Apparently, someone he knew lured him into the alley to kill him and steal his shoes. The brand new Nike Air Jordan Solidify shoes, which retailed for $110, were coveted by someone willing to kill for them.

CHALLENGE Deuteronomy 5:21 lists things a person is not to covet, many of which do not apply to your students! Divide your group into pairs and have each pair rewrite that list for teens today.

Food Fights

Our world is filled with conflicts—wars overseas, political battles at home, and economic struggles worldwide. Many conflicts are fought with adults by adults. But there is a struggle raging that affects younger people as well. It is the battle of the waistline, and some statistics seem to show that even the youngest citizens of the U.S. are suffering defeat.

In a recent study, the Centers for Disease Control and Prevention reported that about 32 percent of young people between the ages of 6-19 were overweight but not obese, 16 percent were obese, and 11 percent were extremely obese. In total, they say nearly six out of every ten have a weight problem!

So how is the food industry taking leadership to win this battle? Pediatrician David Ludwig and nutrition professor Marion Nestle wrote in the *Journal of the American Medical Association* that they are not. In fact, say Ludwig and Nestle, the food industry cannot be trusted to help win the battle of the waistline.

Ludwig and Nestle point to many reasons for their conclusion. One reason is that almost $2 billion is spent each year to advertise unhealthy food to kids. Even when the industry gives the appearance of promoting alternatives to junk food, the alternatives may be less than healthy. In 2006, for example, major beverage makers agreed to remove sugary sodas from school vending machines. But the industry persuaded lawmakers to allow sports drinks and vitamin waters that are just as packed with sugar and calories as fizzy soft drinks are.

Another reason is that processing healthy foods makes them less healthy, but more profitable for the food industry. For example, fresh apples have an abundance of fiber and nutrients that are lost when they are processed into applesauce. Apple juice, which is even more processed, has had almost all of the fiber and nutrients stripped out. This same stripping out of nutrients, says Ludwig, happens with highly refined white bread compared with stone-ground whole wheat bread.

Finally, the food industry gives a great deal of money to those who evaluate the health concerns about their products. The American Dietetic Association, for example, accepts money from companies such as Coca-Cola. In exchange, Coca-Cola is given the opportunity to influence food and nutrition experts. Ludwig concluded that studies looking at the health effects of milk, juice, and soda would be more favorable to the industry if food manufacturers funded the research. "If a study is funded by the industry, it may be closer to advertising than science," he says.

QUESTIONS TO CONSIDER:

■ How do you react to the research that states that about six out of every ten young students are overweight? Do you think this research is overly harsh or right on target? Explain your answer.

■ Who do you think should be taking leadership roles in making sure that young people receive proper nutrition? Of the people and organizations discussed in the article above, choose one and tell why you think that that person or organization is showing positive or negative leadership. Think of leaders you know. List characteristics that you think make either good or poor leaders.

■ We may not always agree on what makes a good leader, but we are always looking for one. Let's look at how a woman in the Bible proved herself to be a good leader.

INSTANT **STUDY 17** ■ **OLD**TESTAMENT

BIBLE TRUTHS

BIBLE**TRUTH** 1

Deborah recruited Barak into God's service.
JUDGES 4:4-7

■ **List the things that need to be done for your church to meet each week. Why is delegation important to accomplish this?**

INSIDE STORY: The time of the judges was one of rampant amorality (Judges 21:25). Israel would often stray from worshiping God. God would withdraw his protection and the nation would fall into the hands of the enemy. The people of Israel would cry out to God for help, and he would raise up a judge to offer justice, defeat the enemy, and bring peace.

At the time of Deborah, Israel was suffering under the rule of a Canaanite, King Jaban, and the army of his general Sisera. God called Deborah to save his people. Then Deborah received word from the Lord. She summoned Barak to battle Sisera. Barak was to take ten thousand men from the tribes of Zebulun and Naphtali to defeat Sisera and his forces.

A good leader recruits others to the cause. They do not do it all. As Paul said to Timothy, "And the things you have heard me say in the presence of many witnesses entrust to reliable men who will also be qualified to teach others" (2 Timothy 2:2).

BIBLE**TRUTH** 2

Deborah assisted Barak in ministry as necessary.
JUDGES 4:8-10

■ **Tell about a skill you have learned because someone showed you how it was done.**

INSIDE STORY: Barak would obey on the condition that Deborah would accompany him. He agreed to recruit the others from the tribes of Zebulun and Naphtali, but insisted that the judge come into battle with the army. She agreed, but added that the honor of victory would not go to him, but to a woman (Judges 4:8-10).

Great leaders refuse to subscribe to the "do as I say, not as I do" school of thought. God's victories are won when leaders are willing to stand on the front lines with the enlisted men. Paul regularly told the churches he led to follow the example he had set (Acts 20:35; Philippians 4:9; 2 Thessalonians 3:7-9). Deborah did not hesitate but went into battle with the recruits. Leaders just don't stand on the sidelines barking orders; they join the fight!

BIBLE**TRUTH** 3

Deborah gave Barak direction as necessary.
JUDGES 4:11-16

■ **What is the difference between a suggestion and a command? Give examples of times when one of those is better than the other.**

INSIDE STORY: Leaders recruit and leaders serve as examples, but sometimes leaders must lead by giving direct, authoritative commands. Heber, an Israelite traitor, played informant to General Sisera, giving him details of Deborah and Barak's military moves. Sisera's nine hundred iron chariots moved into position at the Kishon River, a riverbed that was often dry but could become a raging torrent in the rainy season. Knowing that Jehovah would send rain and trap Sisera, Deborah issued a direct order to Barak, "Go! This is the day the LORD has given Sisera into your hands" (v. 14). Deborah was able to give clear direction to Barak at a crucial time, assuring victory.

CHALLENGE

During the week before this study, enlist the help of a person actively involved in some type of mentoring. Have the speaker challenge your teens to become a mentor to someone.

INSTANT**STUDY 17** . . . CONTINUED

EVEN THE MOST UNLIKELY INDIVIDUALS CAN RECEIVE GOD'S MERCY.

CONFIDENTIAL SOURCE:
JOSHUA 2:1-4, 8-13, 17, 18, 21

Rahab— A Life Changed

Tales of the Unexpected

Sometimes things occur that you never would expect to happen. Here are a few of them.

Kitty care—We might assume that dogs and cats are natural enemies. A terrier in Australia must not have gotten that memo, however! During a house fire, Leo refused to leave the side of a litter of newborn kittens until firefighters came to their rescue. "Leo wouldn't leave the kittens, and it nearly cost him his life," fire service Commander Ken Brown told reporters. Firefighters have nicknamed the unlikely hound hero "Smoky."

Living luggage—Delta baggage workers in Atlanta might have thought that the biggest danger in tracking down luggage was dealing with angry passengers. They learned differently when they opened a jetliner's cargo door and found a cheetah running loose amid the luggage!

Two cheetahs were being flown in the cargo area of a Boeing 757 passenger flight from Portland, Oregon, to Atlanta when one escaped from its cage. While the airline never expected to have to deal with such an occurrence, they handled the problem without incident. They summoned help from Zoo Atlanta, and experts rushed to a closed airport hangar and tranquilized the escaped animal. They then took both big cats to the zoo. While the excitement caused a delay in getting luggage to passengers, the fugitive feline did not damage any baggage.

Puppy provisions—Pet lovers usually do not consider the impact of a bad economy on their animals. Yet when faced with a choice between feeding a family and feeding pets, people may discard their furry friends. A soup kitchen in Germany has taken steps to address the problem. The Animal Board shelter has opened its doors in Berlin, providing a free meal to pets of the homeless and unemployed.

Despite the fact that people do not expect to see a soup kitchen operated for dogs, director Claudia Hollm dismissed any criticism of her project. "Making sure dogs don't go hungry is just as important as making sure that people don't starve," she asserted.

The opening of the soup kitchen follows last month's launch of a new bus service in Berlin for dogs, which shuttles furry friends to a luxury doggy day-care center.

QUESTIONS TO CONSIDER:

■ List some unexpected events mentioned in the animal stories above. Why do you think a logical person would not expect some of these things to happen?

■ Sometimes we draw what we feel are logical conclusions about other people. But these conclusions can be wrong. Think of some assumptions you make about others. Then complete this sentence: "The last person I would expect to see in church today is _____." Why did you fill in the blank this way?

■ Logic is a helpful tool. But God works beyond our logic. When we consider the way God can work in the hearts of people, we need to expect the unexpected. In the Bible we read about Rahab, a woman that few would ever expect to become a follower of God.

BIBLE**TRUTH** 1

Rahab turned from following human authority.
JOSHUA 2:1-4

■ **What are some common practices among your peers that you choose not to do? Why is that difficult at times?**

INSIDE STORY: Canaan was pagan through and through. Abominable practices like child sacrifices occurred (Deuteronomy 18:9, 10). Temple priestesses were prostitutes, performing in ritual sexual acts with pagan worshipers. Rahab was this type of prostitute (Joshua 2:1). When the Israelite spies came her way, she made a crucial decision. She defied the military authority of her nation to protect the men of Israel (vv. 2-4).

We often use the word *repent* simply to mean *to feel sorry for*. The word used in the New Testament literally means to *think against* the way that one thought before. It indicates a total change in worldview. This is exactly what Rahab did. She turned her back on her culture. She took the risk of defying the local king and sent his henchmen on a wild goose chase.

BIBLE**TRUTH** 2

Rahab trusted God's power to save. JOSHUA 2:8-13

■ **Why would it be hopeless to follow God if he were not all-powerful? How does his power give you courage?**

INSIDE STORY: The miracles in Egypt preceding the Exodus and those accompanying the Israelites' march to freedom surely had circulated in Jericho. Rahab had heard all of the stories. She, like her fellow-citizens of Jericho, was filled with fear at the approach of the Israelites. But she allowed her fear to bring more than panic. She concluded that the mighty acts accompanying these people came from

a Mighty God (Joshua 2:9-11). She asked the spies to save the lives of her and her family (vv. 12, 13). God had led these spies not only to a place where they'd be less likely to be detected, but also to the home of a woman who was ready to bolt from her old way of living and her old gods for a new and powerful God. It was not her fear that brought the change; it was her bold faith (Hebrews 11:31).

BIBLE**TRUTH** 3

Rahab remained faithful to the promises she made to God. JOSHUA 2:17, 18, 21

■ **How do you recognize members of other religions? How do those marks differ from those that identify you as a Christian?**

INSIDE STORY: In arguing that faith includes acts of obedience, James used this incident as evidence (James 2:25, 26). Note that Rahab did more than promise to remain faithful to the God of the Israelites. She marked her household with a scarlet thread, a visible sign that she accepted the salvation of Jehovah (Joshua 2:21). Rahab's salvation was complete as she remained faithful day-by-day to her new God. As a testimony to that renewed lifestyle, we find her name in the lineage of Jesus (Matthew 1:5).

CHALLENGE

In the week before this study, tape a short segment of the PBS TV program *Antiques Roadshow*. Include a segment in which someone discovers that an item that they paid very little for was a great treasure. Help students think of someone in their lives who may be a similar unlikely treasure in the eyes of God.

STUDY 18 . . . CONTINUED

Woman of Loyalty
Ruth–A

Question of Loyalty

The quiet Ohio counties lived in fear because of the random sniper attacks. Thomas Lee Dillon killed five people in five rural counties in northern Ohio from 1989 to 1992. His victims were two hunters, two fishermen, and a jogger.

Dillon was caught after his friend, Richard Fry, was frightened by conversations he had with Dillon. Fry said that Dillon had once asked him if he thought Dillon had ever killed anyone. Statements like that, along with the fact that Dillon had been killing hundreds of farm animals, caused Fry to go to authorities with his suspicions. After the tip, FBI found evidence linking Dillon with the murders.

When asked why he killed, Dillon said he was bored. When bored, he'd take his gun and go shooting electric meters, cows, dogs, and sometimes people.

Walter Wilson, the county sheriff of Tuscarawas County who was a former detective on the Ohio case, said that the public's help is imperative in sniper cases. "They are the eyes and ears of law enforcement. In your normal homicide, there's a connection between the killer and victim. When you don't have that tool, you have to depend on a friend or loved one to do the right thing," he said.

QUESTIONS TO CONSIDER:

■ What is loyalty?

■ When Richard Fry turned in his friend Thomas Dillon to the police, he was being loyal to his government by helping authorities solve the case and loyal to his community by saving them from future killings. Discuss other circumstances when loyalty to friends isn't as important as loyalty to doing the right thing.

■ When is it important for you to be loyal to your friends? to your family? to your school? to your church? to God?

■ In this study we're going to look at Ruth, a woman who showed great loyalty to her family and to God.

INSTANT**STUDY** 19 ■ OLDTESTAMENT

BIBLE TRUTHS

BIBLE**TRUTH** 1

Ruth valued loyalty over personal security.
RUTH 1:8-13

■ **Have you ever betrayed a friend? Why did you do so?**

INSIDE STORY: A famine in Judah forced the family of Elimelech to sell their property and start afresh in the neighboring land of Moab (Ruth 1:1, 2). Elimelech's sons took Moabite brides, a controversial decision since Jews saw the Moabites as the products of a sinful relationship (Genesis 19:30-38) and were forbidden by the law of Moses to worship or even get along with them (Deuteronomy 23:3-6). Within ten years, Elimelech and his sons died, reducing the family to three impoverished widows (vv. 3-5).

When situations improved in Judah, Elimelech's widow, Naomi, proposed that she would return to Judah and survive on the charity of her countrymen. She encouraged her Moabite daughters-in-law, Orpah and Ruth, to find security by remarrying in Moab (vv. 6-9).

The thought of separation from Naomi caused Orpah and Ruth grief. They promised to travel to Judah with her despite the consequences (v. 10).

BIBLE**TRUTH** 2

Ruth remained loyal despite peer pressure.
RUTH 1:14, 15

■ **Name some times when peer support helped you accomplish a difficult task.**

INSIDE STORY: According to Jewish law (Deuteronomy 25:5, 6), Ruth and Orpah's prospects for marriage in Judah would be limited to Naomi's male offspring. The ludicrous thought of waiting for an elderly widow to become pregnant and for those sons to reach marriageable age

painted a grim picture (Ruth 1:11-13). Perhaps even a life of celibacy, poverty, and discrimination could have been tolerable if one could turn to someone with a common heritage. Yet Orpah made this impossible. By going back to her family, culture, and religious heritage, she left Ruth with no peer support (vv. 14, 15).

BIBLE**TRUTH** 3

Ruth's loyalty to others came from her loyalty to God. RUTH 1:16-18

■ **Do you think a person's religion or lack of one affects his or her behavior? Defend your answer.**

Ruth found something in her relationship with Naomi that she found more valuable than the comfort of financial security and peer support. In Ruth's short reply (vv. 16, 17), she mentioned deity three times. The untold story of Ruth obviously took place in those ten years between verses two and three of this chapter. During that time, Ruth witnessed the difference the God of Israel could make in the life of a family. Naomi must have treated Ruth with kindness and acceptance. Though she weathered poverty and great sorrow, the Jewish matriarch must have exhibited a courage and inner strength that intrigued her daughter-in-law. Ruth rejected the gods of her homeland and trusted the God of Israel.

CHALLENGE Brainstorm different weather terms with your students (cold, cloudy, foggy, etc.). Have students use one of those terms to describe the kind of friend they have been at times.

A Woman of Gratitude

Hannah—

THE BIG TRUTH

HANNAH HAD AN ATTITUDE OF GRATITUDE.

CONFIDENTIAL SOURCE:
1 SAMUEL 1:10, 12-18, 20, 24-28

Grateful Hostage

Her story captured our imagination, gave us hope, and made us grateful for the little things we enjoy each day. Ashley Smith told of a harrowing experience and how God used it in her book, *Unlikely Angel*.

Smith's story is a compelling one. Early on Saturday morning, March 12, 2005, this single mother in suburban Atlanta found herself face-to-face with a killer. The day before, Brian Nichols had escaped from Atlanta's Fulton County Courthouse, shooting a judge, a court reporter, a deputy, and a federal agent. For more than seven hours, Nichols held Smith hostage. During that time, Smith befriended her captor, cooked him breakfast, read to him from the inspirational best seller, *The Purpose-Driven Life*, and finally convinced him to surrender to the police.

Unlikely Angel is a fitting title for Ashley Smith's story. Smith struggled with drug abuse and was trying to wean herself off of speed, pot, and Xanax at the time of her ordeal. In her book, Smith admits that she still had methamphetamines in her apartment and even gave them to her captor after he demanded drugs. During her ordeal, Smith became convinced that God sent Nichols to straighten her out and ultimately save her from her self-destructive behavior.

During an interview with WXIA news in Atlanta, reporter Brenda Woods asked Ashley why she so openly admitted in her book that she had drugs in her home. "You could have gone to your grave and never have told this, and nobody would have ever known," Woods said. Smith responded, "No lives would have been changed either. My hope was that if I tell the truth, then other people will come forward and help themselves and their addictions."

Unlikely Angel touched many readers. "I did a book signing . . . in Augusta," said Smith. "People were just coming up to me in tears saying, 'Thank you, for what you've done. You've helped me change my life.'" An online reviewer expressed similar thoughts by saying, "It is a wonderful story about how a woman finally realizes that she needs to put her faith in God and begins to realize that he is there for her even through the hard times. . . . This book is also great just to look at someone's outlook on life and maybe feel how wonderful it is just to be alive and healthy."

QUESTIONS
TO CONSIDER:

■ If you were Smith, do you think you would have been so candid in writing this book? Why or why not?

■ An online reviewer wrote that reading Smith's book made her "feel how wonderful it is just to be alive and healthy." What do you think of that statement? How has learning about another person's problem made you realize that you take some of your blessings for granted? Name some things that you often take for granted.

■ It is easy to forget to be grateful for our blessings. In this lesson we will look at the life of a woman who lived centuries before Ashley Smith. This woman, Hannah, was blessed by God and expressed gratitude in three specific ways. Let's examine her story and see what we can learn from it.

INSTANT STUDY 20 ■ OLD TESTAMENT

BIBLE TRUTHS

BIBLE**TRUTH** 1

Hannah developed a grateful attitude.
1 SAMUEL 1:10, 12-18

■ **What puts you in a bad mood? How might you correct that?**

INSIDE STORY: Hannah was childless. To make matters worse, her husband Elkanah had married an additional wife, and she had given him many sons and daughters (1 Samuel 1:1-4). Nevertheless, Hannah worshiped the Lord. Every year when her husband went to the designated place of worship, Hannah went as well (vv. 3, 7). Her bitterness caused her to seek God even more! On one such trip to worship, Hannah was weeping bitterly and poured out her soul to the Lord (vv. 9-11). As Hannah prayed, Eli the priest took notice. Eli assumed that Hannah had dealt with her grief with alcohol (v. 13). When Eli rebuked her, Hannah explained that she had been praying out of great anguish and grief (v. 16). The brother of Jesus would later write that in our disappointments we should seek God through prayer (James 5:13-16). The Spirit will bring results that the distilled spirits cannot (Ephesians 5:18).

BIBLE**TRUTH** 2

Hannah expressed her gratitude to others.
1 SAMUEL 1:20, 24-27

■ **Sometimes we have such great news we can't help but share it. Tell about a time that happened to you.**

INSIDE STORY: In her worship, Hannah vowed that if God would look upon her misery and give her a son, she would dedicate the boy to his service (1 Samuel 1:11). Eli had joined his prayer with hers (v. 17). God answered both prayers. Hannah conceived and gave birth to a son (v. 20). God had answered her prayer, and she chose the name Samuel (meaning *heard of God*).

Hannah told her husband that she had promised to take Samuel to Eli (v. 22). He knew the importance of keeping a vow made to the Lord (v. 21), and agreed. So after the age of weaning (three or four years of age in that culture), Hannah gave Samuel to the service of God. She testified to God's faithfulness with a sacrifice (v. 24). She also reminded Eli of the vow she had made and testified that the Lord had granted her what she had asked (vv. 25-27).

BIBLE**TRUTH** 3

Hannah's gratitude allowed her to sacrifice that which was most precious to her. 1 SAMUEL 1:28

■ **How do you say "thank you" to someone by your actions?**

INSIDE STORY: We cannot exaggerate the difficulty of this next act of Hannah. She did not just testify of God's answer to her prayer. She followed through on her promise. She was willing to give back to God the very gift for which she had prayed (1 Samuel 1:28). This is a mark of a grateful heart. Jesus' disciples were trained by him and given the ability to work wonders in his name. But they did not use those gifts to enrich themselves (Matthew 10:8). The disciples, like Hannah, used their blessings to bless others. Her gift was given, "not reluctantly or under compulsion," but willingly as a "cheerful giver" (2 Corinthians 9:7).

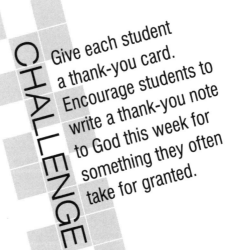

CHALLENGE Give each student a thank-you card. Encourage students to write a thank-you note to God this week for something they often take for granted.

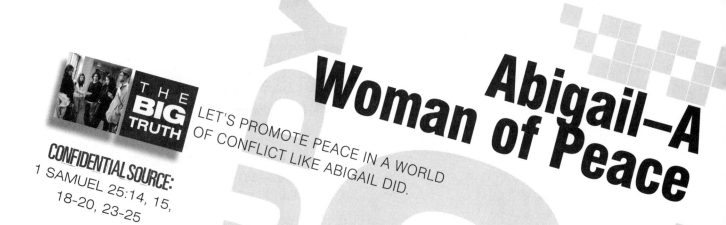

THE BIG TRUTH

LET'S PROMOTE PEACE IN A WORLD OF CONFLICT LIKE ABIGAIL DID.

CONFIDENTIAL SOURCE:
1 SAMUEL 25:14, 15, 18-20, 23-25

High School Battlefields

They used to be dismissed as harmless outlets for student anger. But in recent years, student "hit lists" have been a reason for expulsion from school and even arrest.

On March 30, 2001, a list, labeled "hit list" and containing only the names of twenty students and teachers from Pasco High School in the state of Washington, was found in a girls' restroom at the school. The next school day the author of the list, a sixteen-year-old girl, was expelled.

When a similar list was found scrawled on the restroom wall at Hopkinton High School near Boston in October 2003, the police sought to charge the freshman girl who wrote it with a felony for violating antiterrorism laws.

In January 2005, an eighth-grade girl from Pointe South Middle School near Atlanta was suspended from school and arrested for disorderly conduct for the same offense.

A Magoffin County (Kentucky) teacher found a "kill list" at South Magoffin Elementary School in October 2008 inside a sixth grader's notebook. The list contained the names of twenty-two students. Police charged the girl with twenty-two counts of terroristic threatening and sent her to the Breathitt County Juvenile Detention Center.

This violent trend seems to only be increasing.

QUESTIONS TO CONSIDER:

■ Has a hit list ever been found in a school near you? How would you feel if you were in that school? How would you feel if you were on that list? Why do you think students make such lists? If you found out a friend of yours made such a list, what would you do?

■ Name the last conflict you can remember. Who was it with? What caused the conflict? How was it resolved—who initiated peace? Now name a time when you had to break up a conflict between other people. Describe how you tried to bring peace to the situation.

■ We live in a world nearly boiling with conflict. The Bible tells us about a woman named Abigail who brought peace to a potentially explosive situation. Let's determine how she was able to promote peace when conflict was evident.

INSTANT**STUDY 21** ■ OLD**TESTAMENT**

BIBLE TRUTHS

BIBLE**TRUTH** 1

Abigail was aware of situations that held the potential for conflict. 1 SAMUEL 25:14, 15

■ **List some clues that could give you the impression that a fight is about to break out. What can you do when that happens?**

INSIDE STORY: Abigail was an intelligent and beautiful woman married to Nabal (which means *fool*), an ignorant, mean-tempered man (1 Samuel 25:3). Nabal was shearing sheep when David sent men to ask for food (vv. 4-8). But Nabal rudely refused this request, greatly angering David (vv. 9-13). Fearing the worst because of their master's abrasiveness, one of Nabal's servants told Abigail about the problem (vv. 14, 15).

David's son Solomon may have been thinking about this very incident when he wrote: "The way of a fool seems right to him, but a wise man [or woman!] listens to advice" (Proverbs 12:15). Unlike her husband, Abigail seemed to have a reputation of one who was "quick to listen" and "slow to speak and slow to become angry" (James 1:19). By doing just that, Abigail took the first step toward peace.

BIBLE**TRUTH** 2

Abigail did not hesitate to take action when conflict arose. 1 SAMUEL 25:18, 19

■ **How do you treat someone who is angry with you? Why do you take that approach?**

INSIDE STORY: Abigail immediately took action by preparing a feast for David's men and arranging to have it delivered (1 Samuel 25:18). She did this without consulting Nabal (v. 19).

Years earlier, Jacob was preparing to meet his estranged brother Esau. Jacob took similar preemptive action, sending gifts to the brother who once wanted to kill him (Genesis 32:6, 13-21). Jesus would likewise recommend making peace with someone who is angry (Matthew 5:23-26). Quick, benevolent action can save the day.

BIBLE**TRUTH** 3

Abigail was not afraid of confrontation.

1 SAMUEL 25:20, 23-25

■ **Police officers often say that one of their most dangerous duties is to break up a family conflict. Why might that be true?**

INSIDE STORY: Boldly, Abigail made herself vulnerable by delivering the food to David's vengeance-bent army (1 Samuel 25:20). When she reached David, she got off her donkey and bowed with her face to the ground (v. 23). She humbly accepted all the blame for failing to see David's men arrive. She admitted that her husband was "wicked" and a "fool," just like his name (v. 25).

A peacemaker needs to show such humility, doing everything in his or her power to advance the cause of peace (Romans 12:18). This may include confessing fault to someone with whom he or she is at odds (James 5:16).

CHALLENGE

Write pax vobiscum (paks vo BIS kem) on the board and distribute note cards and pens. Ask students to write that Latin phrase meaning peace be with you on one side of their cards. On the other side have them write the name or initials of someone they need to make peace with. Then ask them to write one way they can help promote peace in their relationship with that person.

David— Confident in God

My Enemy's Enemy Is My Friend

Al-Qaida in Iraq was once confident that anti-American sentiments would be enough to keep Iraqi insurgent groups (those who are rebelling against the Iraqi government) on their side. American forces and the Iraqi government tried to prove that this confidence was unfounded. They did so by trying to persuade what they labeled "reconcilable insurgents" to take a stand against the terrorist network.

As he was resigning his post, U.S. ambassador to Iraq, Zalmay Khalilzad, explained how diplomacy was being used to win the war there. "We have had discussions with those groups," Khalilzad told reporters in Baghdad. "They are continuing to take place, and I think one of the challenges is how to separate more and more groups away from al-Qaida."

Al-Qaida suicide bombers had been responsible for hundreds of deaths in Iraq. But those victims had largely been innocent civilians, not U.S. or Iraqi military personnel. Many tribal leaders and even some insurgents saw that the terrorists were killing the very people they claim to represent. More and more of these insurgents became willing to take a stand against terrorism. The U.S. embassy tried to help that trend to continue and to grow.

"Iraqis are uniting against al-Qaida," Khalilzad said. "Coalition commanders have been able to engage some insurgents to explore ways to collaborate in fighting the terrorists. These insurgents are also in touch with the government seeking reconciliation and cooperation in the fight against the al-Qaida terrorists and joining the government in a reconciliation program." Khalilzad would not

give any details as to which tribal leaders and insurgent groups had been contacted, however. Such publicity would certainly make such leaders terrorist targets.

Afghan-born Khalilzad made these statements in his farewell news conference. He left this post because he was appointed to be the U.S. ambassador to the United Nations. His replacement, Ambassador Ryan Crocker, continued that line of diplomacy.

QUESTIONS TO CONSIDER:

■ Summarize the strategy of trying to turn the loyalty of insurgents and tribal leaders in Iraq away from al-Qaida. What do you think are the strengths of such a plan? What do you think are the weaknesses of it?

■ Should this strategy be successful in the long run, it will certainly shake the confidence terrorists have had in the anti-American groups in Iraq. What was the reason for their confidence? Why might this confidence prove to be unfounded?

■ Tell about a time when you placed your confidence in a person or a plan, but things did not work out as you expected. If you were to live that time over again, what would you have done differently? In what or in whom would you have placed your confidence?

■ Sometimes those people or ideas in which we place our confidence prove to be unreliable. The biblical account of David and Goliath tells that same story. Let's look at it now.

BIBLE TRUTHS

BIBLE**TRUTH** 1

Goliath had confidence in his own abilities.
1 SAMUEL 17:4-7

■ **Whom do you know who is confident because of his or her physical characteristics? How good of a reason is that? Why?**

INSIDE STORY: Goliath had reason to boast. He stood over nine feet tall (v. 4). His armor weighed 125 pounds and the head of his spear was as heavy as a bowling ball (vv. 5-7). For forty days, Goliath challenged the Israelites to choose a champion to battle him (vv. 10, 16). Goliath's confidence was rooted in pride. He knew that he was physically impressive and that he had been trained as a warrior since childhood (v. 33). But pride is a shaky basis for confidence. There are a lot of people in the world, and of them, many probably have equal or superior skills and training to the one boasting. For that reason, the Bible warns, "Pride goes before destruction" (Proverbs 16:18), and "A man's pride brings him low" (Proverbs 29:23). John commented that, "the boasting of what he has and does—comes not from the Father but from the world" (1 John 2:16).

BIBLE**TRUTH** 2

The Israelites had confidence in human reasoning. 1 SAMUEL 17:24, 32, 33

■ **It is said that the common sense of one generation is nonsense to another. What does that mean to you?**

INSIDE STORY: When the Israelite army heard the giant's challenge, they ran (v. 24). Even when the king offered his daughter in marriage and freedom from taxes for the soldier's family, no one dared to face the Philistine (v. 25). King Saul, who was a head taller than any of his men (1 Samuel 9:2), was also afraid to put on his armor and take up the challenge. When David volunteered for duty, Saul dismissed him as "only a boy" (17:33). Their reason for confidence was pragmatism or common sense. The risks seemed to outweigh the rewards.

What they forgot was that they served a God who could overrule common sense. Was it reasonable that the Israelites could escape the well-armed Egyptian army by passing through a body of water on dry land (Exodus 14:15-31)? Was it logical to believe that a whole nation marching through the desert could be fed with food falling from the sky (Exodus 16:4)? Would the odds-makers believe that the fortified walls of Jericho could be destroyed simply by parading around them and blowing a trumpet (Joshua 6:2-5)? As Paul would ask years later, "Has not God made foolish the wisdom of the world?"(1 Corinthians 1:20).

BIBLE**TRUTH** 3

David had confidence in a God who keeps his promises. 1 SAMUEL 17:34-40, 45, 47

■ **Sometimes people see faith and prayer as tools of last resort. Why do you agree or disagree with that opinion?**

INSIDE STORY: Despite Goliath's boasts and Israel's fear, David was confident. He was confident in his God. He explained to Saul how he had defended his father's sheep from both a lion and a bear, so now he would defeat this Philistine who had defied the armies of God (vv. 34-36). David could be confident in himself because he was confident that God would empower him. Just as the Lord had delivered him from the paw of the lion and the paw of the bear, he would deliver him from the hand of this Philistine (v. 37). David did not need the armor of the king (vv. 38, 39); he only needed his familiar sling and five smooth stones (v. 40). In the end, David stood victorious because he was confident God would empower him.

CHALLENGE

Illustrate confidence in an unseen God this way. Put a blindfold on a volunteer. Then have the rest of the students guide that person around the room with verbal directions.

A GODLY FRIEND IS ONE OF LIFE'S TRUEST RICHES.

David and Jonathan—Real Friendship

Friends and Partners

Nelson Gonzalez and Alex Aguila were childhood friends who grew up playing video games together. It seemed like no computer was ever new enough or fast enough, so they were always upgrading their machines to play the latest games. They dreamed of building the ultimate gaming computers.

More than a decade ago Gonzalez worked for a small computer company and Aguila was a medical technician. Neither had any real business experience. Neither had a great deal of money. But they had friendship and their vision of creating and selling high-end computers. One bank after another turned down their applications for loans. The idea of making expensive computers when computer companies were slashing their prices did not seem like a good idea. Also, the name Gonzalez proposed for the company, "Alienware," was just too "X-Files" for lenders to take seriously!

So Aguila and Gonzalez cleaned out their own bank accounts to create their company without any other help. Within ten years, Alienware became a highly-respected company with hundreds of employees and hundreds of millions of dollars in yearly sales.

With towers that resemble alien heads and names like "Area 51" (named for the supposed landing site of a UFO in Roswell, New Mexico), Alienware gained a reputation for manufacturing computers for the serious gamer. Although they have recently offered less expensive models, their top-of-the-line computers sell for nearly $10,000. Their "build it as if it were your own" philosophy of business has earned them a loyal customer base.

[Ten years ago] "I was there and all the walls were black . . . and the phones were sitting there and not ringing. And I'm thinking, 'What did I do?'" said Aguila. "Initially the expectation was [selling] fifty machines a month, maybe a 100," said Gonzalez. But now these two friends have seen their trust in one another pay off and their dreams become reality.

But they insist that success has not changed them or their friendship. "We're . . . nerds and geeks at heart," Gonzalez claims.

QUESTIONS
TO CONSIDER:

■ From the article above, describe the friendship of Nelson Gonzalez and Alex Aguila. What characteristics of a good friendship do you see in their relationship? How did their shared vision for high-quality computers build their friendship? What risks did they take for one another? Would you take such risks for a friend? Why or why not?

■ Who was your best friend five years ago? Is that person still your best friend? Why or why not? What characteristics do you look for in a friend? How do those characteristics make for lasting friendships?

■ True and lasting friendships are built upon solid foundations. The most solid friendships are built upon a shared faith in something greater than the individuals themselves. Let us take a look at three characteristics of friendships built upon a shared faith in God.

BIBLE TRUTHS

BIBLE**TRUTH** 1

Friends are committed to one another.

1 SAMUEL 18:1-4

■ **Imagine two guys who had been friends since childhood. In middle school, one joined the basketball team and the other gained the reputation as a computer geek. What challenges might threaten their friendship? How should they respond to those challenges?**

INSIDE STORY: Jonathan, the son of King Saul, was heir apparent to the throne (1 Samuel 14:1). David was a commoner, the youngest son of a herdsman (1 Samuel 16:11). To make things worse, David had become a rival to the throne. Samuel had anointed David as king, even though Saul was still in power (16:1, 13). After he defeated Goliath, David became so popular that he was seen as a threat to King Saul (1 Samuel 18:6-9). One would expect Jonathan and David to be rivals, even enemies. Yet that was not the case.

Centuries later Jesus would say, "Greater love has no one than this, that he lay down his life for his friends" (John 15:13). In a real sense, Jonathan showed his commitment to David by giving up his royal aspirations for his friend. Jonathan "loved him [David] as himself" (1 Samuel 18:1, 3). He showed his love by giving David his robe and weapons (v. 4). A prince's robe was the mark of his position, and his weapons were the mark of his power. Jonathan was willing to place his friendship to David above both.

BIBLE**TRUTH** 2

Friends warn one another of danger. 1 SAMUEL 19:1-3

■ **What do you think is the hardest thing for a friend to do? Why?**

INSIDE STORY: An old saying proclaims, "Blood is thicker than water." This is another way of saying that family relationships take precedence over any other relationship. Apparently Jonathan disagreed with this saying. King Saul's jealousy of David became so great that he ordered his son to kill David" (1 Samuel 19:1). Instead of obeying his father's

order, Jonathan warned David and gave David information to protect his life (vv. 2, 3).

While family relationships are extremely important, true friends will not let one another come to ruin. This was a time when David needed a friend who "sticks closer than a brother" (Proverbs 18:24). Getting someone through difficult times is a primary purpose of friendship (Proverbs 17:17). Sometimes a true friend will have to tell another what he does not want to hear in order save him from danger (Proverbs 27:6).

BIBLE**TRUTH** 3

Friends should include God in their relationship.

1 SAMUEL 20:16, 17, 42

■ **Do you think there is a difference between Christian friends and non-Christian friends? What might some differences be?**

INSIDE STORY: David's son, Solomon, would later define friends as those who work together to make a job easier and help one another when they are injured, attacked, or in need (Ecclesiastes 4:9-12a). Solomon ended his definition by saying: "A cord of three strands is not quickly broken" (v. 12b). While a good friendship weaves two lives together, a "three strand" friendship knits God into the fabric of the relationship. David and Jonathan promised "friendship with each other in the name of the LORD" (1 Samuel 20:42). In other words, they invited God to examine their friendship and to keep it strong and true. Jonathan promised to submit to God's will in his treatment of David, even if it meant asking God's judgment on his own father (1 Samuel 20:16).

Friends are often chosen because of shared interests or similar backgrounds. Yet the body of Christ contains people of "every tribe and language and people and nation" (Revelation 5:9). When God is in the center of a friendship, social, ethnic, and racial divisions can be overcome.

CHALLENGE

Ask students to create a logo that would symbolize their relationships with their best friends.

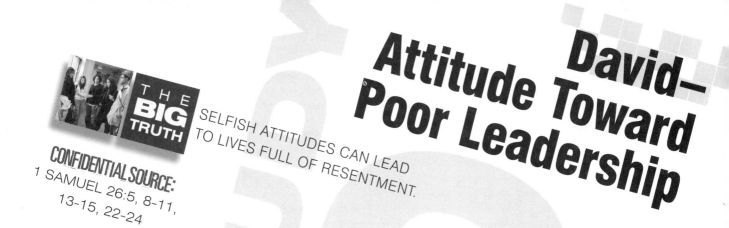

David—Attitude Toward Poor Leadership

Don't Call!

Sometimes it's hard to remember to stop and look at both sides of an issue. So let's start now:

On one hand you have a family sitting at home in the evening. The phone rings right as they begin to eat dinner. There's the dilemma: should they answer it? It could be an emergency, they think. So Dad picks up the phone. After a pause, he rolls his eyes and sighs. "It's a telemarketer," he hisses to his family.

Yes, the "dreaded" telemarketers have called. But now millions of Americans can add their phone numbers to a national government do-not-call list. When on the list, telemarketers must not call those numbers or face a fine of up to $11,000. One exception is that non-profit organizations are still able to call people on the list. Another exception is that companies who've had previous business relationships with customers are still able to contact those homes.

Although many of us may understand the feeling of dread every time the phone rings, we said there was another side to this issue, right? Right.

On the other hand, there are the people who make a living by making those phone calls. Tina Nagel has been a telemarketer for ten years and doesn't understand why people get annoyed with sales calls. "What I'm doing is a valuable service," she said. "I'm telling people what their options are in life."

The telemarketing industry estimates that there are about 450,000 people who make calls for a living. That's just the number of employees in specific businesses that focus on phone soliciting—it doesn't include other businesses that have their own telemarketers on staff. If these callers don't have anyone to call, what will happen to their jobs?

The telemarketing industry has struggled since the do-not-call list has taken effect. Companies must find a way to make sure the billions of dollars made in phone sales calls won't diminish with these restrictions.

QUESTIONS TO CONSIDER:

■ Do you think the bad attitudes of people who felt harassed by telemarketers played a role in the government approving the do-not-call list? Explain. If you were a telemarketer who was greatly affected by the list, would you have a bad attitude toward the government's decision?

■ With which group of people do you most easily identify—the people bothered by sales calls or the people who make these calls for a living? Can you understand the other point of view?

■ Name a time in your life when a situation caused you to have a bad attitude. How did that attitude affect the other areas of your life? What did you do to get beyond that attitude?

■ Today we're going to study the story of Saul and David. We'll see that David demonstrated three ways to keep a good attitude even when he was treated unjustly.

BIBLE TRUTHS

BIBLETRUTH 1

Refuse to compromise your values. 1 SAMUEL 26:9, 11

■ **The comic character, The Incredible Hulk, appears when Bruce Banner gets angry. How do you change when you get angry?**

INSIDE STORY: The victory of David over Goliath (1 Samuel 17) made David a celebrity (18:6, 7) and caused King Saul to view David as a threat to his throne (18:8, 9). Saul attempted to take David's life several times: by sending him on a suicide mission (18:17); by recruiting his daughter and son to betray David (18:20, 21; 19:1, 2); by trying to skewer David with a spear while David was playing the harp (19:9, 10); by slaughtering eighty-five priests who sided with David (22:17, 18); and by recruiting a hit squad of 3,000 soldiers to kill him (24:1, 2; 26:1, 2).

When hiding in the valley of Ziph, David's scouts warned David that Saul had arrived (26:3, 4). David and his nephew Abishai discovered Saul sleeping in the middle of his camp surrounded by a sleeping army (26:5). Abishai asked David for permission to kill Saul (v. 8). David would have none of it. His purpose—even after all the injustice done to him—was to affirm allegiance to the king (vv. 9, 11).

BIBLETRUTH 2

Trust God to act justly. 1 SAMUEL 26:10

■ **Agree or disagree: Believing in a just God changes the way I handle anger.**

INSIDE STORY: Pressed between the marauding Philistines and a demented king with murder on his mind, David held to his convictions in an amazing show of integrity and confidence in God. If God wanted to make David king, he would do it in his time, not David's (v. 10). David's faith proved to be well founded. Later in Saul's reign, his army was trapped on Mount Gilboa. Saul was critically wounded in battle and died by his own sword (1 Samuel 31:1-6). David did not have to exact

vengeance. He trusted that the words of Moses years earlier were true: "It is mine to avenge; I will repay. In due time their foot will slip; their day of disaster is near and their doom rushes upon them" (Deuteronomy 32:35).

BIBLETRUTH 3

Let godly character be your only defense. 1 SAMUEL 26:22, 23

■ **When do you feel you need to strike back at someone? How might it affect your reputation were you to do so?**

INSIDE STORY: David took Saul's spear and water jug to prove that he could have just as easily taken the king's life (1 Samuel 26:12). Then he confronted Saul from a safe distance (vv. 13-17). Saul quickly apologized (v. 21). David did not trust this instant change of heart—he had heard it all before (1 Samuel 24:16-21). David returned Saul's spear and simply stated that a man is rewarded by righteousness and faithfulness to God. He repeated again that he would not harm the Lord's anointed (26:22-24). Saul's profession did not match his actions. David knew that. Saul continued to be a threat to David. Saul counted on his own strength to secure his throne. In contrast, David remained safe because of his reputation for righteousness. Perhaps David's son recalled this incident years later when he would write, "The memory of the righteous will be a blessing, but the name of the wicked will rot" (Proverbs 10:7).

CHALLENGE

Ask your students to rate their attitudes toward their enemies on a scale of one to ten. Ask a few volunteers to explain their ratings and to tell one thing that if corrected would raise their scores.

INSTANT**STUDY 24** ... CONTINUED

54

Solomon— Wisdom From Above

KNOWLEDGE FILLS THE HEAD;
WISDOM CHANGES THE HEART.

Intelligent Loner

The members of Westfield High School's science club were known as intelligent, techno-geeks. One of these students, Chris Davids, described a classmate by saying, "He seemed like a really bright guy." The intelligent student to whom Davids referred was Seung-Hui Cho, a Virginia Tech student who murdered thirty-two people and wounded twenty-five others in a shooting on that campus on April 16, 2007.

No one doubted Cho's intelligence. He took advanced classes in high school. Virginia Tech only accepts the academically capable—their average student scores 1200 on the SAT. Even a physician who proclaimed Cho a danger to himself in 2005 did not question Cho's intellect, writing: "His insight and judgment are sound."

But what roadblocks kept Cho from being a productive member of society? What obstacles led him to commit the worst mass shooting in US history? The situation is complex and does not hold easy answers. But one factor in Cho's profile keeps emerging. He showed an inability to interact with others.

People from various parts of the gunman's life echoed the same observations. "I thought he was just really shy," recalled Westfield High science club member, Davids.

"When I told his mother that he was a good boy, quiet but well behaved, she said she would rather have him respond to her when talked to than be good and meek," said Kim Yang-Soon, Mr. Cho's eighty-four-year-old great-aunt.

Luice Woo, a senior at Virginia Tech who was in Cho's high school calculus class, said: "I thought he was a 'F-O-B' (fresh off the boat) . . . a recent immigrant who didn't know English because he was so quiet."

"It was almost as if he was backed into a corner whenever you tried to talk to him," said Patrick Song, another Virginia Tech classmate of Cho's. "You took it as like he just wants to be left alone."

Though many will attempt to explain the behavior of Seung-Hui Cho, he will surely remain a horrible contradiction. Cho was an intelligent student who maintained good grades at a prestigious university yet remained a troubled loner who hid from the world behind his dark glasses.

QUESTIONS
TO CONSIDER:

■ Does it surprise you that a mass-murderer could be described as intelligent and having good judgment? Why or why not?

■ What are some differences between being "book smart" and being "street smart"? Can someone be intelligent without being wise? Describe some differences between the two.

■ If the Virginia Tech tragedy illustrates nothing else, it shows that wisdom is not the same as intelligence. The Bible describes King Solomon and the attributes of godly wisdom. Let's see what they are.

55

BIBLE TRUTHS

BIBLE**TRUTH** 1

A wise person is grateful for what he has.
1 KINGS 3:5, 6

■ **Tell about a time when you wanted something so badly that you did something stupid.**

INSIDE STORY: Solomon needed help to measure up to the high standard set by his father David. While worshiping at the altar of Moses at Gibeon (1 Chronicles 21:29), Solomon received a surprising "blank check" from God" (1 Kings 3:5). Before asking for anything, Solomon thanked the Lord for the gifts he already possessed—the throne of his father David (v. 6). This itself was an act of grace, because the true heir to the throne would have been David's eldest son. Recognizing that whatever one has is a gift from God is a characteristic of wisdom.

Paul would echo Solomon's wisdom years later when he told Timothy, "Godliness with contentment is great gain" (1 Timothy 6:6). Before seeking more and more, truly wise people take a blessings inventory. As Paul would say, Solomon recognized that "We brought nothing into the world, and we can take nothing out of it. But if we have food and clothing, we will be content with that" (1 Timothy 6:7, 8).

BIBLE**TRUTH** 2

A wise person recognizes his dependence upon God. 1 KINGS 3:7-9

■ **What do we mean when we call someone a *self-made man*? Is there really such a thing? Explain.**

INSIDE STORY: Solomon freely admitted that he did not know how to carry out his duties as king (v. 7). Therefore he asked for the thing he needed most: a discerning heart to distinguish between right and wrong so he could wisely govern the people. Centuries later, the church in the city of Corinth would lack wisdom. Paul echoed the wisdom of Solomon in saying, "Now it is required that those who have been given a trust must prove faithful" (1 Corinthians 4:2).

Christians, like Solomon, have been given tremendous responsibilities in God's kingdom. We are wise when we ask God's help in fulfilling those duties. Here we see the difference between being wise and being a know-it-all. One who is truly wise is quick to admit that he or she does not have complete knowledge. Godly wisdom seeks God's aid in the task of serving him.

BIBLE**TRUTH** 3

A wise person does not forget that God is the source of his success. 1 KINGS 3:10-15; 11:4-6

■ **What do we mean when we say, "Don't bite the hand that feeds you?" Give an example of someone behaving that way.**

INSIDE STORY: God was pleased that Solomon had asked for wisdom, rather than making selfish requests (3:10, 11). Therefore God promised to give him a wise and discerning heart. God would also give Solomon what he had not requested—riches and honor. When the Queen of Sheba visited Solomon, for instance, she saw firsthand his unsurpassed wisdom, wealth, and splendor (10:1-29). Solomon would have no equal among earth's kings. As long as he kept God's commands, he would also be given a long life (3:14).

But on this point we see a flaw in Solomon's wisdom. Though God gave Solomon unparalleled success, the king lost sight of God in his later years. "As Solomon grew old . . . his heart was not fully devoted to the LORD his God . . . he did not follow the LORD completely" (11:4-6). Success tempted Solomon to forget the source of his blessings.

CHALLENGE Write these questions on the board: Are you grateful for what you have? Are you depending on God? Do you remember that God is the one who gives you success? Close with students silently meditating on one or more of these questions.

THE BIG TRUTH

WE DO NOT HAVE THE AUTHORITY TO MAKE OUR OWN RULES.

Jeroboam— Making It Up as He Went Along

Incarcerated American Princess

She called her sentence "cruel and unwarranted." Her attorney claimed, "She's been selectively targeted because she is who she is." But despite the spirited protests, twenty-six-year-old hotel heiress and infamous partier Paris Hilton was sent to jail.

The storyline in the Paris Hilton soap opera began months before her incarceration. The socialite was first arrested in Hollywood at that time for driving under the influence of alcohol. Four months later, Hilton pleaded "no contest" to reckless driving. The judge sentenced her to three years of probation and ordered her to go to an alcohol education program. Yet just days later, police pulled Hilton over for driving with a suspended license. Less than a month later, she was stopped still another time for speeding and driving without headlights.

When a judge asked her why she continued to drive even though she had signed a document acknowledging that she knew that she was not supposed to drive, Hilton answered, "I just sign what people tell me to sign." When asked why she did not believe she needed to know what the document said, she testified, "I have people who do that for me."

Nevertheless, Hilton could not send "her people" to serve jail time for her. She was scheduled to report to a county jail in suburban L.A. to serve forty-five days for violating the terms of her probation in the alcohol-related reckless driving case. In jail, Hilton was supposed to live in a 12-by-8-foot cell with tight limitations.

"She will have an hour outside every day, where she can watch TV, but she won't have any cell phones or any of the luxuries that many people have become accustomed to," said sheriff's department spokesman Steve Whitmore at that time. Criminal defense attorney Dana Cole described the heiress's sentence in much more dramatic terms. "Forty-five days in L.A. County jail is really rough. Conditions are miserable—people take showers under cold dripping water; the food is completely inedible."

Many expressed doubt that a short jail term would change Hilton's behavior. West Hollywood psychologist Jeremy Ritzlin, remarked, "It's going to make her very unhappy because she's not used to this. She couldn't buy her way out of it. But one forty-five-day trip to jail is not going to change her behavior."

Hilton was released after only serving a fraction of her sentence due to unnamed medical reasons. She was subject to house arrest for the remainder of her sentence.

QUESTIONS TO CONSIDER:

■ What parts of Paris Hilton's behavior lead you to believe that she sees herself as being above the law? Describe someone else you know who acts as if he or she is above the law. (No names are necessary; just describe the person's behavior.)

■ Have you ever wanted to have absolutely no rules for your life? Tell about a time when you were tempted to act as if rules didn't apply to you.

■ Everyone struggles with obeying authority, whether he or she is a famous heiress or just an ordinary person. Let's look at how an Old Testament king acted as if no one could tell him what to do—even God! We'll see three ways that he ignored God's authority.

BIBLE TRUTHS

BIBLE**TRUTH** 1

Jeroboam replaced God's rules with his own.
1 KINGS 12:31-33

■ **Tell about a time when you disobeyed instructions and did something your own way. How did that work out for you?**

INSIDE STORY: After Jeroboam led the ten northern tribes in a successful rebellion against King Rehoboam of Judah, he realized he had a problem. The people of his northern kingdom would have to return to Jerusalem to worship, increasing the possibility of losing the political as well as the religious allegiance of his people (12:26, 27). Jeroboam solved his problem by building not one, but *two* temples in the north, one at Dan and the other at Bethel. He placed a golden calf at each temple and created a priesthood to serve at these and other worship sites (vv. 28-31). He went so far as to create religious festivals similar to those celebrated in Jerusalem (vv. 32, 33). The independence and arrogance of Jeroboam are remarkable. He replaced God's ordained Levitical priesthood (Numbers 3:1-13) with one of his own. He replaced the temple designed by God (1 Kings 5:5) with two of his own. Jeroboam even declared a religious holiday on "a month of his own choosing" (12:33).

BIBLE**TRUTH** 2

Jeroboam became angry when his sin was exposed. 1 KINGS 13:1-6

■ **Sometimes people who do not believe in God are angry when someone says that they are violating God's will. Why do you think that happens?**

INSIDE STORY: An unnamed man of God was sent from Judah to Bethel to rebuke King Jeroboam. He cried out, promising that a future king of Judah would sacrifice the rebel priests on that very spot and burn their bones. (This was later fulfilled in 2 Kings 23:15-20.) As proof, the altar would be split apart by God (v. 3). Outraged by this rebuke, King Jeroboam stretched out his hand and said, "Seize him!" Instantly the royal hand became shriveled and paralyzed. Simultaneously the altar was split apart, just as the man of God predicted (vv. 4, 5). These two miracles were enough to cause the king to cry out for healing. That request was granted (v. 6).

Jeroboam's reaction was typical of one who accepted the "no one can tell me what to do" myth. Instead of taking correction, Jeroboam became angry and tried to attack those who pointed out his wrongdoing.

BIBLE**TRUTH** 3

Jeroboam refused to change his ways after being corrected. 1 KINGS 13:33, 34

■ **Read the graphic words of Proverbs 26:11. Try to state this proverb in other words.**

INSIDE STORY: Jeroboam heard the prophecy and saw it fulfilled. Soon thereafter, he learned of the fate of the unnamed prophet. Even that man was judged for his disobedience, a clear message to Jeroboam that God will not tolerate the flaunting of his commands by anyone (1 Kings 13:11-26). But what was Jeroboam's response? He continued to live as he had (v. 33). A third mark of someone who refuses to obey God's rules is this type of insolence. Even though the consequences were clear, Jeroboam refused to change his ways. This hardness of heart is described throughout the pages of Scripture. Paul wrote that people who reject God will literally lose their minds (Romans 1:28). Those afflicted with HIV continue the same dangerous behavior that exposed them to the disease. Those whose lives are shattered by alcoholism still seek another drink. This king of Israel continued to create his own illegitimate priesthood that led to his downfall (1 Kings 13:34).

CHALLENGE Have your students define the terms independence, indignation, and insolence and consider how those attitudes of Jeroboam can appear in their own lives.

INSTANT**STUDY** 26 ... CONTINUED

58

Elijah— Courage to Stand

Laci's Law

On March 25, 2004, President George W. Bush signed a bill into law called the Unborn Victims of Violence Act. The act is the result of cases such as the Laci Peterson murder in December 2002, where her unborn son Connor was also killed. The bill states that the unborn child has rights, and a person who kills a pregnant woman can be charged with two crimes in such cases.

Before the law was signed, twenty-nine states already considered unborn children as victims if they are killed. In California, where Laci and Connor Peterson were murdered, Scott Peterson was charged with two murders. But the Unborn Victims of Violence Act (also called by some the "Laci and Connor Act") brought about a national standard of recognizing the rights of unborn children. After the bill was a law, it allowed for criminal charges to be filed on behalf of a fetus that is injured or killed "at any stage of development" during an attack on federal property. (This includes any of sixty-eight different crimes, such as acts of terrorism, attacks that happen on federal property or military bases, or drug-related shootings.)

Even before the law was drafted, many people supported the idea of protecting unborn children's rights. In a Newsweek poll taken in May 2003, 84 percent of people said they agree that if a mother and fetus die, the criminal should be charged "for two murders instead of one."

But the bill caused lots of controversy. Many people who are pro-abortion believe that giving rights to an unborn child will eventually lead to overturning Roe vs. Wade, which made abortion legal back in 1973. However, the bill is specifically worded to eliminate abortion and other acts a mother commits on herself from being included in this law. So this act alone would not overturn the legality of abortion.

QUESTIONS TO CONSIDER:

■ Why do you think the Unborn Victims of Violence Act caused such controversy? What are the arguments for and against the bill? What could be the long-term effects of this bill? Where do you stand on such arguments? What would you have done if you were in President Bush's position? Defend your answers.

■ Have you ever taken a stand on a controversial issue? Describe what happened. How does it make you feel to think about taking a stand when you know lots of people will disagree with you? (Scared, intimidated, etc.) Have your feelings ever prevented you from taking a stand when you had the opportunity to speak out? Describe the situation.

■ The prophet Elijah took a courageous stand during a very challenging time. Let's read in 1 Kings to discover the characteristics he had that helped him take such a stand.

INSTANT**STUDY 27** ■ OLD**TESTAMENT**

BIBLE TRUTHS

between the hundreds of prophets of Baal and himself, the lone prophet of God. The false prophets were to call on Baal to send fire from Heaven to burn their sacrificial bull. Elijah would call upon the God of Israel to send fire to burn Elijah's sacrificial bull. "The god who answers by fire—he is God," said Elijah (v. 24).

BIBLE**TRUTH** 1

Elijah could clearly tell right from wrong.
1 KINGS 18:18

■ **When have you had trouble arguing against an idea that you knew was wrong? Why do you think that happened?**

INSIDE STORY: During his twenty-two-year reign, Ahab did great evil. He built a temple to the false god Baal and sacrificed on its altar. He set up places of honor to the false goddess Asherah and promoted idolatry and thus led Israel into sin (1 Kings 16:33). God punished that disobedience with a drought that devastated the nation (1 Kings 17:1). Ahab went on the offensive when he saw Elijah, blaming the problems of Israel on the prophet (18:17)! Ignoring such a ludicrous charge, Elijah put the blame where it belonged (v. 18).

The apostle Paul wrote, "Indeed I would not have known what sin was except through the law (Romans 7:7). Elijah knew right from wrong because he knew God's Word. In the same way Ahab blamed Elijah for Israel's trouble, people today try to blame believers for the fruit of their own sins. We must not be fooled by this blame game. We must, like Elijah, have moral clarity from studying the Scriptures so we can confront sin.

BIBLE**TRUTH** 2

Elijah challenged his countrymen to do right.
1 KINGS 18:20-24

■ **Are you more likely to affect the behavior of unbelievers, or are they more likely to affect your behavior? Explain.**

INSIDE STORY: Elijah was ready and willing to challenge the crowds to turn their hearts to the Lord. "How long will you waver between two opinions? If the LORD is God, follow him; but if Baal is God, follow him" (1 Kings 18:21). When his first challenge was met with silence (v. 21b), Elijah proposed a way to clearly test God's superiority over the values of the culture. Elijah hosted a "grudge match"

BIBLE **TRUTH** 3

Elijah was confident that God's power would overcome evil. 1 KINGS 18:36-38

■ **When have you doubted that God was with you in a particular situation?**

INSIDE STORY: Though the foolish prophets of Baal danced and prayed, begged and pleaded, and even cut themselves, there was no one to answer. Baal was a myth. But God is real and Elijah trusted him completely. He trusted God so much that he changed the rules of the contest to make God's response even more remarkable! He had the moderators of the contest douse the sacrifice with water (vv. 30-35). Elijah stepped forward and prayed a simple two-sentence prayer. As the words left his lips, he and the crowds saw the Lord's fire fall from the sky to nearly vaporize the sacrifice, wood, stones, soil, and water! God is real and fully worthy of our trust and confidence. Christians today may be easily discouraged when they see opposition in high places. But like Elijah, we must confidently proclaim that God's plans will triumph regardless of temporal circumstance.

CHALLENGE

Hand a single paper safety match to each student. Ask them to write "1 Kings 18:21" on the stem of the match. Read that verse together and have students keep that single match with them as a reminder to stand confidently for God and allow the Holy Spirit's fire to work through them.

Overcoming Loneliness: Elijah—

THE BIG TRUTH

GOD PROVIDES US THE MEANS TO CONQUER LONELINESS.

CONFIDENTIAL SOURCE:
1 KINGS 19:1-9, 15-18

The Rumors of My Death

Have you ever felt that no one even knows that you are alive? Eighty-one-year-old Myron Manders of Cleveland, Ohio, understands that feeling well. He had to spend weeks trying to prove to the United States government that he was still around!

Manders was released from University Hospital of Cleveland where he had been treated for pneumonia. Manders and his wife, Eunice, were leaving the hospital when they heard the bad news. Social worker, Lynne Seese told the couple that their insurance company refused to pay the hospital bill because their records showed that Mr. Manders had died about a month earlier!

Seese immediately called the insurance company and Social Security saying, "The patient was clearly alive. I'll say that with no hesitation." But her observation did not satisfy the government. Manders had to go to the local Social Security office where he reported, "Here I am alive, and you have me down as dead."

Yet problems continued. The bank called Mr. and Mrs. Manders weeks later, telling them that Manders' Medicare benefits were cancelled and that payment had been stopped on his last three Social Security checks. A few days later, the Department of Veterans Affairs expressed their condolences to Mrs. Manders and informed her by letter, "You are entitled to monthly widow's benefits," and told her how much she would receive.

Eunice remembered that at first she reacted angrily to the news of her husband's supposed death but began to see some humor in it. "*I* never laughed about it," Myron Manders countered.

Finally, five months after the ordeal began, the problem seemed to have neared resolution. Social Security's Cleveland office spokesman, William Jarrett, apologized for the mistake, which he attributed to an erroneous report of Myron's death from either a hospital, a funeral home, or another third party.

After his "death" was no longer an issue, Mr. Manders was free to resume his life. He considered returning to his insurance agency from which he is semi-retired. Ironically, the business is located on *Chagrin* Boulevard in Cleveland.

QUESTIONS TO CONSIDER:

■ Describe some of the feelings of chagrin (distress) that Mr. Manders probably experienced over the few months he was considered to be dead. How do you think that the support from his wife made the situation a little better for him?

■ We have all felt isolated, alone, and helpless at one time or another. Describe a time when you had such feelings. What are some other reasons why teens might feel that no one knows or cares that they exist? What other problems might those feelings cause?

■ We all feel lonely at times. It's how we deal with that loneliness that makes a big difference. Today let's look at how a biblical prophet felt and how he addressed his feelings of isolation and abandonment.

BIBLE TRUTHS

BIBLE**TRUTH** 1

A feeling of loneliness often occurs after a tremendous, positive experience. 1 KINGS 19:1, 2

■ **Have you ever felt alone in a crowd? Describe such a situation.**

INSIDE STORY: Elijah had an impressive string of successes. His prayer brought a three-year drought (1 Kings 17:1-6; James 5:17). He exposed Queen Jezebel's false prophets as frauds (1 Kings 18:16-39). But his success heightened the opposition from the Queen (19:1, 2) and caused Elijah to become fearful and depressed.

A deep valley often follows a mountain top experience in Scripture. Moses experienced God giving the law on Sinai, only to feel abandoned and betrayed when his own brother created a graven image to worship (Exodus 32:15-19). Jesus' true nature was seen in his transfiguration (Matthew 17:1-4). But then Jesus had to scold his disciples for being an "unbelieving and perverse generation" (vv. 14-17). We can expect that even the most positive experiences can be followed by an emotional letdown resulting in stress, depression, and loneliness.

BIBLE**TRUTH** 2

A feeling of loneliness often causes us to neglect our basic, physical needs. 1 KINGS 19:3-9

■ **In the film *The Matrix* (1999) the Oracle responds to Neo's feelings of loneliness and depression by offering him a cookie. Does such a solution ever help? Explain.**

INSIDE STORY: Elijah fled the country out of fear, probably not considering eating and sleeping to be his first priority. At the end of his trek into the Judean desert, Elijah collapsed and literally felt like dying (1 Kings 19:3-4). God put Elijah back on a regular schedule of eating and sleeping (vv. 5-7). After God's angel intervened, Elijah was able to resume a very taxing schedule (vv. 8, 9).

A similar thing happened to Jesus' disciples. Jesus sent them out on a successful preaching tour (Mark 6:7-13). The

excited apostles came back from this high to hit a new low when they learned that John the Baptist had been executed (vv. 14-29). Jesus responded by ordering them away from the crowds to get some rest (vv. 30-32). Loneliness and depression will often disrupt sleeping and eating patterns. Then, not getting enough rest and sleep only deepens the dark mood.

BIBLE**TRUTH** 3

A feeling of loneliness often causes us to separate ourselves from the people who can assist us. 1 KINGS 19:15-18

■ **Agree or disagree: The best way to have a friend is to be one. Defend your answer.**

INSIDE STORY: When God asked Elijah to explain why he was running, Elijah launched into a pitiful tirade. "*I* have been very zealous . . . *I* am the only one left . . . they are trying to kill *me*" (1 Kings 19:10). Elijah's loneliness was an "I" problem. The prophet felt sorry for himself. God showed the prophet that he had friends who shared his zeal. Elijah was to anoint two kings who would battle with Ahab as well as another prophet who would assist and then succeed him. God even told Elijah that there were 7,000 others still on his side (1 Kings 19:15-18).

When Jewish Christians were feeling like they were all alone, they were counseled to meet together for mutual encouragement (Hebrews 10:23-25). Just as God told Elijah that plenty of people were still on his side, the writer of Hebrews lists a "cloud of witnesses" from history that will always be on the side of God's servants (Hebrews 11:4–12:1). Periods of loneliness are unavoidable. Choosing to be a loner is another matter.

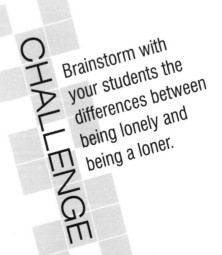

CHALLENGE

Brainstorm with your students the differences between being lonely and being a loner.

Esther—Power Has a Price

Tween Power

They don't drive yet. They don't even have jobs. Most of the money they spend comes from their parents. But students between the ages of nine and twelve (called by many "tweens" since they are between childhood and the teen years) are some of the most powerful consumers in the country today. And companies are fighting for their loyalty. Stop by your local mall and you'll quickly see the evidence.

"Statistics document the rising trend in 'tween' power—spending patterns of those who are not quite teenagers, but who wield a good deal of influence over spending and purchase choices," said Carol Kaufman-Scarborough, a professor of marketing at Rutgers University-Camden campus. "There are stores who cater specifically to this group, with clothing and makeup parties just for them." Thus we see Abercrombie & Fitch with its subsidiary, abercrombie, for this age group. Likewise, The Limited developed a younger oriented store, Limited Too, that did so well that about six years ago, it became an independent corporation.

But it's not just spending on clothing and items for their own usage—now marketers are documenting the powerful influence tweens have on large purchases made for the entire family. "Today around one in four kids are advising their parents about purchasing a DVR and which cell phone plan is best. We've seen this trend increasing in the past year. Now, marketers must learn to appeal to the growing sense of individualism and resurgence of influence among teens and tweens to harness this power," said Cary Silvers, vice president of GfK NOP Consumer Trends, a market research company.

A Canadian study is seeing the same trend up north. "Parents will make the final decision, but they'll take advice from their kids when it comes to buying a computer, a DVD player, a car, a family vacation, and so on," said Sally Tindal, director of publicity and media relations for Corus Entertainment.

Now marketing efforts are shifting their focus. "Advertisers are bypassing the gatekeeper (parents). Young people are potential adult users of brands, so advertisers are instilling brand loyalty at a younger age," said Cathy Wing, director of community programming for Canada's Media Awareness Network.

Peter Rose of the U.S. marketing consulting firm Yankelovich, Inc., agrees that companies not only need to get parents' attention but must also appeal to the tweens in the family as well. He offers this advice to companies: "Provide kids with the information they need so that they can take it to mom and dad for team decision-making. . . . Where kids are passionate, let them be your brand ambassadors and spread the word for you."

QUESTIONS TO CONSIDER:

■ Did you know that tweens were such a powerful buying force? What things did you spend money on when you were that age? What influence did you have at that time over your parents' spending? What influence do you have now over family purchases?

■ This article described tweens as having power. Why do people desire power? What kind of power would you like to have and why?

■ There are many kinds of power and just as many ways to use it. Today we'll read in the Bible about Queen Esther and discover what we can learn from her story about gaining and using power.

BIBLE TRUTHS

BIBLE **TRUTH** 1

God directed circumstances to bring Esther to power. ESTHER 2:17

■ **Tell about a time when things worked out better than you could have imagined.**

INSIDE STORY: At the time when the Jews were scattered among nations and ruled by King Xerxes of Persia, Xerxes invited his chief nobles and officials to a six-month extravaganza to show off his wealth and power (1:3-4). During this boisterous affair, Xerxes wanted to display his beautiful queen to a room filled with drunken men. Queen Vashti refused—an act that cost her the throne (1:12-19). When Xerxes was ready to select a new queen, he chose a Jewish orphan, Hadassah (Esther). Her cousin Mordecai, a minor official at the palace, advised her to keep her heritage a secret. Despite the fact that the Jews were the subjects of a pagan king, God placed a Jew on the throne of the Empire in a quick and bloodless coup (2:17)!

BIBLE**TRUTH** 2

God allowed circumstances to occur that required Esther to use her power. ESTHER 3:13, 14

■ **Tell about a time when you were in the right place at the right time.**

INSIDE STORY: Nearly the same time that God placed Esther in power, Xerxes made Haman the Agagite prime minister of the Empire (3:1). He was cruel and capricious and was an Amalekite, one of the perennial enemies of the Jews (Exodus 17:16). Mordecai defied a royal decree and would not bow to Haman (Esther 3:2-4). Enraged, Haman plotted to have all Jews in Xerxes' territories exterminated (vv. 13, 14). God did not give Esther power simply for her enjoyment. He anticipated the enemy's attack and already had his soldier in position!

BIBLE**TRUTH** 3

God expected Esther to assume risks when using her power. ESTHER 4:13-16

■ **Tell about a time when you took a risk to do the right thing.**

INSIDE STORY: Mordecai begged Esther to go before the king and plead the cause of the Jews even though approaching the king's throne without invitation was against the law and could mean death (4:11). Mordecai argued that God expected her to take that risk because he had given her a royal position (4:14). After a three-day fast Esther agreed and took that risk (4:16).

BIBLE**TRUTH** 4

God blessed Esther's use of power by granting victory. ESTHER 8:3, 4

■ **Sometimes sports stars publicly thank God for allowing them to win. What do you think of that practice?**

INSIDE STORY: Xerxes received Esther gladly, and she requested only that he come to a banquet with Haman (5:1-4). Esther then baited Xerxes with a second dinner, at which time she revealed Haman's genocidal scheme (7:1-4). Haman was hung from the gallows he had built for Mordecai, and Mordicai was awarded Haman's honors (7:5-9). Xerxes reversed his irreversible decree by allowing the Jews to arm themselves (8:11). As a result, the Jews won an overwhelming victory over their enemies (9:1-17).

CHALLENGE Write these words on the board: service, prayer, godly example, moral voice. Discuss how your students have these sources of power. Have them give examples of how to use each one.

INSTANT **STUDY** 29 ... CONTINUED

64

Job–Satan and Suffering

Tragedy in the Tube

On July 7, 2005, four bombs were detonated in the transportation systems of London. A total of fifty-six people were killed and around 700 were injured. The suicide bomber who got on bus No. 30 that day and took twelve lives plus his own was eighteen-year-old Hasib Hussain. In the weeks that followed, details of Hasib's life have been pieced together as authorities try to determine why this young man was involved in such a tragedy. "Why?" is a question his family, especially his parents, have been asking themselves through their tears.

Differing accounts describe Hasib's last few years. Neighbors to the Hussain family say that two years ago Hasib "went a bit wild," drinking and using bad language. He then left school without needed academic qualifications. Friends say that Hasib used to escape by playing soccer, but two years ago he seemed to disappear into another world. During that time, people say that Hasib spent some time in his native country of Pakistan. Some believe it is there that Hasib picked up radical Muslim ideas. A man who said he was Hasib's cousin explained, "I thought he had been brainwashed. I do not know who by."

Another friend said Hasib grew a beard and began to wear traditional Muslim clothes in the last two years. That same friend last saw Hasib about eight weeks before the bombing with his beard shaved off. When the friend asked why, Hasib gave him a vague answer. "He said it was a long story and that he did not like one mosque saying one thing and another mosque saying that was the wrong way. When he heard so many arguments he thought 'Forget it. I will go my own way,'" said Hasib's friend. Those who've studied al-Qaeda say that shaving a beard may indicate someone's intention to join in terrorist activities.

But Hasib's parents paint a different picture. His parents describe him as a young man who was improving academically and preparing to go to the University of Leeds. He also had an upcoming arranged marriage with a girl from Pakistan. They said Hasib didn't display any radical Islamic behavior. Another close family member said, "There was absolutely no sign of him becoming devoutly religious. He wore jeans and trainers, just like me." A man who said he was Hasib's uncle gave this perspective: "He was a nice lad. He was really nice. He wasn't the type of guy to do it. . . . He wouldn't do it. I wish in my heart he was still alive."

Hasib's father clings to the hope that Hasib truly was not the bomber on bus No. 30. His father described Hasib as gentle. "If a fly came into the house, he would catch it and take it outside. If there was a caterpillar in the garden, he would make sure it was safe. I can only imagine that he was brainwashed into doing this. I keep thinking that this must be some kind of mistake. That it must have been someone else who did this. If I am wrong, [he] will face his reward in the next life."

QUESTIONS TO CONSIDER:

■ We read mixed accounts of Hasib's life. But one thing is the same—Hasib's parents find it extremely hard to understand how their son could participate in such disaster. Name a difficult situation in life that you find hard to understand.

■ Sometimes there are no easy answers. The same happens in our lives when we experience suffering. We may wonder why bad things happen. We're going to study about a man named Job—a man who suffered greatly and yet didn't understand why.

65

BIBLE TRUTHS

BIBLE**TRUTH** 1

Suffering can be an act of aggression by Satan.
JOB 1:6-11

■ **Tell about a time when a bad thing happened to someone you consider a very good person.**

INSIDE STORY: Job's story began when God's angels presented themselves in the courts of Heaven (Job 1:6). Joining them on that occasion was Satan, whose very name means "adversary." Ever since the Garden of Eden, Satan had been roaming the earth as the enemy of God and man. Job was "blameless and upright," all the things that Satan had failed to be (Job 1:8; 2:3). Angered by Job's righteousness, Satan accused Job of serving God only because it was profitable for him (v. 9) and implied that if God were to take away Job's blessings, Job would curse him (v. 11). So God agreed to a contest. Bad things would happen to Job, but he would not know why.

Satan is the declared enemy of the righteous. Satan was a murderer from the beginning (John 8:44). The first homicide victim was Abel, who was murdered simply because of his worship (Genesis 4:4-8). Satan continues to be on the prowl, desiring to destroy the righteous (1 Peter 5:8). Many good people suffer because Satan has declared war on those who obey God (Revelation 12:12, 17).

BIBLE**TRUTH** 2

Suffering is always limited by God. JOB 1:12-19

■ **Tell about a time when someone said, "Things could be worse!"**

INSIDE STORY: Four waves of tragedy swept over Job (vv. 13-19), and he was devastated. Yet God was still in control, limiting Satan's power. Satan was not allowed to touch Job himself (v. 12). Some religions teach that there are equal forces of good and of evil in the world. These forces do battle, and the result is uncertain. This is *not* the message of the Bible. Satan is not God's equal. God is in control and will not allow evil to win the final victory. While Christians do have struggles and temptations, God knows how much

we can handle and places a limit on our trials (1 Corinthians 10:13). The child of God is not a pawn of Satan. When we put up a resistance to him, we are promised that Satan will retreat (James 4:7). No matter how dark our times of troubles may be, we can be assured that our advocate is stronger than our enemy (1 John 4:4).

BIBLE**TRUTH** 3

Suffering can help us define our priorities.
JOB 1:20-22

■ **Tell about an important lesson you learned the hard way.**

INSIDE STORY: How did Job respond to his suffering? He tore his robe and shaved his head as expressions of deep mourning. Then he fell to the ground in worship (vv. 21, 22). To Satan's great surprise, Job did not sin by charging God with wrongdoing. In fact, the tragedies forced Job to consider what he believed. In doing so, Job's faith actually became stronger. Satan was defeated in round one of this bizarre contest.

When people suffer, some believe that God is treating them unfairly. Jesus told his disciples that they should *expect* to suffer. After all, if he, their leader, was going to suffer, shouldn't they expect the same (John 15:18, 19)? Peter told Christians that suffering was not "something strange . . . happening to you" (1 Peter 4:12-14). James continued that thought, saying that suffering actually helps a Christian mature (James 1:2-4).

CHALLENGE Distribute a large adhesive bandage and a marker to each student. Have them write: "Testing of your faith develops perseverance" (James 1:3) on their bandages and keep them as a reminder of God's presence.

66

Job's Friends— Helping the Hurting

Student Teacher

Rebekah Nathan was beginning to feel out of touch with her students. An anthropology professor at a large state university with fourteen years of teaching experience, Nathan saw her students acting "like people from a different culture"—a culture completely foreign to her own.

With the intention of better understanding college students, Professor Nathan implemented her own research project. She took a year leave from her job and became an "undercover freshman," enrolling as a student at her own university. She lived in a dorm, attended classes, and socialized with her fellow students. Her cover story was that she was a recent divorcee who was going back to school.

During her year as a student, Nathan took notes of what she learned from her interactions. The results of her research can be found in *My Freshman Year: What a Professor Learned by Becoming a Student,* by Cornell University Press.

Although her intentions were good, Professor Nathan received fierce criticism for gathering information in the way she did.

"Legal or not," wrote J. Langer on the faculty of City University of New York, "the author has crossed some serious ethical lines. Shame on her." Margaret A. Eisenhart, a professor of educational anthropology and research methodology at the University of Colorado at Boulder found the book "ethically ambiguous." While Eisenhart believes that in extraordinary circumstances an anthropologist could justifiably mislead her subjects to get information, those circumstances did not exist in this case.

"I think she could have gotten the information without the disguise," Eisenhart wrote.

Nathan says that the results of her project justify her deception. "Now I see students in a much more human way, with more compassion. And I'm doing different things in the classroom." Yet teachers and students continue to ask, "When does research cross the line and become spying on your students?"

QUESTIONS TO CONSIDER:

■ What do you think of Professor Nathan's research project? Is there a need for teachers to better understand students? Explain. How would you feel if you discovered that someone you trusted as a friend was simply gathering information from you? Do you think Nathan could have gathered her information in a different way? Why or why not? Do you think that this book will help or hurt her relationships with her students over the long run? Explain.

■ Have you ever done something with the best of intentions but later got criticized for *how* you did it? Tell about it.

■ When dealing with relationships, *what* we do is every bit as important as *why* we do it. Today we will read about Job's friends who started out well, taking some very good actions with their good intentions to help Job who was suffering. Let's discover what they did right.

BIBLE TRUTHS

BIBLE**TRUTH** 1

Set aside time for a hurting friend. JOB 2:11

■ **It is said that the best way to spell** *love* **is**
T-I-M-E. What does that mean to you?

INSIDE STORY: When tragedy struck Job's life, the bad
news soon reached three of his friends, Eliphaz, Bildad,
and Zophar.

The three "met together by agreement" to console their
friend (Job 2:11). In other words, this was a planned
meeting. They cleared their personal calendars and set time
aside for this purpose.

Simply taking time is the first step in helping the hurting.
Solomon would later write that friends and relatives should
be available anytime to show love (Proverbs 17:17). Jesus'
Parable of the Good Samaritan illustrates this point. A Jew
was attacked and seriously injured. His own "brothers,"
fellow Jews, passed by without helping. The priest and the
Levite would not take the time for the injured traveler (Luke
10:30-32). But someone outside of the family of God, a
Samaritan, took the time to tend to the man. Although the
man's brothers would not stop, the Samaritan acted as a
neighbor and gave him necessary treatment (vv. 33-37). In
the words of Solomon, "better a neighbor nearby than a
brother far away" (Proverbs 27:10)!

BIBLE**TRUTH** 2

Openly express grief with a hurting friend.
JOB 2:12

■ **List some typical ways people behave**
at a funeral. Why do you think they act
in this way?

INSIDE STORY: The second step for helping the hurting is
being willing to show grief. Job was so covered with sores
that Job's three friends could hardly recognize him! They
wept aloud, tore their robes, and threw dust on their heads
(Job 2:12). Having a good cry with someone who is hurting
is very biblical. When Jacob died, Joseph wept openly. Even

though Joseph was the second highest-ranking official in
the country and a foreigner as well, the Egyptians "mourned
for him seventy days" (Genesis 50:1-3). When Aaron died,
Moses grieved for his brother. Supporting Moses, the rest of
the Israelites mourned with Moses for thirty days (Numbers
20:29). Likewise, when Moses died, the Israelites observed
thirty days of weeping and mourning (Deuteronomy 34:8).
After the death of Lazarus, Jesus openly wept with Lazarus's
sister Mary (John 11:33-35). Although Jesus would raise
him moments later, Mary needed immediate sympathy.

BIBLE**TRUTH** 3

Keep advice and attempted explanations to a
minimum. JOB 2:13

■ **Tell what is meant by the old saying,**
"Silence is golden."

INSIDE STORY: Upon seeing Job's pitiful condition, Job's
friends sat on the ground with Job and did not say a word for
seven days and nights (Job 2:13). Many people avoid those
hurting because they do not know what to say. The fact is,
silence is much more helpful than unsolicited advice.
Talking too much just gets one in trouble. "When words are
many, sin is not absent, but he who holds his tongue is
wise" (Proverbs 10:19). Speaking just for the sake of
speaking is like giving someone a drink of stagnant water
(Proverbs 18:4). Even words spoken with the best intentions
can be taken the wrong way, if someone is not ready to hear
them (Proverbs 27:14). Clichés and simplistic truisms can
only fuel resentment. Silence can be truly golden when
ministering to the grieving.

CHALLENGE Enlist your minister's help in
finding a person who doesn't
have regular visitors. Put
today's lesson into practice
by adopting the person as
a class and planning ways
to offer comfort over the
next several months.

Job–Faith Despite Pain

Olympic Disappointment

Liu Xiang and the entire nation of China looked forward to this moment for years. Liu became his country's first male Olympic track champion in Athens in 2004 and was China's best chance for track gold in 2008. But the hope of this sports hero and the hopes of the people of China turned to hopelessness in a matter of seconds before his appearance in the 2008 Olympics held in Beijing.

The defending Olympic champion lined up to run the 110-meter hurdles at the Beijing games. He didn't even get to race. Grimacing and rubbing his troublesome right hamstring before getting into his crouch, Liu pulled up lame just steps into the first round of qualifying, leaving the summer games' host country without one of its biggest stars—and far and away its biggest star in track and field.

Liu's personal coach for twelve years, Sun Haiping, wept. So did some Chinese journalists. Some fans reacted in anger. "Afraid of [losing], so fake an injury?" a comment on an Internet message board read. "Play your role of a coward and people around the world will look down upon you." Other fans reacted in grief. "Everyone was crying, my mother, my father, my cousin and my friends around me," read another Internet comment. "Liu Xiang became the symbol of new China. Even 10 more gold medals would not compensate for the loss of this gold." Some fans decided to give up on the rest of the Olympics after this injury. Sixty-seven-year-old retiree Liu Guixiang complained, "After Liu Xiang's injury, I won't bother coming back to the Bird's Nest (the stadium in which the games were held) for more."

Liu Xiang is the son of a Shanghai truck-driver. Liu was selected by the Chinese government at age seven on the basis of bone measurements to be trained as a future track star. He began to train as a high jumper but later took to hurdling. Liu became an overnight star and multi-millionaire after winning Olympic gold in 2004. He became China's best-known sportsman, and his face adorns billboards throughout the country. But in an instant, everything he lived his life for seemed out of reach.

"Liu was very, very upset," said China's head coach Feng Shuyong. "He would not have withdrawn unless the pain was intolerable."

QUESTIONS TO CONSIDER:

■ Do you follow the Olympics when they are played? If so, what do you enjoy the most about them? What are your thoughts as you read this story? How do you think you might have reacted if you were a Chinese citizen watching the race?

■ Tell about a time when you felt hopeless. How did you react when you were going through such a low point in your life? Compare and contrast your reactions to the reactions of Liu Xiang and the Chinese people after the track star's injury.

■ We all face situations that seem overwhelming. We may react in tears. We may react in anger. We may react with apathy, just not caring anymore. We see all of these reactions in the article above. In the Bible, Job also reacted strongly in the midst of his suffering. But perhaps we can note a difference in his final responses as we read his story today.

BIBLE TRUTHS

BIBLE**TRUTH** 1

God may seem far away to those who suffer.
JOB 23:1-3, 8, 9

■ **Do you think suffering and loneliness often go together? Explain.**

INSIDE STORY: Job's friends started well when comforting their friend. Quickly, however, they slipped from their original mission and began offering advice. The ill-chosen words of these misguided friends finally caused Job to explode with hostility. In Job 23, Job seems to turn that hostility toward God.

One reason for Job's anger is a perception that God had abandoned him. "If only I knew where to find him" (v. 3). "If I go to the east . . . if I go to the west . . . when he is at work in the north . . . when he turns to the south, I catch no glimpse of him" (vv. 8, 9). Job was simply crying out, "God is avoiding me!"

The psalms of David often express a very similar frustration. "Why, O Lord, do you stand far off . . . [and] hide yourself in times of trouble?" (Psalm 10:1). "Will you forget me forever? How long will you hide your face from me?" (13:1). "Why have you forsaken me? Why are you so far from saving me? . . . I cry out by day, but you do not answer" (22:1, 2).

BIBLE**TRUTH** 2

God may seem unpredictable to those who suffer.
JOB 23:13-17

■ **Have you ever argued with God? Why might someone who is suffering feel like doing just that?**

INSIDE STORY: Job further charged that God acted on his whims, changing his affection toward people as capriciously as an overly romantic junior high student! "He does whatever he pleases. . . . That is why I am terrified before him" (vv. 13, 15). The prophets of the Old Testament also made similar charges. When God was about to allow Judah to be conquered by Babylon, Habakkuk was furious. "Why

are you silent while the wicked swallow up those more righteous than themselves?" (Habakkuk 1:13). At about the same time, Jeremiah had a similar complaint. "Why does the way of the wicked prosper?" (Jeremiah 12:1).

Job was "blameless and upright" (Job 1:1), yet he was in misery—a misery that many of his most corrupt peers never had to taste. Judah was not a perfect nation, but surely she was more righteous than the blatantly pagan Babylon, a nation the Bible elsewhere referred to as "the mother of prostitutes" (Revelation 17:5)! When we suffer, it is easy to believe God to be terribly unfair.

BIBLE**TRUTH** 3

God remains just, even when people suffer.
JOB 23:4-7, 10-12

■ **Do you know of someone whose faith grew stronger because of suffering? Tell about that person.**

INSIDE STORY: Satan wagered that if even the most righteous man were forced to endure great pain, that person would totally give up any loyalty to God (Job 1:11; 2:4). But even at Job's lowest point, it was obvious that Satan had lost the wager. Note Job's faith in the justice of God: "I would state my case before him. . . . he would not press charges against me. . . . I would be delivered forever from my judge. . . . I will come forth as gold" (Job 23:4, 6, 7, 10). Again, this is consistent with views expressed elsewhere in Scripture: "Give ear to my words, O Lord. . . . I lay my requests before you and wait in expectation" (Psalm 5:1, 3). "Hear, O Lord, my righteous plea. . . . May my vindication come from you" (Psalm 17:1, 2). "Vindicate me, O Lord (Psalm 26:1).

CHALLENGE Help students think of ways they react to suffering. Ask them to compare their reactions to a kind of animal (ex. an ostrich who hides its head from trouble or a bulldog that snarls at trouble).

INSTANT**STUDY 32** . . . CONTINUED

CONFIDENTIAL SOURCE:
JOB 38:4-7; 39:1-4;
40:8-14

WE CAN TRUST GOD, EVEN WHEN WE DO NOT UNDERSTAND ALL OF HIS WAYS.

Job—Trusting God

Too Good to Play?

Jericho Scott, age nine, was asked by the Youth Baseball League of New Haven (Connecticut) to no longer pitch for his league team. Surprisingly, it's not because Jericho has done anything wrong. It's the opposite—he has done everything right, and he has been deemed too good for the league. Jericho's pitches were hard and topped out at 40 mph.

"Most of the kids in our league have never played before," said Peter Noble, attorney for the baseball league. "We have a lot of young players and even girls, and there is a fear factor. The league is designed for the development of the players, and we don't want them to be afraid." Noble did note that Jericho throws on target and has never hit another player with his pitches.

Before barring Jericho outright, the league told Jericho's coach, Wilfred Vidro, that Jericho had to play another position other than pitcher. Jericho played second base for a game, but then Vidro put Jericho back on the mound the next game. When the opposing team saw Jericho, they forfeited. The league threatened to disband Jericho's team and put all the players on other teams or return the league fees they paid.

But the team refused to disband, and all players, parents, and Coach Vidro showed up to their next scheduled game. Attorney Noble cancelled the game, saying he was afraid the adults would begin fighting and create an "unhealthy environment."

"I feel sad," Jericho said. "I feel like it's all my fault nobody could play."

"I think it's discouraging when you're telling a 9-year-old you're too good at something," said Jericho's mother, Nicole Scott. Jericho's father, Leroy Scott, said, "If you keep these kids on the field, you keep them off the streets. I'd rather have [Jericho] in the midst of this controversy on the field than dealing drugs on a street corner."

There was a rumor of conspiracy. Jericho's mom said that league officials approached the family, asking Jericho to play in the league because of his fast pitching. They wanted him to join one of the strongest teams in the league. But Jericho's mom and dad wanted him to join a team that had less talent so that Jericho could be a benefit and stay humble. Jericho joined that lesser team, and they were on an 8-0 winning streak and headed for the playoffs when the league asked Jericho to stop pitching. The Scotts and Coach Vidro think the decision to eliminate Jericho was made because the number two team in league standings is sponsored by a company connected with one of the league members.

QUESTIONS TO CONSIDER:

■ Consider the league's decision to ban pitcher Jericho Scott from the following perspectives: Jericho, his teammates, opposing players, parents of all players. How might each feel about this decision?

■ The league is basically saying Jericho must quit pitching "because we said so!" Have you ever heard "Because I said so" from a parent or teacher or someone else in authority? Do you think that's a good response to a problem? Why or why not? Is there a time when that could be a good response?

■ When Job was suffering and asked why, God responded in a way similar to: "Because I said so." Let's find out what Job learned from that experience.

INSTANT**STUDY 33** ■ OLD**TESTAMENT**

71

BIBLE TRUTHS

BIBLETRUTH 1

God is mighty enough to create and sustain the physical universe. JOB 38:4-7

■ **Some people relieve stress by retreating to a quiet spot in the woods or mountains. Why might that be effective?**

INSIDE STORY: After hours of Job's friends' misguided instruction and Job's angry reactions, God interrupted the debate. Out of a storm, the Lord told why he is worthy of trust. The first reason was an appeal to God's power in creation. "Where were you when I laid the earth's foundation?" God challenged (Job 38:4). Job had reared a family and built a business empire, but those achievements pale in comparison to the engineering feat of creating and sustaining the universe.

The Bible teaches that God's work is obvious when a person observes the order in the universe (Romans 1:20). "For who in the skies above can compare with the LORD?" asked the psalmist. "You rule over the surging sea; when its waves mount up, you still them" (Psalm 89:6, 9). In fact, that very power over the natural order convinced Jesus' disciples that he was like no human teacher (Mark 4:41).

BIBLETRUTH 2

God is compassionate enough to care for the most seemingly insignificant wild animal.
JOB 39:1-4

■ **Tell about a favorite pet. What might be some reasons people have pets?**

INSIDE STORY: When Job was feeling that God did not care about his suffering, God reminded Job that he is the supervising physician of the birth of every animal on the planet (Job 39:1). He not only brings life to this planet, but he also meets the needs of his creatures (Psalm 145:16).

Jesus told his disciples that faith in a compassionate God is the antidote to stress and worry. "Look at the birds of the air; they do not sow or reap or store away in barns, and yet your heavenly Father feeds them. Are you not much more valuable than they?" (Matthew 6:26).

BIBLETRUTH 3

God is fair enough to see that human beings receive justice. JOB 40:8-14

■ **List some of the most brutal dictators in history. Where are they now? How did their rule end?**

INSIDE STORY: Finally, God also takes an active interest in seeing that human beings receive justice (Job 40:8, 9). Jesus told his disciples that difficult times would come before he comes again in glory. But during that time we can pray confidently, knowing that God will not allow injustice to triumph (Luke 18:7). We can confidently state with the apostle Paul, "What then shall we say? Is God unjust? Not at all!" (Romans 9:14).

Opening a history book can also help us during times of suffering. Herod tried to destroy the apostles, but his life was taken instead. Adolf Hitler cruelly persecuted anyone who opposed his rule, including believers like Corrie ten Boom. But Hitler's reign was cut short. Idi Amin brutally persecuted Christians in Uganda during the 1970s, but he was driven into exile after a few short years.

CHALLENGE

Read Job's response together in Job 42:1-6. Then sum up the rest of the story—God honors Job and gives him even more than he had before (children and possessions), and Job lives a long life (140 years more). Challenge your students: How can we allow our sufferings to draw us closer to God? How can we be humble and realize God knows better than us? How can we remain faithful despite our pain? After some discussion, offer closing prayers.

THE BIG TRUTH

WE CAN BE PART OF THE GREATEST FAMILY—THE FAMILY OF GOD!

CONFIDENTIAL SOURCE:
PSALM 78:1-8

Family Traditions

Families who work together, play together, and support one another are often in the news:

Generosity—On May 29, 1953, Sir Edmund Hillary and his Sherpa guide, Tenzing Norgay, became the first people to reach the summit of Mount Everest in the country of Nepal. More than half a century later, the explorer's influence continues to be felt in that mountainous Asian nation. Hillary's granddaughter, Amelia Hillary, has followed in her family's footsteps by helping the Sherpa people of Nepal. Sir Edmund Hillary devoted much of his life to helping the Sherpa people and founded the Himalayan Trust to build many schools and hospitals in this remote region of the Himalayan Mountains. Amelia has already worked with her father, Peter Hillary, on several Himalayan development projects and wants to continue the work of her family.

Education—Moments after Robert Quinn accepted his bachelor of science degree from Cabrini College, he rushed to join his sister and parents so they could dash over to the Mann Music Center for his mom's graduation from Philadelphia University on the same day. While equally proud of each other, the experience has left the twenty-two-year-old son with a new appreciation and respect for his fifty-four-year-old mom. "I had a hard time at school as it was. I couldn't imagine filling her shoes and taking care of a family and college and full time job," said Robert.

Fortune—Ian Fleming created the fictional super spy, James Bond. Long after Fleming has stopped writing, Bond continues to enrich the Fleming family fortune. Writer Sebastian Faulks said that some of the profits from his novel, *Devil May Care*—the twenty-third authorized Bond novel not written by Fleming—will be paid to Fleming's survivors. "Ian Fleming comes from the Fleming family, who are one of the richest families in Britain," Faulks said. "But like a lot of people they have remained very keen on making lots more money —that's the difference between rich people and us!"

Fun—Many families have a tradition of a family game night when the whole family plays board games together. But game pieces often get lost. Game manufacture Hasbro has created a solution for that problem by converting classic board games so that they can be played on the Wii and PS2. The company released Hasbro Family Game Night, a video game hosted by Mr. Potato Head. Up to four players can compete in Battleship, Yahtzee, Boggle, Connect Four, and Sorry! on their family's TV screen.

QUESTIONS
TO CONSIDER:

■ List some of the benefits of being a part of a family that you find in the stories above. What other benefits of being a part of a family would you add? Why are you glad to be part of a family?

■ Some businesses claim that their clients are treated like family. What do they mean? Why is that an attractive promise?

■ We do not have to be related by blood to be family. That is what the family of God is all about! We are related by the blood of Jesus. And the benefits of being a part of that family are great indeed. Let's look at what it means to be a part of God's eternal family.

INSTANT **STUDY 34** ■ OLD TESTAMENT

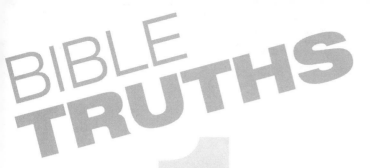

BIBLE TRUTHS

of worship music (1 Chronicles 6:31, 39; 15:16-19; 16:4, 5). Asaph used his ministry of music to pass on the lessons of the past to future generations. In a review of Asaph's psalms (Psalms 73–83) we see that this theme dominates. His songs review the ups and downs of the kingdom of Israel, promising to a future generation that God will be as faithful tomorrow as he was in the past.

BIBLE**TRUTH** 1

Godly believers of the past teach us today.
PSALM 78:1-3

■ **Tell a favorite story about something that happened in your family that all of your family members recall.**

INSIDE STORY: Families pass stories of family history down from generation to generation. The psalmist says that the same is true about the family of God. As believers we can connect to the past of our eternal family. We need to listen when the believers of the past "utter hidden things, things from of old" (v. 2). Like stories of our human families, the oldest stories of the Bible, preserved for generations, reveal our family identity and values. From the story of creation we see the power of God and the unique station of human beings. From the account of Adam and Eve we see the root of our willful nature and the cost of sin. By reviewing the experiences of Noah, we see both God's justice and his provision for those who turn to him. The tower of Babel teaches us about the cost of unchecked pride. These stories have not been lost but have been passed down from generation to generation. From them we learn of the unchanging stain of sin and the unchanging redemption of God. We learn of who we really are and who we desire to become.

BIBLE**TRUTH** 2

Believers today prepare to pass the lessons of the past to our children. PSALM 78:4-6

■ **List three things that you think that every parent needs to teach his or her children.**

INSIDE STORY: In these verses the author of this psalm moves from the past to the present. Since the stories of our eternal family history are so important, we must "tell the next generation" (v. 4) so that "children yet to be born . . . [will] tell their children" (v. 6). This psalm was written by Asaph, one of the Levitical priests King David put in charge

BIBLE**TRUTH** 3

Generations to come can remain faithful to God's plan. PSALM 78:7, 8

■ **Tell about a family tradition. How do you think it became a tradition? How important is it?**

INSIDE STORY: Essayist George Santayana wrote, "Those who do not remember the past are condemned to repeat it." No human mistakes are new mistakes. As Paul said, "No temptation has seized you except what is common to man" (1 Corinthians 10:13). People are people and have commited the same types of sin throughout history.

From the history of our eternal family we can see mistakes others have made and learn how to avoid them. By learning about the past and telling God's story to the present generation, we can make sure that future generations will "not forget his deeds but would keep his commands" (Psalm 78:7). It is the job of this generation of the family of God to warn those who will come after us "not [to] be like their forefathers—a stubborn and rebellious generation" (v. 8).

CHALLENGE Plan a class project or two. Do one that offers a time of thanks to the older generations of the church for the way they've taught younger people about Jesus. Another event you could plan is one that helps your students take on the role of teaching a younger generation.

INSTANT **STUDY** 34 . . . CONTINUED

74

THE BIG TRUTH — WORSHIP IS AS MEANINGFUL AS WE ALLOW IT TO BE.

Psalms—Meeting God Through Worship

Star Struck

Celebrities. We want to see them. We want to talk to them. We want to be like them.

What's Cooking?—Celebrity reality shows have proven themselves to be a hit. Millions have tuned in to see sports stars, music idols, and soap opera actresses find their way around a ballroom on *Dancing with the Stars*. Many watched with anticipation when former sitcom stars hit the ice in *Skating with Celebrities*. Others gasped when watching one-time teen idol Donny Osmond get buried under a pile of bugs and actress Kelly Preston straddle the top of a speeding bus on *Celebrity Fear Factor*.

For three evenings, celebrities joined famous chefs to learn how to prepare gourmet meals in *Celebrity Cooking Showdown*. Viewers watched as soap opera actress Alison Sweeney burned her hand on a hot pan. They marveled that NFL football player Tony Gonzalez could cook a three-course meal. They wondered whether the cooking of comedian Tom Arnold or of country music star Big Kenny Alphin would impress the judges more.

Wedding Rumors—For several weeks, celebrity-crazed Americans had heard that Oprah Winfrey was planning to host a multi-million dollar wedding for Jennifer Aniston and Vince Vaughn. In order to put an end to these rumors, Aniston made a phone call to the *Oprah Winfrey Show*.

"The rumors are so unbelievable," Aniston complained. "For us, I guess, at a certain point, you have no other choice but to think it's funny." Stories have spread that Oprah was helping the couple find a home in her neighborhood, that master cellist Yo-Yo Ma would play the "Wedding March" for the ceremony and that Oprah was planning on giving a million-dollar gift to the couple.

Film Spoof—The pop idol culture was lampooned in the movie *American Dreamz*. In this story, more people seem to know the names of the contestants of an *American Idol*-like show than they do the president of the United States. In fact, in order to correct this, the president signs up to be a guest judge on this program. Of course, it is entirely fictional. But judging from the excesses of our celebrity-crazed society, who knows what the future holds!

QUESTIONS TO CONSIDER:

■ Who is your favorite celebrity? What do you think the appeal is of watching such a star on a reality show or hearing details about that person's private life?

■ Imagine that you could spend an hour with your favorite star. What would you do? What would you talk about? How would you prepare for such a meeting?

■ Few of us will get an opportunity to know a film, sports, or music star personally. But as Christians we have an even greater opportunity. In worship, we can come into the presence of the creator of the universe! Do we take this privilege seriously? How should we prepare for this meeting? Let's examine what the Bible says about meeting God in worship.

BIBLE TRUTHS

BIBLE**TRUTH** 1

In worship we praise God for his constant presence. PSALM 96:1, 2

■ **How might a person's life change if he or she were convinced that God was always near?**

INSIDE STORY: *Singers and audience.* Corporate worship is time when a congregation sings together, recognizing that it is serving as a voice for "all the earth" (Psalm 96:1). The Psalms regularly picture worship as a worldwide event (Psalm 47:7; 66:4; 98:4; 100:1). We sing together with all creation, and God himself is our audience.

Description, occasion, and content. The fact that worship requires the singing of a *new* song is repeated over and over in Scripture (Psalm 33:3; 40:3; 96:1; 98:1; 144:9; 149:1; Isaiah 42:10). The occupants of Heaven and the redeemed on earth continue to sing up-to-the-minute praises until the very last days (Revelation 5:9, 14:3).

BIBLE**TRUTH** 2

In worship we will tell each other about God's nature and work. PSALM 96:3-6

■ **Tell about a time when someone complimented you on a job well done. How might God like hearing words like that?**

INSIDE STORY: *Adoration.* Worship is a time in which we reflect on how God has worked through history (Psalm 96:3; 105:5). The festivals of the Jews were times in which they remembered important God-events such as the exodus from Egypt. The Lord's Supper has always been an important part of Christian worship, declaring that God saves us through the sacrifice of Christ (1 Corinthians 11:17-34).

Exhortation. Worship is also a time in which we warn each other to stay true to God (Psalm 96:6). We are often tempted to "trust in chariots and . . . horses" (Psalm 20:7). In worship we tell one another that the things in which we often put our trust are only idols and have no power to create or sustain (Psalm 96:4, 5).

BIBLE**TRUTH** 3

In worship we more fully give ourselves to God. PSALM 96:7-9

■ **Although salvation is free, is there a cost in being a follower of God? Explain.**

INSIDE STORY: *Surrender of importance.* Worship is a time of giving (Psalm 96:7, 8). In our lives it is easy to give the spot of first importance to ourselves. When we worship, however, we take ourselves out of the driver's seat of our lives and promise to surrender control to God once again.

Surrender of property. When we make an offering that will be used to further God's work, we are taking money that could be used for our own pleasure and surrendering it to God. Merely saying that we surrender our hearts to God is meaningless until we surrender our wallets. Jesus told us that what we treasure determines the loyalty of our hearts (Matthew 6:21).

CHALLENGE Ask students to create an acrostic poem with the word worship in which each line begins with a letter of that word and describes what biblical worship should be.

INSTANT**STUDY 35** . . . CONTINUED

76

What Can One Superstar Do?

Sometimes the news shows us that our world faces a variety of problems that even celebrities seem powerless to change.

A "Rocky" trip—Actor Sylvester Stallone, known for portraying muscle-bound heroes Rambo and Rocky, ran into legal trouble when traveling to Australia a while ago. The actor was formally convicted of importing restricted muscle-building hormones into Australia and was ordered to pay $10,651 in fines and court costs. New South Wales state Deputy Chief Magistrate Paul Cloran said Stallone failed to show that he had a valid prescription for dozens of vials of human growth hormone found in his luggage when he arrived in Sydney for a promotional tour.

The Global "Warm-inator"—Actor and California governor Arnold Schwarzenegger and his fellow Republican, Governor Jodi Rell of Connecticut, accused the U.S. government not long ago of "inaction and denial" on global warming. "It's bad enough that the federal government has yet to take the threat of global warming seriously, but it borders on malfeasance for it to block the efforts of states such as California and Connecticut that are trying to protect the public's health and welfare," the governors wrote in *The Washington Post*. These two states and ten others had approved plans for tougher standards than those imposed by the government to limit vehicle emissions of the greenhouse gases. But the states cannot put the new standards into practice without permission from the Environmental Protection Agency (EPA).

Hard to "Justify"—Vocalist Scott Stapp, formerly of the group Creed, was arrested at his home and was charged with assault related to domestic violence, authorities said. The singer of the hit song "Justify" was charged with one count of domestic assault with intent to commit a felony and was being held without bond, according to an unnamed Palm Beach County Jail official. Stapp was married for a little more than a year to former Miss New York, Jaclyn Nesheiwat. Nesheiwat declined to comment on the incident at the time.

QUESTIONS
TO CONSIDER:

■ What are some of the problems mentioned in the news stories above? How do the famous people mentioned seem incapable of dealing with these problems?

■ What are the most serious problems, in your opinion, that our world faces today? Have you tried to address any of these world problems? What have you done? How successful do you think one person can be in solving such problems? Do you think any of these problems will be fully solved in your lifetime? Why or why not?

■ Sometimes the problems in our world seem so overwhelming that we feel powerless to change them. But the Bible teaches us that one person *can* make a difference in the world. In fact, God *expects* us to make a difference. Let's learn how.

INSTANT**STUDY 36** ■ OLD**TESTAMENT**

BIBLE TRUTHS

BIBLE**TRUTH** 1

It is our responsibility to call others to God.
EZEKIEL 33:7, 8

■ **List some responsibilities you have in your life. What happens if you do no perform them?**

INSIDE STORY: The Lord described the duty of Ezekiel as guarding the gates of an ancient city. A watchman needed to be alert, daring not to miss the slightest rustle in the bushes or the glint of enemy armor in the moonlight. Furthermore, the watchman needed to be decisive, quick to sound the alarm when he saw danger. The comparison was apt. Ezekiel needed to point out sinful behavior that would lead to the destruction of his countrymen. He would be responsible for their demise if he did not do so.

For Christians, evangelism is not optional. Judgment will come. As John the Baptist warned, "The ax is already at the root of the trees" (Matthew 3:10). And while this message is not ever popular, Christians must always be prepared to deliver it, "in season and out of season" (2 Timothy 4:2). The watchman wasn't called to fight the battle by himself, but to rouse the troops. Likewise, we are not called to solve every world problem, but to proclaim the message (Matthew 28:19, 20). To ignore this clear duty is to sin (James 4:17).

BIBLE**TRUTH** 2

It is the responsibility of others to come to God and his message. EZEKIEL 33:9

■ **What does the old saying, "You can lead a horse to water but you can't make him drink," mean to you?**

INSIDE STORY: Those who have God's message have the responsibility to share it. But does that mean that it is our sole responsibility to save the world? The watchman might sound the alarm, but some might prefer to ignore it and go back to sleep. Others may try to hide within the gates rather than join the battle. Those choices will lead to destruction, but the fault is not the watchman's. People *do* ignore the message of God. Those who do not have a formal Christian

background have been told the message of the power and character of God through nature. Their lack of response is on their own heads (Romans 1:20). Likewise many, especially in the western hemisphere, have grown up in a world in which churches and Bibles abound. It is not the fault of the watchman if these people ignore the message available to them (Romans 2:13-15).

BIBLE**TRUTH** 3

It is the responsibility of God to care about those choices. EZEKIEL 33:10, 11

■ **Your friend tells you, "I can't believe in a God who loves sending people to Hell." How do you respond?**

INSIDE STORY: The "take it or leave it" approach described above must not be misunderstood. God provides evangelists and gives people the opportunity to hear, but he *does* care what decision is made. There is much treasure in God's words, "I take no pleasure in the death of the wicked" (v. 11). Although God places responsibility on the believer to tell the message and on the unbeliever to accept it, he takes the greatest responsibility himself.

While major world religions teach that God takes the lives of those who disobey him, the Bible teaches something quite different. God *gives his life* for those who disobey him! "Christ died for the ungodly" (Romans 5:6). He "made us alive with Christ even when we were dead in transgressions" (Ephesians 2:5). While the rest of the world fears a God who cannot wait for mortals to err so he can judge them, the Bible tells another story. To this day God "is patient . . . not wanting anyone to perish" (2 Peter 3:9).

CHALLENGE With your students, look over a list of ministries your congregation performs and supports. Take some time and ask God to show them an area of service for them.

Shadrach, Meshach, and Abednego—Loyal Believers

Misguided Loyalty

Is loyalty a good quality? One might say it all depends upon to whom or what someone is loyal. The story of a cult from decades ago paints a picture of devotion gone horribly wrong.

The Peoples Temple started innocently enough in the American Midwest in the 1960s. James Warren "Jim" Jones was born in a small town in Indiana, obtained degrees from Butler University and Indiana University, and began a church in Indianapolis. His Wings of Deliverance Church was later renamed the Peoples Temple. While the Peoples Temple was making great strides in the areas of racial equality, feeding the needy, and social justice, some danger signs soon emerged. Jones began to preach that there were errors in the Bible, that he was the reincarnation of Jesus, Buddha, Lenin, and others, and insisted that his followers call him "Father."

In the summer of 1977, Jones and most of the 1,000 members of the Peoples Temple moved to the South American country of Guyana. Jones told his followers that they would form a perfect community in the jungle, free from racism and unfair treatment. (The settlement would become known as "Jonestown.") In truth, part of the reason Jones wanted to move was to avoid charges of drug addiction, physical and sexual abuse, and tax evasion.

The tragic story ended a year later. In November 1978, U.S. Congressman Leo Ryan led a mission to Jonestown to investigate alleged abuses. Ryan's delegation spent three days interviewing residents. As Ryan's party were leaving the country with fifteen members of Peoples Temple who wished to return to the United States, a truckload of Jones's armed guards arrived and began to shoot at them.

Representative Ryan, a TV cameraman, a TV reporter, a photographer, and a former Peoples Temple member were killed. After the attack, Jones ordered all of his followers to commit "revolutionary suicide" by drinking a fruit-flavored soft drink laced with cyanide. Over 900 people died that day. People still refer to blind obedience to an evil leader as "drinking the Kool-Aid®," in reference to this horrific act.

Rebecca Moore, now a professor of religious studies at San Diego State University, was interviewed for the film, *Jonestown—The Life and Death of Peoples Temple*. Her two sisters and a nephew were three of those who died in Jonestown. "We date our lives 'before Jonestown and after Jonestown,'" said Moore.

QUESTIONS TO CONSIDER:

■ Have you ever heard of the Peoples Temple? Why do you think this tragedy occurred? What is the difference between loyalty and blind obedience in your opinion?

■ What are some positive instances of loyalty and devotion that you know of? How can one be loyal without being used or manipulated by evil?

■ Unthinking loyalty is foolish, but true devotion is a precious virtue. Let's look at the nature and results of true loyalty by examining a familiar story from the book of Daniel.

BIBLE TRUTHS

BIBLE**TRUTH** 1

Shadrach, Meshach, and Abednego remained loyal to God even when peers were against them.
DANIEL 3:1, 8-12

■ **How has peer pressure negatively affected your behavior in the past? Why do you think peer pressure is so powerful?**

INSIDE STORY: Shadrach, Meshach, Abednego, and their pal Daniel were taken captive from Jerusalem into Babylon around 605 B.C. They had to balance loyalty to God and country with their new responsibilities of serving the pagan King Nebuchadnezzar. The four young men rose to high positions in the Babylonian government.

When Shadrach, Meshach, and Abednego refused to bow down and worship the king's golden statue, some astrologers who served with them as advisers to the king saw a golden opportunity. But the pressure from these astrologers, along with all the rest of the crowd that bowed and scraped before the statue, had no effect on the three friends' loyalty to God. Pressure from their peers was nothing new to the young men. Just after their captivity, they were enrolled in the king's "college" where they were compelled to think like a Babylonian (learning the language and literature), sound like a Babylonian (their names were changed), and even look like a Babylonian (their diet was to be changed, though they succeeded in avoiding that).

BIBLE**TRUTH** 2

Shadrach, Meshach, and Abednego remained loyal to God even when power sought to seduce them. DANIEL 3:13-15

■ **Tell about a particular authority figure you have feared at one time. How did the presence of the person shape your behavior?**

INSIDE STORY: Nebuchadnezzar was one of the most powerful and feared rulers who ever lived. Imagine what it must have been like for these three men to be dragged before

the furious despot, with the crowd on one hand and the blazing furnace on the other. Whatever they faced, Shadrach, Meshach, and Abednego had determined to worship only the God of Israel. They stood before the wrath of the great king, fiercely loyal to the King of kings. Shadrach, Meshach, and Abednego displayed calm under fire (even *in* the fire) because they developed and maintained a strong faith in God that led to unbreakable loyalty.

BIBLE**TRUTH** 3

Shadrach, Meshach, and Abednego remained loyal to God even when pain seemed inevitable.
DANIEL 3:16-18

■ **Civilized countries ban the use of torture, even in times of war. Why do you think that is? What is the purpose of torture?**

INSIDE STORY: In response to the king's demands, Shadrach, Meshach, and Abednego explained the basis of their faith.

We serve God. This was the foundation of everything they experienced with the Lord. They truly loved God. Love for God is one reason we desire to be loyal.

God is able to save us. The three knew that God had power over not only the king but the fire as well. An accurate knowledge of God's character is another reason for our loyalty.

God will rescue us. Shadrach, Meshach, and Abednego knew that God was loyal to them. This is yet another reason to remain true to God.

Even if he doesn't, we will stay loyal. They well understood that there is only one God. The gods of Babylon were false and of no use. As we come to learn that God is our only hope, our loyalty to him grows in strength.

CHALLENGE Work with your students to create personal pledges of allegiance to God. Help them consider what should be in such a loyalty oath.

INSTANT **STUDY** 37 . . . . CONTINUED

80

Daniel–Devoted to the Lord

Dangerous Devotion

Loyalty. This important concept causes people to act in a variety of different ways. This is no more clearly illustrated than it is in the case of Thomas Hamill of Macon, Mississippi.

Hamill was a forty-three-year-old man devoted to his family. In the midst of the Iraq War, that loyalty led him to sell his struggling dairy business and to take a dangerous job. In order to get his family out of debt, Hamill agreed to drive fuel trucks in Iraq for a year.

"He just got behind with low milk prices and all and high feed prices, had to close the dairy out," explained another dairy farmer, Victor B. Allsup. "I'm sure he knew there was a danger of going to a war zone."

A friend of Hamill, Jim Robbins said, "He was more concerned about his wife at the time. He's a hard-working man, totally dedicated to his family and community."

Hamill's devotion caused him to cross paths with those with a rabid political loyalty. Iraqi rebels attacked the fuel convoy Hamill was guarding and kidnapped him. Hamill's captors threatened to kill him unless U.S. troops ended their assault on the city of Fallujah.

The citizens of Macon, Mississippi, then demonstrated their devotion toward Hamill and his family. The community gathered outside the county courthouse to pray for the safe return of Hamill. Hundreds of participants wore yellow ribbons and wrote notes of support for his family.

"We're just all pulling together for this man," said Macon Mayor Dorothy Baker Hines. "This is a small town," said longtime Macon resident Marion Gilbertson. "It hits us hard. God bless him, he's just trying to make a living for his family." Hamill's grandmother stated that she was "just praying." "I trust in God," Vera Hamill declared.

About three weeks later, that trust was rewarded. Hamill escaped from his captors and was found by a convoy of American troops.

QUESTIONS TO CONSIDER:

■ This article describes the loyalty of three different people or groups of people. What does being devoted mean to each of these people or groups? What has loyalty motivated them to do? Of these three, with whom do you have the most sympathy? Why?

■ Describe some other examples of acts of loyalty that you have witnessed or experienced. From whom do you expect devotion? Who expects loyalty from you? Explain.

■ Devotion to a person or cause may be beautiful or it may be deadly. But a total devotion to God is always powerful. Daniel had a devotion to God that had three distinct results.

BIBLE TRUTHS

BIBLE**TRUTH** 1

His devotion to God caused Daniel to be noticed by others. DANIEL 6:1-5

■ **Look at the person next to you. Tell that person something outstanding about him or her. How does it feel to get positive recognition?**

INSIDE STORY: The best and the brightest of the young Jewish men were taken to the royal court in Babylon, where they would be trained to help govern the people for the king (Daniel 1:1-5). Daniel and three of his friends stood out from the rest because of a bold stand for their faith (vv. 8-17).

Positive notice—Daniel came to be a trusted adviser to King Nebuchadnezzar, his heir Belshazzar, and Darius the Mede. He was such a distinguished administrator that Darius, the new king, planned to set him over the entire kingdom (Daniel 6:1-3). Daniel's devotion caused him to be noticed by those in power.

Negative notice—The other administrators, along with minor officials called "satraps," became jealous of Daniel (v. 4). They tried to find some bit of corruption or negligence in Daniel's service, but there was none. They soon decided that the only way they could bring Daniel down was to pit his devotion to God against his loyalty to the king (v. 5). Daniel's devotion to God not only brought admiration, but also bred jealousy.

BIBLE**TRUTH** 2

His devotion to God forced Daniel to take a stand when confronted. DANIEL 6:6, 7, 9-13

■ **Has anyone ever shown jealousy toward you? Tell about that time.**

INSIDE STORY: The jealous officials convinced Darius to decree that for thirty days all prayers must be offered only to him (v. 7). Any offender would be thrown into the lions' den. The trap was set. When Daniel heard about the decree, he had three choices: he could direct his prayers to Darius, he could continue to pray to God, or he could try to hide so that no one would see him pray at all. Without hesitation Daniel went to his house and prepared to pray to God as usual. With windows opened toward Jerusalem (which was over five hundred miles to the west), he knelt and prayed to God, just as he had done before (v. 10). The jealous rivals saw that Daniel prayed to his God as always, so they reported him to the king (vv. 11-13). King Darius was distressed to hear what Daniel had done and tried to think of a way to save him, but the king was trapped by his own words.

BIBLE**TRUTH** 3

Daniel's devotion to God was rewarded.
DANIEL 6:15, 16, 19-23, 26, 27

■ **Think about a time when it was really hard to do the right thing. Why was it difficult? What did you do?**

INSIDE STORY: The king gave the order and Daniel was thrown into the lions' den (v. 16). At the crack of dawn the king rushed to the lions' den. "Daniel," he cried cautiously, "has your God . . . been able to rescue you?" (v. 20). To everyone's astonishment, Daniel was fine. God had sent an angel to protect him, because he was innocent of any wrong (v. 22). The king saw that there was not a scratch on Daniel "because he had trusted in his God" (v. 23). Although he was a pagan, Darius correctly perceived that the living God endures forever and his kingdom will not be destroyed (v. 26). God can work miracles in Heaven and on earth; he rescued Daniel from the lions (v. 27).

CHALLENGE Go around the room and have everyone share a time when they could've been more devoted to God and were not and a time when they showed their devotion to God and what happened as a result.

FORGIVEN PEOPLE CAN DARE TO FORGIVE OTHERS.

CONFIDENTIAL SOURCE:
JONAH 1:2, 3; 4:1, 2, 6–11

Jonah— Roadblocks to Forgiveness

Brain Change

If you have difficulty reading, you'll be comforted by a new study that demonstrates how your brain can change! A Yale University study showed that intensive training helps to activate a certain part of the brain known as the word-form region. This gives hope to people who have dyslexia or people who have trouble reading for other reasons.

The study scanned the brains of seventy-seven children from ages six to nine. In that group, forty-nine were poor readers and the rest were good readers. In the poor readers group, a large section of the children received intensive training at least two hours a week, focusing on phonics. A smaller section of the poor readers received the general treatment of one hour of training a week. This was the first study to compare the normal treatment vs. the intensive treatment both before and after the students received the training.

After one year, the children who went through intensive training showed improvement in several areas. Brain scans afterward showed that these children had activated the part of their brains that caused them to recognize words right away and understand them rather than struggle a bit at a time to piece words together. The students who received the typical training fell further behind.

Dr. Sally E. Shaywitz, one author of the study said, "If a child is not a fluent reader, he or she will avoid reading; it's too effortful."

Sally's husband, Dr. Bennett Shaywitz, indicated that the results seemed to last. "We know that at least one year after intervention ended that the brain systems for reading are intact and look the same as for readers who have no problem reading," he said.

Sally said this study shows "teaching matters and good teaching can change the brain in a way that has the potential to benefit struggling readers."

QUESTIONS TO CONSIDER:

■ Did you remember learning to read? Did you enjoy it or was it hard for you? Who taught you? (Parents, teacher, etc.) Do enjoy reading now? Why or why not? Do you think you would have benefited from receiving extra help as described in this article?

■ For many children, experiencing difficulty in reading can affect the rest of their lives. It's like a roadblock that causes them to take another path that might not lead in good directions. How can overcoming this roadblock now help these children in the future?

■ Have you ever experienced a roadblock that tried to keep you from your goals? What was it—a circumstance, a temptation, a person? Did you overcome it? How? How did it make you feel to get past the roadblock and head toward success?

■ This article shows how a roadblock in reading is now being overcome. We all experience both roadblocks in our lives. Circumstances or people can keep us from achieving our goals. Today we're going to talk about Jonah. We'll see that he had three major roadblocks in his life.

BIBLE TRUTHS

the humility of Christ as he prayed for Jerusalem (Luke 19:41-44). Jesus wept because one city would not repent. Jonah was angered when another city *did* repent!

BIBLETRUTH 1

Fear drove Jonah away from those who needed God's forgiveness. JONAH 1:1-3

■ **The thought of evangelism scares many people. List some of those fears.**

INSIDE STORY: Jonah was sent to the Ninevites around 785 B.C. Nineveh was a large city, enclosed in a massive 40-foot wall nearly eight miles in length. Why did Jonah dread the Assyrians at Nineveh? The Assyrians were cruel and warlike, Israel's most feared enemy. The prophet Nahum fills in the details: They regularly stood in opposition to the Lord (Nahum 1:9); they killed to fill their own wants (2:12, 13); they practiced prostitution, slavery, and witchcraft (3:4); they spoiled the environment (3:16); they were cruel to their adversaries (3:19). History tells us they tortured captives by blinding them and skinning them alive. If they conquered a city, they would pile the skulls of the men in the town square as a sign of their ferocity. Jonah's revulsion is understandable. He didn't want these people to turn toward God—he wanted God to turn against them!

BIBLETRUTH 2

Pride built resentment toward God and those he chose to forgive. JONAH 4:1-3

■ **Prejudice causes people to treat others as less valuable as themselves. Think of some examples of prejudice.**

INSIDE STORY: As humans, we can understand Jonah's fear of these dreadful people. But Jonah did not appear to understand grace and compassion, even after God rescued him from drowning. How could he be so thankful for God's grace to him (Jonah 2), yet so opposed to God's grace toward the pagans of Nineveh?

Jonah thought himself to be far more worthy of God's favor than the Ninevites. Furthermore, he felt foolish because his prophecies of destruction were not fulfilled because of the repentance of the Ninevites. Contrast Jonah's arrogance with

BIBLETRUTH 3

Selfishness caused Jonah to value his own comfort over the salvation of others. JONAH 4:6-11

■ **Change requires sacrifice. Tell about a time that circumstances changed in your life. How were you inconvenienced?**

INSIDE STORY: The last few verses of the book of Jonah contain a wonderful object lesson. In response to Jonah's discomfort in the hot sun (his skin may have been severely damaged during his ordeal in the gastric juices of the fish), God provided the welcome shade of a thick vine. Jonah was very pleased—until God destroyed the vine with a parasite and scorching wind. The sun beat down on Jonah, driving him to thoughts of death.

God's point? Jonah was more than willing to accept the Lord's compassion for himself, but rebelled against God shedding his grace on the people of Nineveh. The lesson was clear: Jonah, you care more about your temporary comfort than for the eternal salvation of others.

How many Christians have avoided taking the gospel to people in need for these same reasons? How many congregations limit the effectiveness of the youth minister because, "We don't want those kids messing up our building?" How many congregations oppose innovative programs to win the lost because they do not want to change their routines? How true are the words of John when he said, "If anyone loves the world, the love of the Father is not in him" (1 John 2:15).

CHALLENGE

Use orange paper to create small traffic cones. Have students write aspects of their attitudes that serve as roadblocks to their forgiving others inside their cones.

INSTANT **STUDY 39** . . . CONTINUED

84

CONFIDENTIAL SOURCE:
MALACHI 3:6-10

Malachi— Robbing God

Greed, Envy, Deception

It seems like there are no end to the ways people try to cheat one another.

Another reason to avoid the fried wonton—A factory manager in China was arrested for using grease from garbage, sewage, pesticides, and motor oil to make cooking lard. Ying Fuming, a manager at the Fanchang Grease Factory in Taizhou, China, sold the lard to hotels and restaurants at half the price of other wholesalers. He promised his buyers that his product met safety standards. Under Chinese law, only pure fat from hogs can be used to produce edible lard. An anonymous tip indicated that the plant used large amounts of recycled grease instead. The factory was shut down and local health and food authorities began an investigation. A police raid discovered 83,000 pounds of used grease and 11,600 pounds of lard. "Some was recycled edible grease, such as oil refined from swill and cooked oil," reported the *Shanghai Daily,* a state-run newspaper. "Some was grease rendered from sewage, and some was recycled industrial grease."

"Tired" of being poor—Mourners in a Chicago-area funeral home went outside to find that the tires of their cars were punctured. This was part of a three-day tire-slashing spree of sixty-three-year-old Robert S. Evans. Evans walked through parking lots of funeral homes, grocery stores, and apartment buildings with his cane in one hand and a pocketknife in the other.

Evan's "reign of tire" ended when a thirty-two-year-old man heard a "popping and hissing" outside of his apartment and went to investigate. The man found Evans with knife in hand by his pickup truck. When Evans refused to drop his weapon, the truck owner punched Evans in the face twice and called the police. Evans was charged with eighteen counts of criminal damage to property, aggravated assault,

battery, and unlawful use of a weapon. "He [Evans] was out of work and decided to lash out at people with money," explained police Commander Dennis McEnerney.

Bring my gnome home!—One Sunday evening, an unusual kidnapping occurred. A sixty-five-pound lawn jockey belonging to Carol Roberts of Port Charlotte, Florida, was stolen from her yard. The thief left a ransom note that read, "If you ever want to see your gnome again, leave $1,000,000 by the bridge!"

"Someone gave him to us as a housewarming gift when we moved here twelve years ago," Roberts said. Promising not to press charges if the decoration was returned, the victim pleaded, "I don't care where they put him. Just put him somewhere on the lawn."

QUESTIONS TO CONSIDER:

■ What ways of taking property from others are described in these stories? List some other ways people try to cheat and steal from one another.

■ Have you or anyone you know ever been the victim of fraud or theft? Tell how you or that person felt because of that crime.

■ Human beings are good at stealing from one another! It is not surprising that the Bible tells us that people also try to cheat God. Let's learn why an Old Testament prophet, Malachi, said this.

BIBLE TRUTHS

The well-known story of Ananias and Sapphira is a New Testament parallel to this event in Malachi (Acts 5:1-4). This couple in the early church withheld money they pledged to the work of God's kingdom and publicly lied about it. To this day, believers embezzle from God's business dealings by withholding offerings.

BIBLE**TRUTH** 1

God keeps his promises to his people. MALACHI 3:6, 7

■ **Who is the most trustworthy person you know? What promises has that person made and kept?**

INSIDE STORY: Instead of merely preaching, Malachi held a mock trial. God is the plaintiff and Judah is the defendant. The prophet starts, as a modern-day tort attorney would, by demonstrating that the plaintiff did nothing to deserve the poor treatment of the defendant. "I the LORD do not change," Malachi began (v. 6). In other words, God had always kept his end of the bargain with the descendants of Jacob, even when they did not keep theirs. Furthermore, he is still willing to bless Judah if they repent and keep their obligations (v. 7).

Over and over again Scripture tells us about God's eternal, unchanging nature. "God is not a man, that he should lie" (Numbers 23:19). "He who is the Glory of Israel does not lie" (1 Samuel 15:29). Our salvation is promised by "God, who does not lie" (Titus 1:2). In fact, "it is impossible for God to lie" (Hebrews 6:18).

BIBLE**TRUTH** 2

We do not deal justly with God. MALACHI 3:8, 9

■ **Tell about a time you were tempted to be dishonest. What caused you to feel that way?**

INSIDE STORY: In stark contrast to God's eternal justice and love, the heart of man is totally corrupt and deceitful (Jeremiah 17:9). The people of Israel were guilty of robbery by withholding their tithes and offerings (Malachi 3:8, 9).

Malachi was writing during the time of Nehemiah. Jews came back from exile, rebuilt the temple, and reinforced the fallen walls of Jerusalem. At that point, many felt that they no longer owed God anything. As a result, the Levites, the tribe of Israel chosen to maintain worship in the temple, were not getting paid. To avoid starvation, many had stopped serving in the temple and made a living by farming (Nehemiah 13:10, 11).

BIBLE**TRUTH** 3

God will reward our financial faithfulness to him. MALACHI 3:10

■ **What are some qualities of a good investment? Have you ever made a good investment? Tell about it.**

INSIDE STORY: In his closing arguments, Malachi makes a recommendation as to how the case can be settled. If the people of Judah would make good on their obligation, God would "throw open the floodgates of heaven" (v. 10). God is not looking to bankrupt his opponent in court, as seems to be the case in a typical lawsuit. Rather, he seeks to impart wealth! The people of Israel were commanded not to till their fields every seventh year (Leviticus 25:3-5). If Israel would make that sacrifice, God would triple the production of the fields on the sixth year (vv. 20, 21). A trusting people on the way to the promised land saw "the doors of the heavens" open and food literally rain down (Psalm 78:23, 24). Paul said that God will still "make all grace abound" for the Christian who is "generous on every occasion" (2 Corinthians 9:8-11). The floodgates of Heaven are still open to Christians who give knowing that "every good and perfect gift is from above" (James 1:17).

CHALLENGE Have teens list important words and phrases from this lesson text as you write them on the board. Lead in a time of individual prayer. Encourage students to use at least one of the listed words or phrases in those prayers.

SCRIPTURE INDEX

OLD TESTAMENT

NEW TESTAMENT

SCRIPTURE TOPIC INDEX

STORY TOPIC INDEX